PENGUIN REFERENCE

THE SLANG THESAURUS

Jonathon Green is Britain's leading lexicographer of slang and jargon. Among his language-related publications are the *Cassell Dictionary of Slang*; *Neologisms: New Words since 1960*; *Slang Down the Ages: The Historical Development of Slang*; the *Dictionary of Jargon*; and *Words Apart: The Language of Prejudice*. He has also written a history of lexicography, *Chasing the Sun: Dictionary Makers and the Dictionaries They Made*.

THE SLANG THESAURUS

Jonathon Green

SECOND EDITION

PENGUIN BOOKS

PENGUIN BOOKS

Published by the Penguin Group
Penguin Books Ltd, 80 Strand, London WC2R 0RL, England
Penguin Putnam Inc., 375 Hudson Street, New York, New York 10014, USA
Penguin Books Australia Ltd, Ringwood, Victoria, Australia
Penguin Books Canada Ltd, 10 Alcorn Avenue, Toronto, Ontario, Canada M4V 3B2
Penguin Books India (P) Ltd, 11 Community Centre, Panchsheel Park, New Delhi – 110 017, India
Penguin Books (NZ) Ltd, Cnr Rosedale and Airborne Roads, Albany, Auckland, New Zealand
Penguin Books (South Africa) (Pty) Ltd, 24 Sturdee Avenue, Rosebank 2196 South Africa

Penguin Books Ltd, Registered Offices: 80 Strand, London WC2R 0RL, England

www.penguin.com

First published in Great Britain by Elm Tree Books/Hamish Hamilton 1986
Published in Penguin Books 1988
Second edition 1999

3

Copyright © Jonathon Green, 1986, 1999

Set in Monotype Plantin
Typeset by Rowland Phototypesetting Ltd, Bury St Edmunds, Suffolk
Printed in England by Clays Ltd, St Ives plc

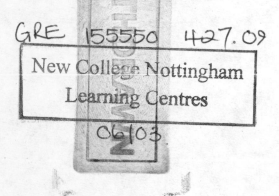

For Lucien and Gabriel

Contents

Contents

Introduction

Dr Peter Mark Roget published his *Thesaurus of English Words and Phrases* in 1852 with the intention of classifying and organising the English Language. His topic encompassed the great spread of standard English, and for all that the Thesaurus has become a basic adjunct to anyone seeking a polished style, his initial aim was to reveal through the relationships of words a new and simpler means of communication for everyone.

Since then, the Thesaurus has gone through a number of revisions, the most recent being published in 1982. It remains a vital helper for every type of writer – both professional and general – who seeks the most apt, the most accurate, the most telling and the most elegant expression of their thoughts. In essence, a comprehensive wordlist, arranged as to topic – with all the words that deal with the same idea (and sometimes their opposites and correlatives alongside them) grouped together – the Thesaurus format remains massively popular.

The intention of *The Slang Thesaurus* is the adapting of the thesaurus technique to the slang vocabulary. Unlike a dictionary, which provides a meaning for a given word, the thesaurus provides a variety of words, all of which express a given meaning. As the editor/compiler of a number of dictionaries of alternative language, including *Newspeak: A Dictionary of Jargon* (1982) and *The Dictionary of Contemporary Slang* (1984), I have come to realize that there exists a definite, and often-voiced demand for a book that would provide just such a 'reverse dictionary'. This book attempts to meet that demand.

The range of slang that has been amassed in the *Thesaurus*, with the particular effect of grouping like with like, is intended to offer a variety of appeals to scholars and less professional logophiles, as well as all those many people who simply enjoy browsing through such collections of more or less arcane, exotic and even obscure words and phrases. As the tabulation of the contemporary slang lexicon gradually developed it became interesting to note the way in which certain areas of human life create seemingly disproportionate vocabularies. While all aspects of the language – taking in the prosaic as well as the more dramatic – have been duly included, specific categories do stand out.

'The chief stimuli of slang are sex, money and intoxicating liquor,' opined Dr J. Y. P. Greig in 1938. Bowing to current events one must add drugs to that list. Coupling such pleasures with a good ration of blasphemy, scatology and euphemism, one has a fair cross-section of slang origins. And, given those additions, Dr Greig's sources are still remarkably constant, as the word lists make clear. There remain only a few parts of the body, and a limited number of functions for their employment, but the language such parts and functions create is still evolving without restraint. Although my intention has been to restrict the *Thesaurus* to contemporary usage, many of the words originate in earlier periods. Slang, like more standard usage, develops over the years, responding in kind to the vagaries and developments of the society in which it is created and used. Listing it in this form only underlines such development.

The *Thesaurus* is divided into sections and groups of categories based roughly on, although obviously not completely following, those used for *Roget's Thesaurus*. These are arranged according to the principal or dominant idea that they convey. Within the sections of these categories are words and phrases that are definitely synonymous; they are entered in alphabetical order. In such cases that the words within a given section require a more specific definition other than that offered by the keyword, this will be given. All categories and sections and the vocabulary listed in them will be cross-referenced whenever necessary. As well as the usual abstract categories – 'Volition', 'Emotion' and the like, I have added listings of several specialist vocabularies – 'Crime', 'Prostitution', 'Commercial Sex', 'Drugs', 'Commerce' and 'Gambling'. All of these fall outside the purlieus of the traditional Thesaurus but are repositiories of large amounts of popularly used slang and therefore demand inclusion.

A thesaurus, by definition, is a compilation of facts – in the form of listed, connected words – rather than of etymologies, discursive explanations of the development and origin of a word or of similar philological exposition. For such information one must look to the ordinary slang dictionaries. On the other hand, this comprehensive organisation into specific categories and sections of the enormous body of slang is designed not merely to appeal to wordsmiths but to have, like any of its peers, a practical function. The genesis of *The Slang Thesaurus* was in the requests of those who said to this compiler 'I enjoy the definitions in a slang dictionary, but what I really want is the reverse, something that gives me the slang for the normal word.' Such appeals have been many. It is the aim of *The Slang Thesaurus* to meet them.

The bulk of the material included in the *Thesaurus* has been derived from my own *Dictionary of Contemporary Slang*, much enhanced by subsequent delvings and accretions. To thank each individual for their contributions would be impossible, grateful though I certainly am, but I must thank David Robbins for opening up an area that had hitherto defeated me, notably the patois used by West Indians in England.

Finally I offer my profound thanks to John Nicolson, without whose invaluable efforts, clichéd acknowledgement though this may be, the compilation of the *Thesaurus* would truly never have been possible.

Jonathon Green
March 1986

Abbreviations

abbrev.	*abbreviation*	occ.	*occasionally*
adj.	*adjective*	orig.	*originally*
adv.	*adverb*	phon.	*phonetic*
aka	*also known as*	prep.	*preposition*
approx.	*approximately*	phr.	*phrase*
Aus.	*Australian*	poss.	*possible*
backsl.	*backslang*	pron.	*pronounced*
betw.	*between*	ref.	*referring (to)*
Can.	*Canadian*	restaur.	*restaurant*
derog.	*derogatory*	rhy.sl.	*rhyming slang*
dial.	*dialect*	RN	*Royal Navy*
eg.	*example*	S.Afr.	*South African*
esp.	*especially*	sp.	*spelling*
euph.	*euphemism*	Sp.	*Spanish*
excl.	*exclamation*	spec.	*specifically*
facet.	*facetious*	synon.	*synonymous*
fr.	*from*	UK	*United Kingdom*
Ital.	*Italian*	US	*United States*
Jam.	*Jamaican*	USMC	*United States Marine Corps*
Lat.	*Latin*	usu.	*usually*
lit.	*literally*	v.	*verb*
Mex.	*Mexican*	v.i.	*verb intransitive*
milit.	*military*	v.t.	*verb transitive*
mod.	*modern*	Yid.	*Yiddish*
n.	*noun*	WI	*West Indian*

Abstract Relations

TIME

1. Duration

n. 1. *period of time:* go, kathleen mavourneen (Aus.), space, stretch, trick
2. *long time:* blue moon, born days (all one's), coon's age, month of Sundays, quite a while, yonks
3. *short time:* bit, brace of shakes, couple of ticks, divvy, half-a-crack, half-shake, jiffy, less than no time, pig's whistle, short stop, two shakes of a lamb's tail, in a tick, wake-up, wet week; spec. mo, sec; short (short service commission)
4. *work time:* hitch (milit.), forty-eight, (milit.), gaol break (movies), graveyard shift, lobster shift, swing shift, R&R (milit.)
v. 5. *spend time:* spec. 29 and a wake-up (prison use: period betw. receiving notice of parole and release)
adj. 6. *new, novel:* been there, done that, brand spanking, bran-new, cherry, crisp, fresh as paint, hot, hot off the press, wen (backsl.)
7. *old:* dillo (backsl.), has-been, over the hill, past it
adv. 8. *during; while:* punch the clock
9. *for a long time:* for donkey's years, for yonks, since God knows when
10. *forever:* for keeps, till the cows come home, till hell freezes over
11. spec. short (near the end of prison term/milit. service)

2. Relative Time

n. 1. manana
2. *crucial time:* nick (of time)
v. 3. *to be late:* stand up

adv. 4. *formerly:* already; spec. space, while back
5. *long ago:* donkey's years, way back, year dot
6. *after:* later! when morning comes (US Black.)
7. *now:* on the dot, this is where we came in (the same time)
8. *soon:* in a brace of shakes
9. *any time:* any old
10. *immediately, shortly:* before you can say Jack Robinson, chop-chop, first crack out of the box, in a jiffy, a jiffy, in a brace of shakes, in less than no time, like a shot, like a shot out of hell, one-two-three, on the knocker, on the nail, PDQ (pretty damn quick), pronto, right off the bat, stat (medical)
11. *suddenly:* bam, bang, bang off, blam, caplunk, kerblam, kersmack, plop, plunk, pop, powee, slap, slap-bang, slap-dab, smack, smack-dab, smacko, socko, wham, whang, zap, zoom, zowie
12. *seldom, occasionally:* once in a blue moon, – a coon's age, a month of Sundays; since God knows when
13. *early:* bright and early; previous
14. *prompt, punctual:* in the nick of time, Johnny on the spot, on deck, on the dot, – nail, – nose, – the spot, pronto, right there
15. *late:* Harry Tate (rhy.sl.)

3. Divisions of Time

n. 1. *day:* good day for it, – for the race; spec. roaster, scorcher, swelterer (a hot day); nice day for ducks (a wet day)
2. *days of the week:* when the crow shits (Aus. payday), Mother's Day (US Black), poet's day (piss off early today),

TGIF (Thank God It's Friday); spec. sickie (Aus.: a day's sick-leave)
3. *festival days:* hols, Xmas; spec. buck's night (Aus.: stag night)
4. *week, month:* moon; spec. Hell Week (US college); leo-time (August); play-away (UK society use: weekend in country); beno (menstrual period, there 'be no' fun); wallflower week (menstrual period)
5. *seasons:* dog days, lamb time, silly season
6. *weekend:* dirty weekend
7. *morning:* ack emma, morning after the night before, rooster time, small hours, sparrow fart
8. *afternoon:* arvo (Aus.), pip emma
9. *night:* crash time, flop time, hay time; spec. dog-watch (media: post-midnight broadcasts)
10. *hour:* half (in telling time: half-five, -six, etc.); spec. happy hour (cheap drinks period in a bar); mad minute (milit. use: free-fire test period for weapons)
11. *minute:* cock linnet (rhy.sl.)

ORDER

4. Arrangement; Order; State of Affairs

n. 1. *conditions:* how-do-you-do, kettle of fish, lay of the land, lie –, size of it, way the wind blows; spec. lineup, set-up
2. *orderliness, good condition:* apple-pie-order, apples (Aus.), apples and rice (Aus. rhy.sl. = nice), fine as wine (US Black) hunky-dory, jake, nice going, squeaky-clean, ticketty-boo, top whack
3. *cleaning, neatening:* doing up, pearl diving (washing dishes in restaur.), policing (milit.), tarting up
v. 4. *to arrange, to clean:* do up, doll up, police up, pretty up, tart up
5. *be consistent:* hang in there, – together, – tight, – tough, hold water, get in line, put one's money where one's mouth is, stand up
adv. 6. hitting on all four (cylinders), up to scratch, – snuff; spec. runner (of a second-hand car)
7. *orderly:* in apple-pie order, kosher

8. *consistent:* according to Hoyle, boilerplate, by the book

5. Disorder

n. 1. Chinese fire drill, dog's dinner, grunge, Horlicks (UK upperclass use), pig's ear, pit, (right) two-and-eight (rhy.sl. = state), scrunge, schmutz, what the cat brought in
v. 2. *to get out of order, get into a mess:* make a dog's dinner (out of), screw up
3. *to disarrange:* arse (ass) up, ball up, foul up, fuck up
4. *to dirty, to soil:* crap on, – over
adv. 5. *messy, out of order:* all to cock, all over the place, – the shop, any how, arsy-versy, cockeyed, everywhichway, fouled up, fubar (fucked up beyond all recognition), gfu (general fuck-up), gmbu (grand military balls-up), gmfu (– fuck-up), grungy, out of whack, raspy (US Black), ratty, samfu (self-adjusting military fuck-up), sapfu (surpassing all previous fuck-ups), screwed up, screwy, scruff, sky-west and crooked, sleazy, snafu (situation normal, all fucked up), susfu (situation unchanged, still fucked up), tarfu (things are really fucked up)
6. *infested:* crawling (with)

IMPROVEMENT

6. Improvement

v. 1. *to improve:* be on the mend, – on the up-and-up, get oneself into shape, – together, get one's act together, – arse (ass) in gear, – shit together
2. *recover:* perk up, pull oneself to pieces (facet.), pull oneself together, pull out of it, pull through, snap out of it
3. *repair, mend:* do up, rev, revamp
4. *strengthen:* beef up, jack up, jazz up

7. Impairment

n. 1. *defective object:* dead duck, fuck-up
2. *accident:* balls-up, cobblers, cock-up, howler, mons
3. *wreck, collision:* pile-up, smash-up
4. *ruin, destruction:* blooie, blow-out, blow up, blue ruin, brodie, bust, bust-up, conk-out, fold-up, knock-out, smash-up, washout

v. 5. *deteriorate:* conk (out), die on the vine, pull a fadeout, fade, go blah, peg out, peter –, spec. deteriorate rapidly: do a brodie, go down the chute, – the tubes, hit the skids, take a nose-dive

6. *get out of order, break:* blow (up), bust, conk (out), crack (up), crap out, fold up, get out of whack, go blah, – blooie, – on the blink, – haywire, poop out, screw up

7. *to degenerate, go to ruin:* (to be) all up, (be) washed up, conk out, fold up, go boom, – phfft, – phut, go to the devil, – to the dogs, – to the deuce, – to hell, – to pieces, – to pot, – to smash, – to the pack (Aus.)

8. *to spoil, disorder:* balls up, blow, do up (brown), bugger up, foul up, fuck up, gum up (the works), louse up, put the kibosh on, – the skids under, queer up

9. *to hit:* bash, whack

10. *to ruin, destroy:* belt out, christen, clean out, crab, diddle, ding, dish, do, – a job on, – brown, – in, – over, – up (like a kipper), gimp, knock off, murder, put the kibosh on, – the skids under, sew up, total, trash, wipe out

11. *have a crash:* have a bust-up, – crack-up, pile up, smash-up, total; spec. collide: collect (Aus.), run smack-dab into, tear into

12. *to spoil, upset:* crab, piss on one's parade

adj. 13. *broken, out of order:* arsed up, ballsed up, banjaxed, beat up, bollixed, bollocksed (up), buggered up, bust (up), clapped out, cockeyed, fouled up, fucked (up), gone blooie, – haywire, – to fuck, – (all) to shit, on the blink, – the fritz, out of whack, screwy, shot, upgefucked

14. *in poor condition:* all wet, beat up, cheesy, crappy, crummy, low rent, punk, trashy

15. *ruined:* all to hell, – to pieces, – to smash, bought and sold (and done for), done, – up, conked out, finito, fucked, gone phut, – to the devil, – to hell, – to the dogs, – to pot, – to smash, (all) shot, washed up

phr. 16. that's torn it

SEQUENCE

8. Sequence; Succession

n. 1. *list:* sked(s), slate

2. *turn:* go, hand, stretch, whack; spec. buying drink: shout; Buggin's turn (next in line for a job)

v. 3. *to follow:* gumshoe, pussyfoot, string along, tag, tail

4. *continue:* go with the flow, hang in (there), keep the ball rolling, stay with it

adv. 5. *in succession:* on the trot

9. Beginning; Commencement

n. 1. first base, first crack (out of the box), git-go, (on the) ground floor, ground zero, jump, jump street, square one, starters

2. *preface:* openers; spec. opening remarks: er, gosh, hell, I mean, look, you know

v. 3. *to begin:* cut loose, dig in, do it, fire away, get the lead out, – the show on the road, – one's arse in gear, – one's finger out, – on one's bike, go for it, hit it, kick off; spec. jump the gun (to begin prematurely)

4. *at the beginning:* early bird, from the word go, in front, off the top, right from the giddyap, when the balloon goes up

10. End; Termination

n. 1. blowoff, curtains, end of the line, in the death, – the stretch, kiss off, payoff, wrap

2. *stop, cessation:* bust-up, fold, knockoff, quits

3. *conclusive end:* all bets are off, capper, clincher, crunch, end-around, KO, living end

4. *suffixes used in slang words:* -aroo, -eroo, -erino, -ette, -fest, -iferous, -ino, -terino, -inski, -itis, -nik, -o, -ola, -ski

v. 5. *to end:* ace it up (Aus.), bust up, conk (out), fold (up), go over the top, – the limit, take the count

6. *to cease, stop:* call it a day, – quits, drop (it), get one's cards, hand in one's chips, hang it up, knock (it) off, pull the plug (on), put the brakes on, stow it, wind up

7. *to terminate:* break (it) up, call all bets

off, clean up (on), floor, fold, knock (it) on the head, polish off, put (it) away, – on ice, – the brakes on, say goodbye (to), wash up, wind up; spec. kill (turn off lights, machinery, etc)

adv. 8. *ended:* all over bar the shouting, all bets are off, all torn up, all up (with), done (for), down the drain, – the pan, – the tubes, in the bag, kiboshed, pegged out, up the spout

excl. 9. can it!, cheese it!, come off it!, cut it out!, drop it!, forget it!, hold on!, hold up!, kill it!, knock it off!, – on the head!, ace it up! (Aus.), lay off!, leave it out!, – off!, – over!, less of it!, stow it!

phr. 10. curtains for you, that's your lot, the deal's off

CHANGE

11. Change

n. 1. *experience:* picnic, set-up; spec. dead man's shoes (US Black: an unavoidable unpleasant experience); university of life (learning by experience)

v. 2. *to alter:* go through changes, snap out of (it); spec. go fish (gay use: to act as a woman)

3. *to happen, to turn out:* come down, go down, pan out; spec. peak (to reach the limit of an experience)

12. Substitution

n. 1. *substitute:* dupe, front, ringer, switcheroo

v. 2. *to replace:* ad lib, cover up, double (for), front for, pinch-hit, ring (in)

adj. 3. *fake:* bogue

13. Permanence

v. 1. hang in there, – tight, stay with (it)

RESEMBLANCE

14. Kind; Sort

n. 1. character, lot, number, piece; spec. situation: layout, outfit, scene, set-up

15. Similarity

n. 1. *likeness:* dupe, lookalike, (dead) ringer

2. *duplicate:* ditto, dupe; spec. knockoff (antiques/clothing trade)

3. *imitation:* copycat, takeoff; spec. shamateur (sporting use)

v. 4. *resemble:* not tell t'other from which, stack up (with)

5. *to copy:* make like, me-too

adj. 6. plastic, strictly from

QUANTITY: SIMPLE

16. Quantity; Number

n. 1. *collection:* ballpark figure, caboodle, grab-bag, whole kit and caboodle, whole bag of tricks, – ball of wax, – bang shoot, – boiling lot, – shebang, – shooting match

2. *zero, nought:* damn all, dick, diddley-squat, doodley-squat, jack shit, nisht (Yid.), not a sausage, squat, sweet FA, – Fanny Adams, zilch, zip, zot; spec. cricket: blob, duck, pair of spectacles (two scores of 0 in the same match)

3. *small denominations:* flach (backsl. = half), country cousin (rhy.sl. = 12), oat (backsl. = 2), roaf (backsl. = 4), net (backsl. = 10), ace, deuce, tray, finif, fiver, nickel (5 as number or quantity), neves (backsl. 7), half a dollar, – a bar, – a sheet, – a yard, – a cock (£5), half saw, sawbuck, quid, tenner, cock and hen (rhy.sl. = ten), cockle and hen, pony

4. *large denominations:* big bucks, telephone number(s), Nelson (111), big one, C, century, G, grand, K, ton, monkey, yard, mill; spec. gambling: nickel ($500), dime ($1000), big nickel ($5000), big dime ($10000)

5. *indefinite numbers:* points (percentages), tall (US Black use: large numbers, often of cash), jillion, squillion, umpteen, zillion

v. 6. *count:* dope out, figure out, guesstimate, reckon, tote (up)

mod. 7. one (as in 'You won't get dime one out of me!')

17. Degree

n. 1. cut above, notch above

adv. 2. *to a degree:* that (when = extent: 'I was that pissed!'), the devil, – deuce,

– hell, on earth (when preceded by 'what . . .')

3. *at the most:* tops

QUANTITY: GREATNESS

18. Greatness

n. 1. *something large:* blockbuster, boomer (Aus.), cheese, gorilla, humdinger, monster

2. *large amount, many:* all sorts, and then some, bags, barrels, heaps, loads, oodles, devil of a lot, heck –, hell –, hulluva, thumping, fat lot, gobs, lashings, more than you can shake a stick at, neat sum, tidy –, pile, pot (of), rafts, scads, tons, wads

3. *something/body important:* ace, biggie, big cheese, – deal, – enchilada, – league, – noise, – shot, – stuff, – time, – wheel, – wig, full two bob (Aus.), something to write home about, your (yer) actual; *spec.* important facts: brass tacks, nitty-gritty

4. *eminence in degree:* (preceded by 'as', 'like', etc) all creation, all getout, beans, billy-o, blazes, a house on fire, nobody's business, in spades

v. 5. *to be important:* beat all, – the band, cut a lot of ice

6. *to feature:* headline, put in lights, – on the map, hit the high spots

mod. 7. *large, huge:* bumper, ginormous, gross, humungous, dirty great, tearing, thumping (great), whopping, whacking

8. *great in degree:* almighty, bally, big-time, blankety, blazing, blessed, blinking, bloody, blooming, boiling, clinking, crying, father and mother of, flaming, heavy, hellacious, hell-fired, holy, motherfucking, mollyfogging, motherless, mother-raping, pepper-kissing, perishing, rip-snorting, ruddy (great), serious, some

9. *to a great extent:* and how, and then some, damn tootin', darn (durn) tootin', as all getout, something awful, – fierce, – terrible, to beat all creation, the worst way, over the fence (Aus.), up the gazoo

10. *very, exceedingly:* all-fired, bang, beastly, blame, blankety, bleeding, blind, blinking, bloody, bust-out, darned, dashed, dead, double, dynamite, ever so, fonky, for sure, goddam, Harry . . . -ers, hell-fired, helluva, pigging, powerful, right, screaming, slamming, spanking, socking, sodding, steaming (great), stiff, stinking, stone, TNT (US Black = dynamite), thundering, veddy, way, well, whacking, whopping (great), wonelly

11. *excellent:* raspy

19. Smallness; Insignificance

n. 1. *something small:* (big) hunk of nothing, (long thin) streak of piss, no great shakes, nothing to shout about, – to write home about, not worth a plugged nickel, – a bumper (Aus.), – a hill of beans, small potatoes, small-time

2. *something worthless:* boloney, blah, bushwa, crap, garbage, trash

3. *small amount:* dribs and drabs, bits and bobs, smidgeonette; *spec.* cough and a spit (theatre: a small role)

v. 4. *not to matter:* cut no ice, (don't) hold no air, no great catch, – great shakes, not amount to a hill of beans, not worth a bumper, not worth a fart in a noisemaker, – a fart in a thunderstorm, – a hill of beans, – a light, – a pisshole in the snow

5. *to lose importance:* to go down the chute, – the tubes, to hit the skids, poop out

adj. 6. *small, insignificant:* airy-fairy, chickenfeed, dinky, footling, half-cocked, – -pint, – -portion, one-horse, milk and water, penny-ante, piddling, pissy-ass, popcorn, sawn-off, teensie-weensie, thin on the ground; *spec.* -ette (suffix)

7. *cheap:* bargain basement, dime-a-dozen, dime-store, five-and-dime, nickel-and-dime, reach-me-down, two-bit, weak

---

QUANTITY: COMPARATIVE

20. Superiority

n. 1. *act of surpassing:* licking, fading, screwing, shafting, skinning, whitewashing

2. *the best:* A1, capper, cream, daddy,

grade A, gravy, monte, payoff, pearler, topper, tops

v. 3. *to beat, surpass:* beat all to hell, – eight ways from Sunday, – out, give a black eye, get the jump on, hammer, have one cold, hype (US Black), kick (one's) arse, knock for a loop, knock sideways, – the spots off, – the stuffing out of, lick, run rings round, put away, – one's nose out of joint, put it over (on), steal the show, sweep the board, take the shine off, whitewash

4. *to be best:* beat all, – all get out, cop the lot, take the cake

adv. 5. *superior to:* ahead of the game, a cut above, two jumps ahead

6. *best:* A1, ace, top of the tree, tiptop, up in the paints

phr. 7. *I've won:* read them and weep

21. Inferiority

n. 1. spec. sport: wooden spoon

v. 2. *to be surpassed:* licked, skinned, get on the short end, take a bath, – a back seat, – it on the chin, – one's lumps, – the fall, – the gas, – the knock, (to be) taken to the cleaners

adj. 3. *inferior:* bush, out of the money, – the picture, not in the game, – the picture, – the same league, pipped

QUANTITY: COMPLETENESS

22. Completeness; Sufficiency

n. 1. *sufficiency:* earful, enuff, full house, noseful, nuff

2. *superfluity:* bellyful, chokka, enough and then some, too much of a good thing, up to one's neck, skinful, snootful

3. *everything:* ballgame, business, everything but the kitchen sink, full monte, full two bob (Aus.), guntz (Yid.), hook, line and sinker, issue (Aus.), SRO (standing room only), whole bag of tricks, – ball of wax, – bang shoot, – boiling lot, – kit and caboodle, – shebang, – schmeer (Yid.), – shooting match, – works

adv. 4. *satiated:* lousy with, jam-packed, crawling with

5. *excessive:* gross, mondo, over the top, OTT, far out, too much, out of sight, outasite, mega-, too-too

6. *complete:* all-fired blinking, blooming, dead, plumb, regular, straight-out, straight-up

7. *completely:* abso-bloody-lutely, bang up, clean (to), clear to hell, flat, from arsehole to breakfast time, from soup to nuts, – the ground up, – the word go, slam,

23. Incompleteness; Insufficiency

n. 1. *share:* cut, divvy, piece (of the action), slice, split, whack

2. *quantity used in a given portion:* crack, edition, go, jag, shot, slug, sniff, throw, toot, toss, whack

3. *nothing:* bugger all, not a lick, – a smell, – sniff, sod all, sweet fuck all, sweet FA, zero, zilch, zip all

v. 4. *to lack:* be clean out of, fresh out of, shy of, light, to be hungry for, hung for

QUANTITY: VARIATION

24. Increase

v. 1. throw in

phr. 2. all that jazz

25. Decrease

n. 1. dent (in one's wallet), knockdown, knockoff, letup

2. *riddance:* brush-off, the big E, – dust, – elbow, – rubout, – runaround, – slip

v. 3. *separate, divide:* cut up, cut up touches, divvy up, go halves, – fifty-fifty

4. *eliminate, discard:* axe, blow (out), boot (out), can, chuck, chunk (US Black), clean house, count out, cut loose, deep six, ditch, dump, get shot of, give the air, – the bump, – the hook, – the brush-off, – the elbow, – the slip, – the (old) heave-ho, – the heave, – the knife, put the skids under, – rollers under, – the shears to, scarf (US campus), unload; spec. censorship, editing: blue-pencil; throw the baby out with the bathwater (to discard the useful along with the useless)

adv. 5. *used up:* all out (of), all shot, done for, fresh out (of), washed up

26. Equality

1. *inequality:* another story, a something else (again), a whole new ballgame, two other guys, a horse of a different colour
2. *on equal terms:* even-Steven, fifty-fifty, halvers, quits

---

QUALITY

27. Goodness

n. 1. *something excellent:* ace(s), beaut, bee's knees, bells (US Black use), belter, the berries, big time, bobby dazzler, but good, cat's pyjamas, – whiskers, corker, cracker, daisy, dilly, duck soup, fave rave, the goods, gravy, humdinger, jim-dandy, kayo (KO), lily, lulu, McCoy, oldie but goodie, pea (Aus.), peach, pip, pippin, real McKay, real McCoy, rip-snorter, scorch (US Black use), shovel city (which one really 'digs'), some thing to shout about, – to write home about, topper, trimmer (Aus.)

v. 2. *to be excellent:* beat all, – the band, go over big, – like a million bucks, hit the spot, make it big, take the cake

adj. 3. *excellent, first-rate:* A1, all fine and dandy, all wool and a yard wide, AOK, apples (Aus.), – and rice (Aus.), awesome, back of the net, bad, baddest, bagged, bang on, – up, bat, beaut, bitchen, bitchin, bitchin-twitchin, blinding, bod, boffo, bonaroo, bonzer, boss, brahma, brill, bully, cas (casual), choice, classic, clearly, cold, completely, cool, copacetic, crackerjack, crazy, d, dandy, dead set (Aus.), def, death, deaf (US Black), doog (backsl.), doog eno (backsl.), ducky, dynamite, electric, ex, fab, fantabulous, foxy, gaff, gear, godawful, good as all getout, great shakes, grouse (Aus.), groovy, handsome, hellacious, high-tone, hot-shit, hotsy-totsy, hunky-dory, irey (Jam.), jolly d., just like mother makes it, – the job, – the ticket, – what the doctor ordered, keen(-o), killer, king, knockout, live, mad (Aus.), magic, major, marvy, massive, mean, mega-, mind-blowing, mondo, nasty, neat, number one, numero uno, on the money, outasite, out of sight, – state, – the box (Aus.), – this world, peachy, peachy-keen, pimp, primo, rad (radical), rich, right up one's alley, righteous, ripper, scrummy, serious, sexy, shit-hot, smashing, socko, solid, spiffy, splendiferous, spot on, superfly, sweet, swell, TB (très brill), that's the ticket, to die, tons, top drawer, top hole, top notch, top shelf, total blowchoice, totally, tough, triff, trippy, tubular, unreal (Aus.), v., vg., vicious, Wee Georgie Wood (rhy.sl. = good), wicked, wizard, yummy

excl. 4. encore!, far out!, fuckin(g) A!, perfecto!

5. *quite good:* better than a poke in the eye with a blunt stick, – a slap in the belly with a wet fish, close but no cigar, not so dusty

28. Badness

n. 1. *something bad:* asshole, baddie, baloney, bomb, bosh, bum, bushwa, chazerai (Yid. = rubbish), cheapie, cold, cold case, crap, crock (of shit), crumb, dead duck, double-whammy, doodley-shit, dreck, kaker (Yid.), no big deal, nowhere, pain (in the arse), – (in the neck), schlock, small beer, – change, – potatoes, snot, stinker(oo), tinhorn

adj. 2. *poor, mean, second-rate:* bad-ass, basic, bit previous, blamed, blankety, bodger (Aus.), bum, brummy (Aus.), bush league, chump-change, coffeeand, cold, cotton-picking, crappo, crappy, Crow McGee, cruddy, crumbum, crumby, crummy, dashed, dicky, dipshit, ditso, dodgy, dog-ass, g, godawful, gross, gnarly, half-baked, hard-boiled, hole-in-the-wall, iffy, jerkwater, low down, – rent, mean, Mickey Mouse, naff, NG (no good), NBG (no bloody good), no bon, no go, not much chop (Aus.), number ten, on the outer, pisspoor, poxy, punk, rank, ribby, rinky-dink, ropey, schlocky, shag, shitty, stinko, suck-ass, ticky-tacky, tinhorn, two-bit, two-bob (Aus.), unreal, upta (Aus. = up to shit), yucky, zero minus

3. *mediocre:* half-assed, – cocked, Wall
Street didn't jump
excl. 4. base!

ATTRIBUTES

29. Weight
n. 1. *something heavy:* gorilla, wodge
adj. 2. gross, nuggety, thumping,
whopping

30. Flexibility; Texture; Colour
adj. 1. blue (US Black: dark-skinned)

31. Temperature
mod. 1. *hot:* hot as a bastard, – a bitch,
– buggery, – hell, hotter than hell
2. *cold:* cold as a bastard, – a bitch, – a
well-digger's arse, – a brass monkey, – a
witch's tit, cold enough to freeze the
hind leg off a donkey

32. Strength
n. 1. get-up-and-go, guts, juice, legs,
steam
2. *physical strength:* beef, the doings,
elbow grease, jism, meat, muscle, what it
takes
3. *directed force:* bang, biff, boot, flash,
ginger, guts, jolt, kick, oomph, pep,
powie, smackeroo, smacko, snap, sock,
sockeroo, swack, wallop, zip
v. 4. *to exert strength:* put beef into,
– muscle into, – one's back into, – one's
elbow into, strongarm
5. *to be potent:* have a shot in one's
locker, – lead in one's pencil
adj. 6. *strong:* ballsy, big ass, built like a
brick outhouse, – brick shithouse,
bullet-proof, heavy, mean, ruggsy, warry

33. Weakness
v. 1. *to be weak:* can't cut it, – fight one's
way out of a paper-bag, – get it together,
– hack it, – knock the skin off a
rice-pudding, – take it, doesn't cut the
mustard
2. *to weaken:* bottle out, cave in, chicken
out, conk out, crack (up), hit the skids,
honk out, lose one's bottle, pull a
fadeout, wimp out
3. *make powerless:* bash, bugger up,
botch –, do –, do over, do the business on,
– up (brown), gum –, put the kibosh on,
– out of commission, queer one's pitch,
put a spanner in the works, screw up
mod. 4. *weak, flimsy:* weak as catspiss,
wet as a dishrag
5. *unsteady:* cockeyed, dotty, groggy,
skewiff, wonkey
6. *effeminate:* faggy, he-she, la-de-da,
nance, pansy, pantywaist, queer, swish
(see also Homosexuals: 404)
adj. 7. *vulnerable:* up for grabs,
wide-open
8. *weak:* candy-ass, chickenshit

APPEARANCE

34. Appearance; Looks
n. 1. front, getup, phizog, stackup,
turnout
phr. 2. *unhealthy appearance:* looking
green about the gills, – like a dog's
dinner, you look like I feel

35. Beauty
n. 1. class, dog, spiff
2. *something beautiful:* beaut, cutesie,
cutesiepie, dream, dreamboat, corker,
daisy, dish, eyeful, hot stuff, looker,
nifty, peach, pip, pippin, spanker,
stunner, sweetie
3. *ornaments:* fixings
4. *attractive figure:* built, classy chassis,
stacked, plenty of what it takes
v. 5. *to look beautiful:* (to be) easy on the
eyes, knock dead, – one's eyes out,
– out, look a knockout, – fit to kill, – a
million bucks, – some, stack up nice
6. *to decorate:* doll up, spiff up, tart up
adj. 7. *beautiful:* beaut, cute, cutesie,
dishy, dreamy, dreamboat, fit, foxy,
ginchy, hot, keen looking, knockout,
neat, no slouch, peach, wow

36. Ugliness
n. 1. *something ugly:* a bag, fit to stop a
clock, no oil painting, – prize, something
the cat dragged in
adj. 2. *ugly:* bagged out, corroded (US
Black), grisly, groaty, grody, – to the
max, gross, grotty, gucky, hard on the
eyes, – to take, hurtin' for certain, icky,

manky, pitty, ragged out, ratty, rough, rugy, scrungy, skrungy, scummy, scuzzy, tacky, white bread

phr. 3. *disregarding ugliness for sex:* you don't look at the mantlepiece when you're poking the fire

Space

DIMENSIONS

37. Dimension
adj. 1. *thin:* beanpole, herring-gutted, ribby, skinnymalink, weedy
2. *short:* hammered down, knee high to a grasshopper, – jack rabbit, sawn-off, tee-tee, titchy
3. *fat:* beefy, broad in the beam, built like a brick outhouse, – shithouse, cornfed, double-gutted, fat-assed, pot-bellied, two-dinners
4. *measure of dimension:* wall-to-wall, yea (as in 'yea high', 'yea big')

38. Distance
n. 1. along, chance, piece, ways
2. *long distance:* good way, – piece, long chalk, neat step, tidy –, back of beyond, back of Bourke (Aus.), beyond the rabbit-proof fence (Aus.)
3. *short distance:* close shave, hop and a step, near as dammit, near thing, piece, (in) spitting distance, near squeak
v. 4. *to be near:* be hot, – warm
adv. 5. *far:* back of beyond, cold, to hell and gone, faraways
6. *near, close:* bang up (against), breathing down one's neck, as near as no matter, – dammit, texan rude (backsl. = next door), under one's nose, (by a) nose, up one's daily (rhy.sl. = daily mail = tail = behind), ringside, upside (US Black)
7. *measurement:* klick (kilometer), mike-mike (millimeter)

SHAPE

39. Straightness
n. 1. beeline
adv. 2. *straight:* down the alley, in the groove, on the beam

40. Crookedness
adv. 1. *crooked:* all anyhow, assbackwards, cockeyed, crinched, everywhichway, gimped (in), hell west and crooked, screwy, six ways from Sunday, skewiff

PLACE

41. Situation; Location
n. 1. posish, sitch
2. *ground:* deck
3. *small place:* manhole (US Black)
v. 4. *to put, place:* dock, park, plant, spot
5. *lay down, put down with force:* bing, blop, bop, chuck, flop, kerplunk, lam, nail, peg, plank, plop, plunk, slap (down), smack, sock, swack, whang
6. *to be in a place, to reside:* (drop) anchor, hang out, – up one's hat, park one's carcase, perch, pitch camp, roost
adv. 7. *where:* anywheres, somewheres, any place, some –, on deck, at (as in 'where are you at?')
8. *everywhere:* all over, – the map, – the shop, from hell to breakfast
9. *in the wrong place:* off one's manor, – patch, – turf, on the flip side, on the Jersey side

42. Town; City
n. 1. big city, burg, met, metrop
2. *small town:* jerkwater (town),
one-horse town, sticks, tank town,
whistle stop
3. *suffix:* -ville

43. Cities: Nicknames
n. 1. Apple (NYC), Bay City (San
Francisco, Calif.), Bean Town (Boston,
Mass.), Berdoo (San Bernadino, Calif.),
Big A (Amarillo, Tx. or Atlanta, Ga.),
Big Smoke (Sydney, Aus.), Big T.
(Tucson, Ariz.), Cowboy City
(Cheyenne, Wyo.), Dago (San Diego,
Calif.), Guz (Devonport, UK), Hip City
(US Black: Cleveland, Ohio), Jew York
(derog: NYC), Nueva York (NYC),
Nap Town (Indianapolis), P-Town
(Philadelphia), Pompey (Portsmouth,
UK), Rubber City (Akron, Ohio), Shaky
City (Los Angeles), Sin City (Las Vegas,
Nev.), the Smoke (London), Tinseltown
(Hollywood, Calif.), TJ (Tijuana,
Mexico), Windy City (Chicago, Ill.),
Yidney (derog: Sidney, Aus.)
2. *imaginary cities:* Shitkicker, Ohio,
Woop Woop (Aus.)
3. *areas:* Bible Belt, Borscht Belt, gin
and Jaguar belt, scampi belt

44. Cities: Districts
n. 1. Chocolate City (any black ghetto),
the Coathanger (Sydney Harbour
Bridge, Aus.), the Drain (the London
Underground), Dream Street (47th St,
NYC, betw. 6th and 7th Avenues),
Foggy Bottom (the State Department,
Washington, DC), Forty-Deuce (42nd
Street, NYC), the Bush (Shepherd's
Bush, London W12), the Gate (Notting
Hill Gate, London W11), the Grove
(Ladbroke Grove, London W10, W11),
the Junction (Clapham Jnct, London,
SW4), Kangaroo Valley (Earls Court,
London, SW10), Rods (Harrods of
Knightsbridge), Swone One (London
SW11), Silicon Glen, Silicon Valley, up
West (the West End of London), the
Water (the River Thames, London)
2. *spec. college use:* Big Green
(Dartmouth), Big Red (Cornell), Bruno
(Brown U.), Crimson (Harvard U.), Eli

(Yale U.), Farmington (Miss Porter's
School), Old Nassau (Princeton U.),
St Grotlesex (a fantasy amalgam of US
prep schools)
3. *spec. prisons:* the Island (Parkhurst,
IOW), the Scrubs (Wormwood Scrubs,
London W14), the Ville (Pentonville,
London N1)
4. *spec. homosexual use:* Boystown (the
gay area of West Hollywood), Queen's
Row (Boston, Mass.), Swish Alps
(Hollywood Hills), Vaseline Heights
(gay centre of Portland, Ore.)

45. Countries: Nicknames
n. 1. Bananaland (Queensland, Aus.),
Big Ditch (Atlantic Ocean), Blighty
(UK), Down Under (Australia),
Honkers (Hong Kong), Jamdung
(Jamaica), the World (the USA as seen
by troops in Vietnam)

46. Region; Locality
n. 1. boonies, boondocks, manor, nabes,
neck of the woods, patch, side (W1),
stamping ground, turf
2. *unpleasant place:* armpit, bottoms (US
Black), craphouse, creepsville, dump,
lavatory, Motel Hell, muckhole,
nowhere city, shitheap, skid row, toilet,
wrong side of the tracks
3. spec. blue feature (water area on a
map); civvy street, Cloud 9

47. Thoroughfare
n. 1. *road:* blacktop, double nickel, drag,
frog and toad (rhy.sl.), M-way; spec.
milit. use: redball (enemy road, in
Vietnam)
2. *street:* bricks, drag, field of wheat
(rhy.sl.)
3. *main street:* Afro set, fast lane, front
line, front street, main drag, – stem, set;
spec. bread and butter (rhy.sl. = gutter),
Johnny Horner (rhy.sl. = corner)
4. *meeting place:* meat market, – rack;
spec. homosexual use: cottage, tearoom

48. Enclosure
n. 1. bullpen, hootch, shovel and broom
(rhy.sl. = room); spec. office (any
workplace – pilot's cabin, pimps' bar,
etc.)

2. *house:* cat and mouse (rhy.sl.), gaff, joint, pad; spec. deri, derry (derelict house), fancy crib, mahogany flat (US Black)

3. *sleeping place:* doss, doss house, flop, – house, kip, – house

4. *residence:* crib, dorm, fleabag, padding crib; spec. slaughter house, whip shack (US Black: a place for sex); animal house (US campus: the least fashionable fraternity house)

5. *garden:* Dolly Varden (rhy.sl.)

6. *spec. places:* bone yard, silent city (cemetery); cooler (mortuary); caff, greasy spoon, takeaway (café); chippy (chip shop); labour (labour exchange); tekram (backsl. = market); farm, funny farm, giggle-house (Aus.), loony bin, – farm, nut house (mental hospital); prison: nick; sport: end (of a football ground); crime: flat joint (gambling), honky-tonk, slaughter (a dump for stolen goods); uni (university); bog, crapper, dike, john, loo, shitter, snakes' house (lavatory), grubber (Aus.); spike (vagrants' hostel); trap (club); slide (transvestite club)

7. *homeless:* on the bricks, – stones, – street

8. *unpleasant, dirty place:* pisshole, shithole

MOTION: VELOCITY

49. Speed; Swiftness

n. 1. action, the double, get-up-and-go, go, hot-foot, hustle, lick, pep, quick-time, rabbit fever, zip

2. *going fast:* hot-footing, scoot, scram, skedaddle, spin, whirl; spec. white line fever (driving fast)

3. *something fast:* bat out of hell, blue streak, greased lightning, scorcher, streak of lightning; spec. wham bam thank-you mam (quick intercourse)

v. 4. *to go fast:* ace, ball the jack, barrel (it), belt along, blow ass, broom, do a fair lick, get one's skates on, go full blast, – like a bat out of hell, – a blue streak, – a bomb, – a house on fire, – a shot out of hell, – greased lightning, – like hell, – like nobody's business, – like the clappers, – through like a dose of salts, hightail (it), hit it, – the wind, hoof it, move one's ass, neckbreak (US Black), pour it on, rattle one's dags (Aus.), rip (along), scoot off, shoot off, – over, – through (Aus.), skedaddle, snap it up, streak (off), take a powder, take a runout powder, tear ass, – off, turn it on, up and dust, whizz (off), zip, zoom (off)

5. *to hurry:* fall (all) over oneself, get a move on, get one's arse in gear, get the lead out, get weaving, look sharp, make it snappy, move it, – yourself, shake a leg, shift arse, snap it up, step lively

6. *to run:* beat feet, cut dirt, fan one's butt, flap the heels, hightail (it), lay 'em down, pick 'em up

7. *to accelerate:* hop on it, jump to it, let her rip, put the skids under

8. *to make go faster:* put the skids under

adj. 9. *fast:* at a rate of knots, chop-chop, double quick, hot and strong, hot cross bun (rhy.sl. = on the run), lickety-split, like a bat out of hell, like a dose of salts, like a rat up a drain, like winking, off like a bride's nightie, on the double, on the hop, on the hurry up, on the trot, toot sweet, zippy

excl. 10. where's the fire!

11. *full speed:* all the way, all out, at full bat, wide open

12. *hurry up!:* snap it up, wake it up

50. Slowness

v. 1. *to be slow:* dog it, drag –, go nowhere fast, leadfoot, mosey (along), slowpoke

2. *not hurry:* hold one's horses, hold one's water, keep one's shirt on, take it easy

3. *to slow down:* put on the anchors

adj. 4. *slow:* doggy, drag-arse, lazy-arse

MOTION: DIRECTION

51. Direction

n. 1. U-ie (u-turn)

v. 2. *go straight:* make a beeline (for)

3. *change direction:* flip-flop, hang, hang a Lilly, – a Louie, – a Ralph, – a U-ie

adv. 4. *moving:* back to square one, on the hoof

5. *in all directions:* all over the shop, everywhichway, hell west and crooked, six ways from Sunday
6. *from both directions:* double-doored (Can.)

52. Approach

n. 1. *arrival:* blow in, check-in, drop in
v. 2. *to arrive:* beat (one) to the punch (US Black use = to arrive first), belly up to, blow in, breeze in, drop in, – by, hit, lob in (Aus.), make the scene, roll in, – up, sneaky-pete, tool in; spec. working use: clock in

53. Entrance

v. 1. *to enter:* barge in, blow in, bob up, breeze along, – in, bust in, drop in, – by, duck in, ease in, ooze in, pop in
2. *enter forcibly:* bust in, crash in, gatecrash, muscle in, nose in
excl. 3. emok nye! (backsl. = come in!)

54. Departure

n. 1. blow, bow-out, check-out, the fade, kiss-off, send-off
2. *hasty departure:* bunk, bust (out), hightail, jump, lam, one-two, powder, runout, – powder, scoot, scram, scrambola, scramskie, skedaddle, skip, vamoose
v. 3. *to leave:* amscray, bail (out), beat feet, – it, beetle off, be missing, blow, – out of, boogie-woogie (US Black), book (US Black), break in, broom, bugger off, bug out, bunk off, buzz off, check out, choof, clear off, cut (out), cut along, – loose, do a bunk, – a powder, – a runner, fade away, flake off, fly the coop, fuck off, get lost, – on one's bike, – the hell out of Dodge, hat up, haul ass, have it away, – on one's dancers, – on one's toes, heel on (US Black use), hightail (it), hit the bricks, – the road, – the street, – the trail, – the wind, hive off (Aus.), honk on, hop the wag, iris out, jam (US Black), leg it, let's boogie, light out, make it, mug up (US Black), nick off, pedal one's dogs, piss off, pop off, pull up stakes, push along, – off, put it in the wind, raise up (US Black use), roll out, run out (on), Scapa Flow (rhy.sl. = to go), scarper, scat, scoot

(off), scram, shoot off, shoot the coop, shoot through (Aus.), shove off, skedaddle, skip, sky, sky off (US Black use), sling one's hook, slope off, sod off, split, take a hike, – a powder, – a runout powder, – it on the lam, – off, – the air, – the wind, tear off, – loose (US Black use), toddle off, up and dust (US Black use), vamoose, whizz off, zoom (off); spec. move one's belongings at night to avoid rent: shoot the moon; hand in one's dinner plate (resign from a job)
4. *sneak off:* do a bunk, duck out, ease out, gumshoe, iris out, skip (out), squirrel off, take it on the creep; spec. jump the gun (start off prematurely)
adv. 5. *departing:* ready for the off, off with a bang
excl. 6. *leave!:* be missing!, blow!, break it up!, bugger off!, buzz off!, case off!, eff off!, fuck off!, get lost!, – rooted! (Aus.), go pound salt up your arse!, – to hell!, hop it!, kaycuff foe! (backsl.), naff off!, on your bike!, piss off!, push off!, rack off! (Aus.), scram!, shove off!, sod off!, take a hike! vamoose!; spec. lead on, Macduff (exhorting another person to take the initiative)
7. *spec. goodbye:* Abyssinia, catch you later, toodle-pip, TTFN (ta-ta for now)
8. spec. AWOL (milit. absent without leave)

55. Ascent

n. 1. stiff pull
v. 2. *ascend:* shimmy up, skin up, zoom (up)
excl. 3. alley-oop!, upsidaisy!

56. Descent

n. 1. *fall:* bop, brodie, cropper, flop, header, kerplump, nose-dive, plop, plump, purler, spill
v. 2. *to fall:* come a cropper, – a purler, go arse-over-appetite, – arse-over-tit, go kerplunk, hit the deck, take a spill, – a brodie, – a flier
3. *to sit down:* give the dogs a rest, grab a chair, – a flop, park yourself, – your carcase, take it easy, – a log off (your feet), – the weight off your feet
adv. 4. *head-over-heels:* arse-over-appetite, arse-over-tit

57. Irregular Motion
n. 1. bumpity-bump, flitter-flutter, pitapat
v. 2. bobble
3. *to jerk:* yank

MOTION: TRAVEL

58. Travel in General
n. 1. *wanderer:* mumper
v. 2. *to wander:* bat around, (go on the) bum, case (it) around, cat around, knock about, mooch, slap the pavement, swan around, tool around, tromp (around), truck; spec. island-hop: the Grand Tour (campus use); pack (live as a female tramp)
mod. 3. *moving:* on the go, – the trot

59. Walking
n. 1. ball and chalk (rhy.sl.), footslogging, Guy (Fawkes) (rhy.sl.), leg work, yomping; spec. UK royal family: walkabout; US Black use: Memphis glide, pimp stride, slidewalk
v. 2. *to walk:* air out, ankle along, bop, diddy-bop, foot it, poke along, ride shanks' pony, walk the dogs

60. Riding
n. 1. *ride:* hitch, spin, whirl; spec. run (Hell's Angels outing)
2. spec. banker (cab-driver's regular route), burn-up (fast riding of a motorcycle), chicken run (teenage virility ritual involving cars), Hollywood swoop (US Black use, one vehicle halts the other by passing and then cutting in front of it)
3. *speed of ride:* herbs (Aus.), horses (horsepower)
v. 4. *to drive fast:* ball the jack, belt it, burn rubber, buzz, caravan, deadhead, do a ton, floor, give (it) the gun, – the herbs (Aus.), gun (it), hammer, hit the gas, jam it, lay rubber, let her go, – her out, peel out, pill out, put the hammer down, rev, romp it, sandbag, screw it on, thrash (Aus.), wind her up
5. *to ride in a car:* spec. ride punk, ride pussy, ride the bitch's seat (US Black: a woman seated between two men);

ride tough (US Black: drive a smart car)
6. spec. hot-wire (to start a car without an ignition key), kojak (to find a parking place easily), nerf (to collide with another car), put on the anchors (brake), run out of road (to crash, after failing to take a corner), (have a) shunt (to collide), soup up (to improve the car's performance), tailgate (to follow too closely)
7. *to hitchhike:* bum, go on the thumb, hitch, push the thumb, ride one's thumb, thumb it, thumb-trip
8. *spec. surfing:* to ride the planks
phr. 9. *what do you drive?:* what are you pushing? (US Black)

MOTION: TRANSFERENCE

61. Transference
v. 1. *to transport, haul, carry:* cart, hump, pack, tote
2. *to pull:* schlep (Yid.), snake, yank
3. *to reach for:* make a long arm
4. *to raise:* hike

62. Throwing
n. 1. chuck, shy; spec. cricket use: dollydrop, skier, steepler
2. *hard throw:* bullet, hot one, hotshot, hummer, ripper, scorcher, sizzler, smoker, steamer, streaker, whizzer, zipper
v. 3. *to throw:* bung, chuck, cut loose (with), let go (of), rifle (it in), shy, smoke, uncork

63. Ejection
n. 1. *discharge, dismissal:* the air, the axe, big E, boot, boot-out, bounce, brush (off), bump, bum's rush, chuck, dust, elbow, gate, KB, kiss-off, knock-back, order of the boot, Spanish archer ('El Bow'), walking papers
v. 2. *to dismiss:* blow out, boot (out), bounce, bump, call it a day, chuck, ditch, eighty-six (rhy.sl. = nix), elbow, give the air, – the sack, – the belt, – the brown envelope, – the (old) heave-ho, – the elbow, axe etc. (see n. 1), hoof out, put the skids under, – the screws to, sack, see the back off, send away with a flea in one's ear, send packing, show the

door, – the gate, sling out, turf out; spec. kick upstairs (move to a senior but less important job)

3. *to be dismissed:* get the chop, – the bullet, – the order of the boot, – the sack, etc. (see n. 1)

adv. 4. *dismissed:* booted, out on one's ear, – one's arse

Matter

GEOGRAPHIC CONDITIONS

64. World; Earth
n. 1. the great outdoors, Mother Nature

65. Heavens; Space
n. 1. upstairs, up there
2. *the sun:* bath bun, currant bun
(rhy.sl.), rays, UVs
v. 3. *to sunbathe:* catch some rays

66. Natural Phenomena; Weather
n. 1. *hot weather:* blazing (down), peas in
the pot (rhy.sl. = hot), roaster, scorcher,
sizzler, swelterer
2. *cold weather:* brass monkey weather,
cold snap, dirty weather, filthy weather,
freezer, Naughton and Gold (rhy.sl.),
potatoes in the mould (rhy.sl.), taters
3. *wet weather:* bucketing down, pissing
down
4. *rain:* Andy Cain (rhy.sl.), pleasure
and pain (rhy.sl.); spec. send her down,
Hughie (Aus.: an appeal for rain, or
good surfing)
5. *fog:* peasouper
6. *winds:* Irish hurricane (dead calm)
v. 7. *to rain:* bucket down, piss down,
rain cats and dogs, spit
8. *to be windy:* blow great guns

FLUIDS

67. Liquids
n. 1. *water:* Adam's ale, fisherman's
daughter (rhy.sl.)
2. *sea:* big ditch, – lake, briny, Davy
Jones' locker, deep, ditch, drink, frog

pond, oggin, pond, puddle; spec. surfing
use: Big Kahoona (a perfect wave)
3. *waves:* spec. white horses (white caps
on choppy waves)
4. *ice:* rocks
5. *petrol:* gas, juice; spec. hot rod use:
nitro
6. *oil:* black gold, crude, lube
7. *thick, sticky liquid:* dope, gism, glop,
goo, goop, guck, gunk
8. *glue:* dope, goo

MATERIALS; DEVICES

68. Raw Materials
n. 1. *things in general:* stuff
2. *spec. oil rigs:* mud; iron-, glassworks,
etc. grog (refractory material)
3. *gold:* red stuff, yellow stuff
4. *silver:* white stuff
5. *stone, brick:* Irish confetti (when
thrown at others)
6. *silk:* squeeze
7. *lead:* bluey

69. Devices; Implements
n. 1. *equipment:* fit-up, gear, kludge,
lashup, layout, rig, rig-up, set-up,
shebang, works
2. *indefinite objects:* bits and bobs,
dingbat, dingus, doings, dojigger,
do(o)-dad(s), doodah, do(o)-hickey,
gitty-gap, gizmo, gubbins, jig, junk,
majigger, motherfucker, oojah, shebang,
so-and-so, stuff, thingummibob,
thingummijig, thingy, whamdoodle,
what-d'you-call-it, whatchamacallit,
whatnot, whatsit, whodjamaflop, you
know, you know what

3. *new object:* wheeze, wrinkle
4. *tool:* April fool (rhy.sl.), ratfucker (home-made starting handle)
5. *prizing tool:* jemmy, jimmy
6. *hammer:* Birmingham screwdriver, Irish screwdriver
7. *wrench:* knuckle buster, monkey
8. *household equipment:* asswipe (lavatory paper), B-52, church key (can-opener), band of hope, Cape of Good Hope (rhy.sl. = soap), hottie (hot water bottle), jerry, Ted Frazer (rhy.sl. = cut-throat razor); spec. homosexual use: trick towel (used by male prostitute to clean up after a client)
9. *knife:* axe, blade, charming wife (rhy.sl.), chiv, cutter, flick, nigger-flicker, shiv, slicer
10. *scissors:* snips
11. *shovel:* banjo, Lord Lovel (rhy.sl.)
12. *drill:* kanga
13. *keys:* church key (can opener), twister (house key)
14. *saw:* bear's paw (rhy.sl.)
15. *nails:* monkey's tails (rhy.sl.)
16. *matches:* cuts and scratches (rhy.sl.), strikers
17. *clock:* dickery (dock), hickory dock (rhy.sl.), ticker
18. *stationery, etc.:* blotch (blotting paper), bungy (eraser), nerd pack (holder for pens)
19. *cleaning:* honey cart, – wagon, pooper-scooper
20. *carriers:* cock sparrow (rhy.sl. = barrow), esky, poly bag (polythene)
21. *covering:* Auntie Ella (rhy.sl. = umbrella), brolly, tarp (tarpaulin)
22. *lights:* finsburies (rhy.sl. Finsbury Park = arc), glim, Harry Randall (rhy.sl. = candle)
23. *vehicles:* body and soul lashing (sailing use); George (automatic pilot)
24. *musical instruments:* axe, bull-fiddle (double bass), joanna (rhy.sl. = piano), Strat (Stratocaster electric guitar), taps (drums)
25. *record players, etc.:* boofer box, chatter box, ghetto blaster, Third World briefcase, wog box; nigger box (TV); sides (records)
26. *technology:* bug (surveillance device); spaghetti (a mass of wires), stinger (a

light socket extension); number-cruncher (large computer)
27. *contraceptive devices:* flying saucer (diaphragm), French letter, – tickler, frenchie, frenchy, rubber, rubber boot, – johnny, safe, scumbag

---

WEAPONS; EXPLOSIVES

70. Weapon
n. 1. *weapon:* enforcer, heat, persuader, piece, tool
2. *clubs:* life preserver, sap, slug
3. *brass knuckles:* brassies, iron mikes, knuckle dusters, knucks, maulers
4. spec. pimp sticks (a whip made of wire coathangers)
5. *pocket knife:* chiv, toothpick

71. Firearm
n. 1. action piece, bad news, barker, belly gun, Betsy, cannon, chopper, chunk, equalizer, gat, grease-gun, heater, hog-leg, iron, peacemaker, piece, poker, pom-pom, rod, roscoe, Saturday Night Special, speaker, tool, zipgun; spec. thirty-eight (.38), forty-five (.45), Mag (Magnum); pump (pump-action shotgun); sawed off (sawn off shotgun)
2. *machine gun:* Chicago piano, – typewriter, chopper
3. *spec. military use:* arty (artillery), Bouncing Betty (a mine that springs into the air), chopper (helicopter), dick gun (a rubber bullet gun), fast mover (F-4 fighter-bomber), flat top (aircraft carrier), frag (fragmentation grenade), Huey (HU-1 helicopter), Leaping Lena (see Bouncing Betty), MA (mechanical ambush), slicks (helicopters), the gun (M-60 light machine gun), thumper (M-79 grenade launcher), tin can (naval destroyer), toe popper (M-14 anti-personnel mine), willie peter (white phosphorus)

72. Ammunition; Explosives
n. 1. ammo, buck (buckshot), hardware, lead, rockets; spec. pineapple (bomb or grenade)

73. Explosion; Shot

n. 1. bing, boom, bong, bop, bust, pam, plink, plunk, pow, whoomp, whomp
2. *gunfire:* Chicago lightning; spec. lit up (under fire), incoming (hostile gunfire)
v. 3. *to shoot:* bust caps, hose down, lead (down), pop (off), turn on the heat; spec. dry-snap (to fire a weapon without ammunition)
4. spec. frag (to assassinate a fellow soldier with a fragmentation grenade)

74. Armed

n. 1. drop (being able to draw a weapon before a rival)
v. 2. *to be armed:* pack iron, – a gat, – a rod, etc.
adv. 3. *armed:* heeled, loaded for bear, packing iron, etc., rodded, tooled up
phr. 4. spec. rock and roll (milit.: firing an automatic weapon in a steady burst)

VEHICLES AND MOTORS

75. Vehicle

n. 1. *car:* auto, boat, buggy, flivver, heap, iron, jam jar (rhy.sl.), john-john (WI), motor, ride, short, wheels
2. *large car:* Al Capone ride (US Black use), big boat, brougham (US Black use), cruisemobile, gangster doors, – ride, gas-guzzler, limo, pimpmobile, spivmobile; spec. black taxi (Aus. official limousine)
3. *old car:* banger, bone-shaker, clunker, jalopy, junker, rust-bucket
4. *specific cars:* Bird (thunderbird), cad, caddy (Cadillac), Connie (Lincoln Continental), deuce 25, deuce and a quarter (Buick 225), DV (Cadillac de Ville), geetoh (GTO), Jag (Jaguar), Jew Canoe (derog: Cadillac in US, Jaguar in UK), kitty-cat (US Black: Cadillac), LD (Cadillac Eldorado), Masers (Maserati), Merc (Mercedes), rado (Cadillac Eldorado), Roller, Woler (Rolls-Royce), Vette (Corvette); black and white (US police car thus painted); crummy (transport in logging camps); ringer, tweedler (UK criminal use: illegitimate cars); passion wagon (car used for seductions); dump truck

(derog: car full of lesbians); woodie (wood-panelled station wagon); ringer (stolen and disguised second-hand car)
5. *trucks:* rig, ute (Aus. utility trucks)
6. *motorcycles:* ass hammer, chopper, garbage wagon, hog, machine, one-lunger; spec. wheelie (trick riding on a motorcycle)
7. *aircraft:* coffee grinder (old, unstable aircraft)
8. *ships:* halfpenny dip (rhy.sl.), tub, the tubs (transatlantic liners)
9. *railways:* Bedpan line (railway line between Bedford and St Pancras)
10. *bicycle:* do as you like (rhy.sl.)
11. *ambulance:* blood wagon
12. *public transport:* drain, rattler (London underground trains); swear and cuss (rhy.sl. = bus)
13. *cabs:* fast black, flounder and dab (rhy.sl.), spin; spec. bill (a taxidriver's licence)
14. *collision:* pile-up, prang, rear-ender, shunt
v. 15. *to crash:* prang, shunt, total, write off

76. Automotive Parts

n. 1. *engine:* cams (camshaft), carb (carburettor), crank (crankshaft), headers (manifold)
2. *brakes:* anchors
3. *accelerator:* hammer
4. *seats:* buddyseat (pillion on motorbicycle), shotgun seat (next to driver), pimp post (US Black: armrest between front seats)
5. *tyres:* gangster walls (whitewalls)
6. *handlebars:* apehangers (high, extra-long motorcycle handlebars)
7. *interior:* black on black (US Black: black car with black interior)
8. *exterior:* rag top (soft top)
v. 9. decoke (to clean spark plugs)
adv. 10. dressed (US Black: a car with every conceivable accessory)

77. Motor; Engine

n. 1. boiler, kettle, pot, hog, mule, donkey; spec. four-, six-banger, four-, six-lunger, kicker (outboard motor)
adj. 2. *specially engineered:* hopped up

BUILDINGS AND FURNITURE

78. Building

n. 1. dive, dump, hole, joint, layout, shebang, spot
2. *house, home:* back-a-yard (WI), crib, drum, eemosh (backsl. = house), kip, pad; spec. crash-pad (house where one can sleep temporarily); condo (condominium); pseudy Tudy, stockbroker Tudor (fake 'Elizabethan' architecture)
3. *apartment:* shotgun flat, walkup
4. *lodging house:* doss, – house, kip, – house
5. *hotel:* spec. Hojo (Howard Johnson's)
6. *public house:* battle-cruiser (rhy.sl.), boozer, rubbidy, rub-a-dub (Aus.); spec. drinker (after hours club); public (public bar); balloon (rhy.sl. = saloon bar); nineteenth hole (a golf-club bar)
7. *café, club, etc.:* caff, carry-out, takeaway, takeout; spec. clip-joint (club that defrauds its customers); slop chute (USMC bar)
8. *place of entertainment:* bughutch, fleapit (inferior cinemas); cherry hogs (rhy.sl. = dogs = greyhound tracks)

79. Parts of Houses

n. 1. *lavatory:* altar, bog, can, crapper, dunnee, dunnigan, flush, jakes, john, karsy, lav, lavvy, little boy's/girl's room, little office, loo, pisshole, pisshouse, shithouse, shit jacket, shitter, snakes' house, throne, thunder-box; spec. head(s) (naval)
2. *outside lavatory:* one-, two-holer
3. *lavatory paper:* asswipe, bumf, bum fodder, wipe
4. *window:* burnt (cinder) (rhy.sl.)
5. *fire:* Anna Maria (rhy.sl.)
6. *stairs:* apples and pears (rhy.sl.), wooden road to Bedfordshire
7. *floor:* Rory (rhy.sl. = Rory O'Moore)

80. Camp

n. 1. spec. jungle (US hobo camp)

81. Furniture

n. 1. fixings, sticks
2. *bed:* kife, kip, sack, Uncle Ned (rhy.sl.)
3. *pillow:* weeping willow (rhy.sl.)
4. *table:* Cain and Abel (rhy.sl.)
5. *chair:* lion's lair (rhy.sl.), ryache (backsl.)
6. *mirror:* snake in the grass (rhy.sl. = looking glass)
7. *clock:* dickory dock (rhy.sl.)
8. *style:* Jewy Louis (derog: over-ornate)
phr. 9. *shut the door:* put the wood in the hole

DRESS

82. Clothes

n. 1. duds, clobber, doodads, drapes, fronts, pieces, rags, rig, schmutter, threads, togs, traps, wrapping; spec. clear cut (US Black use: stylish clothes); night clothes (criminal use: dark clothes used for robberies at night)
2. *suit:* piccolo and flute, whistle and flute (rhy.sl.), vine
3. *formal dress:* d.j., monkey suit, soup and fish, tails, tux
4. *best clothes:* best bib and tucker, glad rags, go to meeting clothes, silks (US Black)
5. *old clothes:* grubbies, tat
6. *second-hand clothes:* hand-me-downs, reach-me-downs
7. *uniform:* spec. colours, originals (patches, jeans and jacket worn by Hell's Angels); rabbit skin, sheepskin (academic tippets)
8. *civilian clothes:* civvies, dog-robbers (suits worn by off-duty officers)
9. *skirts:* midi, mini, maxi
10. *underwear:* Alan Whickers (rhy.sl. = knickers), BVDs, didies, east and west (rhy.sl. = vest), fleas and ants (rhy.sl. = pants), Harolds (pants), kecks, long johns, passion killers, skivvies, snuggies, UBs (underbodies); spec. falsies; VPL (visible pantie line)
11. *trousers:* bins, council houses (rhy.sl.), daks, kicksies, loon pants (very baggy), petrols (Aus. rhy.sl. petrol bowsers), round the houses (rhy.sl.),

strides (Aus.), trou; spec. baggies (shorts worn for surfing)

12. *coat:* benny, boolhipper (US Black: leather), crombie, leather piece, nanny goat (rhy.sl.), rod, smother, weasel (and stoat) (rhy.sl.); spec. bum-freezer (short jacket); pussy (fur coat)

13. *swimming costume:* cossie (Aus.)

14. *pyjamas:* jim-jams, pjs

15. *shoes:* beetle-crushers, boppers, bovver boots, brothel creepers,
– stompers, daisy roots (rhy.sl. = boots), dogs, howd'ye dos, reptiles, roach-killers, shit stompers, stomp(ers), waffle-stompers, winkle-pickers; spec. air hose (shoes worn without socks); thousand eyes (US Black: heavily perforated leather shoes); wellies (wellingtons)

16. *running shoes:* chucks, daps, quick starts (US Black)

17. *hats:* chimney, titfer (rhy.sl. tit for tat); spec. boonie hat (soft military hat for jungle use), skidlid (crash helmet), steel pot (steel helmet)

18. *shirts:* dicky dirt, Uncle Bert (rhy.sl.); spec. fag tag, fruit loop (small loop sewn to back of shirt)

19. *pocket:* bin, Lucy Locket, sky (rocket) (rhy.sl.)

20. *sportswear:* jock, jockstrap (athletic supporter)

21. *tight sweater:* shrink; spec. boob-tube (narrow cylindrical garment, encircling breasts)

83. Accessories

n. 1. *gloves:* turtle (doves) (rhy.sl.); spec. mittens (boxing use)

2. *handkerchief:* bubble duster, snotrag

3. *cane:* whangee

4. *tie:* fourth of July (rhy.sl.), Peckham (rhy.sl. Peckham Rye)

5. *socks:* almond (rocks) (rhy.sl.); spec. pimp socks (US Black: socks with thin vertical lines)

6. *spectacles:* cheaters, Lancashire lasses (rhy.sl.), shades (dark glasses)

7. *bag:* diddy-bag

8. *wallet:* dummy, goitre, leather, poggler, poke

9. *watch:* Gordon and Gotch (rhy.sl.)

10. *jewellery:* bobbles, glass, ice, jim, red stuff, rocks, Simple Simon (rhy.sl. = diamond), sparkler(s), tom, tomfoolery (rhy.sl.), tot (WI); spec. patacca (fake, rubbishy jewels)

11. *sanitary towels, etc.:* diaper, do rag, G-string, jam-rag, jelly sandwich (US Black), rag, sling shot

12. *contraceptives:* bag, French letter, frog, johnny, rozzer (US Black), rubber, rubber johnny

13. *cosmetics:* lippy, slip

14. *braces:* airs and graces (rhy.sl.)

84. Dressing

v. 1. *to dress:* get dolled up, – togged up, pile into

2. *to dress up:* dike down, dog it, doll up, look sharp, put on the dog, spiff (oneself) up, tart (oneself) up, tog (oneself) up

adv. 3. *dressed up:* (in one's) best bib and tucker, buttered (US Black), choked down (US Black), dap, dressed to the nines, dressed up like a dog's dinner, – like a pox doctor's clerk, dolled up, dyke down, flossed up (of a woman), fonked out heavy (US Black), full buf, got up, kitted out, laid out, laid to the bone (US Black), piss elegant, pressed (US Black), pimped down (US Black), pooned (up), ragged down (heavy) (US Black), suited (down) (US Black), spiffed (up), tabbed (US Black), togged to the bricks; spec. drag (dressing in the clothes of the opposite sex)

4. *smart:* clean, clean to the bone, fonky –, mod –, ragged –, silked –, tabbed (US Black), neat, nifty

5. *colourful:* jazzy

85. Undress

n. 1. dishabilly

2. *nudity:* the altogether, birthday suit, (stark) bollock naked, (in the) buff, (in the) raw

v. 3. *to undress:* drop the duds, – the gear (Aus.), peel, – down, – off, shuck down, strip (off)

4. *teenage pranks:* drop trou, hambone (Aus.), moon, press ham

5. *to undress someone:* debag, pants

adj. 6. *naked:* bare-ass, peeled, raw, starkers

phr. 7. Charlie's dead (your slip is showing)
8. it's one o'clock at the water-works (your fly is undone)

FOOD

86. Food

n. 1. belly timber, choff, chop, chow, chuck, eats, feed, fixings, fodder, fuel, grease, groceries, grub, hash, munga, munger, nosh, peck(s), scoff, scran, tack, tuck, tucker; spec. junk food (fast food)
2. *bad food:* crap, dog's dinner, dog vomit, garbage, glop, gunge, slop(s), shit, vom; spec. burnt offering (burnt food)
3. *bread:* needle and thread, Uncle Fred (rhy.sl.), tommy
4. *sandwich:* butty, sango (Aus.), sarnie
5. *meat:* beemal (backsl. = lamb), cold (frozen meat), delock (backsl. = cold), feeb (backsl. = beef), kayrop (backsl. = pork), piano (US Black, spare ribs), teekay (TK = town killed); spec. Kate and Sidney (rhy.sl. = steak and kidney)
6. *sausages:* snorker, snags, swags; spec. red-hots (frankfurters with chilli)
7. *poultry:* elwoff (backsl. = fowl)
8. *stew:* Mulligan stew (tramp's assembly of available foods)
9. *mince:* shit on a shingle (minced meat on toast)
10. *spreads:* marj (margarine), stammer and stutter (rhy.sl. = butter)
11. *potatoes:* murphies, praties, spuds, taters; spec. bimps (french fries)
12. *cake:* Joe Blake, Sexton Blake (rhy.sl.); spec. sinker (doughnut)
13. *mayonnaise:* mayo
14. *watermelon:* African golf ball, culture fruit
15. *cheese:* bended knees, stand at ease (rhy.sl.)
16. *sugar:* sand
17. *breakfast cereals:* burgoo, soggies
18. *vegetables:* veggies; spec. prison use: has-beens (rhy.sl. = greens)
19. *kipper:* Jack the Ripper (rhy.sl.)
20. *pizza:* za
21. *pickles:* Harvey Nichols (rhy.sl.)
22. *pasta:* spag bol (spaghetti bolognese)
23. *gravy:* army and navy (rhy.sl.)
24. *salad:* rabbit food
25. *soup:* loop-the-loop (rhy.sl.)
26. *foreign food:* (an) Indian, (a) Chinese, Chink chow
27. *egg dishes:* Adam and Eve, – on a raft (of toast), – on a raft and wreck 'em (scrambled eggs on toast), two looking at you (two fried eggs), sunny side up (eggs fried on one side only), two down, – with their eyes closed, over easy, (eggs turned over), two on a slice of squeal (two eggs on fried ham)
28. *prison tea:* diesel
29. *ice cream:* scream
30. *chilli:* red

87. Beverage: Drink (non-alcoholic)

n. 1. *coffee:* java, joe
2. *tea:* brew, cuppa, Rosy Lea, – Lee (rhy.sl.), splosh, you and me (rhy.sl.)
3. *cocoa:* ki (RN use)
4. *milk:* cow, Grade-A
5. *lemonade, soda, etc.:* pop
v. 6. *to drink:* chugalug, dip the beak, gargle, inhale, knock back, put away, wet the whistle

88. Preparing and Serving

v. 1. chase up, dish up, rustle –, scare –, fix; spec. shackle up (tramp use, cooking lunch), brew up (to make a pot of tea)
2. *to serve food:* hash, jump tables, sling hash
3. spec. spud-bashing (peeling potatoes)
4. *to boil:* Conan Doyle (rhy.sl.)

89. Eating

n. 1. *daily food:* three squares
2. *catered food:* take away, take out
3. *breakfast:* brekker; spec. Mexican breakfast (a cigarette and a glass of water)
4. *dinner:* din-din, Jimmy Skinner, Lilley and Skinner (rhy.sl.), Tommy Tucker (rhy.sl. = supper)
5. *feast:* beano, blow-out, bust-out, gross-out, grubfest, nosh-up, spread, tuck-in; spec. pig heaven (gross over-eating)
v. 6. *to eat:* chow down, feed one's face, get one's eating tackle around, gnaw a

bone, grab a bite, grub up, hook down, lower (it), peck, put away (the groceries), put on the feed bag, – the nosebag, spoon, stoke up, stow away, tie on the feed-bag, – nosebag
7. *to eat greedily:* blow (oneself out), cram, dig in, eat like a horse, fill one's face, gross out, go for the groceries, grub it up, guzzle, hog it (down), ibble out, knock (it) back, lay into, mac out, pig out, pitch in, pork out, scarf (up), scoff, shovel (it) down, slop (it) up, stack (it) away, throw (it) down, wade into, whack (it) back; spec. guzzle (choke)
8. *to eat a small meal:* catch a bite, tear off a bite
phr. 9. *calls to eat:* chow down!, come and get it!, dig in!, pitch in!, grub('s) up!
abbrev. 10. FHB (family hold back)

90. Appetite; Thirst
n. 1. inner man
2. *hunger:* spec. munchies (cannabis-induced cravings for food)
3. *lack of appetite:* spec. chuck horrors (loathing of food that follows withdrawal from heroin)
mod. 4. *hungry:* peckish

91. Cooking and Dining Utensils
n. 1. *eating utensils:* Duke of York (rhy.sl. = fork), eating irons; sunbeam (Aus. a clean item of cutlery on the table); drugstore (the cutlery trolley in a restaurant)
2. spec. doggie-bag (a bag provided in some restaurants to take away leftovers)

LIQUOR: PERSONS

92. Liquor Dealers and Drinkers
n. 1. *alcohol seller:* mine host
2. *barman:* apron, barkeep, mixologist
3. *drunkard:* barfly, booze artist, – hound, boozer, bottle baby, dredge-head, jarhead, jickhead (US Black), jughead, juice-freak, – head, lush, piss artist, pisspot, plonky, rum-dum, rummy, rumpot, sauce hound, soak, souse, tosspot; spec. bottle-a-day man, two-bottle man, etc.
phr. 4. *free:* on the house

93. Abstainers and Prohibitionists
v. 1. to go on the wagon
mod. 2. TT (teetotal)
phr. 3. off the bottle, on the wagon

LIQUOR: ALCOHOL

94. Liquor (general)
n. 1. alky, bevvy, booze, the creature, eel juice, gargle, grog, hooch, juice, jump steady (US Black), neck-oil, oil, piss, sauce, shicker, swag (US Black), tea; spec. hard stuff (spirits as opposed to beer, wine)
2. *superior liquor:* (just) what the doctor ordered, a little of what you fancy, the (real) goods, the real McCoy, – stuff
3. *inferior liquor:* cat's pee, – piss, dishwater, gnat's pee, – piss, rat's pee, – piss
4. *illegal liquor:* jungle juice, kong, moon, moonshine, nigger-pot, panther piss, potato jack, white lightning
5. *effects of liquor:* bang, boot, buzz, jolt, kick, lift, oof, oomph, pep, powee, punch, smack, sock, wham, zing, zip, zowie
6. *measure of liquor:* shot

95. Varieties of Liquor
n. 1. *beer:* amber fluid, – liquid, – nectar, apple fritter (rhy.sl. = bitter), beevos, brew, brew dog, brewha, brewhaha, brewski, buffalo piss, chilly, chilly dog, cold gold, cornflakes in a can, Crimea (rhy. sl.), dreadnought, drinkage (US campus), eightball, forty (US Black), forty ounce (US Black), forty-dog (US), Germaine Greer (rhy.sl.), green, greenie, ha, haha, icy pop, joy juice, jug, micro-beer, milk, nine (a nine-gallon flagon), oh my dear (rhy.sl.), pub pet, reeb (backsl.), road brew, sixer (a 'six-pack') skimmish, square rigger, stage fright (rhy.sl. = light ale), suds, Tex Ritter, tin, toilet-water, tube, twack (a 'twelve-pack'), wallop, wobbly pop; spec. Nigerian lager, photo finish (rhy.sl.), plain (Guinness stout)
2. *wine:* berries (US Black), plonk, pluck (US Black), schoolboy scotch (US Black), smash, vino

3. *cheap wine:* Red Biddy, dago red, muski (muscatel), railroad whisky, sixteen-year-old after-shave, smoke, sneaky Pete

4. *champagne:* boy, bubbly, champers, fizz, poo, pop; spec. the Widow (Veuve Cliquot)

5. *whisky:* brownie, the creature, gay and frisky (rhy.sl.), gold watch, pimple and blotch (rhy.sl. = scotch)

6. *cheap spirits:* dog juice, redeye, rotgut

7. *brandy:* fine and dandy, Jack-a-dandy (rhy.sl.)

8. *gin:* mother's ruin, Vera Lynn (rhy.sl.)

9. *port:* didn't ought (rhy.sl.); spec. WPLJ, shake-'em-down (white port and lemon juice)

10. *rum:* Tom Thumb (rhy.sl.)

11. *abnormal drinks:* blob (Aus. mix of brandy, wine and hot water); corporation cocktail (coalgas in milk); metho, smoke, white lady (Aus. metholated spirits)

96. Mixed or Adulterated Drink

n. 1. spec. bloody (bloody Mary)

phr. 2. on the rocks (with ice), back (on the side, i.e.: 'soda back')

LIQUOR: DRINKING

97. Drinking (general)

n. 1. boozing, hitting the bottle, lushing (it up), swilling, tying one on, wetting one's whistle

2. *a drink:* bracer, drop (of the creature), gargle, hit, jag, jolt, liquid lunch, night-cap, rosiner (Aus.), shot, slug, snifter, snort, squirt game, tincture, tonic, turps (Aus.), wet; spec. eye-opener, phlegm-cutter (first of the day); leg opener (drink when used for seduction); hair of the dog (an anti-hangover drink); one for the ditch, – for the road (a farewell drink); pick-me-up (invigorating drink)

v. 3. *to drink:* bend one's elbow, booze, – it up, chug, chug-a-lug, crack a bottle, – tube (Aus.), dip the bill, – the snoot, farm, gargle, get a load on, get a snootful, get an edge on, – one's nose painted, – one going, hit the booze, – the

bottle, – the jug, – the sauce, hoist one, inhale (a snort), irrigate the tonsils, knock (one) back, lush, – it around, – it up, oil the tonsils, put one/a few back, – down, shicker (Yid.), slop (some) down, sneeze, splice the mainbrace, suck the bottle, swig, swill, take a drop, – a few, – one, – a wet, etc., throw (one, a few, etc.) down, tie one on, tip, wet one's whistle; spec. brownbag (to drink from a 'hidden' bottle when public drinking is banned); fall off the wagon (to resume drinking after a period of abstinence); wet the baby's head (to celebrate by drinking)

adv. 4. *drinking:* on the bash, on the bottle; D&D (drunk and disorderly)

phr. 5. it's the beer talking (an excuse for breaking wind)

98. Spree; Party

n. 1. bat, batter, bender, binge, blind, booze-up, bout, gig, shitface, shindig, shindy; spec. down to Larkin (free drinks); BYO (Aus. 'Bring Your Own' drink to a party); beer bust, beer fest (beer-drinking only)

v. 2. *to go drinking:* cut up, go on a bat, – a bender, etc., hell around, raise hell, paint the town red, pull to a set (US Black)

adv. 3. *on a party:* on a bat, – a batter, – a bender, – a bust, – a toot, on the lush, – the piss, – the randan, – the razzle, – the tiles, – the tipple

99. Toasts; Drinking Invitations

phr. 1. best of luck!, bottoms up!, bung-ho!, cheerio!, cheers!, chin-chin!, down the hatch!, good luck!, here's how!, here's looking at you!, here's mud in your eye!, more power to your elbow! 2. *invitations to drink:* get them in, it's your corner, what's your poison?, your shout, you're in the chair

100. Temperance; Abstinence

v. 1. to get straight, go on the wagon

LIQUOR: EFFECTS

101. Drunkenness

n. 1. affliction, blind staggers, edge, glow, skinful, snootful, staggers, thick head

v. 2. *to be drunk:* to be addled, – afflicted, – afloat, – basted, – blasted, – bevvied, – bowsered, – boxed, – canned, etc. (see 101.3), bet one's kettle, burn with a low blue flame, – one's shoulder, get a jag on, – one's shoes full, go Borneo, – for veg, – to Mexico, hang one on, have a buzz on, – a few too many, – a heat on, – a skinful, – one's back teeth afloat, – one's pots on, kill one's dog, lay US Black), lose one's rudder, pepper 'em up (US Black), show it, squiff out, tank, walk on one's cap-badge, – on rocky socks, watch the ant races

adj. 3. *drunk:* about right, addled, afflicted, afloat, aled up, alkied, all at sea, all mops and brooms, – wet, arseholed, arse on backwards, awash, awry, back teeth afloat, badered, bagged, bashed, basted, belly up, below the mahogany, belted, bevvied, blasted, bleary, blind, blitzed, blown, blown out, bobo, boiled, bombed, booed and hissed (rhy.sl. = pissed), boohonged, boozed, – up, bottled, bowsered, boxed, Brahms and Liszt (rhy.sl.), buckled (Irish), bug-eyed, bullet proofed, bummed, buoyant, buzzed, caked, canned, can't find one's arse with both hands, – hit the ground with one's hat, – see through a ladder, carrying a load, chateaued, choked, clobbered, cock-eyed, comatose, comboozelated, commode-hugging (drunk), corked, corned, crocked, crocko, cross-eyed, cunted, cut, damaged, damp, decks-awash, dizzy, drunk as a bastard, – a bat, – a beggar, – a besom, – a big owl, – boiled owl, – brewer's fart, – a cook, – a coon, – a coot, – a cooter, – a dog, – a fiddler, – a fiddler's bitch, – a fish, – a fly, – a fowl, – a Gosport fiddler, – a hog, – a king, – a little red wagon, – a log, – a lord, – a monkey, – a Perraner, – a pig, – a piper, – a poet, – a rolling

fart, – a sailor, – a skunk (in a trunk), – a sow, – a swine, – a tapster, – a tick, – a top, – a wheelbarrow, – dogshit, – to the pulp, elephant's trunk (rhy.sl.), elevated, embalmed, exalted, FUBAR (i.e. *f*ucked *up b*eyond *a*ll *r*elief), faced, faded, fallen off the wagon, far gone, feeling funny, – good, – high, – no pain, – right royal, fired (up), flaked, flako, fluffy, flummoxed, flushed, flying blind, forteyed (has drunk a *forty*-ounce bottle of beer), foxed, fractured, frazzled, frazzled out, fried, full, full as a boot, – a bull, – an egg, – a fairy's phonebook, – a fiddler, – a goat, – a googy egg, – a lord, – a pig's ear, – a seaside shithouse on Boxing Day (Aus.), – a state school hatrack, – the family po, – a tick, – two race trains, – to the gills, gaga, gassed, geed (up), gesuip (S.Afr.), giffed (from TGIF: Thank God It's Friday), ginned (up), glad, globular, glowing, golfed, goofy, groggy, half-cut, – gone, – seas over, – slewed, – shot, – the bay over, hammered, heated, hiddy, high (as a kite), hit and missed (rhy.sl. = pissed), iced to the eyebrows, inked (Aus.), in one's cups, – orbit, – the bag, the ditch, – the tank, – the wrapper, invertebrated, jarred, jiggered, John Bull (Aus. rhy.sl. = full), juiced, laced, laid out, lame, legless, likkered, listing to starboard, lit, – to the gills, lit up, – lit up like Broadway, – a Christmas tree, – Main Street, – a store window, – Times Square, – London, loaded, loaded to the barrel, – the earlobes, – the gills, – the guards, – the gunnels, – the hat, – the muzzle, – the Plimsoll mark, – the tailgate, looped, loose, low in the saddle, lubricated, lushy, maggotty, maggoty, mashed, maxed (out), melted, mindfucked, mizzled, mulled (up), muzzy, nailed, newted, not all there, off nice, oiled, on a brannigan, – a skate – a tipple, on the booze, – the floor, – the fritz, – the grog, – the piss, – the sauce, one over the eight, OOC ('out of control'), OTT ('over the top'), otis (? play on OTT), out of control, out of one's head, out of one's mind, out to lunch, over the top, paralytic, paved, pervin' (US Black), petrified, pickled,

pie-eyed, pissed, – as a fart, – as a newt,
– as a parrot, – as a rat, – to the ears,
– up, pixillated, plastered, polluted,
pop-eyed, potted, primed, pummelled,
putrid, ramped, ranked, rat-arsed,
ratted, reeking, rigid, ripe, ripped (to the
tits), ripped out of one's gourd,
ripskated, roaring, rocked, rolling, rotten
(Aus.), saturated, sauced, schizzed,
seeing double, – bats, – the bears, – pink
elephants, etc., shellacked, shickered,
shitfaced, shredded, skulled, skunked,
skew-whiff, slammed, slaughtered,
slewed, slopped, sloshed, smashed,
snockered, snootered, soaked, sodded,
soused, sozzled, spifflicated, squashed,
squiffy, steamboated, steamboats,
stewed, – as a prune, – to the eyebrows,
– to the gills, stiff, stinking, stinko,
stoked, stoned, stonkered, stretched,
stung (Aus.), stupid, swacked, swacko,
tanked (up), tattered, ted, teed up, teeth
under, thrashed, three sheets to the
wind, through, tiddly, tipsy, tired, tired
and emotional, toe, toe up (US Black
pron. 'tore/torn up'), top heavy, topped
up, torn up, torqued, totalled, trashed,
trolleyed, trousered, tubed, tweaked,
tweeked, twisted, under the influence,
under the table, under the weather,
vegetable, vrot (S.Afr.), wasted,
wazzocked, well away, well-oiled,
whazood, whipped, whooped, whupped,
wollied, woozy, wrecked, zippered

102. Hangover
n. 1. DTs, head, Joe Blakes (Aus.
rhy.sl. = shakes), morning after (the
night before), pink elephants, shakes
v. 2. *to feel ill:* have a mouth like the
inside of an Arab's underpants, – the
bottom of a bird's cage, – a Turkish
wrestler's jockstrap
3. *a drink to recover:* hair of the dog

LIQUOR: MANUFACTURE; SALE

103. Manufacture and Sale
n. 1. spec. wash (WI: mash used in
home-distilleries)
v. 2. *to work in a bar:* behind the stick

104. Drinking Establishment
n. 1. battle-cruiser (rhy.sl. = boozer),
booze joint, boozer, dive, drinkery,
filling station, jack (rhy.sl. = jack tar =
bar), jinny, juice house, leeky store, LIQ
(US Black), rescue station, rubbidy,
rub-a-dub (rhy.sl. = pub), scatter,
vineyard
2. *illicit establishment:* blind pig, blues
(WI), shebeen, slygrog (Aus.)

105. Drink Container
n. 1. *liquor container:* perch (pint),
trophy (half a gallon), puppy (small
bottle)
2. *wine bottle:* crop (fifth of a gallon),
mickey, short dog
3. *beer:* frosty, minnow, stubby, tinnie,
tube
4. *empty bottle:* dead, – man, – marine,
– soldier

TOBACCO

106. Tobacco
n. 1. baccy, salmon (and trout)
(rhy.sl. = snout), snout
2. *cigarette:* burn, butt, ciggie, coffin nail,
dub, dubber, fag, gasper, Harry Wragg
(rhy.sl. = fag), oily (rhy.sl. oily rag =
fag), rette, straight, weed
3. *end of a cigarette:* bumper, butt,
dog-end, fag-end, short, shorts, snipe
4. *hand-made cigarette:* roll-up,
roll-your-own
5. *cigarette papers:* papers, skins
6. *cigarette lighter:* flint
7. *cigar:* la-dee-dah (rhy.sl.), stogie;
spec. guinea stinker (a cheap cigar)
v. 8. *to pass cigarettes:* flash the ash, toss
the squares (US Black)
9. spec. defug (to get fresh air into a
smokey room)

107. Tobacco Using
n. 1. *a puff of a cigarette:* drag
v. 2. *to smoke:* take a drag, – puff, – pull,
suck on; spec. bog, niggerlip (to wet the
end of a cigarette when smoking)
3. *to light a cigarette:* spec. match me!
4. *share a cigarette:* do a twos (WI)

Animate Existence

LIFE

108. Life

n. 1. school of hard knocks, university of life; spec. good run, long innings (long life)

109. Pregnancy

n. 1. pudding club
2. *foetus:* little stranger
v. 3. *to make pregnant:* knock up, put in the family way, – in the club, – up the duff, stork; spec. break an ankle, cheat the starter (to become pregnant out of wedlock)
mod. 4. *pregnant:* a bun in the oven, clucky (Aus.), egg in the nest, fat (US Black), in pig, in the (pudding) club, in the family way, infanticipating, knocked up, on the hill, – the nest, poisoned (US Black), preggers, priggling, pu the elop (backsl. = up the pole), the rabbit died, up the creek, – the duff, – the flue (Aus.), – the pole, – the spout

110. Birth

n. 1. blessed event

111. Age

n. 1. *old age:* anno domini
v. 2. *to be old:* be over the hill, – past it, have whiskers, make old bones, seen better days; spec. senior out (to abandon the young lifestyle)
adj. 3. *young:* wet behind the ears
4. *old:* no chicken, one foot in the grave, over the hill, past it, seen one's best days; spec. on the shelf (of an ageing woman, still unmarried)

DEATH

112. Death

n. 1. big sleep, (big) chill, (final) curtain, curtains, end of the ball game, fadeout, kickoff, kiss-off, last farewell, – goodbye, – muster, – roundup, long goodbye, (final) pushoff, the (grim) reaper, send off; spec. Roman candle (milit. use: death when a parachute fails to open)
2. *corpse:* cold meat, dead –, goner, rags and bones, stiff, wormbait
3. *cemetery:* bone yard; spec. Davy Jones' locker (a watery grave)
4. *coffin:* six-foot bungalow, pine overcoat, wooden kimono, – overcoat
v. 5. *to die:* answer the last roll-call, – the last muster, – the last round-up, be thrown for a loss, bite the dust, buy the farm, call it a day, – quits, cash in one's chips, check out, come to a sticky end, conk out, crap out, croak, curl up one's toes (and die), cut one's cable, drop off the twig, – the cue, feed the worms, get (as in 'get yours', 'get his', etc.), get it in the neck, give up the ship, go belly up, – for a Burton, – west, go for one's tea, go to the races, hand in one's dinner pail, hang up one's harness, – one's hat, have one's chips, – one's number come up, join the great majority, jump the last hurdle, keel over, kick off, – the bucket, – up daisies, – up dust, lay down one's knife and fork, pass in one's dinner pail, peg out, push up the daisies, put one's checks in the rack, quit, slam off, snuff it, strike out, take the big jump, throw in one's cards, – one's hand, – the sponge,

turn one's face to the wall, – up one's toes, weigh out

6. *to drown:* go feed the fishes, go to Davy Jones' locker, turn into fish food

7. *kill oneself:* do the Dutch, do oneself in, take a Brodie, – the easy way out; spec. gorge out (leap from a high cliff), bump oneself off, put out one's lights, take a powder, top oneself, turn off one's lights, wipe oneself out

8. *bury:* to plant, put six feet under, send home in a box

9. *to be dying:* on one's last legs, one foot in the grave, (have) one's number come up, pegging out

adv. 10. *dead:* across the river, all bets are off, all up, belly up, checked out, counting worms, croaked, dead as a doornail, done for, gone for a Burton, – west, kicked the bucket, – off, one's hash is settled, – number is up, – race is run, out for the last count, – of the picture, – of one's misery, pegged out, popped off, pushing up daisies, rubbed out, shuffled out of the deck, stiff, through, (all) washed out, – washed up, wasted; spec. KIA (milit. abbrev. killed in action)

113. Killing; Murder

n. 1. the business, – big chill, – kiss-off, the bump (off), the chill, hit, one way ticket, rub-out, wipe out, the works; spec. one-way ride, slay-ride; necktie party (a hanging or lynching); contract (a killing arranged for a fee)

2. *death by shooting:* lead poisoning

v. 3. *to be executed:* spec. burn, fry, sit in the hot seat, take the juice (die in the electric chair); swing (for it) (to be hanged)

4. *to kill:* biff, blast, blow away, brush off, bump (off), cancel one's ticket, chill, clean up, croak, cut loose, erase, do in, do the business on, – the job (on), drop, fog, give the business, – the chop, – the rap, – the works, get shot of, grease, hit, ice, knock (US Black), knock off, – out, – over, let one have it, make cold meat of, off, plaster, polish off, put away, put out one's lights, – to sleep, rain on, rip off, rub out, send up the river, snipe (US Black), snuff (out), spifflicate, squib off, stop one's clock,

take care of, – for an airing, – for a ride, – off the count, – out, top, waste, whack out, zap; spec. DX (milit. euph.: direct exchange); make one's bones (Mafia use: perform one's first murder); reimburse (murder someone who will not pay debts)

5. *to shoot:* lead down, plug; spec. gutshoot (to shoot in the belly)

6. *to mark for death:* put a notice on, – the cross on, take out a contract on

---

PLANTS

114. Plants

n. 1. April showers (rhy.sl. = flowers)

2. spec. carnies (carnations, Aus.), glads (gladioli, Aus.)

ANIMALS

115. Animals

n. 1. *dogs:* bow-wow, goddie (backsl.), mutt, pooch, tyke; spec. dachsie, sausage dog (dachshund)

2. *chicken:* chook (Aus.)

3. *birds:* bow and arrow (rhy.sl. = sparrow)

4. *insects:* clinch (bedbug), cooties, creepy crawly, taxi-cabs (rhy.sl = crabs)

5. *dog excrement:* dog, doggy-do, hocky; spec. pooper-scooper (implement for cleaning up after dog)

6. spec. alderman's nail (rhy.sl. = tail)

7. spec. BEM (Bug-Eyed Monster)

8. *donkey:* burro, donk, moke

9. *elephant:* heffalump

10. *horse:* critter, dobbin, dog, gee-gee; spec. screw (an inferior horse); trotter (racehorse)

THE BODY

116. Parts of the Body

n. 1. *the body:* bod, chassis, frame; spec. shaft (the female body considered purely for sex)

2. *hair:* barnet (fair) (rhy.sl.), righteous moss (US Black)

3. *mind:* gourd, thinker, upstairs

4. *head:* attic, bean, belfry, biscuit, block, boko, bonce, chump, coco, conk, crust of bread (rhy.sl.), deache (backsl.), dome, loaf, napper, noggin, noodle, nut, pimple, scone (Aus.), swede, topknot, top storey, wig

5. *face:* airs and graces (rhy.sl.), beezer, boat (rhy.sl. boat-race = face), chevy chase (rhy.sl.), clock, dial, esaff (backsl.), frontage, Jem Mace (rhy.sl.), kisser, lug, map, mug, mush, pan, phiz, phizog, puss, smiler

6. *jaw:* jackdaw, rabbit's paw (rhy.sl.); spec. glass jaw (boxing use: a fragile jaw)

7. *mouth:* bazoo, cakehole, chops, flapper, gob, hole, kisser, maw, north and south (rhy.sl.), puss, smush, trap, yap

8. *teeth:* choppers, eating tackle, Hampsteads (rhy.sl. Hampstead Heath), laughing tackle, pearlies, toothy pegs

9. *nose:* beak, beezer, boko, bugle, conk, honker, hooter, horn, I suppose (rhy.sl.), konk, schnozzle, schnozzola, schnoz (Yid.), snitch, snoot, snout, snoz, snozzle

10. *beard; moustache:* face fungus, fungus, mouser, muff, stache, tash; spec. bum-fluff (light beard of a teenager)

11. *ears:* flaps, lug, lughole; spec. cauliflowers (ears deformed through boxing); tin ear (no ear for music)

12. *eyes:* babyblues, bins, daylights, headlights, minces (rhy.sl. mince pies), optics, peepers; spec. luggage (bags under the eyes); mouse, shiner (a black eye)

13. *stomach:* Aunt Nelly (rhy.sl.), breadbasket, Darby Kelly (rhy.sl.), elly-bay (backsl.), gizzard, kishkes (Yid.), Ned Kelly (rhy.sl.), Newington Butts (rhy.sl. = guts), tum (-tum), tummy, yellib (backsl.)

14. *ribs:* slats

15. *hands:* deenach (backsl.), German bands (rhy.sl.), hooks, lunch-hooks, Mary Anns (rhy.sl.), maulers, mitt, paw

16. *fist:* bunch of fives, dukes, maulers, meathooks

17. *fingers:* bell ringers (rhy.sl.), forks, lean and lingers (rhy.sl.), lunch hooks; spec. presents (US Black: lucky white spots on fingernails)

18. *legs:* bacon and eggs (rhy.sl.), doog gels (backsl. = good legs), drivers, drumsticks, gams, ham hocks, hammers, pegs, pins, Scotch pegs (rhy.sl.), shanks' pony, stumps, timbers

19. *shoulder:* redloch (backsl.)

20. *knees:* biscuits and cheese (rhy.sl.)

21. *neck:* Gregory Peck, bushel and peck (rhy.sl.)

22. *feet:* hoff, mud flaps, plates of meat (rhy.sl.), puppies, trotters

23. *chin:* button, Errol Flynn, Gunga Din (rhy.sl.)

24. *heart:* pump, raspberry tart, ticker

25. *womb:* kidney

26. *skin:* hide, pelt

27. *freckles:* angel kisses

28. *bodily fluids:* claret (blood), axle grease, cream, come, emok (backsl. = come), gissum, gizzum, jam, load, love juice, melted butter, sugar, water of life (US Black), whipped cream (semen); spec. crud (dried semen on sheets or clothes); cheese, crotch cheese, jelly baby (secretions around the penis or vagina)

29. *anus:* arsehole, asshole, backeye, – slice, – slit, blot (Aus.), brown-eye, brownie, bucket, bumhole, bung, bunghole, cornhole, date (Aus.), deadeye, dinger (Aus.), dirt chute, – road, dukie hole (dukie = excrement), freckle, Gary Glitter (rhy.sl. = shitter), gazoo, gripples (US Black), hog-eye, hog's eye, jacksie, jampot, kazoo, keester, keister, leather, poop-chute, quoit, ring, ringpiece, satchel, shit chute, shitter, stank (US Black), winker-stinker

30. *buttocks:* arse, ass, back, batti (WI), bazooka, bottle and glass (rhy.sl.), BTM, bubblebutt, bucket, bum, bumper kit, bunghole, buns, butt, butter (US Black), caboose, cakes, can, chips, cupcakes, Daily Mail (rhy.sl. = tail), date, dinger (Aus.), dusty behind, elephant and castle (rhy.sl. = arsehole), end, fanny (US), glutes (synon. Lat. *gluteus maximus*), heinie, hot buns, jibs, johnson, kab edis (backsl. = backside), kazoo, keechters (Scots), keel, keister, Khyber Pass (rhy.sl. = arse), labonza, North Pole (rhy.sl. = arsehole), parking place, peaches, poop, pratt, quoit

(Aus.), rearview, ring, rusty-dusty, seat, sit-me-down, sit-upon, squatter, sweetcakes, sweetcheeks, tail, tooshie, toches, tuches, tushie (Yid.)

31. *female breasts:* apples, balloons, bazoom, bazoomas, brace and bits (rhy.sl. = tits), Bristol City (rhy.sl. = titty), bristols (rhy.sl. Bristol bits = tits), BSHs (British Standard Handfuls), bumpers, cakes, cats and kitties (rhy.sl. = titties), charlies (Aus. rhy.sl. Charlie Wheeler = Sheila = female, thus breasts), chichi (Mex.), cupcake, dairies, diddies, dubbies, dugs, gazungas, gib tesurbs (backsl. = big breasts), grapes, grapefruits, hangers, headlights, jugs, knobs, knockers, lollies, lungs, mams, maracas, Mary Poppins, milkers, mountains, nay-nays, ninnies, norks, pumps, rack, T and A (tits and ass), tits, titty, TNT (two nifty tits), top bollocks, tremblers, wallopies; spec. eyes (nipples)

32. *genital area:* down there, genials, naughty bits, rude parts, sweet potato pie (US Black), you know where

33. *male genitals:* accoutrements, basket, crown jewels, equipment, family jewels, gear, kit, marriage gear, necessaries, nick-nacks, rig, string and nuggets, three-piece set

34. *penis:* acorn, almond (rhy.sl. almond rock = cock), arm, baby maker, bacon bazooka, bald headed hermit, barney, bazooka, bean (the shape), beaver cleaver, beef (US Black), beef bayonet, big bird, big foot Joe, big one, bird, blue-veined custard chucker, – havana, – junket pump, – piccolo, – porridge gun, – steak, – trumpet, – yoghurt gun, blow stick, bo-dick, bo-jack (US Black), box, bozack (US Black), buddy, burrito (lit. a form of Mexican snack), butcher knife, candy stick, cannon, cherry splitter, chingus (Sp. *chingar,* to fuck), choad (US), chopper, cock, colleen bawn (Irish), Comrade Wobbly, crab ladder, creamstick, curp (backsl.), dagger, dangler, derrick, dibble, dick, dickory dock (rhy.sl.), dingaling, ding-dong, dingus, dinky, dinosaur, dirk, do-jigger, dong, doodle, doover, dopper, dork, dragon, driving post, earthworm, egg roll, end, enob

(backsl. = bone), fanny rat, ferret, flapper, flesh pencil, fleshy flugelhorn, four-eleven-forty-four (US Black), fox and badger (rhy.sl. = tadger), fuck muscle, fuckpole, gigglestick, goob, goober, good time, gooter, gun, gutstick, hairy sausage, ham howitzer, hammer, hammerhead, hampton rock (rhy.sl. = cock), Hampton Wick (rhy.sl. = prick), hang-out, happy lamp, heat-seeking missile, Herman the One-eyed German, hog, hogger, honker, horn, hose, ice cream machine, ID ('let's see your ID'), inch, Irish root, jammy, jigger, Jim Browski, jimbrowsky, jimmy, jimmy dog, – joint, jock, JT, John Thomas, joybone, – prong, – stick, kcirp (backsl.), kidney wiper, knob, lamb cannon, langer, lanyard, licorice stick, liquorice stick, lob, long dong silver, love arm, – pump, – torpedo, – truncheon, lovesteak, lunch, maggot, meat, meat puppet, member, middle leg, midnight lace, milkman, moisture missile, mole, monkey, mouldiworp, mouse mutton, – dagger, Mr Happy, Mr Happy Helmet, mud snake, mutton bayonet, mutton musket, nimrod, nob, nozzle, nudger, oboe, one-eyed brother (US Black), – cyclops, – trouser snake, – zipper fish, p.h.a. ('purple-headed avenger'), peacemaker (US Black), pecker, peenie, peewee, percy, peter, piece, pillock, pink bus, – oboe, pipe, pistol, plonker, plonker pole, pooper, popsicle, pork sword, porridge gun, portable pocket rocket, prick, prod, prong, pud, purple ridgeback, purple-headed avenger, pussy fodder, putz, rabbit, ramrod, reamer, rod, root, salty yogurt slinger, samurai sword, scallawag, scallywag, schlong, sexocet missile, shitstick, short arm, skinflute, snack, snake, sooty jimmy (US Black), spam javelin, stalk stick, sticky spud gun, string, stump, swack, sweetmeat, swipe, tadger, thing, third leg, toad, tockley (Aus.), todger, tommy, tool, trouser mauser, – trumpet, tubesteak, tubesteak of love, tummy banana, turkey neck, Uncle Dick (rhy.sl. = prick), wab, wand, wang, wanger, wang-tang, weapon, weasel, weenie, wienie, willy, winkle, wire, wong, wood, woofer, worm, ying-yang, yoyo, yutz, zack, zipperfish; spec. IBM ('itty bitty meat' = small penis); donkey-rigged, hung (having a large penis); puppy (small penis); stringbean (US Black: thin penis)

35. *erect penis:* Bethlehem steel (US Black), blue vein, bone, colleen bawn, Marquis of Lorne (rhy.sl. = horn), prong, scope; spec. dead rabbit (penis that remains limp)

36. *testicles:* acorns, acher, acre, agates, apples, apricots, back wheels, bags, ballocks, balls, bangers, bannocks, Betty swallocks (rhy.sl. = ballocks), bollocks, bulbs, chimes, Christmas crackers (rhy.sl. = knackers), chuckies, cobs, cods, cojones (Sp.), conkers, eggs in the basket, flowers and frolics (rhy.sl. = bollocks), frick and frack (US Black), General Smuts (rhy.sl. = nuts), goatees, gongs, gonicles, goolies, grand bag, happy sack, jizzbags, Ken Dodds, knackers, love spuds, nadgers, nerds, nerts, Niagara Falls (rhy.sl. = balls), noogies, nuts, orchestra stalls (rhy.sl. = balls), pills, rocks, sack o'nuts, Sandra Bullocks (i.e. ballocks), slabs (backsl. = balls), tommy rollocks (rhy.sl.), yarbles, yongles

37. *foreskin:* lace curtains, snapper; spec. blind, cavalier, near-sighted (uncircumcised penis)

38. *circumcised penis:* clipped, low neck and short sleeves, roundhead

39. *pubic hair:* area, bikini burger, broccoli, brush, bush, carpet, chuff, cotton, Davy Crockett's hat, dickweed, dick wheat, einstein (Albert Einstein's crinkly haircut), fern, Fort Bushy, fuzz, garden, gorilla salad, grass, haddock pastie, lawn, lemon, map of Tassie (Aus., Tasmania resembles the pubic triangle), pubes, pussy hair, rusty bucket (ginger), scrubbing brush, shaving brush, short and curlies, Sigourney Weaver, squirrel, twat-rug, wool, wowser

40. *vagina:* apple, axe wound, baby chute, bacon sandwich, bargain bucket, barge, bear-trapper's hat, beaver, beef, bite, blart, blate, blurt, blut, boat, bob and hit (rhy.sl. = pit), boodle, boogie, booty, boris, box, brasole (Ital. *bresaole*, wind-dried beef), bucket, bug, bunghole, butcher's window, butter, cakes, canyon, catty-cat, central cut, chasm, chopped liver, chuff, chuftie, clout, cock (US South), cock-locker, cod trench, cono, cooch, coot, cooter, cooze, crack, cranny, crevice, cunt, damp, Dead End Street, diddly pout, ditch, down there, drain, fanny (UK), fig, finger pie, fish, fish mitten, fish-tank, flange, fluff, foo-foo, front bottom, – bum, – door, fuckhole, fud, fun hatch, fur, furburger, furrow, furry bicycle stand, – hoop, futy, futz, fuzzburger, fuzzy cup, – lap flounder, G (goodies), gammon, gap, gape, garden, – of Eden (US Black), gash, gee, gib teenuck (backsl. = big cunt), ginch, giz, glamity (WI), glory hole, golden doughnut (Aus.), gorilla burger, gristle-gripper, groceries, growler, grumble and grunt (rhy.sl. = cunt), grummet, gulf, gully (hole), gutter, hair pie, hairy cup, – doughnut, – goblet, – lassoo, hatchi, hirsute oyster, ho cake (US Black), hole, holy altar, honeypot, Irish fortune, Jack an' Danny (rhy.sl. = fanny), jam, jellybox, jing-jang, joxy, joy trail, kennel, kettle, kitty, kitty-cat, Leslie (rhy.sl. Leslie Ash = gash), lips, little sister, love canal, – glove, – hole, – nest, lucky bag, lunch box, Maggie's pie (US Black), magpie's nest (US Black), manhole, maw, meat, met, middle-cut, minge, mink, monkey, mossy cottage, muff, muffin, must-I-holler, mutton, nasty, nest, notch, p (i.e. pussy), package, passion pit, PEEP (perfectly elegant eating pussy), penocha (Sp.), pink velvet sausage wallet, placket, plumber's toolbag, pole hole, poon, poontang, pootenanny, poozle, prime cut, pta (US Black: pussy, titties and armpits), pum-pum (WI), puss, pussy, pussycat, quiff, quim, rag box, rat, rattlesnake canyon, red lane, ring, rubyfruit, scat, second hole from the back of the neck, serpent socket, sharp and blunt (rhy.sl. = cunt), sleeve, slice, slice of life, slit, slot,

snapper, snapping turtle (puss), snatch, snicket (dial. a narrow passage), snot-locker, spadger, spasm chasm, split beaver, – kipper, spunk-pot, stadge, stank, stench trench, stink, stinkpot, stoat, tail, that there, toolbox, trench, trim, trout, tuna, twange, twat, undercarriage, vacuum, vag, velvet tunnel, virginia, where the monkey sleeps, you know where; spec. cherry (maidenhead), horse collar (large vagina)

41. *female pudendum:* ace of spades (US Black), fern, ha'penny, hide, jelly roll, moneymaker, rubyfruit, you know where; spec. cuffs and collars (pubic hair the same colour as head hair)

42. *clitoris:* boy in the boat, button, clit, clitty, dot, joy buzzer, little man, (little) man in the boat, nuts (US Black), taste bud

43. *labia:* beef, curtains, flange, Hottentot apron, piss flaps

44. *throat:* red lane

45. *arm:* Chalk Farm (rhy.sl.)

117. Physical Characteristics

1. *of the weight:* bagels, beer belly, – gut, broad in the beam, fat city, hipsters, love handles, Milwaukee goitre, spare tyre, taff (backsl.), zaftig (Yid.)

2. *skin problems:* Conan Doyle (rhy.sl. = boil), custards, goob (small spot, fr. goober = peanut), zit hickey (love bite)

3. *scars:* glassed (cut in the face), stripe, tram line

4. *of the eyes:* eyes like pissholes in the snow

5. *having a large penis:* hand-reared, straps it to his ankle, well-hung

6. *naked:* bare-ass, (in one's) birthday suit, bollock naked, bollocko, in the altogether, – the buff, – the rude, laid to the natural bone (US Black), nuddy, starkers, stripped to the buff

7. *of the fingernails:* in mourning (dirty)

8. *of the face:* fish-faced, poker-faced, sour-pussed; spec. more chins than a Chinese laundry (fat-faced)

9. *of the hair:* bottle blonde (dyed hair)

10. *bald:* chrome-dome

11. *having a good figure:* built, best-built, stacked

12. *large:* built, built like a brick outhouse, built like a brick shithouse, hunky

13. *having good legs:* leggy, legs up to her arse

118. Bodily Functions

n. 1. *menstruation:* beno (Aus. 'be no fun'), curse, monthlies, on the rag, red dog on a white horse, red Mary (US Black), wallflower week

2. *breaking wind:* beast, breezer (Aus.), fart, guff, raspberry tart (rhy.sl.), thumper

3. *mucus:* dewdrop, lunger, oyster, snot

4. *an erection:* boner, hard (on), stand, touch-on; spec. piss proud (early morning erection); brewer's droop (impairment of erection by alcohol); muddy waters (US Black: loss of erection)

5. *orgasm:* big O, come

6. *vomiting:* school lunch rerun, technicolour rerun, technicolour yawn

v. 7. *to menstruate:* be on the rag, have a little visitor, – the flag out, – the painters in, – the rag on, put the flags out, ride the rag (US Black), stub one's toe

8. *to break wind:* backfire, cheese, drop a beast, – a thumper, drop one's guts, fart, repeat; spec. he who smelt it dealt it

9. *to spit:* gob

10. *to sneeze:* bread and cheese (rhy.sl.)

11. *to achieve erection:* crack a fat (Aus.), flood (US Black), get a boner, – a hard (on), etc. (see 118.4)

12. *to achieve orgasm:* cheese, come, get one's gun off, – rocks off, light off, pop one's nuts, shoot (off) one's load, – wad

13. *to vomit:* barf, blow one's cookies, – doughnuts, – groceries, – lunch, boot, buick, call for Hughie, – Ralph, cat, chuck, chuck a dummy, chunder, cry Hughie, – Ralph, – Ruth, drive the big white bus, drive the porcelain bus, dump one's load, feed the kippers, flash, go to instant boot camp, go the big spit, – big split (Aus.), hack, have a liquid laugh, have a technicolour yawn, heave, hug the porcelain, hurl, kak, kiss the porcelain god, kneel before the porcelain throne, lose one's doughnuts, – groceries, – lunch, park a custard, pray

to the porcelain god, puke, ralph, shoot a cat, spew, – one's guts, – one's ring, spill one's breakfast, spread a technicolour rainbow (Aus.), throw one's cookies, – one's voice (Aus.), throw up, Tom and Dick (rhy.sl. = to be sick), toss one's cookies, – one's tacos, Uncle Dick (rhy.sl.), upchuck, vom, woof

14. *to masturbate:* accost the Oscar Meyer (US: Oscar Meyer wieners), adjust one's set, adjust the bowl of fruit, apply lip gloss, apply the hand brake, appropriate the means, audition the finger puppets, baste the tuna, battle the purple-helmeted warrior, beat off, – one's dummy, – one's hog, – one's meat, – pete, bludgeon the beefsteak, bring oneself off, buff one's helmet, – the banana, – the bishop, – the happy lamp, burp the worm, choke the chook (Aus.), come into your own, dance with johnnie one-eye, diddle the dinky, disobey the pope, do handiwork, – it one's own way, – one's nails, – something for one's chapped lips, – the bachelor's shuffle, – the backstroke roulette, – the Han Solo (pun on *Star Wars* hero), – your own thing, drain the monster, empty the cannon, engage in safe sex, express yourself, fight the champ, fire the wobbly warhead, flap takkie (S.Afr.), friendly fire, get one's nuts off, – one's pole varnished, – the German soldier marching, give yourself a low five, go on Peewee's little adventure, grapple the gorilla, have a Sherman (rhy.sl. Sherman tank = wank), – oneself, ignite the lightsaber (ref. to *Star Wars*), jerk off, jill off (female play on 'jack off'), juice one's fruit, lick the dick, lighten the load, load the cannon, make a rendezvous with Mrs Hand, man the cannon, – the cockpit, molest the mole, perform a self-test (computer imagery), pet one's pussycat, play pocket billiards, play with oneself, polish Charlie Brown, – one's antlers, – one's knob, – one's sword, – percy, – the lighthouse, – the penguin, – the pole, – the rocket, – the sword, – the viper, pound off, pull one's joint, – one's pud, – one's pudding, – one's wire, rub off, – up, sew (US Black), shags, slap high fives with Yul Brynner (the penis and the movie star are both bald), slay the one-eyed monster, snake, spank, stroke one's beef, tickle one's pickle, tootle one's flute, toss off, twang one's wire, varnish one's pole, wank, whip off, – one's wire, whack off, whank; spec. catch a buzz (to masturbate with a vibrator) (see also 360.19)

15. spec. Barcoo salute (Aus. = brushing flies away from the face)

phr. 16 spec. looks like a wet weekend (Aus.: menstruation will make sex impossible)

119. Defecation

n. 1. business, call of nature

mod. 2. *urination:* comical Chris (rhy.sl. = piss), cousin sis (rhy.sl. = piss), Frazer Nash (rhy.sl. = slash), gerry riddle (rhy.sl. = piddle), goodnight kiss (rhy.sl. = piss), gypsy's (rhy.sl. Gypsy's kiss = piss), hey-diddle-diddle (rhy.sl. = piddle), hi-diddle-diddle (rhy.sl. = piddle), hit and miss (rhy.sl. = piss), J. Carroll Naish (pron. 'Nash', thus rhy.sl. = slash), jerry riddle (rhy.sl. = piddle), jimmy (riddle), Johnny Bliss (Aus. rhy.sl. = piss), – Cash (rhy.sl. = slash), leak, lemon tea (rhy.sl. = pee), little jobs, micky/mike bliss (rhy.sl. = piss), number one/ones, pee, pee-pee, piddle, pie and mash (rhy.sl. = slash), pig in the middle (rhy.sl. = piddle), pooley, poolie, quick one, rattle and hiss (rhy.sl. = piss), riddle-me-ree (rhy.sl. = pee), Robert E. (rhy.sl. Robert E. Lee = pee), run-off, slash, snake's hiss (rhy.sl. = piss), squirt, that and this (rhy.sl. = piss), tinkle, wazz, wee, wee-wee, wet, whiz, widdle, you and me (rhy.sl. = pee)

3. *ordure:* big hit (Aus.), – jobs, boom-boom, crap, crash (Aus.), diddley-poo, dookey, dukie (US Black), honey, job, kak, ka-ka, lemon (rhy.sl. lemon curd = turd), number twos, pony (rhy.sl. pony and trap = crap), poo, edopie-plops, Richard the Third (rhy.sl. = turd), shit, tomtit (rhy.sl.), turd; spec. dog, horse apples, road apples (animals); dags, clinkers,

dingleberries (adherent excrement); skid marks (stains on underwear)

4. *urine:* little jobs, number ones, pee, piddle, piss, Robert E. (rhy.sl. = Robert E. Lee = pee), snake's hiss (Aus. rhy.sl. = piss), wee-wee, widdle; spec. golden shower (urolagnia)

5. *diarrhoea:* apple-blossom two-step, arse-piss, Aztec hop, – revenge, – twostep, b.d.t. ('back door trots'), back-door trots, backyard trots, boot-hill two-step, bum soup, Cairo crud, chickenshits, the, chocolate chutney, clart, cocktails, collywobbles, crab-apple two-step, Delhi belly, dirties, dribbles, dribbling shits, drippy tummy, drizzlies, the Edgar Britts (Aus. rhy.sl. = shits), GI trots (US), GIs (US), green-apple quickstep, – trots, – two-step, Hershey squirt/squirts (US; the Hershey brand of chocolate), Gyppy tummy, Jim Britts (Aus. rhy.sl. = shits), jimmies, Jimmy Britts (Aus. rhy.sl. = shits), Hong Kong dog, King Tut's revenge, Mexicali revenge, Mexican foxtrot, – toothache, – two-step, Montezuma's revenge, movies, nicker bits (Aus. rhy.sl. = shits), Patagonian pasodoble, quick step, Rangoon runs, ringburner, runs, the, scoot scoots, shaster, shits, shitters, Singapore tummy, skiets (S.Afr.), skitters, the, sour-apple quickstep, squitters, the, threepenny bits (rhy.sl. = shits), toms (Aus. rhy.sl. = tomtits = shits), touch of 'em (Aus.), trey-bits (Aus./NZ), touristas, trots, two-bob bits, Zachary Scotts (rhy.sl. = trots), Zasu Pitts (rhy. sl. = shits)

v. 6. *to visit the lavatory:* be excused, chase a rabbit, crap, do one's business, give one's bum an airing, (go and) see a man about a dog, go and see uncle, go round the corner, go somewhere, make a piss stop, make a pit stop, pay a call, pick the daisies, pluck a rose, powder one's nose, rake one's cage out, see Mrs Murray, visit Miss Murphy, visit Sir Harry, visit my Aunt Jones, visit my aunt, visit the sandbox; spec. caught short, taken short (desperate to visit the lavatory)

7. *defecate:* Andy Capp (rhy.sl. = crap), bake it, big hit (rhy.sl. = shit), dog, brad, build a log cabin, bury a quaker, choke a darkie (Aus.), cope, cramber, crap, crash, curl one off, despatch one's cargo, do a job, – a job for oneself, – a jobbie (Scots), – a rear, – a rural, – a shift, – a shit, – an agricultural, – big jobs, – one's business, – one's dirty, – one's duty, drop one's load, drown the brown turtle, dump, eartha (rhy.sl. Eartha Kitt = shit), get a load off one's behind, – one's mind, go and sing 'sweet violets', – down to the ground, – for a walk with a spade, – grunts, grot, grunt, have a clear-out, – a hot pie, – a rear, – an Irish shave, heave a Havana, kak, kangaroo it (Aus.; one is squatting), lay a log, lump, open the bomb-bay doors, park a darkie, – one's fudge, pinch a loaf, – one off, pony, poo-poo, pooh-pooh, poop, post a letter, scutter (Irish), shit, – a brick, – bricks, – pickles, sit on the throne, squat, squeeze, squeeze one's head, strain some potatoes, take a crap, – dump, – shit, – squat, take the kids to the pool, tomtit (rhy.sl. = shit); spec. ride the porcelain bus, – porcelain Honda (to have diarrhoea)

8. *urinate:* bleed the liver, drain the dragon, get rid of the bladder matter, have a gypsy's (rhy.sl. = gypsy's kiss = piss), – a jimmy (rhy.sl. jimmy riddle = piddle), – a piss, – a slash, make pee-pee, pee, piddle, piss, point percy at the porcelain, see a dog about a man, see a man about a dog, shake hands with the wife's best friend, shake hands with the wife's best friend, shake the dew off the lily, spend a penny, splash the boots, strain the potatoes, strain the spuds, syphon the python, take a leak, – a pee, – a piss, – a slash, tap a keg, tinkle, visit Miss Murphy, wee-wee, widdle

phr. 9. who cut the cheese (who farted?), SBD (silent but deadly)

THE BODY: CARE

120. Toilet; Hygiene; Grooming

n. 1. *hairstyle:* afro, 'fro, DA (duck's arse), duck's arse, cowlick

2. *parts of the hair:* bugger's grips, sidies (sideburns)

3. *straightened black hair:* fried, dyed and swooped to the side, konk, process
4. *comb:* rack pick (a comb for curly black hair)
5. *wig:* Irish jig (rhy.sl.), rug, syrup (rhy.sl. = syrup of figs)
6. *shave:* dig in the grave (rhy.sl.)
7. *cosmetics, etc.:* axle grease (hair oil), BO juice (deodorant)
8. spec. grease (gay use: KY jelly)
v. 9. *to straighten black hair:* conk, konk, fry one's hair, press one's hair, process, wig bust
10. *dress one's hair:* have a hair-do, rat one's hair (backcomb hair)
11. *to shave:* dad and dave (Aus. rhy.sl.), mow the lawn
12. *apply cosmetics:* put on one's face, – warpaint; spec. flame (homosexual use)
adj. 13. *natural black hair:* nappy
14. *long-haired:* sheepish

121. Physical Exercise

n. 1. *strength and ability:* fire power
2. *exercising:* pumping iron, pushing iron, throwing iron, working out
3. spec. the burn (in aerobics: the pain barrier)

HEALTH

122. Health; Physical Condition

n. 1. feather, fig, form, kilter, shape, way, whack
2. spec. million dollar wound (milit.: wound that does not kill but invalids out of war)
phr. 3. *enquiries as to health:* how are they hanging?, how are you doing?, – going?, how's by you?, how's your head?

123. Good Health

n. 1. fine fettle, – feather, – form, – shape, – whack, tiptop form
v. 2. *to feel well:* feel one's oats, go strong, run on all cylinders
adj. 3. *healthy:* aces, alive and kicking, all there, – to the good, A1, bobbish, bully, chipper, clever (Aus.), feeling one's oats, – right (royal), fit as a

butcher's dog, fit as a Mallee bull (Aus.), full of beans, – piss and vinegar, hitting on all four/six/eight (cylinders), hotsy-totsy, hunkydory, in fine fettle, – form, – whack, in good shape, – good trim, in the pink, keen, primo, one hundred per cent, ripper (Aus.), rosy about the gills, sharp, skookum, slap-up, top hole, – notch, topping, the tops, up to par, – scratch, – snuff, – the mark
4. *replying to enquiries as to health:* can't complain, could be worse, fair to middling, not so bad, nothing to brag about, – write home about, still here, – (alive and) kicking

124. Poor Health

v. 1. *to be ill:* feel a bit green, feel bum, – crook (Aus.), – like hell, – lousy, – off colour, – ratshit, – under the weather, have one foot in the grave, not feel like anything, – too hot, not feel up to scratch, – up to snuff, etc. (see 123.3)
2. *to become ill:* break down, conk out, crack up, fold up, go on the blink, get out of commission, – of sorts, – of whack
3. *fake illness:* come the old soldier, pull an act, swing the lead, work one's ticket
adv. 4. *ill:* below par, blah, bunged up, butcher's (Aus. rhy.sl. = crook), crook (Aus.), crummy, down at heel, in bad shape, – the shit, not so dusty, – so hot, off colour, – form, out of commission, – of sorts, peakish, peaky, punk, putrid, ratshit, run down, seedy, sick as a dog, under the weather, wonky, yucky
5. *dying:* bought and sold and done for, done for, on one's last legs, (with) one foot in the grave, seen better days, – one's best days, (all) shot, through
6. *exhausted, run down:* beat, burned out, dead-beat, dead on the vine, frazzled, fucked, gone smash, wrecked
7. *delirious:* bats (in the belfry), batty, cuckoo, dippy, dotty, gaga, loony, loopy, nuts, nutty, off one's bean, – chump, – head, – nut, – onion, out of one's head, – gourd, – chump, etc., screwy

125. Ailments; Diseases

n. 1. *stomach ache:* bellyache, collywobbles, gutache, tummyache
2. *headache:* a head

3. *cold:* snotty nose
4. *cramp:* Charlie horse
5. *bad breath:* jungle mouth
6. *hepatitis:* hep
7. *cough:* strep throat
8. *cancer:* Big C
9. *cystitis:* honeymoon cystitis
10. *venereal disease:* band in the box (rhy.sl. = pox), clap, cold in the dong, dose, drip, dripsy, gleet, horse (rhy.sl. = horse and trap = clap), jack (Aus.), Nervo and Knox (rhy.sl. = pox), pox, syph, sypho (Aus.); spec. full house (both syphilis and gonorrhoea); nine day blues (incubation period for gonorrhoea); blue balls (testicular swelling)
11. *haemorrhoids:* hems, Nuremburgs (rhy.sl. Nuremburg trials = piles)
12. *fit:* wingding, wobbler
13. *backache:* shagger's back (Aus.)
14. *deaf mute:* D&D (deaf and dumb)
v. 15. *to catch venereal disease:* be jacked up (Aus.), be one of the knights, cop a dose, (get) dosed up, piss broken glass, ride the silver steed, take the bayonet course
16. *to catch a cold:* catch one's death
17. *to faint:* throw a seven (Aus.)
18. *body odour:* BO, the pits

126. Physical Injury
n. 1. *scars:* Mars bars (rhy.sl.)
adj. 2. *lame:* gammy, gimpy
3. *injured:* buggered up, out of commission, – whack
4. *wounded:* fucked up

127. Physical and Mental Breakdown
v. 1. *to have a nervous breakdown:* blow it, – up, come unglued, – unstuck, crack up, fall apart, go smash, go to pieces, – pot
adj. 2. *mentally unstable:* cracked, off one's hinges, (all) shot, all to fuck; spec. Shrinksville (a state of mind that may require professional aid), (see also 138.3 and 147)
3. *disorientated:* spaced out

128. Recovery
n. 1. comeback
2. *spec. medicine:* op (operation), plastic job (plastic surgery), short-arm inspection (inspection of genitals), scrape (abortion), dust-off (milit: medical evacuation)
3. *pills:* apples, daily-daily (US milit.: anti-malaria pills)
v. 4. *improve, recover:* buck up, perk up, on the up (and up)

SENSATION

129. Sensation; Touch
n. 1. *odd feeling:* creeps, jim-jams, shivers, willies
v. 2. *to touch:* goose

130. Taste
mod. 1. *tasty:* scrumptious, scrummy, yummy
2. *distasteful:* icky, yucky

131. Smell
n. 1. niff, phew, pong, whiff
2. *spec. sexual odour:* funk, wolf-pussy (US Black)
v. 3. *to smell:* get a noseful, niff, phew, pong, whiff
4. *to be smelly:* pen and ink (rhy.sl. = stink)
adj. 5. *smelly:* loud, niffy, noisy, pongy, sniffy, whiffy

SIGHT

132. Sight; Look; Glance
n. 1. butcher's (rhy.sl. = butcher's hook = look), Captain Cook, Charlie Cooke (rhy.sl.), darry, decko, dekko, gander, gig (Aus. = a glance), glaum, glom, look-see, lookism, measure, once-over, pipe, shot, shufti, shufty, slant, squizz, up-and-down; spec. coke stare (US Black = aggressive stare); glad eye, goo-goo eyes (amorous glance); hard eyes (unpleasant look)
2. *view:* spec. flash, flash of light (rhy.sl. = sight), free show; theatre use: Mickey Mouse (rhy.sl. = house = audience)
3. *spectacles:* bins, cheaters, gig-lamps, glims, goggles, headlights, -lamps,

peepers, specs; spec. shades (dark glasses)
4. *maps:* comics
5. *assessment:* recce
v. 6. *to look at:* book (the joint), cast one's optics (at), – peepers (at), clock, cop a decko, – gander, – sight (of), eeson (backsl.), eevach a kool (backsl. = have a look), eyeball, gander, gawp, geek, get a load of, get an eyeful, give a going-over, give the eye (to), – the once-over, glaum, glom, goggle (at), have a decko, – a look-see, key in, lamp, orb, pan, peg, pipe, run the eye over, size up, take a flash at, – a gander (at), – a hinge (at), – a measure (of), – a shot at, – a slant at, – a squint at, twig; spec. watch the birdie, – the dickey-bird (admonition from photographer to subject); shoot the squirrel (glimpse a girl's underwear or genitals)
7. *to spy on:* get a line on, gumshoe, snoop, tail
8. *to stare:* double-o, gander, gawk, gawp, gig (Aus.), goggle, rubber, rubberneck, scope, screw, take a screw at
9. *to disappear:* do a vanishing act, go disappearo
10. *show, reveal:* exhib, flash, trot out, uncork
11. *to assess:* case over, check out, have one mapped, keep tabs on, orb, pan, peep one's hole card (US Black), pin
12. *to appear before:* front (Aus.)

133. Light
v. 1. *turn off lights:* douse the Edisons, kill (the lights), pull the juice

SOUND

134. Hearing
n. 1. earwigging, the Earie, the Erie
v. 2. *to hear:* catch, earhole, get a load of, get an earful, peg, take in

3. *listen:* be all ears, bend one's ear, catch a listen, cop –, earwig, get an earful, grab a listen, give (it) the ear
4. *eavesdrop:* be on the earie, – the Erie, have big ears, – long ears
adj. 5. *deaf:* Mutt and Jeff (rhy.sl.)
phr. 6. *loud and clear:* lumpy chicken (milit.)

135. Sound
n. 1. *solid noise (of a blow, or falling object):* bam, bash, biff, blam, blop, bong, bop, cachunk, etc., chunk, dab, flop, flump, kerbam, kerboom, kerchunk, etc., pam, phut, pom, pomp, powie, slam-bam, slambang, smack, smacko, sock, socko, swack, swacko, whack, wham, whammo, whang, zam, zap, zoom, zowie
2. *light, splashing noise:* burble, guggle, slap, slip, slop, slosh, squelch, squidge, squish
3. *loud noise:* biff-bang, biff-boom, racket, slam-bang
4. *sheet music:* maps
5. *records:* discs, plates, platters, sides, slices, sounds; spec. box (tape recorder, record player), wheel (of steel) (record deck)
6. *instrument:* box (guitar)
v. 7. *to play the piano:* tickle the ivories
8. *play records:* spec. toast (WI: for a DJ to add his lyrics to a backing track), spin discs

136. Silence
n. 1. shush
v.t. 2. *to quieten:* put down the soft pedal, – the lid on, turn off
v.i. 3. *to be quiet:* hush one's mouth, – up, (be like dad and) keep mum, put a sock in it, put the lid on, stow it, – the gab
excl. 4. *be quiet!:* can it!, chuck it!, enough!, hold it down!, hush up!, lay off (the racket)!, pipe down!, pull in your ears!, stow it!, take it easy!

Personality

CHARACTER

137. Character; Disposition
n. 1. bag, the likes (of), number, (one's) size, (–) speed
2. *personality:* dope, goods, merchandise, oil, (the old) this and that, what it takes
v. 3. *to be characteristic:* be that way, built that way, be one all over, (about) one's speed, (just) one's speed, right in one's bag, – up one's alley, – down one's street
4. *to have charm:* be on the ball, have it (right) down, have (plenty of) what it takes
adj. 5. *charming:* ducky
phr. 6. where one is at, – one is coming from

138. Idiosyncracy; Eccentricity
n. 1. idiosity
2. *eccentricity:* bats in one's belfry, bee(s) in one's bonnet
v. 3. *to be eccentric:* have a bee in the bonnet, – a screw loose, – bats in the belfry, – bugs in the brain
adv. 4. *eccentric:* barmy, bats, batty, bourbon, cracked, crackers, daffy, doofus, doolally, dotty, funny (in the head), half-cracked, – -crazy, kinky, loopy, nutty, off-beat, off-brand, off the wall, on the edge, out of left field, potty, queer as a coot, – as a nine-bob note, screwy, weird (see also unintelligence 145–147)

REPUTATION

139. Repute
n. 1. front, rep; spec. it (US Black: the quintessence of Blackness); bell (US Black: personal notoriety)
v. 2. *to have a good reputation:* be in, – in good, count, keep one's nose clean, rate
3. *be important:* (see Greatness: 18), be on top of the heap, make a noise in the world
4. *gain importance:* feature, grab one's fifteen minutes (fr. A. Warhol's dictum 'Everyone will be famous for 15 minutes'), headline, hit it big, hit the headlines, make it big, make the front page, pick up brownie points
adv. 5. *reputable:* aces, all wool and a yard wide, kosher, straight, waxed (US Black: anyone who is well known), white
6. *eminent:* (see Greatness: 18), big deal, – cheese, – stuff, etc., high-up, high muckamuck, swell
7. *famous:* big-named, (a) celeb, having one's name in lights; spec. glitterati (international social-literary circles)

140. Disrepute
n. 1. bad rep, – smell
2. *loss of reputation:* climb-down, nose-dive
v. 3. *to lose reputation:* be brought down a peg (or two), blow up, come down a peg, – a notch, get a black eye, go down the chute, – down the tubes, – on the skids, have one's nose put out of joint, hit the skids
4. *to put into disrepute:* smear
adv. 5. *disreputable:* low-down, lowest of

the low, low-life, no-hoper, ornery, past praying for, wouldn't tell you the time of day

6. *obscure, insignificant:* (see Smallness: 19), bottom of the heap, lightweight, low rent, no great catch, – shakes, not amounting to a piss in the ocean, small beer, – change, – potatoes, – time

---

BREEDING

141. Gentility; Culture

adj. 1. *genteel, well-bred:* aristo, blue-blood, blue-book, glitzy, high-hat, high-tone(d), nobby, posh, ritzy, slick, smooth, swanky, tony, upper crust, uptown; spec. Sloane (Ranger), county (UK upper bourgeoisie)

142. Ungentility; Vulgarity

v. 1. *to live in squalor:* pig it

adj. 2. *vulgar:* all dressed up like a pox-doctor's clerk, brassy, flash, – as a Chinky's horse, – as a rat with a gold tooth, jumped up, lairy (Aus.), not backward in coming forward, out of order, over the top, poncy, smart-ass

3. *rustic:* billyjack (US Black), cornball, corny, folksy, jungly

4. *affected:* artsy-crafty, arty-farty

5. *rough:* hard-boiled, leather-necked, rough-and-ready, rough-necked, tin-arsed, wild and woolly

adv. 6. *living in squalor:* pigging it, pig style (US Black)

Intellect

INTELLIGENCE

143. Intelligence; Intellect
n. 1. brains, (little) grey cells, grey matter, gorm, gumption, horse sense, nous, savvy, smart money, smarts
2. *an intellectual:* long-hair, pointy-head
v. 3. *to be clever:* be on the ball, have all one's marbles, – what it takes, know a hawk from a handsaw, know a shilling from sixpence, know a thing or two, know enough to come in and out of the rain, know how many beans make five, know one's age, know one's anus from one's ankle, – one's arse from a hole in the ground, – one's arse from one's elbow, know one's boxes, know one's eccer (Aus.), know one's kit, – one's onions, know one's stuff, know one's way about, – something, – up from down, – what's what, – what's happening, know what time it is, know where one's arse hangs, know whether one is Arthur or Martha (Aus.), know whether it's pancake Tuesday or half-past breakfast time, – which way is up, use one's loaf; spec. to know where the bodies are buried (to have knowledge which gives leverage over others)
4. *to be wise, shrewd:* be bright as a new pin, – nobody's fool, – not as daft as one looks, – not as stupid, etc., have a head on one's shoulders, know what time it is, use the old bean, – chump, – noggin, – turnip; spec. graduate (US Black: to gain knowledge)
adj. 5. *intelligent:* all there, not so dumb, – dusty, on the beam, there with the goods, smart

6. *wise, shrewd, aware:* (be) down (US Black), cool, culture, first cab off the rank, fly, half-wide, hardcore, hep, hip, jerry, long-haired, necklaced (US Black), no flies on . . . , quick on the trigger, ready (US Black), ready-eyed, savvy, sharp, spunko, streetified, street smart, street wise, swift, switched on, tasty, together, triple hip (US Black), turned on, with it
phr. 7. must have swallowed the dictionary, who slept in the knife box? (and is thus 'sharp')

144. Knowledge
n. 1. dope, know-how, nitty-gritty, savvy
2. *identity:* ID; spec. P Check (UK milit.: personality check); Wilkie Bard (rhy.sl. = ID card)
v. 3. *to be aware of, know about:* be hep, – hip, – jerry (to), – on the inside track, – posted, – up on (one's stuff), – wise (to), have a line on, – the inside track, – the goods on, – the stuff on, – dead to rights, – down cold, – down pat, – its number, – it pegged, – it straight, – it sussed, know it backwards, – it down to the ground, – one's stuff, – the ropes, – what time it is, – what's happening, etc. (see Intelligence 143), sus out
4. *to recognize:* burn, get a line on, – next to, – on to, give (it) a tumble, make (it for), peg, rumble, tumble (to)
5. *see one's own interest:* blow wise, get hep, get smart, – wise, – next to oneself, – one's head screwed on, – one's mind right, – straight (to oneself), smarten up, wise up
6. *see through:* be jerry (to), – on one's wavelength, – wise (to), blow wise (to),

have down, – pegged, – cold, – one's measure, – one's number, – one sussed, know what makes one tick, know where one is at, – is coming from, – where one's head is at, – one's wavelength
7. *to ask for identity card:* card
8. *to prophesy:* Kreskin
adv. 9. *intelligent, aware:* down, fly, hep(ped), hip(ped), jerry, next to, on the ball, on to, smart (to), sussed (out), up to, wise (to)

UNINTELLIGENCE

145. Stupidity

n. 1. numbskullery
v. 2. *to be stupid:* be boneheaded, – sapbrained, etc. (see adj. 145), to be a dickhead, – dorkbrain: – dumbo, etc. (see Disreputable: 433), couldn't find one's way to first base, – find his arse with both hands, doesn't know a mule's ass from a lemon, – his ass from a double-barrelled shotgun, – his ass from a hole in the ground, – his ass from his elbow, – his ass from third base, – his butt from a gourd, doesn't know owl-shit from putty without a map, – sheepshit from cherry-seed, doesn't have a clue, – the foggiest, doesn't know enough to come in out of the rain, – to pound sand in a rathole, doesn't know shit from Shinola, – know from Adam, – know from the man in the moon, – know t'other from which, – know up from down, have one's head up one's arse, – shit for brains, isn't ready for people, thinks it's just to pee through
adv. 3. *stupid:* (see 431: Stupid Person); blockheaded, blubberbrained, boneheaded, bonkers, chuckleheaded, clueless, cuckoo, daffy, daffydown dilly (rhy.sl. = silly), daft, dead between the ears, – from the neck up, dumb, dumbarse, dingy, dopey, dorky, fatheaded, flaky, foggy, goofy, goopy, green as owl-shit, half-baked, jugheaded, King Dick (rhy.sl. = thick), lame, lamebrained, lunchy, lunkheaded, muttonheaded, nitwitted, not all there, – ready for people, off one's trolley, old enough to know better, ossified, out to lunch, pig ignorant, sap-headed, silly as a two-bob watch (Aus.), so dumb he couldn't find his ass with two hands at high noon, – he couldn't piss out of a boat, – he couldn't piss without a button hook, soft (in the head), slow on the trigger, thick, untogether, wet behind the ears, young in the head (US Black); spec. addict (one who falls for confidence tricks)
phr. 4. *of the stupid:* some mothers do have 'em
5. *admitting ignorance:* ask a silly question . . . , ask me another, damned if I know, don't ask me, God knows, I haven't the foggiest, I pass, I give up, it's (all) Greek to me, your guess is as good as mine, what's that when it's at home?

146. Foolishness; Nonsense

n. 1. funny business, monkey business, mug's game, shenanigans; spec. scream (ludicrous idea)
2. *nonsense:* ackamaracka, all my eye and Betty Martin, applesauce, apple butter, ballocks, bollocks, bollox, balls, baloney, boloney, bologna, banana oil, bilge, blatherskite, booshwah, borax, bosh, bushwa, bughouse, bull, bullcrap, bull muffin, bullsh, bullshit, bullshine, bullwash, BS, bunk, bunkum, cheese, chepooka, claptrap, cobblers (rhy.sl. = cobblers' awls = balls), cock, cods, codswallop, cowyard confetti, crap, crock (of shit), dookey (lit. 'crap'), dookie, dooky, duck soup, dukie, eyewash, fiddle-faddle, fiddlesticks, flannel, flapdoodle, flubdub, gammon, garbage, guff, hogwash, hokum, hoo, hooey, hooha, hoo-ha, hoohah, hootennany, horsefeathers, horse hooey, horseshit, jiggery-pokery, jim-jam, krazin, (a) load of applesauce, – balls, etc., load of reg, – (old) madam, lunchmeat, magoozlum, malarkey, mishegaas (Yid.), mumbo-jumbo, pants, phonus-balonus, phooey, piffle, pigshit, poop, poppycock, rannygazoo, rhubarb, rollocks, rot, shite, strunz, toffee, tommyrot, tosh, trash, tripe, twaddle, yang yang
3. *foolish talk:* air, ballyhoo, baloney,

blah, blather, bull, gas, guff, hooey, hot air, jive, wind

v. 4. *to play the fool:* arse about, – around, bugger about, fart about, – around, fuck about, – around, grab-arse, piss about, – around, silly arse about, – around, sod about

5. *do something stupid:* (see 146.4); do the crazy act, fuck up, make a bloomer, – a dumb play, – a prick of oneself, screw up

6. *to talk nonsense:* blah (on), bull, bullshit, crap (on), dish the bull, – the crap, etc. (see 146.2), flannel, go off at the mouth, run off at the mouth, hand (out) a line, – of bull, – of crap, etc., let off hot air, ratchet-mouth, rot, shoot the bull, talk balls, – crap, – guff, etc., talk through one's arse(hole), – one's hat, – the back of one's neck, talk shit, – trash, – tommyrot, wank (on)

phr. 7. *stop being stupid:* act your age, be your age, cut it out, – the comedy, – the crap, get your arse in gear, – yourself together, grow up, stop arsing around, – buggering about, etc. (see 146.4)

8. *to make a fool of:* make a monkey of, – a sap of, etc. (see 431: Stupid Person)

adv. 9. *foolish:* (see 145.3)

phr. 10. GIGO (garbage in, garbage out)

excl. 11. *that's absurd!, don't be absurd!:* applesauce!, are you kidding!, arseholes!, bagpipe it!, balls!, blooey!, bull!, bullshit!, coffee and cocoa! (rhy.sl. = I should cocoa), come off it!, crap!, cut it out!, – that out!, – the crap!, did I fuck!, don't be funny!, – fuck about!, – give me that!, – make me laugh!, fiddlesticks!, forget it!, fucking Ada!, fuck that (for a lark)!, gag me with a spoon!, gertcha!, get away (with you)!, – along (with you)!, get wise!, go chase yourself!, – run up a drain!, – shit in your hat (pull it over your ears and call it feathers)!, – take a flying fuck!, I should cocoa! (rhy.sl. = I should say so), in a pig's arse!, knickers!, later (for that)!, leave it out!, leave off!, – over!, less of it!, like fuck!, my eye!, my foot!, never happen!, no way!, nothing doing!, not much you wouldn't!, pull the other one (it's got bells on it)!, quit fooling!, says you!,

screw it!, shut your mouth and give your arse a chance!, skip it!, stick it!, stroll on!, tell it to the marines!, – me another!, turn it up!, up your arse!, – your gazoo!, – kazoo!, up yours!, walk on!, what else is new?, who do you think you're kidding?, you must be joking!, you've got a nerve!

147. Madness

n. 1. barminess, bats in the belfry, lame brains, looniness, (a) screw loose, space case, wack attack, whack attack

2. *mental hospital:* bin, booby hatch, bughouse, crazy house, funny farm, loony bin, nut hatch, nut house

v. 3. *to be insane:* be all over the board, – around the bend, – bananas, etc. (see 147.5); have a screw loose, – a tile loose, – one's wires crossed, – bats in the belfry, not be all there, – have all one's marbles

4. *to become insane:* blow a fuse, – one's cork, – lid, – mind, – top, crack up, flip one's lid, – wig, get out of gear, go balmy, – bananas, – batty, etc. (see adj. 147.5), go off one's bean, – one's chump, – one's gourd, – one's nut, – one's onion, go out of one's bean, – one's chump, etc., go off one's rocker, – the rails, – over the edge, lose one's marbles, shoot one's marbles (US Black), wig out

adj. 5. *insane, crazy:* all over the board, around the bend, asiatic, balmy, bananas, barmy, bathouse, batty, bats, batshit, bats in the belfry, boho, bourbon, bughouse, cuckoo, cracked, crackers, cracko, crazy-arse, cruising with one's lights on dim, daffy, dippy, doofus, doolally, dopey, dorky, dotty, freaky, gaga, gone, half-cracked, – -gone, – -there, harpic ('clean around the bend'), has a few of his pages stuck together, kooky, lakes (of Killarney) (rhy.sl. = barmy), lamebrained, loco, loony, loopy, loose up top, mental, meshugge (Yid.), neuro, non compos, not all there, – quite there, (not having) both oars in the water, not playing with a full deck, not the full quid (Aus.), nuts, nutso, nutty (as a fruitcake), off-beat, off-brand, off one's bean,

– box, – cake, – chump, – gourd, – nut,
– onion, – rocker, off the beam, – the
wall, out of left field, out of one's head,
– mind, – onion, – tree, out of whack, out
to lunch, plumb loco, potty, only eighty
pence in the pound, queer as a coot, – as a
nine-bob note, rum, schitzi, screwy, (one)
shingle short (Aus.), sicko, squirrelly,
stark staring bonkers, troppo (Aus.), two
bricks short of the load, two pence short
of a bob, toey (Aus.), twisted, unglued,
whack-a-doo, whacked out, whacko,
whacky, weird, wig city, wigged out,
wiggy, wild, wild-arse, (living in a) worm
farm, wired, yarra (Aus.)
phr. 6. keep taking the tablets

ATTENTION

148. Attention; Heed

v. 1. *to be alert:* be all there, – fly, – on
the job, get down (US Black), keep
one's eye on the ball, know what's what,
– what the time is, look alive, – sharp,
– slippy, not miss a trick, – take any
wooden nickels
2. *to become alert:* brace up, buck up, get
on the case, – on the job, get with it,
jump to it, snap (it) up, snap out of it,
stand point
3. *to notice:* catch
4. *to point out:* finger, put the cross on
5. *make an obscene gesture (at):* give the
finger, flip the bird, make a V-sign
6. *to be involved:* get in deep
adv. 7. *alert:* alive and kicking, all there
(with the goods), chipper, hot to trot,
Johnny on the spot, live, (up) on one's
toes, on the ball, – the hop, – the job,
sharp
8. *engrossed, obsessed:* behind, crazy for,
have a ring through one's nose (US
Black), hot for, head over heels, into, up
to the neck (in), right in (it), from soup
to nuts, – the ground up

149. Care

n. 1. caginess, leariness
v. 2. *take care of:* keep tabs on, ride herd
(on), ride shotgun; spec. look out for
number one (take care of oneself first)
3. *be careful:* keep one's eyes peeled,

– one's head down, not stick one's head
out, – stick one's neck out, – take any
wooden nickels, watch one's arse
4. *be alert:* be on the job, stay on the job,
cock a weather eye, keep one's eyes
peeled, look sharp, – slippery, watch it
5. *keep watch:* give jiggs, keep cave,
– KV, – chickie, – nit, – one's ear to the
ground, lie doggo
excl. 6. *be careful:* be cool!, don't take
any wooden nickels!, get wise!, hang
tight!, stay loose!, take it easy!, watch it!
– your step!, don't do anything I
wouldn't (do)!

INATTENTION

150. Inattention; Neglect

v. 1. *to neglect, ignore:* brush off, drop
(it), fake on (one) (US Black), give (it)
the go-by, – (it) a miss, let (it) go, – (it)
ride – (it) slide, – it sweat, not to give a
damn, – a fuck, – shit, – a tumble (for),
skip it
adv. 2. *absent-minded:* asleep on the job,
blank, dead from the neck up, – to the
world, not all there, – on the job,
somewhere else

151. Carelessness; Recklessness

n. 1. slapdashery, sloppiness
2. *careless work:* cheap and cheerful, lick
and a promise, quick and dirty, quickie
v. 3. *to perform carelessly:* bang out,
hack –, knock –, slam –, slap –, whack –,
do any which way, – everywhichway,
knock off, not give a damn (for), – a
fuck (for), etc. (see 150.1)
4. *to be reckless:* ball the jack, break a leg,
go off half-cocked, – like a bat out of
hell, – like hell on wheels,
– hell-for-leather, – hell('s)-bent (for),
rip, tear arse
adj. 5. *careless:* slapdash, what-the-hell,
who-gives-a-damn, – -a-fuck, etc.
6. *reckless:* chancy, iffy
adv. 7. *carelessly:* all anyhow,
everywhichway, half-arsed, half-cocked,
slam-bang, slap-bang, slap-dab
8. *recklessly:* harum-scarum, hell(s)-bent,
hell-for-leather, (like) hell on wheels,
like crazy, over the top

phr. 9. fubis (fuck you buddy I'm shipping out), I could care, I don't give fuck

how does that grab you?, – do you like them apples?, like it?

REASON

152. Reason
n. 1. *argument:* argy-bargy, free-for-all, gabfest, set-to, splang (US Black), tangle
2. *conclusive argument:* knockout
v. 3. *to argue:* argy-bargy, chew the fat, chinwag, fatmouth, go to the mat, go head-to-head, – mano-a-mano, – one-on-one, scream some heavy lines, slug it out, weigh in
prep. 4. *why?:* how-come?, why in the name of hell?, – the hell? – heck?

153. Thinking
n. 1. brainwork
2. *idea, thought:* brainchild, brainstorm, brainwave, hot one, wheeze, wrinkle; spec. skulldrag (taxing thought)
3. *opinion:* two cents' worth
v. 4. *to think:* bear down on, beat the brains, chew the cud, figger, figure, hammer away at, have something on one's head besides one's hat, – one's hair, pound (one's) brains, put on the thinker, – thinking cap, run down, skulldrag, use the (old) bean, – brainbox, – chump, – noggin, – thinker, – turnip, use one's loaf, zero in on; spec. run it up the flagpole (and see if anyone salutes) (to put forward an idea)
5. *to think again:* get back (US Black)
adj. 6. crackerbarrel (homespun philosophy)
7. *intellectually demanding:* thick (US Black)
8. *spontaneous thought:* off the top of one's head
adv. 9. *lost in thought:* dead to the world, – the wide, elsewhere, out to lunch
10. *thinking about:* on one's chest, on the brain, under one's hat
excl. 11. *think about it!:* bite on that!, chew on that!, stick that in your pipe (and smoke it)!, stick that in your hat!
phr. 12. *what do you think (of that)?:*

INQUIRY

154. Interrogation
n. 1. *question:* draw, feeler, sounder
2. *cross-examination:* going over, grilling, hot seat, roasting, third degree, workover
v. 3. *to interrogate:* give a going-over, – a roasting, – a workover, go over, go to town on, – to work on, grill, open up on, pump, put in the hot seat, put the cosh on, – the screws to, – the squeeze on, – through the grinder, shake down, sweat, throw the hook into, turn inside out, work over; spec. put the feelers out (to pump for facts)
phr. 4. what's biting you?

155. Inquisitiveness; Curiosity
v. 1. have a stickybeak, – big ears, – long ears, poke one's nose in, Paul Pry; spec. study (gay use: to observe a possible pickup)
adj. 2. *inquisitive:* long-nosed, nosy, sticky(beak), snoopy
phr. 3. what's it (all) in aid of?

156. Investigation; Examination
n. 1. eye, look-see, measure, once-over, the tape; spec. tale of the tape (boxing use: rival boxers' vital statistics)
2. *test, trial:* go, shot, tumble, workout
v. 3. *to investigate:* check out, – over, dig into, figure, line up, size –, give the eye, – the once-over, have a look-see, take a decko (at), – a shufti (at), root about, – around, run the tape over, see how the cat jumps, – the land lies, – the wind is blowing; – which way the wind is blowing; spec. case the joint (cant: to inspect a place that may be robbed)
4. *experiment:* fool (with), fuck around (with), futz around (with), mess (with), play around (with), try it on the dog
5. *to study:* hit the books, oil it

157. Search
v. 1. *search for, hunt:* be after, – on the prowl for, grubble (around), go gunning

for, gun for, look all over the shop, peel the eyes for, scout (around), scout out, sniff out, take a gander (for), turn upside down; spec. declare open season on (to hunt with intent to kill or harm)

POSSIBILITY

158. Possibility; Probability

n. 1. hope, shot
2. *Impossibility:* Chinaman's chance, Chinese chance, dead pigeon, dog's chance, fat chance, longshot, no-no, some chance, – hope, sweet chance
v. 3. *to be possible:* be on the cards, – in the running, can do, run, stands fair to, worth a punt
4. *to be impossible:* be out of the running, not have a hope (in hell), not have a dog's chance, – Chinaman's chance, etc. (see 158.2), not stand a cat's chance in hell, – a snowball's chance in hell
adv. 5. *impossible:* done for
6. *possible:* on the cards
phr. 7. *that's impossible:* forget it, forget you, no dice, not a hope in hell, not an earthly, no soap, no fear, no way I should be so lucky, – I should live so long, not on your Nellie
8. *in emergency:* at a pinch

159. Certainty

n. 1. blue-chip(s), cert, cinch, dead cert, good thing, lead-pipe cinch, monte, a moral, moral certainty, nice one, shoo-in, sure thing
v. 2. *to be certain:* bank on, bet one's life, go bail on, put money on
adj. 3. *certain:* bang to rights, dead sure, dead to rights, (down) cold, in like Flynn, no ifs and buts, no two ways (about it), open-and-shut, stoneginger, sure as eggs is eggs, – God made little green apples
adv. 4. *certainly:* abso-bloody-lutely, abso-fucking-lutely, and how!, as sure as eggs is eggs, – as God made little green apples, def (definitely), fair dinkum (Aus.), for sure, natch, no shit, poz, pozzy (positively), sho' 'nuff

BELIEF

160. Belief; Credence

n. 1. cred, sell, slant, twist, wrinkle
v. 2. *to believe:* Adam and Eve (rhy.sl.), buy, buy the (whole) farm, fall (for), figure, go for, have, swallow
3. *to be credulous:* be an easy mark, – easy, – green (as grass), – raw, bite, go for (it), gobble (it) down, lap (it) up, take the hook, tumble (for), walk into
4. *to be confident:* bank on, bet one's life, – one's bottom dollar, – the lot, – the wad, go bail on
adj. 5. *plausible:* unsus
6. *gullible:* sold, sold on

161. Disbelief; Suspicion

v. 1. *to disbelieve:* not see (it), – go for (it), – swallow (it)
2. *to be suspicious:* be leary, – sus, hawk, rumble, smell a rat, tumble
3. *to act suspiciously:* fancy pants
adj. 4. *suspicious:* fishy, hincty, leary, sus, sussy, wet (US Black)
adv. 5. *incredible:* bit steep, – tall, – thick, – thin
excl. 6. *I don't believe it!*: (see Nonsense 146); all kidding aside, are you for real?, are you kidding?, can it, come off it!, the hell you say!, don't give me that!, don't kid yourself!, – make me laugh!, – shit me!, get along (with you)!, – away!, fuck off!, I ask you!, I don't believe this!, I don't buy that!, I'll eat my hat!, in a pig's eye!, – arse!, my (giddy) aunt!, my eye!, my foot!, no kidding!, no shit!, says who?, sez who?, – you!, tell it to the marines!, tell me another!, there (just) ain't such an animal!, you must be joking!, you've got to be joking!

SOLUTION

162. Solution; Discovery

n. 1. *evidence:* dope, goods (on), lowdown (on), nitty-gritty, stuff
v. 2. *to solve:* blow wise, break, crack, crack wise (to), get outside of, – a line on, – a slant on, have taped, – by the tail, – down, knock over, size up

3. *to discover:* catch up with, clap eyes on, cop, get a line on, – next to, – onto, – wise to, give a rumble, – tumble, glaum, glom, make, nab, nail, nick, nip, peg, slap the peepers on, sniff out, rumble, tumble (to), twig

4. *to meet with, happen on:* barge into, bump into, connect, hit up with, knock into, run into

5. *to catch, catch out:* bust, catch bending, – cold, – on the hop, – with one's pants down, – trousers down, do up (like a kipper), do up right, have bang to rights, – by the short and curlies, – by the short hair, – the dope on, – the goods on

6. *to be caught:* be bowled out, – caught bending, – cold, etc. (see 162.5), dead to rights

adv. 7. *solved:* bang to rights, cinched, cracked, doped out, down cold, nailed, sussed out, taped

163. Judgement; Conclusion

n. 1. at the death, bottom line, clincher
2. *result:* come-out, curtain, end of the line, payoff
3. *estimate:* guesstimate
v. 4. *estimate:* angle, dope (out), get a line on, – the hang of, – the lay of, size up
5. *to deal with:* square away
adv. 6. *estimated:* by guess and by gosh

ACCURACY

164. Accuracy; Truth

n. 1. *facts:* brass tacks (rhy.sl.), nuts and bolts, nitty-gritty, rodge, runabout, (US Black), score, strength, ticket
2. *truth:* the goods, gospel, inside track, legit, straight dope, – goods, – poop, – shit
3. *essentials:* brass tacks, cases, name of the game, nuts and bolts, nitty-gritty, real grit (US Black)
4. *real thing:* aces, cheese, goods, legit, real McCoy, – McKay, stuff, ticket
v. 5. *to be correct:* be right there, – (right) on the ball, hit the spot, have (it) down, – bang to rights, – dead to rights, hit it, nail it

6. *tell the truth:* come across, – – clean, lay it on the line, shoot straight, tell it like it is
7. *promise the truth:* bet one's boots, – bottom dollar, – life (on it), cross one's heart (and hope to die), swear blind, – to God.
adj. 8. *genuine, true:* aces, all wool and a yard wide, as large as life (and twice as natural), blowed in the glass, dinki-di (Aus.), dinkum, eighteen-carat, for real, – sure, legit, no ifs or buts, on the level, – the up and up, pukka, sure enough, sho' 'nuff, solid, straight up
adv. 9. *precisely:* bang on, – up, in the groove, on the button, – the line, – the nail, – the spot
10. *correct:* bang to rights, dead –, bang on, jake, righteous, rodge, (just) what the doctor ordered
11. *directly:* bam, bang, blam, blap, blip, blop, caplump, caplump, casmack, dap, slap-bang, smack-dab, smack, sock, spang, wham
phr. 12. *you're right:* AOK, ain't that so, – a fact, – the truth, and no mistake, back of the net, check and double check, don't I know it, hole in one, 'nuff said, I'll say she does, – you do, no shit, now you're cooking, – talking, righto, Roger, seen (WI), that's telling them, that's the stuff, you ain't just whistling Dixie, you bet, you can say that again, you don't know the half of it, you got it, you know it is, you're dern tootin', you're telling me, you've got me there, you've got something there, you've said it

165. Error; Mistake

n. 1. bad break, balls up, blue (Aus.), bloomer, boob, boob play, boo-boo, bum steer, bust, cropper, dumb play, – trick, fluff, foulup, fuckup, howler, miscue, misfire, plumb, rick, ricket, wrong'un
v. 2. *to be wrong:* back the wrong horse, be all wet, have another guess coming, not hold together, – hold water
3. *to make an error:* ball up, blot one's copybook, boob, bugger (it) up, cock (it) up, cock up, come a cropper, drop a brick, fluff, foul up, fuck (it) up, goof, go off the rails, louse up, make a bloomer,

– boo-boo, etc. (see 165.1), put one's foot in it, – in one's mouth, put on a black, screw up, step on one's dick, – one's prick, zeke (US Black)

adv. 4. *mistaken, wrong:* barking up the wrong tree, cuckoo, daffy, (a) mile wide, off (the) beam, – (the) line, – the tack, screwed up, way off, – out

excl. 5. *you're wrong:* (see 146); are you kidding!, don't kid yourself!, – make me laugh!, in a pig's eye!, – arse!, like fuck!, – fun!, – hell!, etc.

UNDERSTANDING

166. Intelligibility

n. 1. savvy

v. 2. *to understand:* blow wise, crack wise, catch (on), colly (US Black), connect, cop, dig, earwig (rhy.sl. = twig), figure (out), get a line on, – next to, – outside of, – the message, – the picture, – with it, glaum, glom, grok, have a line on, – a slant on, – pegged, – it down, – the goods on, know the score, – the number, – the ropes, – the words and music, latch on (to), make, make the scene, nail, peep one's hole card, spot one out (US Black), sus out, tumble (to), tune in, twig; spec. flash on (to have a sudden moment of comprehension)

3. *to be understood:* talk one's language

adv. 4. *understanding:* into, onto, up one's alley

phr. 5. *I understand:* (see 164.12); AOK, check, – and double check, gotcha, got it, got you, reet, seen (WI), you said it

6. *do you understand?:* are you with me?, comprenny? (Fr. comprenez?), dig?, do you read me?, – get me?, get it?, you get my drift?, – my meaning?

vb. 7. *to read:* crack the books

167. Unintelligibility

n. 1. double Dutch, Greek

v. 2. *cannot understand:* can't figure, – sus, etc. (see 166), don't know from, no can see, no savvy, not have the foggiest, – the first idea

adv. 3. *incomprehensible:* above one's

head, over –, beyond one, clear as mud, geechie (US Black)

excl. 4. *what?:* er?, huh?, says which?, sorry?, what in the hell? – Sam Hill?, etc., what you say?, whatta whatta?, you what?

phr. 5. *I don't understand:* beats me, – the hell out of me, beyond me, don't ask me, fucked if I know, God knows, (I) can't get that together, it's got me, sod that (for a lark), you've got me (there), your guess is as good as mine

168. Bewilderment; Perplexity

n. 1. botheration, backward thinking (US Black)

2. *problem:* bamboozler, curly one, facer, handful, Harvey Nichol (rhy.sl. = pickle), headache, queeb, (bad) shit, shit on a string, teaser

v. 3. *to confuse:* bamboozle, floor, flummox, get (one) going, keep (one) guessing, stump, throw (for a loop)

4. *to be confused:* don't know one's arse from one's elbow, – one's arse from a hole in the ground, – whether one is coming or going, get one's head up one's arse, go into a flat spin, need a foghorn, up a gumtree, – a stump

adv. 5. *confused:* all at sea, – at sixes and sevens, between a rock and a hard place, hot and bothered, on one's beam end, up against it, up shit creek (without a paddle); spec. on the fence (undecided)

169. Bewilderment; Confusion; Disconcertion

n. 1. *muddle:* dopiness, dottiness, fuddleheadedness, fuziness, grogginess, muzziness, wonkiness, wooziness

v. 2. *to be disconcerted, muddled:* (all) balled up, be like a chicken with its head cut off, run around in circles, not know whether you're on your head or heels, walk on one's head

3. *to disconcert, muddle:* discombobulate, drive up a pole, – out of one's brain, – gourd, – skull, etc., faze, flabbergast, flummox, jive, make one's head swim, put all at sea, put at sixes and sevens, – in a flat spin, – on the hop, – on a crosstown bus (US Black), spifflicate

adj. 4. *bewildered:* all behind like a fat woman, all to shit, cockamamie,

discombobulated, dusty (US Black),
fazed, gimped up, in a (right) two and
eight (rhy.sl. = state), in a flat spin,
paranoid, up in the air
5. *muddled:* addled, addle-pated, adrift,
arsed up, at sixes and sevens (all) at sea,
dopey, dotty, frazzled, goofy, in a loop,
in a spin, jingled, muzzy, not all there,
– with it, screwy, twisted, (having) one's
wires crossed, woozy

RECOLLECTION

170. Memory
v. 1. *to stay in the mind:* get under one's
skin, – in one's hair
2. *to reminisce:* cut up old scores
3. *refresh the memory:* beat the brains,
pound the brains, jog the brains, polish
up, sharpen, shine up, wise up
4. *to remember:* wake up
5. *to learn:* mug up
6. *to remind:* ring a bell

171. Forgetfulness
v. 1. *to forget:* bury (it), draw a blank, let
slide in one ear and out the other, lose
the combination, wipe (Aus.)
adj. 2. *forgetful:* foggy, rusty, with a head
like a sieve, with a hole in the head

EXPECTATION

172. Expectation; Anticipation
n. 1. *presentiment:* hunch
v. 2. *to expect:* feel in one's bones, figure,
reckon
adv. 3. *expectant:* all hopped up, hot (to
trot), raring (to go)
4. *as expected:* nothing to write home
about, par for the course

173. Inexpectation; Surprise
n. 1. bombshell, jar, jolt, knockout,
turn, turn-up
v. 2. *surprise:* catch asleep at the wheel,
– bending, – flat-footed, – off-base, – with
one's pants down, – trousers down, give
one a (nasty) jolt, – turn, etc., jump
3. *to astonish, amaze:* blindside, blow
away, – one away, blow one's mind,

knock for six, knock dead, – cold,
– down with a feather, – for a loop,
make one's hair curl, – head swim, psych
out, smoke out (US Black), strike all of
a heap, strike one blind, – dead, – dumb,
– pink, wow, zap, zoom one out
4. *to be surprised:* take the knock
adv. 5. *unexpected:* out of the blue; spec.
unbuttoned (unprepared)
6. *astonished:* all of a heap, blown away,
buggered, flabbergasted, jiggered, on the
ropes, reelin' and rockin'
excl. 7. *what a surprise!:* are you ready!,
are you prepared!, as I live and breathe!,
blow me down (with a feather)!, blow
my nose!, bugger me!, can you beat it!,
can you feature that!, – you hack it!, did
you ever!, for crying out loud!, for a
motherfucker! (US Black), for days!,
heavens to Betsy!, – to Murgatroyd!,
hell's bells!, – teeth!, holy smoke!, (well)
hush my mouth!, if that doesn't beat the
band!, (well) I'll be a monkey's uncle!,
(well) I'll be fucked, lumme!, my word!,
shit a brick!, shit, eh!, (Aus.), sock it to
me!, starve the lizards!, stiffen the
lizards! (Aus.), (well) strike me blind!,
– me pink!, – a light!, (well) strip my
gears!, shiver my timbers!, stone me!,
stone the crows!, swipe me!, this'll pin
your ears back!, that's news!, too much!,
fuck!, too fucking much!, what a
turn-up!, who (the hell) would've
thought it!, yikes!, yipes!, you could have
knocked me down with a feather!, you
wouldn't read about it!, (see Oaths 189);
spec. Mercy Mary! (homosexual use)
8. *imagine!:* fancy!
9. *really!:* do say!, do tell!, don't tell me!,
go on!, he/she did!, he/she didn't!,
izzatso!, no shit!, say it ain't so!, the hell
you say!, you did!

SUPPOSITION

174. Supposition; Conjecture
n. 1. *guess:* potshot, shot (in the dark),
stab –; spec. guesstimate (informed
guess)
v. 2. *to predict:* call it (right), call one's
(best) shot, dope out, figure, hit (it) on
the head, – the nose

3. *to guess:* go it blind, take a shot (at), – stab (at), make a stab (at), whistle in the dark, – in the wind

175. Imagination; Fantasy

n. 1. pie in the sky; spec. thousand-yard stare (the 'lost' look of a combat soldier)

v. 2. *to imagine:* moon around, space out
adv. 3. *fantasising:* moony, spaced (out), sanpaku (fr. Zen), T-zoned (T = transcendental)

Communication

LANGUAGE

176. Language; Speech
n. 1. chat, -ese (language peculiar to a person or profession)
2. *jargon:* gobbledegook, Morkrumbo (journalese)
3. *slang:* slanguage
phr. 4. as she is spoke

177. Word; Letter
n. 1. dickybird (rhy.sl.), peep (as in 'not a peep'), verbals
2. *hard word, big word:* jawbreaker, mouthful, two-dollar word
3. *introductory word:* er, like, look, you know, now, right, say, well
4. *printed character:* dog's cock, – bollocks, screamer (exclamation point)

NAME

178. Name
n. 1. handle, label, monicker, tab, tag, trademark
2. *title:* his nibs, hizzoner
3. *general forms of address:* boyo, boysie, bub, bubby, buddy, buster, cock, cocky, cuz, dad, daddy-o, dearie, digger (Aus.), ducks, ducky, guv, guvnor, hon, honey, Jim (US Black), John, Jack, love, lovey, mac, mate, mister, momma, moosh, mush, my man, pal, squire, toots, tosh, wack; spec. Miss (homosexual use)

179. Nickname
n. 1. *UK football team:* Addicks (Charlton Athletic), Brough (Middlesbrough), Canaries (Norwich), Cestrians (Chester), Dons (Wimbledon), Fifers (East Fife), Filberts (Leicester), Forest (Nottingham Forest), Gills (Gillingham), Glaziers (Crystal Palace), Grecians (Exeter City), Gunners (Arsenal), Hammers (West Ham), Imps (Lincoln City), Latics (Oldham), Lions (Colchester), Moorites (Burnley), Orient (Leyton), Owls (Sheffield Wednesday), Paraders (Bradford), Pilgrims (Plymouth), Rangers (Queen's Park Rangers), Reds (Manchester Utd, Liverpool), Robins (Bristol City), Saddlers (Walsall), Seasiders (Blackpool), Shakers (Bury), Spurs (Tottenham Hotspur), Trotters (Bolton Wanderers), Villains (Aston Villa)
2. *commercial:* Coats and 'Ats (C&A), Freds (Fortnum and Mason), Rods (Harrods), Gucky (Gucci), Moss Bros (Moss Brothers), M&S, Marks (Marks & Spencer), Woolies (Woolworths); spec. Chucks, Cons (Converse basketball boots)
3. *military:* The Andrew (RN), big Deuce (WW2), Kate Karney (rhy.sl. = the army), looey (lieutenant)
4. *US college courses:* blabs in labs (linguistics), shocks for jocks (basic engineering), stones & bones (prehistory), darkness at noon (art history slide show), slums and bums (urban sociology), rocks for jocks (introduction to geology), stars for studs (basic astronomy), chokes and croaks (first aid and safety education), sounds and tunes (campus songs), clapping for credit (music appreciation), physics for

poets (basic physics for arts graduates), jock major (physical education), holes and poles (sex education classes), nuts and sluts (abnormal psychology); spick (Spanish), number-cruncher (involving complex maths), nudes for dudes (art), Plato to NATO (European civilisation), monkeys to junkies (anthropology), gods for clods (comparative religion), Monday Night at the Movies (film school)

5. *UK newspapers:* Daily Excess, – Getsmuchworse (Daily Express), Thunderer (The Times), News of the Screws (News of the World), Grauniad, Garudnia, Grudian, etc. (The Guardian – from its many misprints)

6. *racial:* (see Persons: Inhabitants 383– 4); Johnny- (as in Johnny-Chinaman, Johnny-Pathan, etc.)

7. *first names:* Del (Derek), Tel (Terence)

8. *'inevitable' nicknames:* Agony (Paine, Payne), Betsy (Gay), Blanco (White), Bodger (Lees), Bogey (Harris), Bomber (Harris), Brigham (Young), Buck (Taylor), Busky (Smith), Chalkie, Chalky (White), Charlie (Peace), Chats (Harris), Chatty (Mather), Chippy (Carpenter), Cock (Robins, -son), Dan (Coles), Darky (Smith), Dickie (Bird), Dixie (Dean), Dodger (Green), Dolly (Gray), Doughy (Baker), Dusty (Miller, occ. Jordan, Rhodes, Smith), Dutchy (Holland), Edna (May), Fanny (Fields), Flapper (Hughes), Foxy (Reynolds), Ginger (Jones, Smith), Granny (Henderson), Gunboat (Smith), Happy (Day), Hooky (Walker), Iron (Duke), Jack (Sheppard, -erd, -herd), Jesso (Read), Jigger (Lees), Jimmy (Green), Johnny (Walker), Jonah (Jones), Jumper (Collins), Kitty (Wells), Knocker (Walker, Wright), Lackery (Wood), Lefty (Wright), Lottie (Collins), Mouchy (Reeves), Muddy (Waters), Nobby (Clark, -e, occ. Ewart, Hewart, Hewett, Hewitt), Nocky (Knight), Nutty (Cox), Pedlar (Palmer), Peeler (Murphy), Piggy (May), Pills (Holloway), Pincher (Martin), Pony (Moore), Rabbit (Hutchins, -son), Rattler (Morgan), Sandy (Brown),

Shiner (Black, Bright, Bryant, Green, White, Wright), Shoey (Smith), Shorty (Wright), Slinger (Woods), Smoky (Holmes), Smudger (Smith), Snip (Parsons, Taylor), Snowy (Baker), Spider (Kelly), Spikey (Sullivan), Spokey (Wheeler, Wheelwright), Spud (Murphy), Taffy (Davis, -ies, Jones, Owen and other Welshmen), Timber (Wood), Tod (Hunter, Sloan), Tom (King), Topper (Brown), Tinkle, Tinker, Tottie (Bell), Tubby (Martin), Tug (Wilson), Wheeler (Johnson), Wiggy (Bennett)

9. *rhyming nicknames:* Charlotte the Harlot, Dennis the Menace, Even Stephen, Flo the Chro (Aus.), Giggling Gertie, Hairy Mary, Harriet the Chariot, Harry the Horse, Merv the Perv, Myrtle the Turtle, Nola the Bowler (Aus.), Peter the Poof (Aus.), Phil the Dill (Aus.), Randy Mandy, Roger the Lodger, Terry the Ferry (Aus.), Dizzie, Tizzie Lizzy

10. *of strong men:* Buck, Bull, Butch, Spike

11. *of hair:* Darky; Blondie; Bricktop, Carrots, Ginger, Red; Curly; Baldy

12. *of a slim person:* Daddylonglegs, Lanky, Lofty, Spider

13. *of a fat person:* Chubby, Chubs, Fats, Fatso, Fatty, Jumbo, Tiny, Tub, Tubby, Tubs

14. *of a short person:* Half-Pint, Pee-Wee, Shorty, Tiny, Titch

15. *of one who wears glasses:* Four-eyes

16. *of a foolish person:* Dizzy, Dopey, Goofy, Sappy, Simp

17. *of a conceited person:* (Mr, Mrs, etc.) Knowitall, – Smartarse, – Smartypants

18. *BBC:* Auntie, Beeb, Corp

19. *popular black use:* T-bone

180. Pet Name

n. 1. *names of affection, endearment:* angel, -face, apple-dumpling, babe, baby, babycakes, birdie, blossom, booful, buggins, buggle, bunny, buttercup, chick, -adee, chicken, chicky, cutems, cutesie, -pie, dear heart, diddums, duck, ducks, ducky, fruit pie, honey, – bunny, -child, -pie, -suckle, izzum, -kins (general suffix), lamb, -chop, -pie, little one, – thing, love, lovey, lovey-dovey, oodlum, oozit, peach, pearl, pet, – lamb, piggy, poopsy, precious, – heart, pretty, pudding, pussums, rabbit, snooks, snookums, squidlums, sugar, -bun, -pie, -plum, sweet, sweetie, – pie, sweetness, sweets, toots, tootsie, – wootsie, turtle-dove, -ums (general suffix), wootsie

---

SIGN

181. Sign; Symbol
n. 1. *badge:* buzzer, potsy; spec. pips, stripes (milit. use)
2. *certificate, etc.:* union card (US certificate of one's degree)
3. *medal, award:* gong, ruptured duck; spec. leather medal, wooden spoon (metaphorical award for coming last)

182. Signal
n. 1. flash, high sign, nod, office, tipoff, wink
2. spec. Maggie's drawers (US milit.: on a firing range, the flag that denotes a miss)
v. 3. *to signal:* flash, give the high sign, slip the wink, tip the nod, – wink

---

SPEECH

183. Speech; Talk
n. 1. blab, broadcasting, bunny, crack, gab, gaff, gas, guff, jaw, jaw-jaw, kaylack (backsl.), (mouth) music, noise, patter, rabbit (rhy.sl. = rabbit and pork), rap, tongue-wagging, wind, yap; spec. ji-jibe (US Black: unimportant chatter); fat lip (US Black: unpleasant talk); blooper (embarrassing public verbal error); beef (complaint)
2. *smooth talk:* applesauce, banana oil, blarney, bull, bullshit, BS, bunk, bunkum, chat, (the) con, come-on, eyewash, flannel, gammon, line, (old) oil, riff, soap, spiel, snow (job), speeching (WI), spit-bit (US Black); spec. sob stuff, – story (stories intended to persuade through pity)
3. *complaining:* beating the gums, going on (at), wanking (on)

4. *remark:* capper, crack, whammy, zinger; spec. (the) liquor's talking (to talk unrestrainedly or embarrassingly)
5. *articulacy:* gift of the gab
6. *voice:* pipes
v. 7. *to talk:* beat the gums, bat the breeze, blab, blow, break one's chops, bunny (= rabbit), burble, cackle, chew (the fat), dish, gab, gas, go (as in 'I go . . . and he goes . . .'), jaw, jib (US Black), rabbit, rap, shoot a line, – the breeze, sound off, spiel, spill a line, warble, yap
8. *whisper:* blow down one's ear, talk out of the side of one's neck; spec. deadpan (to speak without expression)
9. *talk loudly:* ballyhoo, blart, blat, bloviate, blow hard, blow off (at the mouth), broadcast, loudmouth, sound off, talk big
10. *to remark:* crack, cut loose (with) dish, let loose (with), out with, shoot (one's wad), sing one's song, spew (it out)
11. *to become abusive:* curse out, get down dirty (US Black), slag off; spec. rub in (to emphasise maliciously)
12. *to talk sincerely:* be one hundred per cent, come flat out (with), get down to brass tacks, let oneself go, pull no punches, make no bones (about), put one's cards on the table, rap on the real (US Black), shoot straight (from the shoulder), show one's (hole-) card, take no prisoners, take the gloves off, talk turkey, touch base with; spec. on one's say-so (on trust); put the bee on (air one's obsessions)
13. *to talk cleverly:* come the smart arse, crack wise, deliver the goods, say one's stuff, spritz (Yid.), talk like a book
14. *to start talking:* fire away, out with (it), shoot; spec. break squelch (milit.: break radio silence)
15. *interrupt:* butt in, chip in, pick up fag ends; spec. pull one's coat (to draw attention)
16. *to talk aptly:* hit the button, say a mouthful, strike home, touch base
17. *offer an opinion:* cop an attitude, put in one's two cents, say one's piece, sound off (about)
18. *speak foolishly:* go off half-cocked,

put one's foot in it, – in one's mouth,
shovel (the) shit; spec. foot in mouth
disease (constant stupidities)
19. *to talk smoothly:* apply the oil,
blarney, bull, bullshit, BS, feed a line,
hand (out) a line, pour on the oil, soft
soap, schmooze, shoot the bull, snow
(under)

184. Talkativeness
n. 1. *chatter:* babble, blarney, blather,
bosh, burble, cackle, dribble, gas, gift of
the gab, guff, gush, hot air, jabber, jive,
natter, schmooze, tosh, wind,
yackety-yak
v. 2. *to chatter, talk idly:* bang on, beat
one's chops, – one's gums, bend one's
ear, blow (off), blow off steam, break
one's chops, burble, chew the rag, flap at
the jibs (US Black), gab, gabble, gas, go
off (at the mouth), go on, jaw, jawbone,
natter, pop off (at), run off at the mouth,
schpritz, shoot blanks (US Black), shoot
off (at one's mouth), spout (off), spruik
(Aus.), talk a blue streak, – the hind leg
off a donkey, waffle, woof (US Black),
yackety-yak, yak, yawp; spec. work the
room (chatter at a party)
3. *to tell a secret:* blow the gaff, let the cat
out of the bag (see also 202)
adj. 4. *talkative:* full of it, gabby, gassy,
gobby, mouthy, yappy

185. Grandiloquence
n. 1. blah, gas, hot air, jazz, wind
v. 2. *talk grandly:* blah, lay it on, pile it on,
splash it on, swallow the dictionary,
swank; spec. do a Melba (announce one's
retirement, glean the publicity, then
continue working)
3. *to boast:* sell a wolf ticket (US Black)

186. Conversation; Discussion
n. 1. bull sesh, – session, chinwag,
confab, dialogue, gabfest, frank and
fearless, pow-pow, rap, sound; spec.
commo (US milit.: communication);
stiffin' and jivin' (US Black: an unreal,
false conversation); bad talk (US Black:
politically unsound talk)
2. *'line', 'pitch':* mack (US Black), riff,
snow job, spiel, stuff (as in 'do your
stuff')

3. *conference:* confab, huddle, pow-wow
4. *explanation:* rundown
5. *response:* comeback, feedback
v. 6. *to discuss:* bat (it) around, chew the
fat, – the rag, kick (it) around,
pow-wow, run down some lines (US
Black), splish and splash (US Black);
spec. say something (US Black: to make
a profound statement)
7. *to 'shoot a line':* come on (to), crack
(something) up, give one a song and
dance, give (one) the old boracic, run
down some lines (US Black), scream
some heavy lines (US Black)
8. *to communicate:* keep the lines open
9. *to discuss again:* rehash
phr. 10. talk to the engineer, not the
oily rag (talk to the boss)
excl. 11. get this!, what's it to you?

187. Public Speaking
n. 1. bitch box (US milit.: Tannoy), PA
(public address system)
2. *publicity:* ballyhoo, hype, promo
v. 3. spec. belt (it) out (to sing loudly)

188. Call; Cry; Shout
n. 1. bleat, boola-boola, hog-caller,
holler, squawk, whoop, yawp, yip
v. 2. barrack, bleat, holler, squawk,
whoop, yawp, yell blue murder, yip
3. *summon:* bell (by telephone), hoy
(Aus.)

189. Cursing; Profanity
n. 1. effing and blinding, four-letter
words, toilet talk
2. *curse:* hex
v. 3. *to swear:* cuss, Lord Mayor, rip and
tear (rhy.sl.); spec. excuse my French,
pardon my French (apologies for
swearing)
adj. 4. *cursed:* all-fire(d), blame(d),
blankety, blasted, bleeding, blessed,
blinking, blithering, bloody, blooming,
blowed, buggering, cocksucking,
consarn(ed), corksacking, cussed,
dad-blasted, dad-gasted, dadgummed,
damnation, dang(ed), dashed, dern,
deuced, doggone, dratted, effing, fizzing,
flipping, freaking, frigging, fucking,
God-blasted, gd, goddam, goldarn(ed),
goldurn(ed), gosh-damned, – -danged,

– -dern, hell-fired, mammy-jamming, mammy-ramming, mammy-tapping, mollyfocking, motherflunking, motherfouling, motherfucking, mothergrabbing, motherhugging, mother-jiving, mother-jumping, motherless, motherloving, mother-raping, pissing, plaguey, shitting, sodding, stinking

excl. 5. *damn!:* balls!, barf!, barf me out!, begorra!, bejabers!, bejazus!, bless me!, – my heart!, – my soul!, blimey!, blow (it)!, botheration!, bugger!, bugger me!, by George!, – golly!, – gosh!, – gorry!, – gum!, – jimminy!, – jingo!, – jove!, – the great horn spoon!, Christ!, – Almighty!, – on a crutch!, Christmas!, Christopher Columbus!, chuck you Farley!, cor!, cracky!, crikey!, criminy!, cripes!, crumbs!, damnit!, – to hell (and back)!, damn my stars!, – sakes!, darn!, dash!, dash it (all)!, dern!, doggone!, drat!, ferchrissakes!, for Christ's sake!, – crap's sake, – cripes' sake, for crying out loud!, – a mother-fucker! (US Black), – gosh sake!, etc., – God's sake!, – heaven's sake!, – landsakes!, – the love of Mike!, – of Pete!, fuck a duck!, – this for a lark!, – for a game of soldiers!, fudge!, gee whillikins!, – whillikers!, – whiz!, glory (be)!, goddam!, goldarn!, goldern!, etc., golly!, gor blimey!, Gordon Bennett!, gosh!, gosh-almighty, gosh-darn!, etc., great Caesar's ghost!, great Scott!, – snakes!, etc., heavens to Betsy!, – to Murgatroyd!, heck!, hell!, hell's bells!, Hogan's ghost! (Aus.), holy cats!, – cow!, – cripes!, – mackerel!, – Moses!, – smoke!, Jesus!, – H. Christ!, Jiminy Cricket!, Judas Priest!, jumping Jehosaphat!, landsakes!, lawd(y)!, lawks!, Lord love a duck!, Mary!, mercy!, motherfuck!, mollyfock!, etc., my (holy) aunt!, my sainted aunt, – eyes!, – gosh!, – hat!, – stars (and garters), nerts!, nuts!, pigs!, pigshit!, radishes!, rats!, sheet!, shit!, shit and derision!, shoot!, shucks!, strewth!, suffering cats!, sugar!, sweet (bleeding) Jesus, tarnation!, the hell with it!, to hell with it!, what the hell!, – the fuck!, – shit!, ye gods! – and little fishes!, your mother!

6. *I'll be . . . !:* I'll be a Chinaman!, – a Dutchman!, – a dirty word!, – a monkey's uncle!, – a (lowdown) son of a bitch!, etc.; I'll be blowed, – consarned!, – darned!, – jiggered!, etc. (see 189.5); I'll be hanged, – shot

7. *curses:* bugger you!, fuck –!, sod –!, damn your hide, go to hell!, rot your bones, the hell with you, – fuck with you, get fucked, – knotted, (go) take a flying fuck!, – a run up yourself!, you piece of crap!, – of shit!, you SOB!, you son-of-a-bitch!, you whoreson bastard!, you scumsucking shit-for-brains!, etc., etc.

WRITING

190. Writing

n. 1. hacking (it out), inkslinging, knocking it out, pen-pushing, pencil-pushing, whacking it out

2. *ticket:* bat and wicket (rhy.sl.), ducat, ducket; spec. Annie Oakley, chinee, Chinese ducket (free, complimentary ticket)

3. *signature:* handle, John Hancock, mauley

4. *handwriting:* fist; spec. chicken scratchings, poultry –, pothooks and hangers (bad writing)

5. *typewriter:* typer

6. *paper:* repap (backsl.)

7. *book:* Captain Cook (rhy.sl.)

v. 8. *to write:* crank it out, hack (it out), knock it out, sling (some) ink, whack it out

9. *to study:* book it, book up, bone up (on), hack (it)

191. Correspondence

n. 1. *letter:* line (as in 'drop a line'), pc (post-card)

2. *invitation:* stiff, stiffie

3. *thanks:* bread and butter letter, thank-you letter, – note

4. *bureaucracy:* bumf, red tape

5. *lovers' codes on envelopes:* SWALK (sealed with a loving kiss), SWAK (sealed with a kiss), SWANK (– a nice kiss), NORWICH (knickers off ready when I come home), SWALCAKWS (sealed with a lick 'cos a kiss won't stick), BOLTOP (better on lips than on paper – next to an X for a kiss), ILUVM (I love U very much), ITALY (I trust and love you), BURMA (be undressed, ready, my angel), HOLLAND (here our love lives and never dies), EGYPT (eager to grab your pretty tits)

6. *love letter:* mash note; spec. Dear John (ending an affair)

v. 7. *to send a letter:* drop a line

INFORMATION

192. Information (inside)

n. 1. dope, goods, hot poop, – stuff, info, line (up), lowdown; spec. beat, scoop (exclusive newspaper story)

2. *inside information:* buzz, hot poop, – steer, – stuff, – tip, inside dope, – stuff, – tip, lowdown, etc. (see 192.1)

3. *reliable information:* cinch, good thing, (the) goods, lead-pipe cinch, real thing, straight goods, – poop, sure bet, – thing; spec. Mister Ed (unimpeachable inside source), deep throat

4. *false information:* bum steer

v. 5. *to inform:* dish (the lowdown), – the dirt, dope up, give the dope on, – the goods on, etc. (see 192.1), let (one) in, – on the ground floor, put a word in one's ear, put in the know, put next to, put on to something good, – something hot, smarten (up), wise (up); spec. kibitz (to offer unwanted information, esp. to a card-player)

6. *to teach:* larn, learn, show the ropes, – a thing or two, smarten up, wise up

7. *to give false information:* bum steer

8. *to become informed:* get a line on, get alongside, get behind, get the hang of, get into, get next to, get onto, get on the inside (track), get wise to, get with (it), sus out

9. *to be uninformed:* not know the score

adj. 10. *of inside information:* hot off the presses

11. *reliable:* blue-chip, gilt-edged

193. Disclosure

n. 1. finger-pointing, (dead) giveaway, let-on, top-off (Aus.), whistle-blowing

2. *rumour:* sniff

v. 3. *to disclose, reveal:* blab, come across (with), come clean, cough, ding, get (it) off one's chest, – (it) out of one's system, give, – (it) a name, go the hang-out route, lay (something) on, loosen up, make a clean breast (of it), open up, put up one's hand, put out, show one's cards, sing, – like a canary, sneeze (it out), spill (one's guts) – the beans, – the works, spit (it out), stand up, unbutton (one's lip), unload

4. *to betray, inform on:* blab, blow the gaff, – the whistle (on), bubble (rhy.sl. = bubble and squeak = speak), deep throat, dob in (Aus.), finger, fink (on), grass (up), nark (on), pin on, put a name up, put one in (Aus.), put the whisper on, rat on, rat one out, shop, snitch, squeal, stool, tip in, torn out (US Black), top-off (Aus.)

5. *to expose:* blow the whistle (on), muckrake, stir up

6. *to reveal one's intentions:* stand up, stick one's chin out, – neck out, tip one's hand, – hole-card

7. *to disillusion:* knock the props from under, pull the rug from under, let down easy, puncture one's balloon

adv. 8. *betrayed:* bubbled, fingered, grassed (up)

194. News; Newspapers

n. 1. dope, gen, griff, info, (hot) poop, SP (starting price); spec. kicker (problematical information)

2. *privileged information:* beat, lowdown, scoop

3. *spec. newspapers, etc.:* bladder, book, funnies, funny pages, – papers, glossy, heavy (serious paper), linen, scream sheet, tab (tabloid), sheet; spec. hatched, matched and dispatched (births, marriages and deaths columns in The Times); bread and butter column (column based on rewritten PR handouts); bulldog (first edition)

4. *'men's magazines':* one-hand magazine, stroke book, tit mag; spec. eight-pager, Tijuana bible (small pornographic comic book)

5. *pin-ups:* beefcake, cheesecake, leg art

6. *journalistic technique:* baby-sitting,

body-snatching (hiding away the human source of a big story); door-stepping (waiting outside the house of a possible interviewee); spoiling (ruining a rival paper's story)

v. 7. *to appear in a paper:* get some ink
8. *(for a story) to happen:* break

195. Television; Telephony, etc.

n. 1. *television:* boob-tube, box, custard and jelly (rhy.sl. = telly), gobble box, goggle box, idiot box, Nervo and Knox (rhy.sl.), tube; spec. God slot (religious programmes), sit. com. (situation comedy), soap opera (very long-running drama series); idiot board (cue board), idiot girl (cue board operator)
2. *film:* flicks
3. *porno film:* cock movie, snuff movie (spec. death), trick flick
4. *still picture:* Beecham's (rhy.sl. Beecham's pill), X-ray
5. *telephone:* blower, dog and bone (rhy.sl.), hook, Molly Malone (rhy.sl.), seven digits (US Black)
6. *rehearsals, etc.:* Acton Hilton (BBC rehearsal studios); mug book (casting directory)
7. *film types:* ear-jerker (featuring the score); weepie (sentimental/romantic); oater (Western)
8. *film director:* lenser, megger
9. *photographer:* shutterbug; spec. blinker (camera)
10. spec. sleeper (media use: slowly developing success)
v. 11. *to telephone:* bell, buzz, give (one) a bell, – (one) a buzz, tinkle, tootle
12. *to watch TV:* tube it
13. *to direct a film:* lens, meg

196. Gossip

n. 1. buzz, Daily Mail (rhy.sl. = tale), dirt, dish, furphy (Aus.), jazz, scuttlebutt, whisper
2. *collective gossip:* bull session, bush telegraph, (the) dirt farm, galah session (Aus.), grapevine
v. 3. *to gossip:* bad-mouth, bad-rap, barber, bat the breeze, bum-rap, clean up the walls (US Black), dish the dirt, get down dirty, – shitty (US Black), hardmouth, put it on the street, put

(one's business) on front street (US Black), put in the poison, set mouth (US Black), shoot the breeze, – the bull, – the regular, – the shit, shovel shit, slay, smartmouth (US Black), stir (it up), talk out of school, – that talk, – trash, throw some dirt (on)
adv. 4. *gossiping:* on the wire

197. Description; Explanation

v. 1. *to explain:* break down (US Black), clue (one) in, daylight (US Black), dope out, fill (one) in, fold one's ears, give, hip (to), lay (the scene) on, light (US Black), mark one's card, run (it) down, school (US Black), whip it on (one), wire up (US Black); spec. kick apart (analyse); knock into (one's skull), – through (one's skull) (to explain to the dull)

198. Story

n. 1. Daily Mail (rhy.sl. = tale), spiel, tell, yarn
2. *unlikely story:* cock-and-bull story, con, fairy story, fish story, song-and-dance, tall story, wind-up; (see Lie 312)
3. *depressing story:* hard-luck story, Newgate gaol (rhy.sl. = tale), sob story, tearjerker
4. *exciting story:* chiller, cliffhanger, shocker, snorter, spine-tingler, thriller; spec. potboiler (story written purely for cash, not art)
5. *romantic story:* bodice-ripper, gay gothic, hysterical historical, sweet savagery; spec. confessional (religious romance)
v. 6. *to tell a story:* spin a yarn, yarn
7. *to tell an unlikely story:* feed (one) the bull, hand a (cock-and-bull) story, – a line, shoot a line, spin a line
8. *to exchange stories:* cut up touches (with)

AFFIRMATION AND DENIAL

199. Assertion

v. 1. *to assert:* lay down the law, – it on the line, take no shit, tell it like it is
2. *to believe absolutely:* eat one's hat,

– one's head, hope to die, swear till one's blue in the face, bet one's bottom dollar, etc. (see 160)

excl. 3. A!, ain't that a fact!, – so!, – it the truth!, all kidding aside!, all reet!, all right!, and don't you forget it!, and that's a fact!, AOK!, awright!, believe me!, betcha!, bet your boots!, blood oath! (Aus.), Bob's your uncle!, check!, – and double check!, damn right!, darn right!, dern right!, etc. (see 164), did I ever!, does a bear shit in the woods?, – the Pope shit in the woods?, fucking A!, go on twist my arm!, harbour light! (rhy.sl. = all right), honest injun!, I ain't just whistling (Dixie)!, I don't mean maybe!, I hear you!, I'll say!, I'll eat my hat!, – my head!, etc., I mean!, I should say so!, Isle of Wight! (rhy.sl. = all right), is that . . . or is that . . . (insert subject as to context), is a bear a Catholic?, is the Pope a Catholic!, lahteeache (backsl. = all right), left off!, lovely grub!, naked!, natch!, no kid(ding)!, no risk! (Aus.), no shit!, OK, okey-dokey, on the level!, right arm!, righto!, right on!, scotia! (US Black), see (backsl. = yes), seen! (WI), (you can) take it from me!, that's the shot! (Aus.), – the ticket!, way to go!, word!, word up!, would I shit you! (you're my favourite turd!), you bet!, you can say that again!, you don't know the half of it!, you('ve) got it!, you know it (is)!, you're dern tootin'

200. Negation

n. 1. blank, KB, knock-back, nix, no-no
v. 2. blank, give the thumbs-down (to), KB, knock-back, nix, no-no
excl. 3. don't make me laugh!, fat chance!, fuck off!, I don't think!, I'll be damned if!, – fucked if!, like fuck!, – fun!, – hell!, nerts!, nix!, no dice!, – sale!, – soap!, – way!, not bleeding likely!, not on your Nellie!, not on your tintype!, nothing doing!, no siree (Bob)!, nope!, not fucking likely!, nuts!, on! (backsl.), some chance!, – hope!, you must be joking!

UNCOMMUNICATIVENESS

201. Muteness

v. 1. *to be quiet, silent:* button one's lip, – up, clam up, dry up, dummy up, freeze, hold one's noise, – water, keep mum, – stum(m), – the cap on the bottle, put a sock in it, shut one's cakehole, – face, – gob, – hole, – trap, zip one's lip
2. *to make quiet:* choke off
3. *to withhold information:* clam up, dummy up, freeze up, hold one's breath, – out (on), keep the cap on the bottle, – the lid on, – them guessing, – it on one's chest, – it under one's hat, keep stum(m), save one's breath, stonewall
adj. 4. mum, stum(m)
excl. 5. *stop talking!:* bag your face!, belt up!, button your lip!, button up!, can it!, cheese it!, cut the chat!, – the crap!, – gas!, – the noise!, drop it!, dry up!, dummy up!, enough said!, forget it!, get back in the knife box!, give your face a rest!, hit me and cut the crap!, hold it!, hold it down!, hold your noise!, hush your mouth!, keep mum!, – stum(m)!, knock it off!, nark it!, nit-nit, 'nuff sed!, put a sock in it!, – the stopper in it!, save it!, – your breath!, shut it!, shut your face!, – gob!, – hole!, – trap!, shut your mouth and give your arse a chance!, stow it!, wrap up!, zip it up!
6. *don't interrupt!:* butt out!, who pulled your chain!

202. Secret

n. 1. cover-up, family jewels, hole card, whitewash
v. 2. *to keep a secret:* clam up, close up, dummy up, hush up, keep it dark, – it down, keep a stiff lip (US Black), – mum, – on the strict q.t., – under one's hat, not let the cat out of the bag, not peep, not spill the beans, play the dummy, put the lid on, tell no tales (out of school)
3. *to suppress:* blue-pencil, put the lid on
4. *to confide in:* blow in one's ear, pull one's coat, put wise (to), wise up
adj. 5. *secret:* closet, hole and corner, hush-hush, inside, on the quiet, – the

q.t., stum(m) and crumm, under the table, – one's hat, under wraps
adv. 6. *secretly:* on the quiet, – the q.t.

203. Concealment
n. 1. cover-up, smoke screen, whitewash
2. *hiding place:* funk-hole
3. *cache:* drop, slaughter (burglar's storeroom), stash
4. *disguise:* front
v. 5. *to hide* **v.t.:** bag, drop, dump, law away, plant, stash

v.i.: 6. *to hide* **v.i.:** dive, duck-out, hole up, keep on the q.t., lay low, lie doggo, – low, lie dead, play dead, – possum, sit quiet, – tight
v.t.: 7. *disguise* **v.t.:** cook up, doctor (up), fake (up), ring
adv. 8. *in hiding:* holed up, lying low, on the lam, playing possum, etc.
9. *disguised:* cooked up, doctored (up), etc., incog

Volition

RESOLUTION; DETERMINATION

204. Resolution

n. 1. balls, guts, stones

v. 2. *to be determined:* barrelass, be out for blood, – for business, do the full sesh, get behind, – down, – into, – (it) on, – one's head down, – some respect (US Black), – stuck in, give one's best shot, go for broke, – (for) the whole shot, – nap on, – overboard, – the limit, mean business, play hardball, put one's head on the block, – foot down, run with the ball, shit or bust, shoot one's bolt, shoot to kill, stand pat, step fast (US Black), stick one's neck out, take care of business, TCB, take no prisoners, take one's best shot, wade in

3. *to make determined:* psych (oneself) up

4. *to determine:* allow, figure, fix (to), reckon

adj. 5. *determined:* ballsy

adv. 6. *determined:* behind, dead set, hell-bent, hells-bent, hot for, into, psyched up, set

excl. 7. *I mean it:* honest (injun)! I ain't just whistling Dixie!, no kidding!, no shit!, would I shit you? (you're my favourite turd)

205. Perseverance

n. 1. stick-to-it-iveness

v. 2. *to persevere:* bang away (at), buck (for), bust a gut, bust one's arse, go down the road (for), hammer away (at), hang in (there), – tight, hit for six, keep the ball rolling, – the show on the road, make the fist (US Black), not give up

the ship, plug away at, run down one's best game (US Black), shag ass, shoot from the hip, – one's best mack (US Black), show the flag, sit tight, steam in, stick one's neck out, stick to (it), sweat (it) out, throw one's hat in the ring, tough it out

adv. 3. *persevering:* shovin' and pushin' (US Black)

206. Obstinacy

v. 1. *to be obstinate:* have one's head up one's arse, put one's foot down, run into the ground, take no shit

adj. 2. *uncompromising:* bloody-minded, bullnecked, cussed, dog in the manger, hard-assed, hard-nosed, mulish, pig-headed

adv. 3. spec. accidentally on purpose

phr. 4. it's my story and I'm sticking with it

IRRESOLUTION; EVASION

207. Irresolution

n. 1. fence-sitting; spec. touch of the seconds (second thoughts)

v. 2. *to be irresolute:* beat about the bush, – around the bush, fart around, fuck about, hum and haw, piss about, – around, pussyfoot, seesaw, shilly-shally, stall

adj. 3. *irresolute:* betwixt and between, half and half, ho-hum, on the fence

208. Caprice

n. 1. *whim:* bee in the bonnet, wheeze

v. 2. *to act madly:* rally

adv. 3. *acting irresponsibly:* triflin' (US Black)

209. Abandonment; Relinquishment
n. 1. chuck, heave-ho, push, shove
v. 2. *to relinquish, abandon:* axe, call it a day (give up), chuck (it) (up), cut loose, ditch, dump, fold, give (it) the (old) heave-ho, give it the chuck, – the elbow, – the E, – the toss, give up the store, hang (it) up, jack (it) in, junk, kiss goodbye, – one's arse goodbye, knock on the head, knuckle down, – under, pack (it) in, put on ice, sack it up (US Black), scrub (it), throw in one's hand, – the sponge, – the towel, top up, wash out, wind up; (see also: Discard 25.4)
3. *to retract one's words:* back down, – out, bow out, call all bets off, chicken out, clam up, crawfish, eat dirt
4. *to alter an opinion:* change one's tune, draw in one's horns, pull in one's horns
5. *to desert, abandon:* break it off (with), cut (out), ditch, do a fade (on), give the brush-off, – the go-around, go bent (on), kiss goodbye, – off, lay down on, leave flat, play the chill (for), take a powder, – a runout powder on, throw overboard, toss overboard (see also v. 2)

210. Evasion
n. 1. dodge, duck, e, elbow, go-around, run-around; spec. AWOL, French leave (absence without leave)
v. 2. *to evade:* back and weave, bob and weave, buck, cock a deaf 'un, duck (out), get cold feet, give the go-by, – the runaround, go AWOL, go cold on, lose one's bottle, oil out, play the duck, – hide-and-seek (with), plead the Fifth, punt off, shake; spec. beat the rap (avoid punishment)
3. *to play truant:* flick (US Black), hop the wag, play hookey, wag off
4. *to avoid:* fight shy (of), give a wide berth, give the go-by, – the runaround, – the miss, steer clear (of)
5. *to avoid work:* come the old soldier, – the tin soldier, dodge the column, flick (US Black), goldbrick, goof off, lay down on the job, soldier, swing the lead
6. *to absent oneself:* go AWOL, take French leave

211. Flight; Escape
n. 1. bunk, disappearing act, vanishing act, el disappearo, powder, skip
2. *narrow escape:* close call, – shave, narrow squeak, near squeak, – go
v. 3. *to escape:* amscray (backsl. = scram), beat it, blow, bunk, buzz the nab, cheese it, cop out, crash out, cut out, do a runner, – a fade, – the disappearing act, – the vanishing act, duck out, fade, fly the coop, fuck off, get out, – the fuck out, – the hell out, go on the lam, go walkabout, have it away, head for the hills, – the tall timber, – the tall trees, – the woods, hightail it, make a break, pull a runner, save one's bacon, Scapa (rhy.sl. = Scapa Flow = go), scarper (= Scapa Flow), show one's heels, skip (it), sod off, take a (runout) powder, – the air, take it on one's toes, take it on the lam, vamoose; spec. flick (US Black: to play truant, to avoid work)

CHOICE

212. Choice; Option
n. 1. bag, bet, cup of tea, cuppa, druthers, fave, – rave, scene, thing
2. *alternative:* any old, between hell and high water, betwixt and between, or else, no two ways about it
v. 3. *to choose:* do one's thing, go for; spec. you pays your money and you takes your choice
phr. 4. *after a decision:* when the chips are down

213. Freedom; Independence
n. 1. open slather (unlimited situation, Aus.), Rafferty's rules (Aus.); spec. indie (entertainment use: an independent TV/film/record company)
v. 2. *to be free, independent:* cut one's own throat, do as one damn well pleases, – one's own thing, footloose and fancy-free, go it alone, go one's own (sweet) way, hoe one's own row, keep oneself to oneself, look after number one, – out for number one, paddle one's own canoe, roll one's own, take care of number one, write one's own ticket

3. *to give freedom:* cut loose, get off one's case, give enough rope, let off the hook
adv. 4. *free:* footloose and fancy-free, on the loose
5. *without rules:* anything goes, no holds barred, no punches pulled, no strings (attached), the sky's the limit
6. *solo:* (all) on one's lonesome, on one's Jack (rhy.sl. = Jack Jones = alone), – one's Pat (Aus. rhy.sl. = Pat Malone = alone), – one's Tod (rhy.sl. = Tod Sloan = alone), under one's own steam

CHANCE

214. Chance; Opportunity
n. 1. breaks, fling, go, hope, main chance, shot, show, slant
2. *good chance:* aces, cinch, clean shot, fair go, fair pop, good thing, natch, runner
3. *poor chance:* crapshoot, longshot
4. *no chance:* on a hiding to nothing, not a Chinaman's chance, – a dog's chance, – an earthly (chance), – a hope in hell, – a cat's chance in hell, – a hope, – a snowball's chance in hell
v. 5. *to take a chance, to risk:* chance one's arm, – one's luck, give it a go, have a fling (at), – a shot (at), lead with one's chin, odds (it), play a hunch, punt (around), punt it (up), sail close to the wind, stick one's neck out, take a stab (at), wing it
6. *to bet:* bet one's bottom dollar, go the whole bundle, – the whole pile, – the whole wad, put one's shirt on
7. *to have a good chance:* have a look-in, – a hope, stand pat
8. *to have little or no chance:* to be on a hiding to nothing, to have a Chinaman's chance, etc. (see 214.4)
9. *to use one's chances:* not to miss a trick, play one's hand
adv. 10. *at risk:* on spec
excl. 11. *no chance!*: don't make me laugh!, you must be joking!

215. Luck
n. 1. beads, breaks, Dame Fortune, dice, ins and outs, joss, Lady Luck, ups and downs

2. *good luck:* break, mazel (Yid), mozzle, muzzle, turnup (for the book)
3. *bad luck:* tough break, – shit, – titties, tzuris (Yid. = problem)
4. *a bad luck totem:* hoodoo, Jonah
v. 5. *to be lucky:* be in clover, – in fat, – on a roll, – on a winner, break the bank, get the breaks, get hot, luck into, luck out, turn up trumps; spec. born with a silver spoon in one's mouth (to be born to riches)
6. *to be unlucky:* be down on one's luck, be fucked, – screwed, etc., crap out, draw a blank, on the outs, not to have the breaks; spec. sizzle (US Black = to be unusually prone to arrest)
7. *to cause bad luck:* hoodoo, jinx, Jonah
adv. 8. *lucky:* hot, in clover, in the fat, on a roll, on a winner
9. *unlucky:* behind the eightball, born under a bad sign, cold, jinxed, hoodooed, fucked, screwed, etc.
10. *destined:* in the cards, – the dice, – the stars

CONTROL

216. Authority
n. 1. clout, final cut, juice
2. *order:* say-so
v. 3. *to have authority:* to be in the chair, – in the driving seat, etc. (see 216.6), call the punches, – the shots, come on strong, crack the whip, have (it) covered (US Black), – one's act together, – one's act down, – one's game uptight, – shit together, – shit down, – it knocked, hold the can, keep ahead of the game, ramrod, ride herd (on), run a tight ship, sit down, toughen (up) one's game (US Black), wear the trousers; spec. go under one's neck (Aus. to usurp another's position)
4. *to give orders:* lay down the law, put one's foot down
5. *to lose control:* blow it, jump the rails
adv. 6. *in authority:* ahead of the game, in the box seat (Aus.), in the chair, in the driving seat, in the saddle, on one's game (US Black)
7. *strict:* death on
phr. 8. don't just stand there, do

something; if it moves salute it, if it doesn't, paint it

217. Force; Compulsion
n. 1. screws, squeeze, third degree; spec. habe (abbr. habeas corpus)
v. 2. *to compel:* blackjack, clobber one with, dump on, put the screws to, – the squeeze on, scare up, strongarm, twist one's arm
3. *to be forced:* like it or lump it, toe the line, walk the plank

218. Restraint; Curb
n. 1. clamp, crimp, damper, freeze, lid, squelch
v. 2. *to restrain:* bottle (up), clamp (down) (on), crimp, put the clamp on, – a crimp into, sit on; spec. dock (to cut wages)
3. *to subdue:* buffalo, bust, take down a peg (or two), take the frills out of
4. *to restrain oneself:* hold one's horses, pull one's punches, slow one's row (US Black), soft pedal
adv. 5. *restrained:* in bondage (US Black), over a barrel

INFLUENCE; INDUCEMENT

219. Influence
n. 1. clout, drag, fluence, juice, mojo, pull, strings, wires
v. 2. *to use influence:* pull strings, pull wires, railroad, tickle palms
3. *to have influence:* draw (a lot of) water, have clout, drag, etc., know where the bodies are buried
4. *to persuade:* do a number (on), get around, grind down, hassle, hook in, pressure, put something over, sell (on), sell a bill, talk a good game
5. *to deceive:* ballyhoo, bamboozle, bullshit, con, get at, get one's hooks on, – one's hooks into, pull the wool over one's eyes, set up, take to the cleaners, three-sheet, wind up
6. *to urge:* ding, drum up, egg on, kack up, kid (along), talk (something) up
7. *to influence emotionally:* get to, put through changes

220. Enticement; Allurement
n. 1. come-on, draw, sucker bait
v. 2. *to entice:* give the come-on (to), pull, smoke out, throw out a line, work (on)
3. *to attract:* bring down
adj. 4. *enticing:* come hither

WILLINGNESS

221. Willingness
adj. 1. *willing:* game
adv. 2. *willingly:* at the drop of a hat, like a shot
phr. 3. I don't mind if I do

222. Consent; Assent
n. 1. go-ahead, green light, OK, thumbs-up
v. 2. *to consent:* give a nod (to), give the go-ahead, – the green light (to), – the OK, – the thumbs-up (to), go with, – the flow, hang loose, lay down (for), roll with the punches, stand still (for), stand up, tip the wink (to); spec. swallow (it) (to accept – often knowingly – lies); choke (it) down (accept reluctantly)
excl. 3. spec. bags I! (schoolboy: yes please!)

UNWILLINGNESS

223. Unwillingness
excl. 1. *I refuse!:* the hell you say!, the hell I will!, the fuck I will!, don't make me laugh!, you must be joking!, in a pig's arse I will!, I'll be damned, – danged, – dashed, – hanged, – shot (if I will)!, I'll see you in hell first!, like fuck I will!, – fun I will!, – shit I will!, etc., include me out!, kiss my arse!, ring the other one (it's got bells on it)!, get fucked!, on your bike!, no deal!, – dice!, – go!, – soap!, not on your life!, not on your tintype!, try and make me!, you've got another think coming!; spec. bags I (baggy) no par! (schoolboy: not me!)

224. Refusal; Rejection
n. 1. big E, elbow, nix, red light, thumbs-down

2. *dismissal:* boot, brown envelope, sack
v. 3. *to reject:* blank, blow out, ding, give the E, – the elbow, – the hard word, give the thumbs-down, – the red light (to), kiss, kiss goodbye, kiss off, turn one's nose up at
4. *to chase away:* hunt (Aus.)
5. *to dismiss:* give the boot, give the brown envelope, give the sack

225. Prohibition
v. 1. *to prohibit:* nix, thumbs-down, zero
adv. 2. *forbidden:* verboten
excl. 3. *no!:* (see 'Stop it' 10.9); forget it!, ixnay!, nix!, – on that (stuff)!, no way!

CUSTOM

226. Habit
n. 1. (daily) grind, nine-to-five, same old same old
adj. 2. *habituated:* hooked, hung up (on) (see also Drugs 503)

227. Convention
n. 1. done thing
v. 2. *to be conventional:* follow one's nose (US Black), get in line, mind one's Ps and Qs, toe the line, watch one's lip, – step
adj. 3. *conventional:* burbed out, button-down, grey

228. Unconventionality
n. 1. spec. the Revo (Revolution)
v. 2. *to behave oddly:* to get away with murder
adj. 3. *bizarre:* craze-o, out of left field, OTT, over the top, way out, weird (see also Madness 147)

229. Fashion
n. 1. *glamour:* pizzazz, Tate and Lyle (rhy.sl. = style)
2. spec. nigger fronts (US Black, very smart clothes)
v. 3. *to be unfashionable:* have whiskers
adj. 4. *fashionable:* glitzy, happening, high-tone, keen, mod, ritzy, sharp, snazzy; spec. early (US Black)

5. *unfashionable:* dead as a dodo, joanie, lunchy, the pits
6. *ostentatious:* flash as a Chinky's horse, – as a rat with a gold tooth (Aus.)

BEHAVIOUR

230. Behaviour; Conduct
n. 1. (where one is) at, bag, (where one is) coming from, doings, goings on, (one's own) thing
v. 2. *to conduct one's life:* do one's own thing, keep one's end up, – one's nose clean, – one's pants zipped, – on the straight and narrow, set to rights, shape up, stack up, wise up; spec. CYA, cover your arse (look after yourself)
excl. 3. *behave yourself!:* act your age!, be yourself!, cut the comedy!, – the crap!, – the funny business!, don't fuck about!, – muck about!, – piss about!, get yourself together!, – your act together!, – your shit together!, – your arse in gear!, lay off!, quit fooling (around)!

231. Misbehaviour
n. 1. carry-on, cold shot (US Black), ego trip, shenanigans, to-do
2. *set-to:* big how-de-do, randan, razzle-dazzle, ruckus, shindy; spec. knock-down drag-out (extremely rough)
3. *social error:* floater
v. 4. *to misbehave:* carry on, come it, – the old acid, – the raw prawn (Aus.), create, cut up rough, – up rusty, draw the crabs (Aus.), hell around, jump bad, kick up hell, raise Cain, – hell, – a racket, – a ruckus, – sand (US Black), throw one's weight about, turn the set out (US Black), trash around, whoop it up; spec. tart about (for a female to act like a tart)
adj. 5. *unpleasant:* boldacious (US Black), bucko
adv. 6. *misbehaving:* all over the board, off the track, out of pocket (US Black), out of order, over the top, OTT

PLAN

232. Plan; Method
n. 1. angle, big idea, gag, hustle, lay, moves, racket, ropes, scam, schmeer, wangle, wheeze
2. *schedule:* layout, lineup, sked, set-up
v. 3. *to plan:* angle, figure, honcho, hustle, plot up, promote, wangle
4. *to plot:* be up to (something) (US Black), cook up, fake up
adv. 5. *anyhow:* all ways to hell, – to shit, anywhichway, everywhichway
excl. 6. *how?:* how (in) the devil?, – (in) the fuck?, – (in) the heck?, – (in) the hell?, – the deuce? – the blazes? – the shit?, etc.
7. *what's happening?:* how about it?, how's about it?, what do you (whaddya) say?, what's the deal?, what's up?, where do we go from here?

233. Prearrangement
v. 1. *to prearrange:* fake (up), fix, put in the bag, – on ice, ready up, set up, sew up, tie-up, wrap up
2. *to reveal a plan:* spring (it)
3. *to succeed in a plan:* click
4. *to go wrong:* blow (it), duff (up), gum things up, – up the works; spec. go in the tank, take a dive (to lose deliberately)
5. spec. back to the drawing board (to replan after a failure)
adv. 6. *arranged:* bagged, boxed, fixed, in the bag, in one's pocket, in the tank, on ice, open-and-shut, sewed up, sewn up, stacked up, tied up, wrapped up; spec. accidentally on purpose

UTILITY

234. Use
n. 1. *useful part:* business end
v. 2. *to use:* cash in (on), keep on tap, play (it) for all its worth
3. *to make useful:* doctor (up), rejig, rev, revamp
adv. 4. *available:* on tap, up for grabs

235. Uselessness
n. 1. *useless object, idea:* crock (of shit), dead duck, – rabbit, washout, write-off
2. *rubbish:* crap, drack (Aus.), junk, leavings, schlock, tripe; spec. honey (human extrement); round file (waste paper basket); airmail (rubbish tossed out of the window)
3. *waste of time:* boondoggle, undertaker job
v. 4. *to waste:* blow, fiddle-faddle away, fool away, footle (away), piddle away, piss away
5. *to waste time:* hack around, piss around
6. *to be worthless:* suck
adj. 7. *spare:* gash
adv. 8. *useless:* crook (Aus.), crude (US Black), down the drain, duff, 4-F, gonzo, no account, on doog (backsl. = no good), sunk, washed up; spec. rumour (irrelevant)
9. *third-rate:* crappy, half-arsed, icky, junky, tacky
phr. 10. ain't worth wiping your ass on, don't amount to a fart in a whirlwind, don't amount to a pisspot full of crab-apples, (as useless as) a spare prick at a wedding, – tits on a bull, not worth a fart in a noisemaker, – a light, – a pisshole in the snow

ACTIVITY

236. Activity; Liveliness
n. 1. game (US Black), goings-on, hustle, jump, lark, play (US Black), tripping, trot
2. *spirit, energy:* bang, bounce, flash, ginger, go, hotcha, hustle, kick, oof, oomph, pep, piss and vinegar, pizzazz, punch, snap, socko, steam, zap, zing, zip, zowie
3. *enthusiasm:* get-up-and-go, hustle, push, spunk, what it takes
v. 4. *to rush around:* bang around, buzz around (like a blue-arsed fly), – like a one-armed paper-hanger, come on (like gangbusters), shazzam
5. *to enliven:* crank (up), hop up, jazz up, pep up, punch up, put some pep, punch, etc. into (it), snap (it) up, stir the

possum (Aus.), stoke the fires, zip (it) up
6. *to draw attention:* draw the heat
adv. 7. *lively:* chipper, chirpy, feeling
one's oats, feisty, full of beans, – of go,
– piss and vinegar, hopped up, on one's
toes, offish, on the go, peppy, zappy,
zingy, zippy
8. *ambitious, enthusiastic:* full of go, – of
pep, – of what it takes, go-ahead,
hard-charging, hungry, Johnny on the
spot, not backward in coming forward,
on the make, pushy, spunky

237. Preparation
n. 1. once-over
v. 2. *to prepare:* clear the decks, gear up,
get set, pepper 'em up (US Black), prep,
ready (up)
3. *to train:* lick into shape, sharpen up,
wise up
4. *to rear:* drag up
adv. 5. *prepared:* armed for bear, fired
up, good and ready, hot to trot, loaded
for bear, up to scratch
6. *unprepared:* half-cock(ed), not cut out
for, not up to scratch

238. Undertaking
n. 1. (tall) order
2. *attempt:* crack, dab, fist, fling, go,
hack, jab, lick, shot, shy, smack, stab,
try-on, whack; spec. good shot (best, if
useless effort), darnedest, Sunday punch
(best effort)
v. 3. *to try:* balloon, give it a burl, – it a
fling, – it a fly (Aus.), – it a go, – it a
tumble, – it a whirl, go for it, have a see
who salutes, take a pop (at), – a shot
(at), etc., try it on
4. *to undertake:* bog in (Aus.), get into,
get one's arse in gear, go out for, go to
bat, motivate, put on the front burner,
take the plunge
5. *to try hard:* be in there pitching,
– slugging, break a blood-vessel, – one's
neck, buck for, bust a grape (US Black),
– a gut, – one's arse, – one's hump,
– one's nuts, get cracking, get down (US
Black), get one's act together, – one's
finger out, – one's shit together, lean
over backwards, pull one's socks up,
turn on the heat
6. *to do one's best:* do one's level best,

– one's darnedest, give (it) all one's got,
go for broke, – the limit, shit or bust
7. *to go to excess:* come it, – on strong,
run (it) into the ground

239. Performance; Accomplishment
n. 1. schtick, shtick, shtik (Yid.), stunt
v. 2. *to do:* cut loose with, hit, pull, talk
talk and walk walk (US Black); spec. go
ahead up (US Black: to do something
together); do it like Mommy (act
domestically)
3. *to do roughly:* bang out, knock out,
toss off
4. *to do well:* blow fire (US Black),
deliver, – the goods, fire on all cylinders,
do it up (right), do one's stuff, do the
works, – the whole bit, go great guns,
go the route, have (it) knocked, hit for
six
5. *to accomplish:* bring home the bacon,
come through (with), cut it, cut the
mustard, get away with, get it together,
get outside of, hack it, lift one's game
(US Black), play past (US Black), pull a
stroke, pull it off, pull one's finger out,
put (it) across, – (it) over, put one's
money where one's mouth is, score,
swing (it), turn a trick
6. *to complete, finish:* be through (with),
call it a day, – it quits, drop the curtain,
hang up one's tools, knock it on the
head, pack (it) in, polish (it) off, put (it)
away, – (it) in cold storage, – (it) on ice,
– the lid down, – the lid on it, top (it)
off, wash up, wind up
7. *to work out:* crack (it), lick (it)
8. *to entertain:* do a bit
phr. 9. *completion:* when all's said and
done

240. Production
v. 1. *to create, concoct:* bodge (up),
– together, cook up, hammer out, hash
up, kludge, lash up, rustle up, toss off,
whip up
adv. 2. *spontaneous:* off the cuff, – the
top of one's head
phr. 3. damned clever these Chinese

241. Work; Employment
n. 1. fag, graft, grind, hang (US Black),
nine-to-five, racket, slave (US Black),

yakka (Aus.); spec. shit detail, shitwork
(unpleasant work)
2. *a job:* meal ticket, spot; spec. chump
job (US pimp: any 'straight' work);
undertaker job (a hopeless job);
foreigner (an illegal second job)
3. *work shift:* swing (4pm–midnight),
graveyard (midnight to 4am), lobster
(early morning), golden hours
(overtime)
v. 4. *to work:* be in harness, graft, punch
the clock, sock the clock; spec. go
around the block (gain work
experience); moonlight (to work two
jobs, one at night); stooge (to work as an
assistant)
5. *to start work:* dig in, fire away, get
cracking, – going, – moving, – off one's
arse, – the lead out, – the show on the
road, hit it, hop to (it), jump to (it),
knuckle down (to), lay into, let rip, light
into, pile in, pitch in, plough into, rip
into, sail into, snap (in)to, turn it up, up
and at 'em, wade into
6. *to work hard, keenly:* bat (it) out,
battle (Aus.), break one's arse, – one's
neck, bust a grape (US Black), bust
one's arse, – one's hump, – one's nuts,
fire, go at it hot and heavy, hammer ass,
pour it on, root hog or die, shake a leg,
sweat it out, work like a black (derog.),
work like anything, – like billy-o, work
one's arse off, – one's butt off, – one's
tail off; spec. gut it (US college: to work
all night); spec. nigger-driving (US
Black: white exploitation of black
workers)
7. *to endure tedious work:* bang away,
grind, hammer away, peg away, whack
(it) out
8. *to end work:* call it a day, – it quits,
clock off, down tools, hang (it) up,
knock off, punch out; spec. chuck
(it) up, go south, jack (it) in (leave a
job)
9. *to defy union rules:* blackleg, fink, rat,
scab, scissorbill
adj. 10. *busy:* at it, at bat, busy as a
one-armed paper-hanger (with the itch),
hard at it, on the ball, – the hop, – the
jump, – the trot, snowed under, tied up,
up to one's eyes, – one's ears, – one's
elbows, – one's neck, etc.

phr. 11. *work hard or don't waste time:*
fish, or cut bait; piss, or get off the pot;
shit, or get off the pot
12. spec. no rest for the wicked; spec.
why keep a dog and bark yourself (use
the available labour force); illegitimis
non carborundum ('Latin': don't let the
bastards grind you down)

242. Hiring

n. 1. *employment bonuses:* golden
handshake (payoff at dismissal or
retirement), golden hello (financial
inducement to a new recruit), golden
parachute (a long-term contract that
must be paid in full even if one is fired)
2. *dismissal:* boot, elbow, heave-ho, sack,
tin-tack (rhy.sl. = sack)
v. 3. *to hire:* sign up
4. *to promote:* spec. kick upstairs (to
promote into inactivity)
5. *to demote:* bump, bust, kick downstairs
6. *to fire:* can, give the bullet
7. *to be fired:* get one's cards, – the boot,
– the slingers
adj. 8. *retired:* spec. bowler-hatted
(retired from the Services)
excl. 9. *I want work!:* gissa job!

243. Fatigue

v. 1. *to collapse:* blow up, burn out,
– down, crap out, curl up (and die), drag
one's arse, keel over, peg out, peter out,
poop out, rock out (US Black), tucker
out
2. *to work to excess:* have too much on
one's plate
3. *to tire out, exhaust:* beat, blow one out,
burn out, do in, do over, fag (out), run
ragged, tucker out
adj. 4. *exhausted:* all in, – shot, at the
end of one's rope, beat, blown out,
burned out, – down, bushed, crapped
out, creased, dead, dead to the wide,
done in, – up, euchred (Aus.), fagged
(out), fit, flaked out, flat (Aus.),
fuckfaced, jiggered, kerried (rhy.sl. =
Kerry Packered = knackered),
knackered, muzzy, one's get-up-and-go
got up and went, on one's last legs, out
of it, out like a light, – on one's feet,
played out, pooped, racked, rooted
(Aus.), rusty, shagged out, shot, stoked

out, stroked (out), sparkers, tuckered, washed up, zoned

INACTIVITY

244. Inactivity; Idleness

v. 1. *to idle, waste time:* arse around, bum around, dog around, – it, duff around, fart about, – around, – off, fartarse around, fiddlefart around, footle about, freeload, fuck off, futz about, ghost (US milit.), goldbrick, goof off, half step (US Black), horse around, jerk off, keep banker's hours, layin' and playin' (US Black), let one's game slip (US Black), lollygag, mess about, muck about, piddle about, – around, play ring a rosie, ponce around, razzle-dazzle (US Black), screw around, scrimshank, shuck and jive, skive (off), sod about, swing the lead, veg out, work one's ticket; spec. punt (US campus: to abandon work)
2. *to remain:* hang about, – around, satellite, stay put, stick around
adj. 3. *inactive:* dead as a doornail, – as a dodo
adv. 4. *unemployed:* at liberty, in dock, on the beach, – the loose, pattin' leather, resting (esp. theatrical)
phr. 5. *you're idle:* don't strain yourself; you'll be a long time dead

245. Laziness

adj. 1. *lazy:* bone idle, born tired, doggy, drag-assed, niggerish (derog.), rum-dum

246. Rest

n. 1. lay-off, lay up; spec. five, ten (as in 'take five' or 'take ten' minutes break)
v. 2. *to rest:* ease it, hole up, lay back, – dead, – up, take five, take ten
3. *to lie or sit down:* flop, park one's carcass, – one's frame, plant oneself, take a pew

247. Sleep

n. 1. beddy-bye, Bo Peep (rhy.sl.), horizontal exercise, kip, rack monster, sack time, shuteye, winks; spec. rack attack (desire to sleep)

2. *nap:* forty winks, zizz
v. 3. *to go to bed:* bunk down, crash down, doss down, fall out, flop, get one's head down, go beddy-bye, – bye-bye, – nighty-night, hit the hay, – the sack, hop in the hay, – in the sack, spark out, turn in
4. *to sleep:* bag (some) Zs, cop (some) Zs, crash (out), get some shuteye, kip, pound one's ear, rack, rack out, sack out, pile up some Zs, Z; spec. do skippers, skipper (sleep in derelict houses, etc.)
5. *to take a nap:* catch forty winks, cop a snooze, grab a little shuteye
6. *to get up:* hit the deck, rise and shine, show a leg
adj. 7. *asleep:* crapped out, flaked (out), on flake, sacked out, Z'd out; (see also Exhausted: 243.4)
excl. 8. *get up!:* hands off your cocks and on your socks!, let's be having you!, rise and shine!, shake a leg!, show a leg!

248. Delay; Postponement

n. 1. hang-up, stand-off
v. 2. *to delay* **v.i.:** hold the phone, put on the back burner, take a rain check, – the scenic route, wag (US Black)
3. *to delay* **v.t.:** let (it) ride, put on hold, – on ice, stall
4. *to be impatient:* bite the carpet, chomp at the bit, foam at the mouth, froth at the mouth, sweat it out
excl. 5. *wait!:* half a mo!, hang about!, hold everything!, – it!, – the phone!, keep your hair on!
6. *stop it!:* ock it!

INTERFERENCE

249. Interference; Meddling

n. 1. back-seat driving, flak, horning in, kibitzing, nosing around
v. 2. *to interfere:* barge in, cut off at the pass, dip in one's business (US Black), horn in, mess with, monkey with, muscle in, nose around, play one too close (US Black), poke one's nose in, shove one's oar in, – one's nose in, stick one's bib in (Aus.), stick one's nose into, snoop

3. *intrude in a conversation:* breeze in, put in one's two cents' worth, – two pennorth, mouth in, – off

excl. 4. *don't interfere!:* butt out!, fuck off!, go bark up another tree!, – blow you own nose!, – chase yourself!, – fish!, – fly a kite!, – fry an egg!, – bag your head!, – join the navy!, – jump in a lake!, – jump off a cliff!, – lay an egg!, – peddle your fish!, – roll your hoop!, – soak your head!, – stick your head in a bucket!, – take a running jump (at yourself)!, – take a walk!, keep stum(m)!, – your nose out!, m.y.o.b.!, pull in your neck!, sit on it and rotate!, slip it where the monkey slipped the nuts!, shove it where the rhino got the javelin!, shove it where Moby Dick got the old harpoon!, what's it to you?

250. Hindrance; Obstacle

v. 1. *to hinder, cause trouble:* ball up, cook one's goose, crab (one's act), cramp one's style, dish, fuck around, – over, gum up, – the works, knock the bottom out of, lumber, put the bag on, – the block on, – the freeze on, – the kibosh on, – the mockers on, – the mozz on (Aus.), – the screws to, queer the pitch, shanghai, throw a spanner in the works; spec. corpse (theatre use: to cause another actor to forget lines)

adv. 2. *hindered, in trouble:* (all) balled up, (all) gummed up, (all) screwed up, up against the wall

---

FACILITY

251. Facility; Ease

n. 1. blow off, breeze, (dead) cert, cinch, cushy number, doddle, duck shoot, – soup, easy game, – ride, – stuff, free ride, gravy train, gut, money for jam, – for old rope, picnic, piece of cake, – of piss, pushover, snap, snip, soft number, tit, tough stuff (US Black), velvet; spec. featherbedding (giving 'jobs to the boys'); sitter (sporting use: an easy catch – cricket; an easy target – hunting)

v. 2. *to make easy:* grease the wheels

3. *to have an easy life:* have it soft, sit pretty

4. *to do easily:* do (it) on one's dick, – on one's head, – on one's prick, have a field day (with), piss it, waltz it

adj. 5. *easy:* as easy as ABC, – as cake and ice cream, – as falling off a log, – as kiss my arse, – as one-two-three, – as pie, – as shooting fish in a barrel, – as taking candy from a baby, – as taking money from a child, – as winking, cheesecake, cushy, easy-peasy, in the bag, pie, pimpsy, plain sailing, right up (down) one's alley, skate, sweet (as a nut), under the odds

6. *easily:* hands down, in a walk, on one's dick, – one's prick, like a house on fire, no sweat, right off the bat

7. *out of trouble:* off the hook

252. Difficulty; Trouble

n. 1. *problem:* bad news, bind, bother, facer, hang-up, hassle, headache, hot potato, hot seat, jam, kick in the pants, Queer Street, screamer, sharp end, skulldrag (US Black), sweat, Tom Mix (rhy.sl. = a fix), TS, tough shit; spec. bear (hard college work)

2. *unpleasant situation:* can of worms, drag, (the) devil to pay, – hell to pay, holy mess, – muddle, jive hand (US Black), (a) nice how-d'you-do, pain in the arse, pretty mess, – muddle, – pickle, rainy days (US Black), (a) right how-d'you-do, shit city, shithouse, (a right) two and eight (rhy.sl. = state), when the shit hits the fan, when the solids hit the air conditioning

3. *unfair treatment:* bumps, hard lines, iron cross (US Black), jack job, more kicks than ha'pence, raw deal, rough end of the pineapple (Aus.), shaft, short end of the stick, static, tough tits, – titty

4. *something difficult:* bastard, bitch, bother, brute, bugger, pain (in the arse), SOB, sod, son of a bitch, tall order, tough nut to crack

v. 5. *to be in trouble:* (be) for it, – in for it, – in the shit, – in the soup, – in shtuck (Yid.), – up shit creek etc. (see: adj. 12 below), catch a cold, catch one's (big fat) tit in a wringer, get one's arse in a sling, go a million (Aus.), have one's cock caught in a zipper, hit some shit, scoff fishheads, scramble for the gills

6. *to cause trouble:* mix (it), put the mozz on (Aus.), shit on from a great height, signify (US Black), stir (it) up

7. *to get into trouble:* get in a hole, – in the shit, – in shtuck, – one's arse in a sling; (be) in a pickle, – a holy mess, etc. (see n. 2 above); spec. it's your little hip pocket (US Black = you're in bad trouble)

8. *to get into trouble:* dob in (Aus.), hit the shit

9. *to avoid, escape from trouble:* beat the rap, crawl out from under, hang tough, land on one's (own) two feet, play it cool, save one's bacon, slide out (of)

10. *to make trouble:* crap around, do over, fuck around, – over, – with, have against the ropes, put (up) against the wall, – in shtuck, – on the spot, etc. (see 7 above), screw

adj. 11. *difficult:* bread and lard (rhy.sl. = hard), no picnic, no laughs (laffs), shitty, sketch, tough

adv. 12. *in trouble:* between the devil and the deep blue sea, – the rock and the hard place, buggered, caught by the short and curlies, cruising for a bruising, done up (like a kipper), floored, fucked, in bother, – a bind, – a jam, – a pickle, – a spot, – a tight hole, – Dutch, – it (for fair), – it (for real), – Queer Street, – Shit Street, – shtuck, – the doghouse, – the shit, – the soup, on offer, on the chopping block, – one's beam end, – the ropes, – the spot, out on a limb, riding for a fall, screwed, shafted, sunk, stymied, under the cosh, – the gun, up against it, up a gum tree, up shit creek (without a paddle), up the creek, up to one's neck, up against the wall, well fucked and far from home

excl. 13. *what's the matter?:* what's eating you?, what's biting you?, what's got into you?, what's the bitch?, what's the beef?, what's up, Doc?, what's with you (him, her, etc.)?

253. Skill; Ability

n. 1. goods, gumption, naus, savvy, smarts, street smarts, what it takes; spec. mileage (experience)

2. *cunning:* curves, fast one, good one, nifty

v. 3. *to be able, skilful:* be all there, – on the ball, – up to snuff, – wised up, come up to snuff, cut it, cut the mustard, hack, have it knocked, – something on the ball, – what it takes, know all the answers, – how many beans make five, – one's arse from one's elbow, – one's onions, – one's stuff, – the ropes, – what time it is, – what's happening, know where it's at

4. *to do well:* be death on, be the berries (at), have a (good) head for, have its number, – it knocked, piss it, stride (US Black), waltz (it)

5. *to be suitable:* hit (it) on the head, – on the nose, – between the eyes, – the bull's eye, fill the bill

6. *to take care of, to deal with:* square, swing (it), TCB, take care of business; spec. hold the baby (to be left to deal with a problem)

adj. 7. *experienced, efficient:* bonified (US Black), fly, hip, hot stuff, keen, keeno, no flies on (him, her, etc.), plugged in, sharp, slick, snappy, up to snuff, wicked

8. *suitable:* about one's speed, just one's speed, right up (down) one's alley, right up one's street, etc.

254. Unskilfulness; Awkwardness

n. 1. butterfingers, muffishness

v. 2. *to be unskilful, make a mess of:* arse about, – around, – up, bollix up, bollocks up, bitch up, bugger up, cack-hand, cock (it) up, cods up, foul up, fuck up, gum up, gum up the deal, – the play, – the works, etc., make a cods of, – a cobblers of, – a hash of, put one's foot in, screw up, stub one's toe

adj. 3. *incapable:* can't cut it, – cut the mustard, – hack it (see Facility 253), half-arsed, lame, no can do, not all there, – playing with a full deck, etc. (see Unintelligence: 145ff.), – up to snuff, out of one's (own) league, playing with the big boys (now)

4. *unsophisticated:* down-home, on fire, square, – to the wood

5. *inexperienced:* amateur hour, green (as grass), half-baked, uncool, unhip, wet behind the ears

6. *clumsy, gauche:* all thumbs, – fingers and thumbs, arsy-versy, gimpsy
phr. 7. *of incompetence:* couldn't run a piss-up in a brewery; couldn't organise a fuck in a brothel

SECURITY

255. Safety; Protection
n. 1. twirl (skeleton key)
v. 2. *to protect:* mind
3. *to protect oneself:* cover your ass, CYA, look after number one, save one's bacon
4. *to stand watch:* give jiggs, keep cave, keep decko, – KV, – jiggers, play chick, – chicken
adj. 5. *safe:* copasetic, in the clear
adv. 6. *secure:* dry land (US Black = all clear), home and dry, on a good wicket

256. Danger
n. 1. bad news, – scene, heat, heavy scene, hassle; spec. trick bag (US Black = unpleasant situation)
2. *warning:* high sign, tip-off, whisper, (the) word
v. 3. *to warn:* tip (off), put the word about, – out
4. *to endanger:* put in the middle, – on the spot; spec. put in the frame (to frame up)
adj. 5. *dangerous:* heavy, iffy, sus, uncool
excl. 6. *look out!:* heads up!, Hey Rube!, nonnus! (backsl. = someone!), kool toul (backsl. = look out), there'll be blue murder if, watch it!
7. *be careful:* don't do anything I wouldn't do, – take any wooden nickels

ATTAINMENT

257. Success
n. 1. fat city, gorilla, hole in one, killing, numero uno, result, score, smash, smasherino, smasheroo, smashola, sock, sockeroo, sockerino, socko, sockola, three-bagger
v. 2. *to succeed:* ace, beat the game, box clever, break the bank, bring down the house, bring home the bacon, click, come through, connect, cop a packet, – the lot, crack it, cream, cut the mustard, do (it) up right, get across, get a guernsey (Aus.), get a result, get clear, get it together, get it to the T, get over (US Black), get places, go over (big), go over like a house on fire, – like a ton of bricks, go great guns, go to town, hack it, have it dicked, – it taped, – it knocked, hit it (off), knock dead, – cold, KO, make a go (of), make a killing, make (it), – it big, – the grade, make out, mop up, play one's cards right, put it all together, register, score, – big, – heavy, sew up, strike it rich, – paydirt, – oil, take the biscuit, – the cake, turn up trumps, whup the game (US Black)
3. *to do successfully:* clean up on, come through, cut it, – the mustard, deliver (the goods), fill the bill, get away (with it), get down, go to town with, hack it, have it big, knock for a loop, make a go of, – it stick, – the grade, put (it) across, – (it) over, – over big, wrap (it) up
4. *to be successful:* be there, – the guvnor, – the boss, – number one, get to the top of the heap, – the top of the tree, have it big, wrap (it) up, have it dicked, set the world on fire
adv. 5. *successful:* ahead of the game, doing a hundred (US Black), going full blast, – great, – great guns, – over big, on the make, – the up and up, on top of the heap, – of the tree, on velvet, quids in

258. Failure
n. 1. bad job, blow-out, blow-up, brodie, bum deal, – trip, bummer, bust, crackup, crapout, crash, croak, cropper, dive, dud, fadeout, fall, fizzle, flash in the pan, flat tyre, flop, floperoo, flopola, flunk, fold, fold-up, frost, fuck-up, goner, lemon, let-down, mess, miss, muff, no dice, – go, – soap, – sale, nose-dive, not a bite, – a hope, – a nibble, poop, raw deal, smash, turkey, washout, wipe-out
v. 2. *to fail:* be all up (with), – all washed up, bite the dust, bomb, – off, – out, cave in, cock off, come to grief, come undone, – unstuck, – a cropper, conk out, crap out, crash (out), die, – on the

vine, draw a blank, fall down on the job, fall flat, fizzle out, flop, flunk (out), fold (up), fuck up, go all to shit, – all to hell, – all to smash, – all to fuck, – all to buggery, – bluey, – bung, – flooey, – down in flames, – down the pan, – down the plug (hole), – down for the third time, – down like a lead balloon, – down the drain, – down the tubes, – hang, – phut, – sour, go to pieces, – to the dogs, – to the pack (Aus.), – under, – up the spout, have two left shoes (US Black), lay an egg, lose out, lose the ball, miss the boat, – the bus, not cut it, – hack it, etc. (see Success: 257), not get past first base, not hit a lick (US Black), peg out, poop out, pull a brodie, score an own goal, shovel shit against the tide, strike out, stub one's toe, suck wind, take a bath, – a fall, – a header, – a nose-dive, – it on the button, – it on the chin, take the count, tube, wipe out; spec. go in the tank, – in the water; spec. take a dive (to fail deliberately)

adv. 3. *failing:* at the end of one's rope, – one's tether, on one's last legs, on the fritz, – kibosh, – skids, riding for a fall

4. *failed:* at the bottom of the heap, blooey, buggered, cold, cooked, cracked, done for, done up, down the pan, – the plug, fizzled out, gone phut, – under, – to hell, – to the dogs, – down the drain, etc., on the rocks, thrown for a loss, upgefucked, up shit creek, up the spout, washed up, wiped out

phr. 5. *resignation:* can't win them all

259. Advantage

n. 1. ace in the hole, – up one's sleeve, beat, card up one's sleeve, drop, edge, hook, inside track, long suit, pull, scoop, set-up, something on one

v. 2. *to have an advantage:* be in on the ground floor, – on the inside, have an ace up one's sleeve, – the inside track, hold all the cards

3. *to put at a disadvantage:* catch bending, come (it) over, do like a dinner, – to a turn (Aus.), fade, have by the short and curlies, – by the short hair, – by the balls, – the edge over, – the drop on, – the jump on, – it over, – cold, – dead to right, – bang to rights, – on toast, – on the run, – one over a barrel, – the drop on

4. *take advantage of:* come something over, give the double-shuffle, put something across, – something past (one), put something over (on), sting, work

adv. 5. *at a disadvantage:* naked

Emotion

FEELINGS

260. Emotion
n. 1. attitude, groove, soul; spec. tude, vibes (one's emotional 'style')
2. *spec. black sensibility:* ebony (US), soul
v. 3. *to undergo emotions:* feel funny, go through changes

261. Sentimentality
n. 1. flapdoodle, goo, gush, hearts and flowers, milk and water, schmaltz (Yid.), slop, slush, sob stuff, sweetness and light, tear-jerking
2. *sentimental talk:* dribble, drool, goo, gush, slobber
v. 3. *to become sentimental:* dribble, drool, gush (over), moon over, slobber
4. *to become mawkish:* give a sob story, go ga-ga, moon about, turn on the water-works
adj. 5. *sentimental:* ga-ga, icky, moony, mushy, sappy, schmaltzy, soppy

EXCITABILITY

262. Excitement
n. 1. fireworks, flap, heat, hoopla, kerfuffle, lather, panic stations, shemozzle, stew, stink, streak, sweat, tizzy, to-do, two and eight (rhy.sl. = state), wind-up
2. *a stimulant:* bang, shot in the arm, turn-on
v. 3. *to be excited:* come in one's pants, cream one's jeans, get a bee in one's bonnet, – one's bowels in an uproar, – one's knickers in a twist, – one's shit hot, – steamed up, go hog-wild, hit the ceiling, – the roof, make a Federal case (out of), run around like a chicken with its head off, wail, work up a circulation, – up a lather, zeek out; spec. let it all hang out (to abandon inhibitions)
4. *to live excitingly:* pace (US Black)
5. *to shock:* blow one out, – one's mind, freak one out
adj. 6. *exciting:* hairy, hairy-assed, smoking (US Black)
7. *excited:* (all) fired up, (all) hot and bothered, all of a doodah, – of a tiswas, – of a tizzy, hepped up, het up, hopped up, in a lather, – a sweat, – a tizzy, – a twitter, on the hop, psyched (to death), rattled, (all) steamed up, up in the air
excl. 8. tonight's the night! (excited expectation)

263. Nervousness
n. 1. ants in (one's) pants, collywobbles, creeps, edge, heeby-jeebies, jimmies, Jimmy Britts (Aus. rhy.sl. = the shits), jitters, jumps, needle, screaming abdabs, shakes, shim-sham, West Hams (rhy.sl. = West Ham reserves = nerves), willies, wim-wams, yikes; spec. flopsweat (stage-fright); yips (golfer's nerves)
v. 2. *to be nervous:* climb the walls, get the jitters, – shakes, – willies, etc., get the wind up, have the breeze up, shizzout
3. *to make a fuss:* do a number, throw a moody, – a wobbler
adj. 4. *nervous:* antsy, busting, edgy, froggy (US Black), hyper, jittery, screaming blue murder, spare, under house, under the cosh, – the gun, windy
5. *unnerved:* climbing the walls, cracked up, frazzled, in a frazzle, on the edge,

shattered, shot (to hell, to pieces), up in the air, uptight
6. *intense:* heavy

264. Impatience
n. 1. lather, stew, sweat
v. 2. *to be impatient:* (to be) champing at the bit, – hot to trot, hurt to, in a lather, – sweat, raring to go, etc. (see adv.)
adv. 3. busting, champing at the bit, hot to trot, hurting, in a lather, – a stew, – a sweat, on tiptoe, raring to go

INEXCITABILITY

265. Calmness
n. 1. cool
2. *emotional freedom:* slack, space
v. 3. *to remain calm:* bite the bullet, chill out, cool down, – it, hang loose, keep a tight asshole, – one's cool, – one's hair on, – the cork on, lay tight (US Black), not turn a hair, stay cool, taken one's best hold (US Black), track
4. *calm down:* cool, – down, – it, – off, – the rock, get one's head together, go off the boil, lighten up, mellow (out), pull in one's horns, simmer down
5. *to calm one down:* cool (off), get someone's head together, mellow out, tune off
adj. 6. *calm:* laid back, mellow, off the boil, on a tight leash, swiss
excl. 7. *calm down*!: cool it!, don't get your bowels in an uproar!, – get your knickers in a twist!, – get your shit hot!, – make a federal case (of it)!, keep your hair on!, – your shirt on!, lighten up!, no muss no fuss!, pull in your horns! quit racing your motor!, simmer down!, steady the buffs!

266. Patience
v. 1. *to be patient:* cool it, hold one's horses, – one's water, – it down
2. *to endure, tolerate:* go (for), hang in (there), keep a stiff upper lip, – one's pecker up, like (it) or lump (it), not let it get to one, – get one down, stand still for, stay the pace, stick with it, take, – it, – it on the chin, – the nose, etc., tough it out

3. *not tolerate:* take no guff, – no shit
excl. 4. *be patient!:* hang on!, hold your horses!, hold your water!, don't shoot the pianist he's doing his best!

INTEREST

267. Interest
n. 1. hots
v. 2. *to be interested:* fall for, flop for, go for, give a tumble, – the time of day, have big eyes for, make a dead set for, rush, tumble for
3. *to interest:* grab, tick (one) off
adv. 4. *interested:* all for, hot for, into, strong on, struck on

268. Desire
n. 1. itch, yen
v. 2. *to want:* choose, do with, go for, have a yen for, hurt for, spoil for, want the worst way
3. *to be selfish:* look after number one, pig it
adj. 4. *desirous:* bursting (for), crazy (for, to), hopped up, hot (for), hung for, hurting (for), itchy, nuts about, nutty, raring (to), screaming (for), sold on, spoiling for, steaming, wild (for, to)
5. *greedy:* grabby, piggy
phr. 6. what's in it for me?

269. Ambition
n. 1. get-up-and-go, pizzazz, stick-to-it-iveness, what it takes (see Enthusiasm: 236.3)
v. 2. *to be ambitious:* to have what it takes
adj. 3. *ambitious:* (see 236.8)

270. Enthusiasm
n. 1. full scream (US Black), go, hotcha, oomph, pep, zap, zing, zip, zowie
2. *craze, fad:* bee in the bonnet, bug, -itis, -mania
v. 3. *to be enthusiastic:* be bugs about, carry on (about), crack on (about), flip for, get it up (for), get stuck into, give a shit, go for, – nap on, – on about, – overboard, – to town (on), max out
adj. 4. *enthusiastic:* cooking, full of beans, gung-ho, hung up, jumping, overboard, skied

adv. 5. *enthusiastic about:* as a (Aus.), as a bean (Aus.), bats about, batty about, crazy for, daffy about, gone on, het up over, hot for, – on, hung up on, (all) in a lather about, – a sweat about, etc. (see Excitement: 262), like a good 'un, like crazy, nuts about, rapt (Aus.), shook on (Aus.), stuck on, tiger (for) (Aus.), up in the air over, wild about, worked up (about), wrapped (Aus.)

6. *fanatically:* bugs about, nuts about

DISINTEREST

271. Indifference

n. 1. what-the-hell

v. 2. *to be indifferent:* go off the boil, not give a damn, – a darn, – a (flying) fuck, – a shit, – a tuppenny fuck, – a good goddam, – a hoot, – a monkey's, – give a rap (for), – a stuff, – a tinker's cuss

3. *to act indifferently:* play it cool, sit on the fence

4. *to make no difference:* cut no ice

adj. 5. *indifferent:* deadpan, on the fence, sniffy, stoneface

6. *nonchalant:* flip

excl. 7. *I don't care:* big deal, break my heart, FIGMO (fuck it, got my orders), fuck you Jack I'm all right, I should care, – worry, it's not my funeral, no skin off my arse, – off my nose, see if I care, so what? that's your bad luck, – funeral, – problem, tough tits, what's the percentage?, who gives a damn?, – a fuck?, etc. (see v. 2), what do I do now, cry? beats me, don't ask me, I don't know, – dunno, – wouldn't know, no biggie, three tears and a bucket (US Black), your guess is as good as mine, you reckon

272. Dullness; Tedium

n. 1. drag, full tour, snooze job, three-hour tour

2. *something tedious:* corn, fag, history, old hat, – stuff, pain (in the arse), yawn

v. 3. *to bore:* bore stiff, – the pants off, have a stick up one's arse

4. *to be bored:* cool off, get jack of (Aus.), (see Disinterest: 271)

adj. 5. *boring:* dead as a doornail, – as a dodo, – from the neck up, on the vine, dopey, drag-ass, gutty, ho-hum, tired

adv. 6. *bored:* bored stiff, – to tears, drug, fed up with, to have a bellyful of, – skinful, – snootful, jack of (Aus.), sick and tired (of), up to here

excl. 7. *I'm bored:* here we go again, ho-hum, that finishes me, what a life, – a pain

---

PLEASURE

273. Pleasure; Delight

n. 1. bang, buzz, charge, kick, knockout, thrill, turn-on, wallop

2. *pleasant situation:* bee's knees, hot stuff, humdinger, lollapaloosa; spec. sight for sore eyes (a welcome appearance)

v. 3. *to please:* be up one's alley, click with, go down, go over (good), hit the (right) spot, make a hit, score, turn on, turn one's crank

4. *to thrill:* bowl over, give a bang, – buzz, – charge, etc. (see n. 1), go over strong, – in a big way, – like a house on fire, – like a million dollars, hit for six, knock dead, – out, – the pants off, lay one out, mow one down, send out of this world, slaughter, slay, throw, tickle (pink), tickle to death, wow

adj. 5. *pleased:* all over oneself, fit to bust, happy as a dog with two tails, – as Larry, – as a sandboy, (see also 274), over the moon, pleased as the devil, – as heck, – as hell, – as punch, stoked, tickled, – pink, – to death, – to pieces

adv. 6. *pleasant:* ace, bully, cute, daisy, darling, divine, ducky, fantabulous, fucking-A, hotsy, jammy, keen, peachy-keen, the tops, too-too, TF much

excl. 7. *I feel happy:* ain't love grand, – that something, – we got fun, and how, baby, boy, boy-oh-boy, (oh) brother, cowabunga!, daddy, diggety damn, – dog, fucking-A, hey, hotcha, hot-cha-cha, hot damn, – diggety, – diggety dog, – shit, love it to death, man, man oh man, oh mama

274. Happiness; Cheerfulness

n. 1. hoopla, hoot, whoopee

2. *a laugh:* boff, gag, yok, yuk

3. *smile:* spec. shit-eating grin (smug smile)

v. 4. *to laugh:* be in stitches, break up, burst, crack one's face, – up, crease up, fall about, – out, goof on, haw-haw, hee-hee, hoot, laff, piss oneself, roll in the aisles

5. *to make laugh:* bowl over, break up, bring the house down, convulse, get a laugh, hand a laugh, kill, knock them in the aisles, paralyse, put away, put in stitches, slaughter, slay, tickle the funny bone

6. *to become happy:* brace up, buck up, chirp up, come out of it, drop it, pep up, pull oneself together, snap out of it

7. *to cheer one up:* brace up, buck up, pep up, perk up, pull together

8. *to be happy:* be full of beans, – full of pep, – Mr Laffs, pop

adj. 9. *happy:* bobbish, breezy, chipper, chuffed, grooved, happy as a pig in shit, – as a king, – as Larry, – as you-know-what, high wide and handsome, in the pink, lunchy, nice (US Black), one hundred per cent, over the moon, perky, rorty, wrapped tight; spec. slap-happy (slightly eccentric); spec. paralytic, spastic (convulsed with laughter)

10. *merry:* feeling one's oats, feisty, full of beans, larky, on the razzle

275. Contentment; Satisfaction

n. 1. *comfort:* easy street, velvet

v. 2. *satisfy:* cut the mustard, fill the bill, go down one's alley, keep (one's) cool, – sweet, play one's tune, sing one's song, talk one's language, walk on one's side of the street

3. *to be satisfied:* have no beef, – no kick, – no squawk

adj. 4. *satisfactory:* ace(s), all reet, AOK, bang on, can't complain, hunky-dory, (right) in there, jake, jerry, kosher, OK, OK by me, – for my dough, okey-doke(y), okay, a (little) bit of all right, no kick, no squawk, no sweat, on the ball, – the beam, – the button, slap-up, solid, up to snuff

5. *comfortable:* cushy, soft

6. *contented:* all the way live, joint-joint (US Black)

phr. 7. *that's satisfactory:* AOK, everything's cool, – hotsy-totsy, – jake, – OK, etc. (see adj. 4), righto, roger, that's affirmative, – a big ten-four, we have lift-off

276. Enjoyment; Fun

n. 1. barrels of fun, barrels of laffs, juice, loads of fun, – of laffs, (a) laugh a line, more fun than a barrel of monkeys

2. *a good time:* (see also Party: 363); action, ball, goof bender, high old time, hot time, shit stopper; spec. the life of Riley (an easy, enjoyable life)

3. *a celebration:* (see also Spree: 98); bat, beano, bender, binge, blast, blow-out, Bushey Park (rhy.sl. = lark), bust, cutup, hi-de-hi, let-go, shindig, shindy, tear, toot, whoopee

v. 4. *to enjoy:* dig, eat up, gas, get down with (US Black), – one's thing off (US Black), – a bang out of, – a kick out of, etc. (see Thrill: 273); get off on, groove (on), – behind, have a high old time, – a hot time, live it up, – the life of Riley, love it to death, party, rally, swing with, tear up (US Black), wig out

5. *to have a good time, celebrate:* bat around, boogaloo, boogie, break loose, cut loose, get one's rocks off, – one's jollies, go bananas, go on a bust, – a shindy, – the razzle, hell around, high-step (it), hit the high spots, jive and juke (US Black), kick ass, – up one's heels, let her rip, – one's hair down, make whoopee, paint the town red, raise a hullaballoo, – a racket, – a ruckus, – Cain, – (merry) hell, – sand (US Black), skylark, step high wide and handsome, swing, whoop it up

6. *to play the fool:* act up, carry on, clown around, cut up, horse around, kick up one's heels, loon about, play funny buggers, play silly buggers; spec. score yoks (to get laughs); mug (make funny faces)

adj. 7. *playful:* feeling one's oats, feisty, full of beans, etc. (see Activity; Liveliness: 236)

8. *enjoyable:* hot

adv. 9. *for fun:* for kicks, – laughs, – the hell of it, – trips
phr. 10. *it's been fun:* it's been a slice

277. Wit and Humour

n. 1. *joke:* boff, boffola, crack, fast one, gag, good one, hoot, laff, laff riot, nifty, scream, shit stopper, shriek, yell, yok, yuks; spec. horse laugh (a bad joke); pisser (a very funny joke)
v. 2. *to amuse:* cop the laughs (laffs), crack (one) up, crease (one) up, tickle one's funny bone
3. *to tease:* hack around, josh
4. *to tell jokes:* crack (wise), gag, pull a fast one, – a nifty, etc. (see n. 1)
5. *to play practical jokes:* come it over, horse around with, put over a fast one (on), send for a left-handed monkey wrench, whip the cat
6. *to pull funny faces:* mug
adj. 7. *funny:* killing, rich, ripe, wacky
phr. 8. *that's funny:* that's a good one, that's a laugh; spec. funny peculiar or funny ha-ha? (do you mean humorous or not?)

DISPLEASURE

278. Displeasure; Disagreeableness

n. 1. *something unpleasant:* barf city, damper, downer, Motel Hell, nowhere, – city, outers, pain (in the arse), – in the neck, piece of crap, – of shit, pit city, pits, puke, stinker, stinkeroo, tack city
2. *unpleasant time:* dog's life, thin time, tough tittie
v. 3. *to act unpleasantly:* play the heel
4. *to displease:* be hard to take, curdle one's guts, get in one's hair, – up one's arse, – up one's nose, give one a headache, – a pain, – a pain in the arse, – in the neck, stick in one's craw, turn one's stomach, – one's tum
adj. 5. *unpleasant:* bit thick, creepy, crumby, crummy, deadly, gut-wrenching, heavy-duty, icky, icky-poo, jive-ass, low-life, low-rent, no-hope, on the nose (Aus.), outers, out of order, putrid, ratshit, ratty, stinking, stinko, tacky, ucky, vomitous
adv. 6. *displeased with:* had it (with), out

with, pissed off (with), up to there with
excl. 7. *of displeasure:* bugger off!, can you stand for that!, don't give me that!, drop dead!, fiddlesticks!, fooey!, fuck off! (out of it), fuck that for a bowl of cherries!, – for a lark!, how do you like them apples?, how does that grab you?, it shouldn't happen to a dog, nuts!, of all the . . . !, on your bike!, piss off!, pull the other one it's got bells on it!, shit!, shoot!, shucks!, sod off!, that's just too bad!, the hell with it, tough shit!, ts, up your arse!, – your brown!, what's the big idea?, who're you screwing!, you and who's army!, you would!

279. Sullenness; Depression

n. 1. long face, misery-guts, sourpuss
2. *depression, misery:* black dog, blues, dumps, Edgar Britts (Aus.), glooms, grumps, hump, jimjams, jimmies, Jimmy Britts (Aus.), mulligrubs, pits, the pip, red arse
v. 3. *to be sullen, depressed:* bellyache, come the old moody, drag one's tail, feel like death warmed up, gripe, grizzle, grump, gutache, shit and wish (US Black – 'shit in one hand, wish in another, see which fills up first'), throw a moody, wear the dog (US Black)
4. *to feel miserable:* be down in the dumps, – down among the wines and spirits, – in a bad shape, – in the cellar, feel blue, – ratshit, – sick, get the hump, get up on the wrong side of the bed, have (a fit of) the blues, – the glooms, – the jimmies, etc. (see n. 1), have one's heart in one's boots
5. *to depress:* bring down
adj. 6. *sullen:* grouchy, grumpy, long-faced, mopey, root-faced, sourpussed, strung out, tight-assed
7. *depressed:* black, blue, brought down, bummed out, cheesed off, choked, down, down in the mouth, drug, fit to bust, hurting, in the dumps, lower than a snake's belly, off one's feed, shafted, shot down, sick as a parrot, torn down (US Black), with one's tail between one's legs; spec. solitary as a bastard on Father's Day (Aus. use: lonely)
8. *depressing:* depresso, pit city

280. Temper; Anger

n. 1. bate, peeve, red ass, red pants; spec. slow burn (gradually rising temper)

2. *explosion of rage:* blow-up, carry-on, conniption fit, fireworks, flare-up, lather, stew, sweat, tizzy

v. 3. *to lose one's temper:* boil over, blow a fuse, – a gasket, – off steam, – one's cool, – one's cookies, – one's cork, – one's gasket, – one's stack, – one's top, blow it, blow off, blow up, bust a blood vessel, – a gut, climb the rigging, – the walls, create, do one's block, – one's nut, – the lolly (Aus.), flip, – one's lid, – one's wig, – out, fly off the handle, foam at the mouth, get a hair up one's arse, – hot under the collar, – mad, – sore, etc. (see adv. 6), – one's dander up, – one's knickers in a twist, – one's shit hot, – one's bowels in an uproar, etc. (see Excitement: 262), – one's back up, – one's nose out of joint, – the ass, – the red ass, – the mohawk, get up on one's hind legs, go ape, – apeshit, – bananas, – haywire, – off one's chump, – off one's nut, – off the deep end, – spare, – up in the air, – up the wall, grow horns, have a bellyful (of), – it up to here, – kittens, – the (dead) needle, – the rag on, hit the roof, kick up a racket, jump down one's throat, jump salty, jump the rails, lose one's cool, – one's hair, – one's marbles, – one's rag, make a (great) to-do, – carry-on, make the fur fly, – the sparks fly, nut up, poke one's mouth off (US Black), pop off, – one's cork, raise a ruckus, – (merry) hell, – Cain, – the roof, reach boiling point, run around like a chicken with its head off, see red, simmer, sizzle, smoke, steam (up), throw a fit, – a wingding, trip out, work up (a head of) steam, zeek out, zoon out

4. *to make angry:* burn, get a rise out of, get one's dander up, – one's back up, – one's nose out of joint, – one's mad up, – one going, needle, piss off, rub up the wrong way, ruffle one's feathers, team up

adj. 5. *ill-tempered:* crusty, feisty, gritchy, grouchy, in a snit, mean, niggly, ornery, out of sorts, peevish, salty, snappy, sour

6. *angry:* apeshit, burned (at), fighting mad, (all) fired up, fit to be tied, gutted, hacked, het up, hopping (mad), hot, (all) hot and bothered, in a lather, – a pet, – a peeve, – a sweat, jacked (Aus.), leery, loaded for bear, mad, – as a cut snake (Aus.), – as a wet hen, miffed, on one's hind legs, on the muscle, peeved, pissed off, POed, pushed out of shape, raving (mad), sore, steamed (up), uptight, wild

281. Grief

n. 1. hurting dance, pit city, sob stuff

2. *crying:* jag, weeps

v. 3. *to cry:* blub, boohoo, pipe one's eye, squawk, turn on the waterworks

282. Disappointment

n. 1. bring-down, choker, dud, false alarm, frost, lemon, let-down, misfire, no dice, – joy, – soap, sickener

v. 2. *to disappoint:* bring down, burn, dish, fall down on, let down, puncture one's balloon, piss on one's parade, stand up, sting; spec. let down easy (to soften the blow)

3. *to be disappointed:* draw a blank, get left, land with a (dull) thud, lose out, miss the boat, take it on the chin

adj. 4. *disappointed:* burnt, dished, let down, screwed, stood up, stung, taken for a ride

phr. 5. *disappointed:* all dressed up and nowhere to go, looks like he/she lost a pound and found sixpence

283. Anxiety; Worry

n. 1. butterflies (in one's stomach), freak-out, joes (Aus.); spec. all points bulletin (plea for help)

v. 2. *to be worried:* be in a lather, – a stew, – a sweat, drop one's bundle (Aus.), fall apart, freak, give a shit, have a bee in one's bonnet, have kittens, – one's heart in one's boots, piss blood, sweat; spec. feel a draught (US Black: to sense racism)

3. *to reveal one's worries:* get it off one's chest, – out of one's system, let down one's hair, spill the beans, take the load off one's mind, unload

4. *to worry:* discombobulate, give one the

creeps, mess one's mind, throw one for a loop

5. *to worry about:* have a hard-on for

adj. 6. *worried:* (all) hot and bothered, at the end of one's tether, bitched, buggered and bewildered, blue around the gills, charlie, down, fucked up and far from home, hot pants, in a mucksweat, – a sweat, – a stew, – the pits, jacked up, jumpy, sick, uptight, wired

adv. 7. *worrying:* eating (someone), heavy

phr. 8. I can't handle this

284. Annoyance; Vexation

n. 1. bitch, burn, needle, pain, pain in the arse, – the neck, (the) pip; spec. slow burn (increasing rage); aggravation (UK: mutual grievances between police/criminals)

v. 2. *to annoy, vex:* be on one's arse, bitch off, bite, brass off, brown off, bug, burn, burn up, cheese off, drive one nuts, – around the bend, – through the roof, – up the wall, get across, – in one's hair, – one's back up, – on one's wick, – on one's goat, – on one's tits, – one going, – under one's skin, – up one's nose, give one a pain (in the neck, arse), give the needle, – the pip, grief, jerk around, – one's chain, make ignorant, miff, nark, needle, peeve, piss off, put one's back up, – one's nose out of joint, rub (up) the wrong way

3. *to be annoyed:* get the hump, – the needle (with), have a mad on with, – ants in one's pants, – a flea in one's ear, – something biting one, – something eating one, jump salty, steam

4. *to be offended:* get on one's high horse

adj. 5. *irritated:* brassed off, browned off, cheesed off, fed up, had it (with), jacked out, miffed, narked, nettled, on the rag, peeved, pissed (off), ratty, salty, stroppy, teed off, twisted, up a tree; spec. OT&E ('over-tired and emotional' – of an irritable child)

6. *sensitive:* tetchy

7. *perfectionist:* finicky

excl. 8. *of annoyance:* buggeration!, come off it!, don't get funny!, – get smart!, don't mind me I only live/work here!, forget it!

APPROBATION

285. Approval

n. 1. the all-clear, the go-ahead, the nod, the OK, nod and a wink, thumbs-up

2. *recommendation:* blurb, boost, build-up, plug, write-up

v. 3. *approve:* be (all) for, – behind, give the all-clear, – go ahead, etc. (see n. 1), have a soft spot for, OK

4. *to recommend:* front for, go to bat for, – to the mat for, go for, – overboard for, put in a (good) word for, stand up for

excl. 5. *of approval:* all the way!, attaboy!, attagirl!, beaut! (Aus.), (God) bless you!, bully (for you)!, dandy!, death!, fair dos! (Aus.), fair enough!, fairy snuff!, for sure!, fucking-A!, good on you! (Aus.), great!, hubba! hubba!, I should be so lucky!, is that good or is that good!, keen, keeno, nice one Cyril!, no sweat!, not half!, not to be sniffed at!, – to be sneezed at!, now you're cooking!, – you're talking!, solid!, swell!, tasty!, that's it!, that's the stuff (to give the troops)!, – telling them!, – the way!, too Irish stew! (rhy.sl. = too true), too right!, what a boy!, – a man!, – a star!, wicked!, you're a pal!, – a peach!, – a prince!, you're darn tootin'!, – singing my song!, you tell them!, you wrote the book!

286. Praise

n. 1. boost, plug, puff, push, rap (Aus.), rave; spec. log-rolling (mutual praise)

v. 2. *to support, enthuse:* beat the drum for, bang the drum for, boost, come on strong (for), crack on, go on about, hype, lay it on (heavy/thick), pile it on (heavy/thick), puff, push, root (for), sell (up), talk (it) up

phr. 3. *spec. praise of a passing woman:* I could do that a favour, whap that thing! (US Black), whacko the diddle-o (Aus.)

287. Flattery

n. 1. applesauce, banana oil, blarney, build-up, bull, eyewash, flannel, grease job, guyver (Aus.), hokum, oil, soft soap; SEG (abbrev. shit-eating grin)

v. 2. *to flatter:* blarney, bull, bullshit,

butter up, con (along), dish out the applesauce, – the oil, – a line, feed a line, grease, hand a line (of bull), jolly (along), kid (along), kiss the blarney stone, lay it on (thick), – with a trowel, pat on the back, plaster, pour it on (heavy/thick), shmeer (Ger. = grease), shoot the bull, – the shit, – a line, soft soap, spread it on (thick)
3. *to toady:* arse-lick, back-slap, bootlick, brown-nose, creep, get in (solid) with, – next to, kiss-arse, make up to, pal up to, play up to, polish the apple, roll over for, schmooze (Yid.), stooge for, suck around, suck-arse, suck hind tit, suck up to, wax up, wipe one's arse, – one's nose, yes, yessir

---

DISAPPROBATION

288. Disapproval
n. 1. frost, nix, the no, thumbs-down
2. *disapproving look:* dirty look, old-fashioned look
v. 3. *to disapprove:* be down on, corrode, give the no, – the thumbs-down, nix, not go for, put the thumbs down, turn up one's nose at
adv. 4. *disapproving:* down on, on the coat (Aus.)
phr. 5. *of disapproval:* all yours!, bobkhes! (Yid. anything absurd or insulting), count me out!, no way!, perish the thought!, that's so ill!, you've got to be joking!, yuck!
6. *spec. disapproval of passing girl(s):* don't fancy yours, I wouldn't touch it with a (ten-foot) barge-pole, I wouldn't touch it with yours

289. Objection; Complaint
n. 1. beef, bellyache, bitch, crab, kick, kvetch (Yid.), moody, squawk, yip
v. 2. *to complain:* ballsache, bellyache, beef, beat the gums, bitch, bleat, blow great guns, buck (against), crab (about), go on (about), gritch, grizzle, howl, kick (about), kick up a fuss, – a racket, kvetch, make a federal case (out) of, – a great how-do-you-do (out of), pitch a bitch, pull one's joint, raise Cain, – a racket, rattle one's beads (gay use),

sound off (about/over), squawk, yell blue murder
adv. 3. *complaining:* crooked on (Aus.), on at, po-faced, snippy

290. Censure; Criticism
n. 1. knock, putdown, roasting, slam, slash; spec. hatchet job (journalism); sledging (cricket: on-field barracking)
v. 2. *to criticise:* come down on, come down fonky (US Black), come down hard, come down heavy, crab, cut up, go for, go to town on, hack up, hammer, haul over the coals, knock, pull to pieces, put down, roast, rub (US Black), savage, slam, slash (up), slice up, take a swipe at, – to pieces; spec. give the duke (to slow handclap)
phr. 3. some people!

291. Scolding
n. 1. bawling out, bit of one's mind, bollocking, calling down, cussing out, dressing down, earful, flea in one's ear, going over, jaw, kick in/up the arse, piece of one's mind, roasting, rocket, rucking, scorcher, serve (Aus.), shakeup, stick, talking-to, toco, what-for, wigging
v. 2. *to scold:* bawl out, – the (living) hell out of, bear down (on), blow the daylights out of, – sky-high, bollick, bring one up (US Black), carpet, chew one's balls off, chew out, climb all over, come down on, cuss out, cut down to size, dress down, drop on, eat one's arse off, get down dirty, – fonky (US Black), give (one) a piece of one's mind, – one a (good) talking to, etc. (see n.1.), – one some curry (Aus.), – one some stick, give it hot and heavy, – one the business, – it the works, go after (right and left), go for, go to town on, haul over the coals, jump all over, – up and down on, – on with both feet, lay down the law, lay into, let (one) have it, light into, lower the boom on, make it hot for, pin one's ears back, pull one's coat, put a flea in one's ear, – one through it, – the fear of God into, – through the mill, – the blast on, raise hell with, – the dickens with, – the devil with, etc., read the riot act, – the Rocks and Shoals, ride ragged, roast, rollick, say a mouthful, sit

on, slag (off), smack down, take a jab at,
– a smack at, talk to like a Dutch uncle,
tear off a strip, – a piece (or two), tear
one's arse, tell a thing (or two), – what is
what, – one where to get off, – where to
go, throw the book at, vamp on, wade
into; spec. read one's beads (gay use)
3. *to be in trouble:* be on the carpet, – on
the mat, catch hell, catch it (hot), get it
in the neck
4. *to nag:* break one's balls, go on at,
hassle, henpeck, stay on one's case
adv. 5. *nagging:* at the micks, on one's
case

292. Disparagement
n. 1. knocking, panning, razzing, (big)
razoo
2. *sarcastic remark:* crack, dig, raspberry,
razz, shot, shy, slam, slant, slap, sock,
swipe
v. 3. *to disparage:* bag, base, blow a
raspberry, fire on (US Black), give the
big razoo, – the finger, knock, pan, pin
one's ears back, put the hammer on,
razz, shoot down, slam, slap, slash (US
Black), take a shot, – shy, etc. (see n. 2),
vamp on, weigh into
4. *scorn:* bucket (Aus.), chump off (US
Black), need like a hole in the head
adj. 5. *sarcastic:* sarky
adv. 6. *scorned:* stuffed
excl. 7. *sarcastic comment:* and you!,
(the) answer is a lemon!, back in the
knifebox!, be your age!, – yourself!, big
deal!, bite the ice!, blow it out (your
arse)!, bully for you!, butt out!, cost ya!,
does your mother know you're out?,
don't ask me, I only work here!, drop
dead!, eat it!, eat my shorts!, – shit!, fag
your face!, famous last words!, get!, get
fucked!, – her!, – him!, – knotted!,
– onto yourself!, – out of my way!,
– stuffed!, give over!, go (and) bark at
the moon!, – boil your head!, – jump in
a lake!, – take a long walk off a short
pier!, go fuck a dead horse!, – fuck
yourself!, – fuck yourself in the ass and
get some brains!, – fuck yourself with a
rubber wienie!, – piss up a rope (and
play with the steam)!, – shit in a pot and
duck your head!, – to blazes!, – shit in
your hat pull it over your head and call it

curls!, go to buggery!, half your luck!
(Aus.), stick it up your jumper!, stop
moing me!, suck it and see!, sucks to
you!, take a flying fuck!, – a running
jump!, thanks a bunch, – a million, TS!,
tough shit!, up your arse!, – your
brown!, – your jacksie!, – yours!, with
knobs on!, you'll be sorry!, you slay me!,
your mama!; spec. shall I put a bit of
hair on it? (to an inept workman); were
you born in a barn?, – in a tent? (to
someone who has left a door open)
8. *contempt:* be hanged, blah!, fuck you!,
huh!, nuts to you!, phooey!, pooh!,
screw you!, the hell with it!, – with
you!

293. Ridicule; Banter
n. 1. Bronx cheer, hee-haw, horse laugh,
panning, raspberry, razz, rib, roast
2. *teasing:* codology, kidology, joshing,
kidding, ragging, taking the Michael,
– the mickey, – the piss
3. *gesture of derision:* the finger, two
fingers of scorn, V-sign
v. 4. *to ridicule:* cast nasturtiums, give
the bird, needle, pan, razz, rib, roast
5. *to tease:* bull, extract the Michael, get
gay with, get one at it, – going, give one
the business, – the leg, haze, howl, jack
around, josh, kid, move one, piss-take,
pull one's leg, – one's pisser, put on, rag,
rib, send up, shoot on, sling off (Aus.),
sound, stick it to, take the Michael, – the
mickey, – the piss, wind up
6. *to make a rude gesture or noise:* flip the
bird, give a Bronx cheer, – a raspberry,
– the finger
phr. 7. *you silly fool:* now you've been
and gone and done it

294. Vilification; Slander
n. 1. spec. dozens, dirty dozens,
momma's game (US Black: ritual
'games' of insult)
2. *slander:* dirt, muck, mud,
mudslinging, poison, shit-stirring, smear
3. *abuse:* bullyrag, (the) hard word,
rough edge of the tongue, verbals
v. 4. *to vilify:* slag off, talk trash; spec.
play the dozens, shoot the dozens (see n.
1)
5. *to slander:* bad-mouth, crap on, dish

the dirt (about), poormouth, put the bad word on, – the hard word on, – out the poison, rank, sling dirt, – mud, – shit, smear, stir shit, stab in the back
6. *to abuse:* bullyrag, call (one) out, chew out, curse out, give the hard word, – rough edge of one's tongue, lay into, let loose on (see Scolding: 291), put down, rubbish, schpritz (Yid.), snipe on (US Black)

COURAGE

295. Courage; Confidence
n. 1. Aristotle (rhy.sl. = bottle), arry, balls, bottle (rhy.sl. = bottle and glass = arse = 'bottom'), brass balls, cojones, face, grit, guts, hair, heart, intestinal fortitude, moxie, rocks, rooks (US Black), spunk, stiff upper lip, stones, what it takes; spec. Dutch courage (liquor-induced bravery)
v. 2. *to be brave:* be a man, have (plenty of) what it takes
3. *to encourage:* brace up, buck up
4. *to encourage oneself:* keep a stiff upper lip, – one's chin up, – one's pecker up
adj. 5. *brave:* ballsy, game (for anything), gutsy, nervy, spunky
excl. 6. *of encouragement:* buck up, it will all come out in the wash, don't make a production out of it, worse things happen at sea, (keep your) chin up!, don't let the bastards grind you down, keep your pecker up, the first hundred years are the hardest, cheer up – the worst is yet to come!, it's a great life if you don't weaken!, be a devil!, go for it!, snap out of it!, stay with it!, hang in there!, up there Cazaly! (Aus.); spec. break a leg! (theatrical)

296. Cowardice
n. 1. dog, funk, yellow streak; spec. edge city (at one's emotional limits)
2. *fear:* blue funk, cold feet, creeps, horrors, white-knuckler
v. 3. *to be a coward:* bottle out, chicken out, cop out, get cold feet, have a yellow streak (right down one's back), lose one's bottle, punk out; spec. can dish it

out but can't take it (usually of a weak bully)
4. *to be afraid:* get the wind up, have one's heart in one's mouth, pack 'em (Aus.), piss (in) one's pants, shit a brick, – bricks, – oneself, wear brown trousers, wet one's pants
5. *to frighten:* freak out, give a bad moment, – a turn, make one's hair curl, psych out, put the fear of God into, – the frighteners on, rattle, scare stiff, – the bejazaus out of, – the pants off, – the shit out of, spook, throw a scare into, weird out
adj. 6. *cowardly:* chicken, CS, chickenshit, chicken-hearted, dripping, gutless, nervy, weedy, wet, wimpy, yellow, yellow-bellied
7. *afraid:* freaked (out), in a blue funk, packing 'em (Aus.), pissing oneself, scared shitless, – stiff, shit-scared, shitting bricks, – oneself, spooked, white about the gills

---

PRIDE

297. Pride; Conceit
n. 1. high-hatting, (old) acid, snippiness
v. 2. *to be conceited, arrogant:* be too big for one's britches, come it, get a swelled head, – above oneself, have one's nose in the air, high-hat, put on dog, strong it, think one is 'it', throw one's weight around, upstage
adj. 3. *arrogant:* all over oneself, boasie (WI), cocky, dickty (US Black), flash, Flash Gordon (US Black), highfalutin', high-toned, hincty, hoity-toity, la-de-dah, on one's high horse, smart-ass, smartypants, snobby, snooty, snotty, stuck-up, stuck on oneself, stuffy, toffee-nosed, too big for one's britches, uppish, uppity
adv. 4. *arrogant:* on one's high horse
excl. 5. *don't be so conceited:* come down off your high horse, – off your perch, come off it, who do you think you're fooling?
phr. 6. more front than Brighton beach, more hide than Jessie (Aus.)

298. Ostentation

n. 1. dog, frills, high-sidin' (US Black), high-steppin' (US Black), side, splash, splurge, swank

v. 2. *show off:* act the nigger (US Black), come on strong, cut a swath, fan, flame (gay use), flash (it about), grandstand, lay it on (thick), ponce about, put on (the) dog, put on jam (Aus.), spread it about, strut one's stuff, tart about, show boat, style, throw one's weight around; spec. put on the guiver (to affect a smart accent)

3. *to ornament:* ponce up, tart up

4. *to put on airs:* high-side, high-step (US Black), get on one's high horse, put on the ritz, put on frills, – one's high hat, put on the dog, put on jam (Aus.), swank

adj. 5. *ostentatious:* flash, – as a rat with a gold tooth, flossy, jazzy, nouveau, piss elegant, saddity, screaming, sidity, swanky, tarty

299. Boasting

n. 1. ballyhoo, blatherskite, bosh, BS, bull, bullshit, flapdoodle, gas, hot air, six-sheeting, three-sheeting, tall talk, wind

v. 2. *to boast:* advertise, ballyhoo, blow black (US Black), blow hard, blow heavy, blah, blow one's own trumpet, broadcast, BS, bull, bullshit, come on like gangbusters, come the big note (Aus.), crack on, crap on, fiend on (US Black), gam (US Black), gas, give it all that, grand (US Black), high-side (US Black), lairise (Aus.), let off some hot air, loudmouth, loudtalk, mouth off, lip off, pop off (at the mouth), put the bee on, run a line, scream some heavy lines (US Black), sell a wolf ticket (US Black), shoot off at the mouth, shoot the bull, shovel shit, skite (Aus.), spread the bull, swank, talk shit (US Black), three-sheet

adj. 3. *boastful:* all mouth and trousers, – piss and wind, mouthy, smart-arse

excl. 4. *boasting:* did I ever!, is the Pope a Catholic!, does the bear shit in the woods!, is the bear a Catholic? does the Pope shit in the woods? watch my dust!

HUMILITY

300. Humility; Meekness

n. 1. back seat

2. *humiliation:* bring-down, climb-down, come-down, crow, putdown, take-down

v. 3. *to be humble:* be on the (strict) QT, eat crow, fly low, keep a low profile, lie low, take a back seat

4. *to humiliate:* bring down, burst one's bubble, come down on, jump on (with both feet), knock (down), – off one's perch, knock the bottom out of, – the stuffing out of, – the kibosh out of, – off one's high horse, puncture one's balloon, put (one) down, put one where they belong, – the skids under, – one's nose out of joint, settle one's hash, squash, squelch, take the wind out of one's sails, – one down a peg, – down a few pegs, – the starch out of, tell where to get off

5. *to be humiliated:* come down to earth, – a peg, – a few pegs, land on one's arse, lower one's flag, take a fall, tuck in one's tail

301. Embarrassment

v. 1. *to embarrass:* burn, get, put in the hot seat, – on the spot

2. *to be embarrassed:* be in the hot seat, – on the spot, feel like a horse's arse, – like nothing on earth, – like hell, – like two cents, wilt

3. *to hurt one's feelings:* get one (where it hurts), get one where they live, step on one's corns, touch a soft spot

excl. 4. *of embarrassment:* I could have died!, I didn't know where to put myself!, was my face red!

302. Submissiveness

n. 1. back seat, cave-in, climb-down, second fiddle

v. 2. *to give in:* back down, break, break it down (Aus.), call all bets off, – it a day, – it quits, chuck it (in), chuck up the sponge, crack, cry uncle!, give up as a bad job, give it a miss, go under the table!, – in the tank, knuckle under, take the count, throw in the towel, – the sponge, – one's cards, – one's hand

3. *to be subservient:* crawfish, dep (act as deputy), eat crow, kiss arse, play second fiddle, play the Tom (US Black), take a back seat, Tom (US Black)

adj. 4. *subservient:* whipped; spec. hincty

(US Black derog. ref. to blacks who ape whites)

excl. 5. *of resignation:* if you can't beat 'em join 'em, that's the ball game, that's the way the cookie crumbles

Morality and Religion

INTEGRITY

303. Morality
n. 1. straight and narrow; spec. Brownie point (an award for 'goodness')
adj. 2. *moral:* tallawah (WI), white
3. *self-righteous:* pi, prissy, stuffy

304. Obligation
n. 1. *responsibility:* load
v. 2. *to be responsible:* pay one's dues, pick up the tab, put one's money where one's mouth is, stand up, stick one's neck out
3. *to make responsible:* wish on, – upon
4. *to deserve:* be in line for, get one's come-uppance, have it coming
adv. 5. *due:* down to

305. Honesty
n. 1. fair go (Aus.), fair shake (Aus.), the handsome thing, no stuff (US Black), square shake, straight poop, – goods, – shit, – shooting
2. *blamelessness:* clean nose, – sheet
v. 3. *to be honest:* act on the square, be on the level, – on the legit, – on the up-and-up, etc. (see adj. 6), lay (it) on the line, – one's cards on the table, play it square, – with a clean deck, shoot straight, – square, toe the line, walk the line
4. *to treat fairly:* be one hundred per cent with, do the handsome thing, give a fair crack of the whip, – a fair shake, – a square shake, play it straight (down the line), – the game, – the white man
5. *to be blameless:* have a clean nose, – a clean sheet, keep one's nose clean, – in the clear, stay kosher
adj. 6. *honest:* clean, dinkum (Aus.), for real, kosher, (on the) legit, on the level, outfront, ridgie-didgie (Aus.), righteous, straight, up and up, upfront, white
7. *frank:* straight from the shoulder, – down the line
8. *trustworthy:* A1, aces, all wool and a yard wide, blowed in the glass, dinkum (Aus.), kosher, the (real) McCoy, the (real) McKay, on the level, – the legit, – the square, one hundred per cent, regular, right, solid, sure-fire, sure-as-shit
excl. 9. *honest!:* fair crack of the whip!, fair dinkum! (Aus.), fair shake of the dice!, on my life!, stand on me!, straight up!, strictly!, you know me Al!

IMPROBITY

306. Immorality; Evil
n. 1. bad news, backmark (US Black), no-no
v. 2. *to become immoral:* crack up, go blooey, – downhill, – down the chute, – down the tubes, – haywire, – smash, – to the dogs, – to the bow-wows, – to hell (on a rocket), – to pot, – to shit, – to the devil, hit the rocks, – the skids, smash up
adj. 3. *immoral:* alias (WI), as bad as they come, – as they make them, left-handed, low-down, low-rent
4. *tough:* hard-boiled, heavy-duty, mean
5. *risqué:* adult, blue, hot, juicy, raunchy, spicy, strong

307. Dishonesty

n. 1. dodge, emag (backsl. = game), funny business, graft, lurk (Aus.), racket; spec. payola (bribery to gain publicity)

v. 2. *to be dishonest:* fall down on, go back on, lay down on (see also Crime: 460 ff)

adj. 3. *dishonest:* bent, – as a nine bob note, fishy, funny, iffy, off, sneaky

4. *untrustworthy:* bent, cronky (Aus.), lurky, wrong

phr. 5. *of distrust:* I wouldn't trust him/ her as far as I could throw him/her

308. Unfairness

n. 1. carve-up, dirty deal, dirty pool, dirty work (at the crossroads), funny business, not cricket, raw deal, the dirty, the shaft

v. 2. *to treat unfairly:* do one dirt, do the dirty (on), hit below the belt, play (one) dirty, pull off a raw deal, – off some funny business

adj. 3. *unfair:* below the belt, crummy, low-down, low-rent

adv. 4. *treated unfairly:* shafted, screwed

309. Dissoluteness; Dissipation; Self-Indulgence

n. 1. the life of Riley, the Life (US Black underworld), the fast lane, – track

v. 2. *to live 'fast':* fly high, go for broke, go it, – the pace, hit the high spots, kick up one's heels, play the giddy goat, rip it up, run in the fast lane, – the fast track, step high (wide and handsome), tear it up, whoop it up

3. *to indulge oneself:* bust loose, kick over the traces, let oneself go, let loose, loosen up, take the lid off

adj. 4. *dissolute:* fast, sporty

DECEPTION

310. Deception; Deceit

n. 1. bill of goods, bull, bullshit, bunk, bunkum, con, crap, eyewash, hanky-panky, jiggery-pokery, jive, kidology, moonshine, put up job, shuck, snowfall, snow job, window dressing

2. *trick:* all done by mirrors, bunco, dirty pool, dodge, fast one, gaff, gag, okey-dokey (US Black), old moody, (one's) little game, racket, ramp, ripoff, sucker trap; spec. crib (examination aid); long con (long-term con trick), short con (short-term con trick) (see also Confidence Tricks: 480)

3. *hoax, swindle:* cod, con, dry shave, fast shuffle, fiddle, gyp, hook, job, mace, number, put-on, shakedown, sell, skin, touch

v. 4. *to deceive:* bamboozle, blag, blow past, chi-ike, chump, con, criss-cross (US Black), deal them from the bottom of the deck, do brown, – down, – in the eye, drop one in it, flimflam, flummox, get the drop on, give (one) a fast shuffle, give (one) the business, hand a lemon, have on toast, have one on, lead up the garden path, play for a sucker, play the con, – the nut role, pull an act, – a fast one, put down a routine, put it across (on), – the shuck on, – one over (on), rat fuck, RF, ring it on, rip off, rope in, run one way and look another (US Black), sam, scale (Aus.), sell a bill of goods, sham on (US Black), show out, shuck, snow, string along, suck, take for a ride, – for a sucker, two-time, work

5. *to fool:* cod, goose, jive, josh, kid, pull one's leg, – the wool over one's eyes, send on a humbug trip (US Black), throw a curve (to), – dust in one's eyes

6. *to defraud:* ace, – out of, beat for, beat (one) out of, burn, chisel, chizz, diddle, do, – a job on, – brown, – over, flim-flam, fuck out of, game, get the fat off (Aus.), gazump, gessump, gyp, give a fucking, – a screwing, hook for, lay for, take for, jip (out of), half-ounce (rhy.sl. = bounce = short-change), have, have one over, – one on, Jew (derog.), knock, mace, milk, nail, pluck, promote, ring the changes, rip off, roll, rook, scale (Aus.), screw, sell (one) a pup, send to the cleaners, shake down, shanghai, shave, skin, stick it up, sting, take to the cleaners, trim, tuck up, weed; spec. gas and run (fill up without paying); walk the check (leave without paying)

7. *to hoax:* BS, bull (along), bullshit, cod, feed a line, – load of baloney, have on a string, hand a line (of bull, baloney, etc.), hokum, jolly (along), josh, keep (one) on

a string, kid (along), lay it on thick, pile it on (thick), play (along), shoot the bull, – a line, string along, toss a line

8. *to be tricked:* be bamboozled, – done up brown, – given a fast shuffle, had, etc. (see v. 4, 6), fall for, get a haircut, – it in the neck, – suckered, go for, jump at, play out of the pocket (US Black), swallow (hook, line and sinker), tumble for

adj. 9. *deceitful:* full of shit, leery, near the mark, snaky

10. *cheating:* macing, stuffing (US Black)

11. *cheated:* done, x-ed out (US Black)

phr. 12. *warning:* don't take any wooden nickels

311. Falsification; Sham

n. 1. bunkum, dud, phony, phonus balonus, ringer, Sexton Blake (rhy.sl. = fake), snide; spec. Oliver (rhy.sl. = Oliver Twist = fist = false entry in a ledger); slum (fake jewellery)

2. *pretence:* act, blind, front, put-on, smoke screen

v. 3. *to falsify:* cook (the books), pad (a bill), ring, sell a pup

4. *to pretend:* come it, come the old soldier, drum up, fake it, go through the motions, make like, play dumb, pull an act, swank; spec. pass (for a Jew to act as a Christian, a gay to act as a heterosexual, etc.)

adj. 5. *false:* brummagem, bent, bum, cheesy, cooked (up), doctored (up), dud, hokey, jive, not all that it seems, phony, snide

adv. 6. *faked:* ain't holding no air (US Black)

312. Falsehood; Lie

n. 1. ackamaracka, balls, BS, bull, bullshit, crap, fanny, fib, fish story, get up, good one, jiggery-pokery, jive, likely story, moody, one (US Black: one big lie), pitch, porky (rhy.sl. = pork pie), sell, snow, snow job, straight shit, tall story, – tale, whopper

v. 2. *to lie:* blow smoke up one's arse, BS, bull, bullshit, clock a daffy (S.Afr.), crap, draw a long bow, feed one a line, – one stuff (US Black), fib, fudge, fly a

kite, give a little leg, jive, lumber, pile it on (thick), play stuff (US Black), prop up, shit through one's teeth, three-sheet

adj. 3. *exaggerated:* gross, howling, thumping, thundering, whacking, whopping

phr. 4. *am I lying?:* can you see green in my eyes? (S.Afr.), would I shit you (you're my favourite turd)?

313. Treachery

n. 1. dirty work (at the crossroads), funny business, the shaft

v. 2. *to be treacherous:* dingo (Aus.), give one some funny business, – the shaft, play (one) dirty, stab in the back

3. *double-cross:* cross, cross up, two-time

adj. 4. *treacherous:* two-faced, two-timing

314. Betrayal

n. 1. squeal, tipoff

v. 2. *to betray:* do the dirty (on), fink (on), front one off (US Black), play Judas, put the finger on, rat on, sell down the river, sell out, spill the beans on, turn in (see also Crime: 473)

3. *to turn against:* go back on, go sour on, lay down on, poop out on

315. Entrapment

n. 1. fit up, fix, frame up, put up job, set-up

v. 2. *to entrap:* drop (right) in, fit up, frame up, put in the frame, set up; spec. plant (to 'discover' false evidence); (see also Crime: 486)

CULPABILITY

316. Accusation; Blame

n. 1. beef, knock, rap

v. 2. *to accuse:* call the turn on, drop on, finger, hang something on, knock, pip (something) on, put the finger on, – the shoe on the right foot (US Black), shift the weight, throw down on (see also Crime: 473)

3. *to blame unfairly:* bark up the wrong tree, put the shoe on the left foot (US Black), smear

4. *to take the blame for:* be left holding the baby, – holding the bag, carry the can (for), take the rap (for)

317. Vindication
n. 1. let-off, let-out
2. *excuse:* blind, (load of) flannel, song-and-dance, stall
v. 3. *to acquit:* give an out, slide; spec. spring (to free a prisoner)
4. *to make an excuse:* alibi out of, clean up (US Black), give a song and dance, stall along
5. *to apologise:* eat crow, – dirt, – one's words

318. Punishment
n. 1. rap
2. *chastisement:* dose, dressing-down, going over, shellacking, trimming, what-for
3. *beating:* anointing, basting, clouting, fanning (one's arse), hiding, larruping, lathering, leathering, licking, polishing, seeing-to, shellacking, strap oil, swishing, tanning (one's arse/hide), toco, welting, whacking; spec. kneecapping (IRA punishment)
v. 4. *to punish:* attend to, bear down on, bust loose on, come down on, crack down on, do, – for, go after, – for, fix, get on one's arse, – one's case, – one's tail, give a dose, – a dressing-down, etc. (see n. 2), give (merry) hell, – it to, – the business, – the works, – one Larry Dooley (Aus.), hang one to the wall, have one's guts for garters, let one have it, – have it in the neck, – have what-for, go at, – to town on, jump on (with both feet), knock it out of, land on, lay on, light into, make it hot for, pour (it) on, nail to the wall, put through the grinder, – through the mill, – through it, – through the hoop, – under the cosh, raise Cain with, – merry hell with, settle one's hash, skin alive, spifflicate, turn inside out, walk into (see Crime: 491, 492)
5. *to beat:* anoint, bash, baste, beat the daylights out of, – the devil out of, – the hide off, beat up, dust one's coat, fan, give a basting, – a clouting, etc. (see n. 3), hammer, knock the stuffing(s) out of,

larrup, lather, lay into, leather, lick the hell out of, – the tar out of, – the pants off, – to a frazzle, nail to the wall, pan, shellac, sock, swack, swish, tan (one's arse/hide), tickle one's tail, wallop, whale the shit out of, – the tar out of, whop
6. *to be punished:* cop it, draw the crow (Aus.), eat shit, get it in the neck, take it on the chin, – one's lumps, – the fall, – the gas, – the knock, catch (merry) hell, catch it, get it (good and hot), get toco; spec. have it coming and going (be punished twice) (see Crime: 491)
7. *to accept one's punishment:* face the music, get what's coming to one, – one's come-uppance, pay the piper, stand up and take it, take it (like a man), – one's medicine, – the rap
8. *to deserve punishment:* be riding for a fall, be for it, – in for it, – on the spot, have it coming, let oneself in for it
9. *to escape punishment:* beat the rap, duck the rap (see Crime: 491.6)

REPARATION

319. Confession
n. 1. come-across, cough (up), squawk, squeak
v. 2. *to confess:* come across (with the goods), come clean, – one's cocoa, – one's fat (Aus.), – one's lot, cough (up), fess up, get (it) off one's chest, – (it) out of one's system, – (it) off one's mind, level (with), open up, out with (it), put up one's hand, sing, spill (it), spill one's guts, – the beans, – it out, squawk, squeak, talk, unload (see also Crime: 490.6)
3. *force to confess:* break (down), crack, – wide open, make one sing, put the arm on, third degree

320. Reform
n. 1. clean-up; spec. Black justice (black self-determination)
v. 2. *to reform:* clean up, clean up one's act, go legit, – square, – straight

RELIGION

321. Religion
n. 1. *spec.* fish-eater, Taig (derog. Roman Catholic); God slot (compulsory religious hour on UK TV)
adv. 2. *religious:* holier-than-thou, nearer-my-God-than-thee, pi

322. Religious Activities
v. 1. *spec. take a collection:* pass the hat

323. Religious Person
n. 1. bible-banger, bible-basher, bible-puncher, Holy Joe
2. *spec. Salvation Army:* Sally Ann, Salvo (Aus.)
3. *preacher, priest:* Holy Joe, sky pilot
4. *charlatan:* mitt man

324. Religious Buildings and Organisations
n. 1. *church:* Godbox
2. *YMCA:* Y
3. *Salvation Army:* Sally Ann, Salvo (Aus.)

325. Supernatural Beings
n. 1. *euphemisms for God:* dad, gad, gawd, golly, gor, gorra, gorry, gosh, gum, Lawd, lawdy, lawks, laws, lor, Lordy
2. *euphemisms for Christ:* Christmas, Christopher (Columbus), crikey, criminy, cripes, gee, geez, jayzus, jeez, Jesus H. Christ
3. *the Devil:* deuce, dickens, divil, Old Bendy, – Billy, – Blazes, – Boots, – Boy, – Cain, – Clootie, – Dad, – Driver, – Gentleman, – Gooseberry, – Harry, – Horny, – Lad, – Ned, – Nick, – One, – Poger, – Poker, – Roger, – Ruffin, – Scratch, – Serpent, – Toast, Sam Hill
4. *ghost:* bogeyman, boogieman, spook

326. Afterlife
n. 1. *heaven:* happy hunting grounds, harp farm
2. *hell:* blazes, blue blazes, Hades

327. Sorcery; Magic
n. 1. hocus-pocus
v. 2. *to put a spell on:* hex, hoodoo, put the hex on

Human Relations

FRIENDLINESS

328. Friendship
n. 1. *welcome:* glad hand
v. 2. *to make friends:* buddy up, chum up, get next to, get one's feet under the table, hit it off, pal up (with)
3. *to get on with:* click (with), knock along with
4. *to be popular with:* be in good with, – on the right side of, – in with, etc. (see adv. 9), rate, stand good with, sit right with
5. *to be overfriendly:* glad hand; spec. press flesh (for a politician to shake hands)
6. *to associate with:* hang around with, hook up with, mob up with, run with, tie in with, – up with
adv. 7. *friendly:* buddy-buddy, chummy, down with, hope-to-die (US Black), in one's corner, one on one, pally, palsy-walsy, running with, thick with, tight with
8. *intimate:* on speakers; spec. just quietly (Aus. between you and me)
9. *popular with:* aces with, in good with, in solid (with), in with, into, next to, on the right side of
excl. 10. *terms of friendship:* ace, amigo, baby, babes, babycakes, bless your little cotton socks, buggerlugs, diddums, ducks, love, lovey, sunshine

329. Kindliness; Consideration
n. 1. TLC (tender loving care)
v. 2. *to be kind:* have one's heart in the right place
3. *to be lenient:* ease up on, let down easy, let up on, pull one's punches

adj. 4. *kind:* big hearted, soft
excl. 5. don't worry it may never happen, upsidaisy, worse things happen at sea, you can't win them all

330. Reconciliation
v. 1. *to reconcile:* square up
2. *to be reconciled:* bury the hatchet, get clear with

HOSTILITY

331. Estrangement
n. 1. break-up, bust-up, splitsville
v. 2. *to become estranged:* break it off, – up, – with, bust up, call it a day, – it quits, chuck, ditch, dump, give one the brush(-off), part brass rags, split (with), throw over, wash one's hands of (see also Rejection: 224, Jilting: 353)

332. Enmity; Disfavour
n. 1. frost, hard word; spec. shit list (black list); spec. Jim Crow laws (racist laws in US)
v. 2. *to dislike:* be down on, – off, go off, – sour on, have a down on, have a hard-on for, – a hate on, – it in for, – no love lost for, not go nap on (Aus.)
3. *to earn disfavour:* get in bad with, – on the outs with; spec. one's name is mud (to be unpopular)
adv. 4. *on bad terms:* in bad (with), in Dutch (with), – the doghouse, – wrong (with), off of, on the outs, on the outer (Aus.), out with, washed up with, went down like a pork chop at a Jewish wedding

333. Jealousy
v. 1. *to be jealous:* eat one's heart out
phr. 2. *of jealousy:* all right for some, I should be so lucky, nice work if you can get it

334. Malice
n. 1. cussedness, shenanigans
2. *grudge:* axe to grind, bitch, bone to pick, down, peeve
v. 3. *to cause trouble for:* louse (one) up, mess over, put the mockers on, rubbish, trash; spec. put the black on (blackmail); set up (place in a vulnerable situation)
4. *to provoke trouble:* gee up, head-hunt (US Black)
5. *to hold a grudge:* be down on, have an axe to grind, – a bone to pick, – a down on, – a peeve with, – it in for
adj. 6. *malicious:* mean, mean-hair, ornery, shitty

335. Retaliation; Revenge
n. 1. comeback, paybacks (US Black)
v. 2. *to take revenge:* come back at, even the score, fix, settle one's hash, settle up, square (it), stuff
3. *to seek revenge:* be out for blood

336. Intimidation
n. 1. big stick, frighteners, screws
v. 2. *to intimidate:* buffalo, bulldoze, bullyrag, come down on, come down fonky (US Black), – heavy, hang tough, hard-talk, heavy, lean on, put the arm on, – the bull on, – the cosh on, – the frighteners on, – the screws on, – the squeeze on, – the wind up, stand over (Aus.), weird out; spec. kneecap (IRA punishment) (see also Cowardice: 296)
excl. 3. *threats:* or else!, I don't mean maybe!, I'll knock your block off!
4. *counter to threats:* oh yeah!, sez who!, you and whose army!

337. Rough Treatment
n. 1. muscle, rough-house, rough stuff, strong arm stuff; spec. heading, nutting; knuckle sandwich
2. *a blow:* backhander, bang, haymaker, lick, old one-two, one (i.e. 'fetch him one'); spec. Christmas hold (on the testicles),

king (Aus. kinghit = knockout punch)
v. 3. *to manhandle:* be rough on, bounce, cut up rough, – up rusty, hand out punishment, – a bit of stick, get tough with, rough up, tough up
4. *to hit:* banjo, barrel (Aus.), bash, bean, belt, boff, boot (around), burst, bust (one) up, clip, clobber, clock, clunk, conk, crown, dance on one's lips, deck, dish it out, do a job on, do over, drive on (US Black), duff over, duff up, duke, dust (one), flatten, get in one's eye (US Black), give a fourpenny one, give one the leather, go down on, go the knuckle (Aus.), go upside one's head (US Black), grunge, hang one on, jam one up (US Black), job (Aus.), kick (one's) arse, kick the stuffing out of, knee, knock one's block off, knock the bejazus out of, – the stuffing out of, lump, nut, paste, pepper one up (US Black), plaster, pop (in the eye), put a hurting on (US Black), put one on, – one's arse in sling, – the boot in, – the leather in, ring one's bell, roak (US Black), run over, run sets on (US Black), run up the side of one's head (US Black), scone (Aus.), scrag, slosh, slug, sock, spank, stick one on, stomp, take a pop (at), tan one's hide, throw a punch, throw hands (US Black), tump over, whack, whale the piss out of, – the shit out of, – the tar out of, whap, whup, wooden (Aus.), work over
5. *to knock out:* cold-cock, cold-deck, drop, kayo, knock cold, KO, lay out, put (one) away, put one's lights out
6. spec. chive, let the daylights into, stick (stab); skullneck (decapitate); stripe (slash)
7. *to shoot:* bang off, blast, blow away, blow one's head off, chop, drill, give it to, – (one) lead poisoning, let have it, nail, perforate, plug, put the blast on, shoot the daylights out of, take a crack at
8. *to wound, hurt:* hurt, nip; spec. mark up (bruise)
9. *to kick:* give the leather, leather
adv. 10. *hit on the head:* boned

338. Attack; Assault
n. 1. *a fight:* aggro, barney, bovver, confusion (WI), ding-dong,

donnybrook, dust-up, fair, fist junction (US Black), kick-up (WI), knock-down drag-out, knuckle, mash-up (WI), pasting, punch-up, rashing (US Black), ruffle (US Black), rumble, scrap, spillin' (US Black), stoush (Aus.), thumb (US Black), up-and-downer; spec. shin battle (a fake battle); spec. queer bashing, Paki-bashing, nigger-bashing (attacks on gays, Pakistanis, blacks)

2. *rape:* drumstick case (US Black)

v. 3. *to fight:* bop, duke it out, get down from the Y (US Black), give the works (to), go from the Y, go from the fists, go from the shoulders, gunzel (US Black), kick (some) ass, lay into, lock arseholes, mess up, mess with, mix it, rain on, rough-house, shuffle, snap arseholes, sort out, straighten

4. *to attack:* beat up (on), blaze on (US Black), do, do up, get tore in, get stuck into, go down, go round with, jack up, make a pass at, muscle in, rip into, sail into, sandbag, sic onto, snag, tear into, tear one a new arsehole, vamp on (US Black)

5. *to beat, defeat:* beat the can off, – the pants off, – the shit out of, boff, bop, break in half, brown-slice (WI), cream, crease, do over, do to a turn, do up (brown), donkey-lick (Aus.), dough-pop, eat up, flatten, floor, give it to (one) good, give lumps, give the chop, give the works to, hang one out to dry, have one's guts for garters, jam one up (US Black), jump all over, knacker, knock bowlegged, – for a loop, – hell west and crooked, – into the middle of next week, – one's socks off, – one's teeth down his throat, – silly, leave for dead, lick, make mincemeat of, mogador (rhy.sl. = floor), mullah, paste, push one's face through the back of one's neck, put (one) away, shove one's fist down his throat, smear all over the map, take to the cleaners, wax one's tail, wax, whale the shit out of, – the tar out of, whip one's arse, wipe out, work over good; spec. mummy (US Black: beat to death)

6. *to rape:* gorilla, jam one up (US Black)

7. *to ambush:* jap, jump, snag

adv. 8. *beaten up:* done over, done up (like a kipper)

9. *aggressive:* scrappy

CO-OPERATION

339. Co-operation

n. 1. cahoots, get-together, hook-up, tie-in, tie-up

v. 2. *join in:* case out, hook up with, lock into, muck in, play ball (with), tie up with, tie into; spec. re-up (US milit.: to re-enlist)

3. *to involve:* get one in (on an act), ring in, rope in

4. *to do one's share:* do one's bit, keep one's end up, pull one's weight, weigh in

5. *to make a deal:* cut up the cake

adv. 6. *united:* crewed up, in cahoots, hooked up, mob-handed, solid, team-handed, tied in, – up

phr. 7. *let's co-operate:* you scratch my back and I'll scratch yours

340. Agreement

n. 1. click, hook-up, tie-up

v. 2. *to agree:* be on, get behind, go a bundle on, go for, go (along) with, swing with, tumble for

3. *to sign a contract:* ink, pact

phr. 4. *agreement:* put it there!, shake!

5. *agreed:* and how, aren't we all, bags I, check, check and double check, count me in, don't mind if I do, I'm on, I'll go for that, I'll say, I'm with you, me and you both, 'nuff said, put it there, shake, same here, that's (for) me, you're on

341. Assistance

n. 1. *help:* boost, leg-up; spec. log-rolling (mutual aid)

v. 2. *to help:* boost, chip in, give a leg-up, pinch-hit, reach (US Black)

3. *to support, back up:* boost, front for, go overboard for, get behind, get one's back (US Black), go to the mat for, stooge for

4. *to defend oneself:* throw a punch

5. *to give a chance to:* give a break, – half a chance, – a squeeze

6. *to let someone get on with:* let the dog see the rabbit

7. *to do a favour:* do a solid (US Black), lemon (rhy.sl. = lemon flavour = favour)

OPPOSITION; CONFLICT

342. Opposition
n. 1. spec. needle match
2. *litigation:* Sue City
v. 3. *to oppose:* thumb the nose at, throw one's hat in the ring
adj. 4. *rebellious:* bolshy, uppity

343. Disagreement
v. 1. *fail to agree:* get out of line
adv. 2. *in disagreement:* no deal, – dice, – go, – sale, – soap, – way, nothing doing

344. Contention
n. 1. *argument, quarrel:* argy-bargy, barney, blow-up, blue (Aus.), bull and cow (rhy.sl. = row), ruck, ruckus, run-in, shoot-out, spat, to-do; spec. demo (demonstration); Mexican stand-off (no-win situation); sporting encounter: blinder
v. 2. *to pursue, compete:* breathe down one's neck, duck-shove (Aus.), go for pinslips, have a hit on, jockey, lock assholes, tangle assholes
3. *to argue:* have it out, pick a bone with, weigh in
4. *feel aggressive:* feel froggy (US Black)
5. *to challenge:* buy a (wolf) ticket (US Black), call (one) out, choose off (US Black), step out on the green (US Black)
adv. 6. *in contention:* head up, mano-a-mano, one-on-one
7. *aggressive:* bad-ass, chippy, hard-boiled
phr. 8. *challenges:* leap and you will receive (US Black), want to make something of it?, who (are) you screwing?

COURTESY

345. Courtesy; Politeness
n. 1. spec. cool (street gang peace)
excl. 2. *social remarks:* age before beauty, be my guest, bully for you!

3. *thank you:* ta, ta muchly, thanks a bunch, – a million
4. *you're welcome:* forget it, keep the change, no sweat, skip it, that's cool
5. *no thank you:* I'll freeze, that's cool

346. Greeting
n. 1. howdy, howdydo; spec. dap, soul shake (ritual black palm-slapping)
v. 2. *to greet with mutual palm-slapping:* give some skin, – spli, give the drummer some, high-five, slap, – five, – the plank (US Black)
excl. 3. *hello:* bhani ghani (US Black), cop a squat, getting any?, hello, John (got a new motor?), hi-de-hi! (response: hi-de-ho), how's it hanging?, how're they hanging?, how's tricks?, lay some on me! (US Black), long time no see, look what the cat's brought in, – the wind's blown in, park your carcase, roll your own (US Black), skin me! (US Black), what can I do you for?, what gives?, what's cooking?, – going on?, – happening?, – new?, – shaking?, – the deal?, what sup?, wotcher; spec. Miss Thing (homosexual use)
4. *goodbye*!: Abyssinia!, (see you later) alligator, catch some rays, – you later, cheerie-bye, cheerio, chin-chin, don't call us, we'll call you, don't do anything I wouldn't do, – spend it all at once, – take any wooden nickels, hooroo (Aus.), oh reservoir, pip-pip, seeya, seeyabye, see you in church, – in court, – the funny pages, so long, stay loose, ta-ta, TTFN (ta-ta for now), teuf-teuf, toodle-bye, toodle-oo, toodle-pip

---

DISCOURTESY

347. Impudence; Audacity
n. 1. *cheek:* brass, chutzpah (Yid.), crust, face, neck, lip, moxie, once a week (rhy.sl. = cheek), piss and vinegar, sass, stalk
2. *cheekiness:* guff, jaw, lip, mouth, sauce, sass
v. 3. *to be impudent:* cock a snoot (at), have a brass neck; spec. gross out (to shock); spec. take tea with (to outwit)
adj. 4. *impudent:* bold, bold as brass,

faastie (WI), fresh, leery, lippy, more front than Brighton beach, mouthy, pushy, rumbunctious, rumbustious, smart-arse, smart-alecky, snotty, wise-ass

excl. 5. *don't be cheeky!:* can you beat that!, what a nerve!, less of it!, of all the . . . ! , don't be smart!

348. Slight; Snub
n. 1. brush (off), cold shoulder, frost, frozen mitt, go-around, kick in the pants, run-around, smack in the eye (see also Ejection: 63)

v. 2. *to slight, snub:* freeze on, give one the belt, – the brush (off), – the cold shoulder, – the freeze (out), – the frost, – the go-around, – the runaround, have a shot at (Aus.), high-hat, see off, send away with a flea in one's ear, shoot down, shine on (US Black), upstage; spec. cold-cunt (lesbian use: ignore)

phr. 3. *of ignorance:* don't know one from a bar of soap (Aus.)

excl. 4. *of contempt:* in your eye!

LOVE

349. Love
n. 1. *infatuation:* crush, pash

v. 2. *to be in love:* be stuck on, fall for (like a ton of bricks), go for, have a thing for, – eyes for, – one's nose open (US Black), – a ring through one's nose, – the hots (for), rush, take a shine to, wear the ring (US Black)

3. *to fascinate:* get under one's skin

adv. 4. *in love with, obsessed:* after, bitten, crazy for, cuckoo over, dead set (on), gooey about, – over, goofy about, gone on, head over heels, in a bad way, in deep, lovey-dovey, mad about, moony (over), nuts about, smitten, snowed over, soft on, sweet on, on a tight leash, wild about

350. Courtship
n. 1. dating, macking, nanny-goating (rhy.sl. = courting); spec. basket picnic (gay use: looking over prospective pickups)

2. spec. heavy date (very important date)

v. 3. *to pick up:* chat up, give the business, hoopdie-swoop (US Black), mack, pluck (US Black)

4. *to appraise sexually:* give the glad eye, make a dead set for, – a play for, prop up, pull a quick park (US Black), put the hard word on, scope (on); spec. cruise (gay use)

5. *to go out:* spec. double (double-date), sit (a woman) (US Black)

6. *to steal someone else's date:* cut out, snake

7. *to interfere with courtship:* (play) gooseberry

351. Caressing
n. 1. (bit of) slap and tickle, bush patrol, finger pie, groping, lovey-dovey, parking, PDA (public display of affection), pecking and necking (US Black), stink(y)-finger; spec. first base (initial sexual contact); ga-ga, jam (gay use)

2. *a kiss:* French kiss, kissyface, hit (rhy.sl. = hit and miss), soul kiss (US Black), smacker, tongue sushi

v. 3. *to caress:* canoodle, climb all over, cock pluck (US Black), cop a feel, dry-fuck, feel up, finger-fuck, get to first base,

4. *to kiss:* chew face, mug, poof, suck face, swap spit

adv. 5. *physically affectionate:* H^2 (hot and heavy)

phr. 6. *rejection of caresses:* not tonight Josephine

352. Flirtation; Philandering
n. 1. *philandering:* catting (US Black); spec. little black book (bachelor's address book)

2. *a flirt:* cock-teaser, cunt-teaser, prick-teaser

3. *flirtatious glance:* bedroom eyes, come-hither look, glad eye, goo-goo eyes

4. *flirtatious talk:* chat, line, lyricising (WI)

v. 5. *to philander:* cat around, cruise, fan one's ass, – one's pussy (US Black), flag (gay use), fool around, give up rhythm (US Black), hit and run, jack around, jazz around, perv about, play around, play the field, put it about, shoot the

thrill (US Black), tomcat; spec. basketeer (gay use: to size up possible conquests); play checkers (gay use: to move around a cinema looking for sex)
6. *to flirt:* play hard to get
7. *to approach for sex:* bumchat, hit on, jeff (US Black), mack on (US Black), make a pass, pick up, sweet-talk, shoot a line, talk business (US Black); spec. front one off (US Black: to seduce for gain, not lust)
8. *to frustrate:* cocktease, pricktease
9. *gay use:* have kidney trouble (solicit in public lavatories)
10. spec. red-light, shell-road (to throw a girl out of a car if she refuses to have sex)

353. Jilting
n. 1. air, brush, chuck, dump, freeze, frost, kiss-off, let-down, push
v. 2. *to interfere in a relationship:* bird dog, cock block, gigolo, play chicken, rank one's style (US Black)
3. *to cheat:* burn, chippie, chippy on, two-time
4. *to have an affair:* carry on, tip out (US Black)
5. *to end an affair:* chuck, dump, give the air, – the brush, etc. (see n. 1), kiss off, run out on, throw over, tip (US Black), unload (see also Reject: 224)
6. *to miss a lover:* carry a torch, torch for
adv. 7. spec. on the rebound

354. Engagement
n. 1. spec. bottom drawer
v. 2. *to be engaged, go out with:* date (Aus.), get it together, go steady, have something going
3. *to propose:* pop the question
adv. 4. *engaged:* dropped, taped up (US Black)

355. Marriage; Living Together
1. ball and chain
2. *living together:* LTR (living together relationship), shack job, shack-up
3. *uncertain relationship:* see-saw (US Black)
4. *marrying someone younger:* baby-snatching
v. 5. *to marry, be married:* be spliced,

– hitched, have papers (US Black), make the legal move, tie the knot
6. *to live together:* bungalow, knock on together, shack (up)
adv. 7. *married:* cash and carried, cut and carried (rhy.sl.), hitched, spliced
8. *unhappily married:* hen-pecked, pussy-whipped

356. Divorce; Parting
n. 1. bust-up, splitsville
v. 2. *to divorce, part:* blow one out, bust up, call it a day, – quits, split
3. *to repel:* turn off

SEX

357. Sexuality
n. 1. *desired object:* cookies
2. *desire, passion:* hard-on, load (US Black), hot nuts, – pants, zazzle (US Black); spec. blue balls (frustration)
v. 3. *to desire:* be hot for, go for, gun for, have hot pants for, – hot nuts for, honk for, lech (after), feel one's oats
4. *to excite:* get one going, get one's nose open (US Black), (this will) put lead in your pencil, prime one's pump, turn on
5. *to be sexually active:* have some rabbit, put it about
6. *to expose the genitals:* flash
7. *to be bisexual:* swing both ways
adj. 8. *sexy:* foxy, hot, raunchy, rude, warm
9. *bisexual:* AC/DC, ambidextrous, bi, half-and-half
10. *pornographic:* adult, blue, hard, strong
adv. 11. *excited:* begging for it, dripping for it, fruity, horny, hot (for), hot to trot, randy, sexed up
phr. 12. as the actress said to the bishop; nudge nudge wink wink know what I mean say no more

358. Sexuality: Homosexual
n. 1. spec. debut (first gay experience); mother-love (gay male's relationship with a heterosexual woman); talking (lesbian use: a relationship when one

partner is in jail); bambi effect (for a young gay male to turn to heterosexuality); second closet (an admission of homosexuality); squelch (sex without affection)

v. 2. *to hide one's homosexuality:* pass, stay in the closet, wear a mourning veil; spec. lose one's gender (to abandon homo- for heterosexuality); wear a cut-glass veil (fail to hide one's homosexuality)

3. *to reveal one's homosexuality:* come out, discover one's gender, drop one's beads, – one's hairpins, lay it out, learn a new way, wear one's badge; spec. be brought out (to be initiated into the gay life); turn the tables (for a homosexual to blackmail a heterosexual)

4. *to act effeminately:* camp, foop, poof about, ruin, swish, wreck

5. *to become homosexual:* turn the corner **adj. 6.** *effeminate:* la-di-dah

7. *homosexual:* bent, camp as a row of tents, chichi, having a dash, lavender

8. spec. longwinded (taking a long time to reach orgasm)

9. spec. on the fence (ambivalent about homosexuality)

10. spec. enthroned (soliciting in a public lavatory), dethroned (ejected from a public lavatory)

359. Intercourse

n. 1. ball, bang, bit of how's-yer-father, – of the other, bunk-up, bush patrol, dash in the bloomers, dead shot (US Black), Donald Duck (rhy.sl. = fuck), fickey-fick, fratting, fucking, fucky-fucky, fugging, ground rations, horizontal jogging, – rumble, horry (Aus.), hot fling (US Black), indoor sledging, interior decorating, Jack in the box (US Black), jig-a-jig, lay, legover, nasty, naughties, naughty, nobbing, nookie, oats, parallel parking, roll in the hay, root, rub-a-dub, seeing-to, thrill and chill (US Black), turking, Ugandan discussions, wellington (Aus. rhy.sl. wellington boot = root), you know what; spec. knee-trembler (intercourse while standing up); straight shot (intercourse without contraception)

2. *spontaneous intercourse:* bip bam thank-you mam, bump, fast-fuck, quicke, wham bam thank-you mam

3. *lunchtime intercourse:* afternoon delight, funch, nooner

4. *place of intercourse:* killing floor, whip shack (US Black)

5. *coitus interruptus:* getting off at Redfern (Aus.), – out at Gateshead, leaving before the gospel

v. 6. *to have intercourse:* ball, bang, beanbag, biff, bust some booty (US Black), cha-cha, charver, chingazo (Sp.), cut a side (US Black), cut a slice off the joint, dance on the mattress, dip it, dip one's wick, – the fly (US Black), dive into the dark (US Black), do, do a kindness, do the do (US Black), – the nasty, – the natural thing, – the pussy (US Black), drill, drop one's load, empty one's trash (US Black), exercise the ferret, feature with (Aus.), fill one up (US Black), frig, fuck, fug, fugh, futz, gee, get a shot of leg (US Black), – into one's pants, – into, – on top of, – one's ashes hauled, – one's cookies, – one's end away, – one's greens, – one's jollies, – one's leg over, – one's oats, – one's rocks off, – some big leg, – some cock, – some pussy, – some tail, – some, give her a length, give her one, – one a tumble, – some body, – the dog a bone, go all the way, go with, grind, have a cut off the joint, have a dash in the bloomers, have a shag, – a slice off the joint, – a tumble, – it away (with), – it in, – one's greens, – one's oats, hide and salam, hide the salam, honeyfuck, honeyfuggle, hop on a babe, hump, jack up, jazz, jump, jump up and down, knock it off, knock it out (US Black), – off a piece, lay, lay some pipe, make it (with), mash the fat (US Black), meddle, mess around, mount, off, pile (US Black), plank, play mothers and fathers, – mummies and daddies, – night baseball, plonk, plough the back forty, plough, poke, pole, pork, prod, punch, ride, roger, root, rout, rump, schtup (Yid.), score between the posts (Aus.), scrape (Aus.), screw, see the King, shaft, shag, skeet (US Black), skin the cat, slip her a length, slip it to, snag, spear the bearded clam (Aus.), stick it to, stoop, stroke (US Black), stuff, take a turn on shooter's hill (US Black), throw, tom, tonk, tumble, twang; spec. roof it (to have sex on the roof); spec. talk fuck (to talk obscenely during intercourse); come across (surrender to seduction)

7. *to copulate enthusiastically:* bang like the shithouse door in a gale, go in out like a fiddler's elbow, go up her like a rat up a drain, rip her guts down (US Black), screw the arse off, shag like a rattlesnake

8. *to have an orgasm:* come, come one's cocoa, – one's fat, cream, pop one's cork; spec. have a double shot (ejaculate twice)

9. *to give an orgasm:* ring one's bell, – one's chimes

10. *to have many sexual partners:* climb trees to get away from it (Aus.), get more arse than a toilet seat, have more pricks than a second-hand dart-board, have to swim underwater to get away from it (Aus.), hump 'em and dump 'em, so busy I've had to put a man on to help (Aus.), swing

11. *to deflower a virgin:* cherrypop, cop a cherry, crack a cherry, cut the cake, pop a cherry, split the cup (US Black)

12. *to seduce:* Georgia, Georgy (US Black), get across, – off with, – next to (US Black), – one's leg over, go case with, have, – it away with, have one over, make, nail, prong, race off (Aus.), reel in the biscuit; spec. strike out (fail to seduce); are you saving it for the worms (an attempt to persuade an unwilling girl)

13. *to lose one's erection:* mess with nature (US Black)

adj. 14. *promiscuous:* fast

15. *seduced:* had

16. *having intercourse without contraception:* bareback

adv. 17. *having intercourse:* at it, firkin, frigging, fucking, in the saddle, on the job, – the nest, – top of; spec. been there (referring to a previous sexual partner); spec. dog-knotted (for partners to be locked together during intercourse through muscle spasm)

18. *satiated:* plucked (US Black)

phr. 19. it takes two to tango

20. *sexual distaste:* don't fancy yours, I wouldn't fuck her with your prick, – with a borrowed prick, I wouldn't touch it with yours, – with a ten-foot barge-pole

360. Varieties

n. 1. *oral sex:* head, lunch, sixty-nine, soixante-neuf; spec. rubbernecking (auto-fellatio)

2. *fellatio:* blow-job, deep throat, face-fucking, gob-job, head, lunch, sixty-eight ('you suck me and I'll owe you one'); spec. punishment (gay use: taking on an extra-large penis); glory hole (a hole in a public lavatory – the penis is pushed through for fellation)

3. *cunnilingus:* box lunch, dining at the Y, dipping in the bush, head, mouth music, punch in the mouth, sack lunch, skull (US Black); spec. red wings (Hell's Angel use: cunnilingus with a menstruating woman)

4. *anilingus:* felch, reaming, ream job, rimming, rim, rim-job; spec. black wings, brown wings (Hell's Angels use)

5. *sodomy:* arse fucking, back jump (US Black), brown-eye, browning, going up the arse, – the chute, – the tan track, etc. (see Parts of Body: 126.29), Greek culture, hoop, ring, trip to the moon (gay use)

6. *group sex, orgy:* all in one, bunch punch, daisy-chain, gang-bang, gang-shag, group grope, team cream (gay use), threesome, three-way deal, triangle; spec. sloppy seconds (a girl moving from one partner to the next)

7. *fringe sex:* B&D, English culture (bondage and discipline), bagpiping (intercourse under the armpit), freak fuck, leg work (intercourse between the thighs), S&M (sado-masochism), Swedish culture (rubberwear), tightbuck (gay use: foetal position used for S&M or bondage)

8. spec. collegiate fucking, Princeton rub (gay use: body-to-body rubbing); flat-fucking (lesbian use: body rubbing)

9. *masturbation:* Allied Irish (Irish rhy.sl. Allied Irish Bank = wank), arming the cannon, couch hockey for one, dusting the duvet, engaging sixth gear, finger

blasting, five-finger Mary, – shuffle, – solo, five-knuckle shuffle, fly fishing, four sisters on Thumb Street, frapple, gusset typing (female), ham shank, han solo (pun on Han Solo of *Star Wars* and 'hand solo'), hand job, hand shandy, hand solo, hard labour, Harry Johnson (i.e. hand job), J. Arthur (rhy.sl = wank), J/O scene, jerking off the jelly juice, jerking the gherkin, Jodrell Bank (rhy.sl.), kit-kat shuffle, knuckle shuffle, Lady Five Fingers, manual labour, manual override, mother fist and her five daughters, Mrs Palm and her five daughters, much goo about nothing, night exercises, Onan's Olympics, one-eye target practice, one-gun salute, one-legged race, one-man show, one off the wrist, one stick drum improvisation, Pam and her five sisters, pocket pool, single dingles, slaking the bacon, squirt 'n' spurt, unloading, wank, whizzing the jizzum, wrist aerobics, wrist marathon; spec. circle jerk (group masturbation); playing chopsticks (gay use: mutual masturbation)

10. *coprophilia:* scat

v. 11. *to have oral sex:* eat, fress (Yid. = eat), give up one's face, go around the world, – down (on), – down south, gobble, take it any way (gay use)

12. *to fellate:* bite one's crank, blow, blow one's cookies, – one's glass, – the skin flute, cop one's bird, – one's joint, deep throat, eat one's meat, feed one's face, french, gam, give cone, – head, gnaw the 'nana, go down on, gobble, – the goo, kiss, – the worm, lay the lip, plate (rhy.sl. = plate of ham = gam), play hoop-snake with (gay use), smoke, suck off, swing (gay use), tongue lash; spec. ride a blind piece (gay use: to fellate an uncircumcised penis); spit out of the window (gay use: to spit out semen); spray the tonsils (ejaculate in the mouth); bag (US Black: swallow semen)

13. *to practise cunnilingus:* blow some tunes (US Black), brush one's teeth (US Black), clean up the kitchen (gay use), dine at the Y, dip in the bush, dive, – in the canyon, drink at the fuzzy cup, eat, – hair pie, – out, face the nation (US Black), go way down South in Dixie, gorilla in the washing machine (US Black), go under the house (US Black), grin in the canyon, have a moustache, scalp (US Black), sip at the fuzzy cup (US Black), sneeze in the cabbage, – in the canyon, tongue (gay use), yodel, – in the canyon (of love), – up the valley; spec. sit on one's face (cunnilingus with the female superior)

14. *to practise anilingus:* eat jam, eat pound cake, go way down South in Dixie, rim (out)

15. *to sodomise:* ask for the ring, ass-fuck, brown, bunghole, burgle, butt-fuck, buy the ring, cornhole, dive into the sky, go up the old dirt road, get some brown, – some brown sugar, – some duke, go Hollywood, hose (gay use), lay the leg, leather (gay use), pack peanut butter, plug, punk, shoot one's star, throw a buttonhole on (US Black); spec. use the English (wriggle the buttocks during penetration)

16. *to permit sodomy:* duck, flopover, pick up the soap for, pratt for, take it up the arse, – up the butt, – up the (poop-) chute, etc. (see also Parts of Body: 116.29), take on some backs (US Black)

17. *to have group sex, an orgy:* gang bang, gang shag, line up on, make a sandwich, turn out; spec. run a double train (for two men to penetrate a woman simultaneously); pull a train (to suffer gang-rape)

18. *to molest:* diddle, touch up

19. *to masturbate (male):* bang the bishop, beat one's little brother, – one's meat, beat off, – one's dummy, – one's hog, – one's meat, belt one's hog, bring oneself off, burp the worm, butter one's corn, choke the chicken, – the chook (Aus.), clean one's rifle, consult Dr Jerkoff, crank one's shank, dinky one's slinky, do oneself off, do a dry waltz with oneself, feel in one's pocket for one's big hairy rocket, file one's fun-rod, fist fuck, fist one's mister, flex one's sex, flick one's Bic (US Black), flip oneself off (Aus.), flog one's mutton, – the dolphin, – the dog, – the log, get one's nuts off, grease one's pipe, hack one's mack, hand-gallop, haul one's own ashes,

hump one's hose, jack off, jerk off, levy (rhy.sl. = Levy and Frank = wank), milk the chicken, pack one's palm, paint one's ceiling, play a flute solo on one's meat whistle, play pocket billiards, – the male organ, – with oneself, please one's pisser, point one's social finger, polish one's sword, pound one's pork, – one's pud, – one's flounder, prompt one's porpoise, prime one's pump, prune the fifth limb, pull one's joint, – one's pud, – one's pudding, – one's taffy, – one's wire, – the pope, rub off, – up, run one's hand up the flagpole, sew (US Black), shake hands with the guy who stood up when I got married, – with the wife's best friend, shine one's pole, shoot the tadpoles, slam one's hammer, slam one's spam, slap one's wapper, spank the monkey, – the salami, stir one's stew, strike the pink match, stroke one's beef, – one's poker, – the dog, talk with Rosy Palm and her five little sisters, thump one's pumper, tickle one's pickle, toss off, twang one's wire, tweak one's twinkie, unclog the pipes, varnish one's pole, walk the dog, wank, watch the eyelid movies, wax one's dolphin, whip off, whip one's dripper, – one's wire, whack off, whank, whip it, wonk one's conker, yang one's wang, yank the yam, – one's crank; spec. catch a buzz (to masturbate with a vibrator)

20. *to masturbate (female):* beat the beaver, buttonhole, clap one's clit, cook cucumbers, grease the gash, hide the hot dog, hit the slit, hose one's hole, make waves, pet the poodle, slam the clam, stump-jump

21. spec. fist, fist-fuck (gay use: to insert the fist into the anus)

22. spec. pick up the vibrations (gay use: watch a gay sex-show); take one's meat out of the basket (gay use: to reveal the genitals to another man)

adv. 23. *aberrant:* geared

SOCIAL LIFE

361. Sociability

n. 1. *'good life':* life of Reilly, sporting life
2. *invitation:* stiffy
v. 3. *to lead a social life:* get around, put oneself about; spec. sit eggs (US Black: overstay one's welcome)
4. *to visit:* blow by, fall by, knock up, pop in, slide by, stop by
adj. 5. *sociable:* chummy, pally, palsy(-walsy)

362. Social Engagement

n. 1. *meeting:* date, meet, one to meet
2. *a meeting place:* hang-out; spec. cottage (gay use); meat market (student use)
v. 3. *to meet:* bump into
4. *to break a date:* duck out, give one a miss, stand up
5. *to have a date broken:* be shafted, stood up
6. *to stay at home:* bing it (US Black)

363. Social Entertainment; Party

n. 1. bash, bean-feast, beano, beer bust, beer-up (Aus.), blast, bunfight, bust, do, gang-shag (US Black), get-together, heller, knees-up, racket, rave, ruckus, rug beat (US Black), shake, shindig, shindy, thrash, turn (Aus.), wing-ding; spec. hen party (all women); stag party (eve-of-wedding men-only party); be-in (hippie gathering)
v. 2. *to go out:* creep, hit the high spots, night-club; spec. party-hop (to move from party to party); get home with the milk (return after a night's revels)
3. *to have a good time:* cut it up, juke, party, whoop it up
4. *to entertain:* do the honours, throw a party, – a bash, – a beano, etc. (see n. 1)

364. Dancing

n. 1. bopping, boogying, cutting the rug, juking; spec. breaking, hip-hop, hoofing
2. *a dance, ball:* bollock, clutch
v. 3. *to dance:* boogaloo, boogie, cut the rug, juke, shake a leg, shake it, strut one's stuff

POSSESSION: ACQUISITION

365. Acquisition; Gains
n. 1. goodies, killing, pickings, rake-off, take
v. 2. *to obtain:* bag, collar, come in for, cop, freeze onto, get one's hooks on, glom, gobble up, land, load up on, mop up, nab, nip, pull down, rope in, rustle up, scare up, snag, sneeze, whistle up; spec. trouser (to pocket)
3. *to take everything:* go the whole hog, sweep the board
4. *to obtain by fraud:* chisel out of, ease out of, promote for, wangle out of, work for (see also Influence: 219)
adv. 5. *gaining:* on a roll
phr. 6. *I want!:* bags I!, dibs on!

366. Possession; Property
n. 1. traps; spec. dead man's shoes (property of a dead person); OPs (other people's property)
2. *luggage:* bindle, keister
v. 3. *to have plenty:* be cochealed, – lousy with, pack, reek with, roll in, stink of, swim in
adj. 4. *supplied:* cochealed, stinking
adv. 5. *well-supplied:* crummy with, filthy with, loaded, long on, lousy with, rolling in, stinking with, swimming in
6. *lacking:* clean out of, fresh out of
phr. 7. *how much do you have?:* how are you fixed?; spec. are you holding? (do you have drugs)

367. Joint Possession; Sharing
n. 1. piece, rake-off, shake, slice, split; spec. Dutch treat (both parties share payment); even Steven (fair shares); short end, – straw (the lesser share)
v. 2. *to share:* chip in, cut up, divvy (up), go Dutch, – fifty-fifty, – halves, – splits, muck in with, split; spec. deck up (drug use)
3. *to give a share:* cut in, deal in, give a cut, – a piece, etc. (see n. 1), ring in, split with
4. *get one's share:* come in for, cut a piece, – a slice, etc. (see n. 1), get a cut, – a piece, – a slice, etc. (see n. 1); spec. get in on the ground floor (get a share at

the outset); hog, muscle into (take an extra share)
5. *to share out:* dish out
adv. 6. *sharing:* even Steven, fifty-fifty, going halves, – Dutch
7. *excluded from a share:* out of the game, – the picture, – the running

368. Borrowing and Begging
n. 1. *a request for something:* bite, hit-up, mooch, shakedown, tap, touch
v. 2. *to beg:* bite one's ear, bludge (Aus.), bot (Aus.), brace up, bum off, coat and badge (rhy.sl. = cadge), fang (Aus.), get into one's ribs, grub, make a touch, mump, ponce off, put the bee on, – the bite on, – the lug on, – the touch on, shake down, soak, stick one for, tap, throw the hooks into, touch; spec. work a crowd (beg from an audience)
3. *to extort:* bleed (white), put the bite on
adv. 4. *begging:* on the bot (Aus.), – the coat and badge (rhy.sl. = cadge)
phr. 5. *lend me some money:* let me hold some change

369. Loss
n. 1. wipe-out; spec. losing streak (continual losses)
v. 2. *to lose:* drop a packet, – a bundle, – one's roll, – one's wad, get the short end (of), kiss goodbye, kiss off, lose one's shirt

POSSESSION: BESTOWAL

370. Giving
n. 1. *gift:* freebie, handout, pressie, prezzie
v. 2. *to give:* chip in, come across (with), come up with, cough (up), deal out, dish out, dob in (Aus.), eevige (backsl.), fork out, – over, hand out, kick in, shell out, sub (up); spec. give one the pink slip (to cede something of value); mash it on (one) (US Black: to give someone their dues)
3. *to contribute:* chip in, kick the tin (Aus.), weigh in with
4. *to tip:* cross one's palm, grease; spec. stiff (fail to tip)

5. *to treat:* blow one to, go for, pick up the tab, shout; spec. my shout (my round of drinks)
6. *to be generous:* spread oneself
adj. 7. *generous:* handsome

371. Reward
n. 1. payoff; spec. pie in the sky (fantasy reward)
2. *deserts:* come-uppance
3. spec. leather medal, wooden spoon (metaphorical prize for the poorest loser)
v. 4. *to give one's deserts:* cook one's goose, give one's come-uppance
5. *to be rewarded:* bring home the bacon, pick the plums, take the cake; spec. get it coming and going (get double rewards)

372. Bribery
n. 1. dash (Nigeria), fix, grease job, kickbacks, payoffs
2. *a bribe:* backhander, bung, drink, hush money, kickback, payoff, straightener, take
v. 3. *to bribe:* bung, get to, grease, – one's palm, juice, oil, palm, patch (Canada), piece off, put the fix in, schmeer (Yid. = grease), sling (Aus.), square one off, stiffen, straighten, take care of
4. *to accept bribery:* be on the take, dip one's beak, get one's hands dirty, take

---

POSSESSION: ECONOMY

373. Extravagance
n. 1. splurging
v. 2. *to be extravagant:* blow one's wad, flash one's dough – one's wad, have a hole in one's pocket, live high off the hog, ride high wide and handsome, splash it about, splosh it on, splurge, throw one's money away

374. Thrift
n. 1 *something in reserve:* ace in the hole, card up one's sleeve
v. 2. *to live on the cheap:* take the bus

3. *to hide away:* keep on ice, put in cold storage, rat-hole
adj. 4. *mean:* cheap, chinky, Jewy (derog.), mingy, tight

POSSESSION: ESTATE

375. Wealth
n. 1. barrel of money, pot of dough
2. *funds:* bundle, pile, roll, wad
v. 3. *to be rich:* have money to burn, live high on the hog, ride the gravy train, roll in money
adj. 4. *wealthy:* cashed up, filthy rich, flush, in the money, loaded, made of money, rolling, stinking, stuffy, up in the dough, – in the money, well in, – away, well-fixed, – -heeled, – -lined
adv. 5. *comfortable:* high on the hog, in clover, in good shape, living off the tit, on a good wicket, on Easy Street, on the sunny side (of the street), on velvet, set, sitting pretty

376. Poverty
n. 1. Queer Street
2. *insufficient funds:* ain't long enough, not a bean, – a brass razoo (Aus.)
v. 3. *to be poor:* be down to one's bottom dollar, – in Queer Street, – in a hole, feel the pinch, have the wolf at the door, not have a pot to piss in, – have a prayer, – a red cent, rough it, scrape the bottom of the barrel, skate on one's uppers, touch bottom
4. *to lose money:* drop; spec. alley-whipped (unpaid for work performed)
adj. 5. *poor:* at the bottom of the barrel, – the end of one's tether, beat, boracic (rhy.sl. boracic lint = skint), bought and sold and done for, broke (to the wide), busted, clean broke, cleaned out, cold in hand (US Black), dished, doesn't have a pot to pee in, done for, – up, down on one's luck, flat as a pancake, – broke, hard-up, heart of oak (rhy.sl. = broke), hung for bread, hurting, in a hole, – a tight corner, nigger-rich, on one's beam ends, – one's uppers, – the Rory (rhy.sl. Rory O'Moore = floor = poor), out (of pocket), poor as a church mouse, – as a

shithouse rat, pushed (for), raggedy-ass, skint, stony (broke), strapped (for cash), touching bottom, up against it, washed up, wiped out; spec. beggar my

neighbour (rhy.sl. visiting the Labour = Unemployment Office)
6. *indebted:* in hock

People

PERSONS: GENERAL

377. People

n. 1. *person:* article, artist, bastard, bim, bimbo, bird, bleeder, blighter, bloke, bozo, cat, civvie, critter, customer, dude, egg, face, fish, fuck (as in 'dumb fuck', etc.), guy, head, jamoke, Joe Blow, joker, Mr Average, momser (Yid.), nosper (backsl.), number, (ordinary) Joe, people, proposition, punter, scout, sort, stiff, ticket, whatshis(her)face, whatshis(her)name; spec. breeders (gay use: non-homosexuals); textiles (nudist use: non-nudists)
2. *self:* yours truly
3. *suffix:* -nik

378. Group; Crowd

n. 1. crew, idrin (WI: brethren), mob, outfit, pack, posse, push (Aus.), team; spec. slag (unpleasant people)
2. *everyone:* all and then some, all hands, – the world and his wife, – the world and his brother, every mother's son, every man Jack, every Tom Dick and Harry, whole kit and caboodle, – shbang, – shooting match, – works
3. *cults, clubs, etc.:* bodgies (Aus.), bopping club, – gang, Brussel sprouts (rhy.sl. = Boy Scouts), greasers, mods, rockers, punks, sharpies (Aus.), skinheads, Sloanes, Valley Girls, widgies (Aus.)

379. Men

n. 1. bloke, bozo, bugger, chap(pie), cock, cove, cuss, customer, dude, geezer, hombre, ice cream freezer (rhy.sl. = geezer), John, joker, meat, moosh, nam (backsl.), old bean, – boy, – chap, – cock, – horse, – top, omee, regular Joe, sport, wallah

380. Women

n. 1. apron, babe, band (US Black), biddy, bim, bimbo, bird, bit of fluff, bitch, booty (US Black), broad, butter (US Black), chick, cock, cono (Sp.), cookie, coot, crack, crotch, cuddle and kiss (rhy.sl. = miss), cunt, dame, dish, doll, dolly (bird), filly, fish, fluff, fox, frail, gash, hairy, haybag, hen, jane, judy, kitty-cat, minge bag, moll, moo, mustang, mystery, nammo (backsl.), nemmo (backsl.), one good woman, oyster, piece, piece of ass, – of tail, polone, potato (Aus. rhy.sl. = potato peeler = sheila), pussy, quail, rag baby (US Black), real woman (US Black), sheila (Aus.), sister, skirt, slit, snatch, sort, squirrel, tart, totty, trout, tuna, twist, womon, wool; spec. -widow (a woman whose husband is occupied elsewhere)

PERSONS: BY AGE

381. Young Persons

n. 1. spec. youthquake
2. *baby:* ankle-biter, chickabiddy, crumb-crusher, – -snatcher, diddums, lambkin, little man, rug rat
3. *child:* dustbin lid (rhy.sl. = kid), gawdelpus, God forbids (rhy.sl. = kids), goober, kiddiwink, kiddo, nipper, pogue, shaver, short, sprog, sprout, snotnose; spec. moppet (young girl);

bub (young boy); drop (US Black: orphan)

4. *young man:* bimbo, geepie, pup(py); spec. queerbait (pretty young man); toy-boy (young boy pursued by older women)

5. *young woman:* bimbo, bint, bobby-soxer, bopper, bubble-gummer, bud, schoolie, teenybopper, yummy; spec. gaolbait, San Quentin quail (sexy underage girl); schlubette (stupid girl); little madam (self-opinionated)

6. *immature youngster:* candy-butt, cootie, poopbutt (US Black), puppy dog, rootiepoot (US Black), young blood

7. *virgin:* cherry, puppy, raw sole (US Black)

382. Old Persons
n. 1. antique, buster, crumbly, dusty, fossil, geri, grunters, oldie, old coot, – timer, wrinkly

2. *old man:* buffer, codger, deelo nam (backsl.), gramps, joskin, mossyback, old buzzard, – cocker, – geezer, – sweat, pop(s), pot and pan (rhy.sl.); spec. DOM (dirty old man), sugar-daddy (provider for a younger girl), (see also Men: 379)

3. *old woman:* battleaxe, boiler, bunty, delonammon (backsl.), drago, leather, old bag, – biddy, – boiler; (see also Women: 380)

PERSONS: INHABITANTS

383. Nationality
n. 1. *American:* septic (rhy.sl. = septic tank = yank), uncle, Uncle Sam, yank, yankee-doodle; spec. WASP (white anglo-saxon protestant)

2. *Australian:* Aussie, digger; spec. Alf, Fred, ocker (unsophisticated Australian); roy (sophisticated Australian)

3. *Canadian:* Canuck

4. *Chinese:* chink, chinky, tiddley-wink (rhy.sl.)

5. *Dutchman:* butterbox

6. *Englishman:* John Bull, jumble, kipper (Aus.), limey, pom(my) (Aus.), pongo

(NZ); spec. expat (expatriate English)

7. *Frenchman:* frog

8. *German:* boche, Fritz, Heinie, hun, jerry, kraut, Otto, squarehead

9. *Greek:* bubble (rhy.sl. = bubble and squeak)

10. *Hawaiian:* kanaka

11. *Indian (US):* spec. breed (half-breed)

12. *Irish:* bogtrotter, green nigger, harp, Mick, narrowback, Paddy, Patsy, tad; spec. lace-curtain Irish (genteel Irish)

13. *Italian:* dago, eyetie, ghinny, ginney, ginzo, guinea, guinzo, mountain wop, spag, spaghetti bender, wop; spec. moustache Pete (early Italian immigrants to US); paisan (fellow-Italian)

14. *Japanese:* nip

15. *Mexican:* bato, beaner, bean eater, chico, cholo, chuc, dago, greaseball, greaser, pachuco, spic(k), taco bender, – head; spec. wetback (illegal immigrant to US)

16. *New Zealander:* Kiwi

17. *Pakistani:* Paki, Pakki

18. *Philippino:* flip

19. *Russian:* Ivan, Russki; spec. commie, commo (Aus.), pinko, red

20. *Scot:* Jock

21. *South African:* rock spider (Afrikaaner)

22. *Welshman:* Taffy

23. *West Indian:* Bimi

24. *Yugoslav:* Yug

25. *foreigners:* ding (Aus.), reffo (Aus.), snow (Aus. Latins)

26. spec. PIGS (Poles, Italians, Greeks, Slavs: US 'ethnics')

384. Race and Religion
n. 1. *blacks (by whites):* boog, boogie, chocolate, chungo bunny, coon, dark meat, darkie, dinge, egg and spoon (rhy.sl. = coon), eightball, groid, harvest moon (rhy.sl.), jig, jigaboo, Jim Crow, jungle bunny, Lucozade (rhy.sl. = spade), nigger, nignog, oogie, Rastus, razo (rhy.sl. = razor blade = spade), sambo, schvug (Yid.), schwartze (Yid.), shadow, shine, silvery spoon (rhy.sl.), smoke, smut-butt, soap dodger, spade, spearchucker, spook, stove lid, swartzer

(Yid.), wog, zigaboo; spec. touch of the tar brush (black ancestry); pickaninny (black child); Afs, munt (S.Afr. use); boong (Aus. aborigine)

2. *blacks (by blacks):* all-originals, black 360°, bleed, blood, boot, brothers, homeboy, homegirl, member, original, skillet, speck, suede; spec. butterhead (US Black: embarrassing person); bungo (WI: fool); royal (WI: non-West Indian black)

3. *spec. dark complexioned black (by blacks):* black bird, – dust, inky-dinky, midnight, smokestack, zombie

4. *spec. light complexioned black (by blacks):* bright, buckwheat, casper, grey, lemon, pinkie; spec. high yaller, – yellow, yellow ass, – girl (mulatto)

5. *spec. rebellious black (by blacks):* bad boy, – nigger, bad-ass nigger, cut-throat, field nigger, hardhead; spec. John Henry (tough, hard worker despite odds); firsts (blacks who are first to invade white purlieus)

6. *spec. subservient or bourgeois black (by blacks):* Aunt Jemima, – Jane, Dr (Mr) Thomas, fade, faded boogie, handkerchief head, house nigger, HN (house nigger), oreo, seddity, shuffle, (Uncle) Tom, yard negro

7. *gypsy:* diddicoi, gyppo

8. *Jews (derog.):* abe, Abie Kabibble, abie, bagel bender, eskimo, fast-talking Charlie (US Black), five-to-two (rhy.sl.), four by two (rhy.sl.), front-wheel skid (rhy.sl. = yid), Goldberg (US Black), goose, half-past two (rhy.sl.), hebe, hooknose, ikey mo, kangaroo (rhy.sl.), kike, lox jock, moch, mockie, quarter-to-two (rhy.sl.), Red Sea pedestrian (Aus.), saucepan lid (rhy.sl. = yid), sheeny, shonk, shonnicker, slick-'em-plenty (US Black), three balls (US Black), Yid, yiddle; spec. JAP (Jewish-American princess)

9. *spec.* Litvak, Polack (immigrant Jews from Lithuania, Poland)

10. *spec. non-Jews (by Jews):* goy, goyim, yoks; flour mixer (rhy.sl. = shikse), shikse (gentile girl)

11. *orientals (derog.):* chopstick, dink, gook, little people, ricer, slant, slit, slope, yellow peril

12. *whites (by blacks):* beast, blanco, chalk, Charlie, devil, fay, fey, gray, hay eater, honk(ie), hunkie, kelt, lily, man with fuzzy balls, Mr Charlie, – Cracker, – Peanut, ofay, paleface, peck, peckerwood, pink, rabbit, whitey, yacoo; spec. gringo (Mexican use); gub, Mr Gub (aborigine use); roundeye (oriental use); pepper and salt (US Black: a mix of blacks and whites); superhonkie (ultra-authoritarian, possibly racist white)

13. *white females (by blacks):* bale of straw, Lady Snow, Little Eva, Miss Amy, – Ann, – Lillian, pinktoes, silk, snow, white meat; spec. gringa (Mexican use)

14. *subservient US Indians (by Indians):* apple (red on the outside, white inside), Uncle Tomahawk

385. Inhabitants

n. 1. spec. banana bender (Aus: Queenslander), brummy (inhabitant of Birmingham, UK), crow eaters (Aus: South Australians); cornpone, cracker (US: poor Southern white), ethno (Aus: any immigrant, usually Italian, Greek, Yugoslav), fly-over people (US: 'middle America'), raddie (UK: Italian living in London), scouse (Liverpudlian), Wooloomooloo yank (Aus. one who attempts to ape US style); yellow-belly (inhabitant of Lincolnshire)

386. Townspeople

n. 1. slicker, townee; spec. town (student use; local residents, rather than 'gown' – students)

2. *neighbour:* Texan rude nam (backsl. = next door man)

3. *resident:* old identity (Aus.)

4. spec. blockbuster (first white or black family to live on a black or white block)

PERSONS: TYPES

387. Person of Importance

n. 1. big cheese, – chief, – deal, – enchilada, – fish, – gun, – noise, – pot, – stuff, – wheel, – wig, biggie, BMOC (big man on campus), Boss Charlie (US

Black), celeb, gaffer, guvnor, hammer
man (US Black), head cook and bottle
washer, headliner, heavyweight, (high)
mucky-muck, high-up, high
monkey-monk, his nibs, honcho, hook,
hot-shot, kingfish, main man, men in
suits, mensch (Yid.), Mr Big, pitch and
toss (rhy.sl. = the boss), pooh-bah,
sachem, shtarka (Yid.), shtarker, the
cheese, – gorilla, – man, top cat, – dog,
wheel; spec. higher-higher (US milit.
use: high command); blue-eyed boy,
fair-haired boy, white-haired boy
(favourite)
2. *conceited person:* doll

388. Insignificant or Petty Person
n. 1. bebopper (US Black), bit of fluff,
crumb, dud, feeb, frip, half-pint,
jobsworth, lightweight, Melvin, no big
deal, – great shakes, nobody to write
home over, one-eyed scribe (US Black),
pint-size, pipsqueak, piss-ant, slob, small
change, stooge, tick, tinhorn, twerp,
zero; spec. grunt (USMC use); shower
(group of insignificant people)

389. Polished and Sophisticated Person
n. 1. cool cat, hipster, jumping cat (US
Black), Mr Cool, smart guy, smoothie

390. Unsophisticated Person
n. 1. booboisie, Great Unwashed,
Johnny-come-lately, square, working
stiff; spec. squaredom (world of
'squares')
2. *peasant:* apple-knocker, boonie, carrot
cruncher, clod, farmer, hayseed, hick,
honyok, hoosier, neck, red, redneck,
rube, shitkicker, swede, woollyback
3. *lout:* ape, baboon, bohunk, boob,
clunk, dumbo, dummy, geek, goop,
honky, hunk(y), jibone, lob, lug, lump,
lunkhead, ox, palooka, plug, swab,
yahoo
4. *socially inept:* diddy-bop (US Black),
ditty-bop, flamer

391. Gullible Person; Dupe
n. 1. boob, chump, fall guy, gobshite,
lollipop, loogan, mark, meal ticket, mug,
pigeon, puppethead, pushover, sap,

soft-cop, soft touch, square, steamer
(rhy.sl. = steam tug = mug), sucker,
Trick Willy (US Black), turkey on a
string (US Black)
phr. 2. there's one born every minute

392. Ill-bred Person
n. 1. grunge, lowlife, sleaze, sleazo,
yob(bo)
2. *snobbish abbrevs.:* NB (no
background), NQOCD (not quite our
class dear), SQPQ (suspiciously quiet,
probably queer)

393. Awkward, Careless Person
n. 1. baggage smasher, butterfingers,
mollydooker (Aus.), shithook, spas(tic),
stumblebum
2. *uncoordinated:* non (US Black)

394. Superior, Admirable Person
n. 1. *admirable:* bottler (Aus.), brick,
cool head, curly wolf, good news, killout
(US Black), natural (born) man/woman
(US Black), notch (WI), regular guy,
straight shooter, through and through
(US Black); spec. soul child (US Black:
high in black consciousness)
2. *superior:* big shot, high mucky-muck,
Mr Big, toff; spec. OMCD (gay use: out
of my class darling)

395. General Terms of Abuse
n. 1. animal, ape, arsehole, asswipe,
ate-your-bun, bag o'wank, ball-buster,
baluba (Irish), basket, beige, big stiff,
big stuff, bliksem! (S.Afr.), blikskottel
(S.Afr.), bliksom! (S.Afr.), bludger
(Aus.), bluxom! (S.Afr.), bog person
(Irish), bogman (Irish), bollockbrain,
bowsie, bowsy, butterhead (US Black),
cack, cheesy-feet, chicken-plucker,
chippy-chaser, clotty (Irish), clown,
cockface, cockhead, cockmunch,
cocksuck, cocksucker, crapbrain, crud,
crud-sucker, cunt, cunt-lapper,
cunt-licker, cuntock, deadpicker,
dickhead, dipwad, dirt bird, dirtbag,
dog, dork, dos a reno (backsl. = sod),
douchebag, dratsab (backsl. = bastard),
drol (S.Afr.), dub, duchill (Ulster),
ducle (Ulster), dum-dum, dumb cluck,
dumb-dumb, dumb fuck, f.b.i.! (fucking

bloody idiot!), faggot, feather-plucker, four-letter man, fuckdust, fucker, fuckwit, gluggar (Irish), gobeen (Irish), gobshite, goorie (NZ), goory (NZ), granny-jazzer, grunge, guban (Irish), hang-out, honkoe (Aus.), hoofler (Irish), hootenanny, horse's arse, horse's ass, horse's neck, horse's patoot, horse's patootie, houtkop (S.Afr.), J. Arthur (rhy.sl. = wanker), jerk, jobbie, jobby, joe (NZ), jughead, kiss of death, knob, knob-shiner, knucklehead, lobster, long thin streak of piss, lug, lummocks, lump of shit, maggot, malco, mammy-jammer, – -rammer, – -hugger, – -tapper, meatbeater, meathead, merchant banker (rhy.sl. = wanker), m.f., milk bar cowboy, mollyfock, momma-hopper, momser (Yid.), mong, mongrel (Aus./NZ), monkey spank, mooch, mook, mother, mother-fouler, – -flunker, – -raper, – -fucker, – -grabber, – -hugger, – -jiver, – -jumper, mug, naus, nellie, nerd, nobscratch, north end of a southbound horse, north end of a southbound mule, oil tanker (rhy.sl. = wanker), out-and-out (US Black), peasant, peck, pencil dick, pheasant plucker, piece of crap, pilcher, pillock, piss artist, piss-cutter, plonker, pluke (Scots), poephol (S.Afr.), poes (S.Afr.), poppa-lopper, ponce, poopbutt (US Black), pootbutt (US Black), possum-guts, prick, pug(gy), putz (Yid.), rat arse, – bastard, – muncher, – prick, – shagger, rat-ass, ratbag, ratter (Aus./NZ), sad bastard, sad cunt, sad fucker, sap, scadger, scheisspot, schlep, schmo (Yid.), scoot, scrote, scud (Ulster), scumbag, scumbo, scumhead, scumsucker, seek-sorrow, shit, shit on a stick (US Black), shitbird, shitbum, shiter, shit-for-brains, slag, sleeping Jesus, smartiepants, smeerlap (S.Afr.), smeghead, so-and-so, SOB, sod, sonofabitch, sonofagun, spaka (i.e. 'spastic'), spackahead, spacker, spankhead, spud, spunk-gullet, spunk-head, stinker, stinkpot, sub, sucka, sucker, sumbitch, tarleather, ticket-of-leaver, titwank, tossprick, trake, triple clutcher, turd in the punchbowl, turkey, twat, twat-scourer, twot, upjump

(Aus.), vark (S.Afr.), vuilgat (S.Afr.), vuilgoed (S.Afr.), wedgeass, whore's melt, wooden ears, wowser (Aus./NZ), yak (US); spec. REMF (US milit.: rear-echelon mother-fuckers), SOHF (UK 'society': sense of humour failure); (see also: Insignificant Person: 388, Ill-bred Person: 392, Contemptible Person: 396, Annoying Person: 397, Selfish Person: 399, Weakling: 403, Homosexuals: 404, etc.)

2. *thug:* ass-kicker, goombah, goon, jibone

396. Contemptible Person

n. 1. bad egg, – hat, – lot, – penny, bastard, beat off, Berkeley Hunt (rhy.sl. = cunt), bitch, bitch's bastard, blood claat (WI), bugger, bum, cocksucker, creep, cunt, dipstick, dipshit, droob (Aus.), fart, flake, fuck, fucker, jel, lower than the spots on a snake's ass, – than whale-shit, merchant banker (rhy.sl. = wanker), Mr Do-You-Wrong, motherfucker, mucker, pain in the arse, piece of crap, – of shit, poison, prick, rat, shithead, shitheel, skull-and-crossbones (US Black), so low he can look up a snake's asshole and think it's the North Star, sod, tick, TL (Yid: tochus-lekker = arse-licker), toe-rag, turd, wanker (see also Insignificant Person: 388, Ill-bred Person: 392, General Terms of Abuse: 395, Annoying Person: 397, Selfish Person: 399, Weakling: 403, etc.)

397. Annoying Person

n. 1. blister, crasher, gangster, gawdelpus, god-help-us, pain in the arse, – in the neck, PITA, pill, poison; spec. mudcrusher (US Black: bully); jobsworth (petty official)

398. Meddler or Inquisitive Person

n. 1. back-seat driver, buttinski, finick, fleabag (US Black), kibitzer, stickybeak (Aus.), stirrer (see also Talker: 420)

2. *obsessive:* neatnik

399. Selfish or Greedy Person

n. 1. *mean:* cheap Charlie, cheapie, cheapskate, clam, crawfish, doggy (US

Black), Jew (derog.) meanie, meany, penny-pincher, piker, skinflint, Scotchman (derog.), tick, tight as Kelsey's nuts, – as O'Reilly's balls, tightwad

2. *egocentric:* jackanape (US Black), jake flake (US Black)

3. *Breedy:* gannet, glut (glutton), gross-out artist, guts, hog, pig; spec. foodie (gourmet)

4. *obstinate:* cuss, donkey, hardhead, hard nut to crack, mule, 'ornery cuss, pighead, tough customer, – proposition

400. Unselfish, Helpful Person

n. 1. good thing, pussycat, softie, soft touch, stand-up guy

2. *helper:* helping hand, meal ticket, rooter; spec. angel (theatrical backer)

3. *representative:* dep, double, stand-in, sub

4. *go-between:* fixer, front

5. *advisor:* back-seat driver, kibitzer, tipster, woppitzer

401. Vain Person

n. 1. *braggart:* all wind and piss, – mouth and trousers, bigmouth, big note artist (Aus.), bilge artist, blatherskite, blowhard, bullshit artist, ear-basher, fatmouth, man with a paper ass (US Black), smart arse, – guy, swellhead, windbag, wise arse, – guy, wisenheimer (see also Talker: 420)

2. *show-off:* bit of a lad, diddy-bop (US Black), hot-dogger, Jack the lad, lair (Aus.), teddy bear (Aus. rhy.sl. = lair)

3. *self-opinionated:* acts like shit would melt in his/her mouth, hard-on (derog.), thinks his/her ass is icecream and everyone wants a bite, thinks he/she shits lollipops, – he/she is so nice his/her shit don't stink

4. *snob:* Lady Muck, Lord Muck, sadit (US Black), stuffed shirt, upways (US Black)

5. *flashily dressed:* butterfly (US Black)

402. Brave and Reckless Persons

n. 1. chancer, fire-eater, redhot, shtarka (Yid.)

2. *street fighter:* diddley-bop

403. Weakling; Coward

n. 1. baa-lamb, bottler, candy-ass, Caspar Milquetoast, chicken, chickenshit, copout, creampuff, creeping Jesus, CS, div, drip, 4-F, fraidy-cat, funk, funker, girl's blouse, jellyfish, lightweight, limp-dick, Mary Ann, microbe, milksop, milquetoast, mollycoddle, mother's boy, namby-pamby, panty-waist, puss gentleman (US Black), pussy, rabbit, scaredy-cat, sheep, snow (Aus.), softy, sook (Aus.), sop, tired people (US Black), wanker, waterboy, weak sister, wimp, wimp-guts, yellowbelly

2. *whining person:* creeping Jesus

404. Homosexuals

n. 1. *male homosexuals (derog.):* arse bandit, arse pirate, ass boy, back-door commando, back-door kicker, badger, balloon-knot bandit, bananas, banjy boy, battyman (WI), beachcomber, bent, birdie, bitch, bone smuggler, bone-stroker, booty buffer, boy-ass, brown artist, – dirt cowboy, – family, – hatter, – pipe engineer, Browning family, – sisters, bruce, bufu (i.e. *butt-fucker*), bugger, buller, bum-boy, bum chum, bum plumber, bunker, burglar, butch, buttercup, buttfucker, cackpipe cosmonaut, Cadbury's canal boat cruiser, Cadbury's canal engineer, cadger, chacha queen, chocky jockey, chocolate runway pilot, chocolate speedway rider, chuff chum, chutney farmer, – ferret, cocksucker, cocoa-shunter, colon choker, colon commando, dead-eye dick, dicky-licker, dinner masher, dirt tamper, donut-puncher, Dorothy's friends, dung-puncher, eye doctor, fag, faggot, fagola, fairy, fancy-pants, fembo, femme, flip, flit, fooper, four-letter man, freak, fruit, fruit loop, fudge-nudger, funny man (US Black), gay, gayola, gender-bender, ginger (rhy.sl. = ginger-beer = queer), grand duchess, haemorrhoid hitman, haricot (Aus. rhy.sl. = haricot bean = queen), he-she, hole-filler, homo, hoop stretcher, hula raider, iron (rhy.sl. = iron hoof = poof), jam duff, jobby jouster, jocker, ki-ki, lavender cowboy, lily, log-cabin raider, log-pusher, manhole inspector, Marmite driller, Marmite miner, mouser, muzzler, nance, nancy-boy, navigator of the windward passage, nellie, nelly, nola, nudger, off-colour, omee-polone, one of those, pansy, peanut buffer, pickle kisser, pillow biter, pilot of the chocolate runway, pipe smoker, pixie, poo percolator, – pusher, – packer, – stabber, poof, poofta, poofter, poove, (powder) puff, putty pusher, quack (US Black), queen, queer, rear seat gunner, rectal ranger, rectum ranger, ring master, – raider, ripe fruit, sausage jockey, – smuggler, scatman, shandy (rhy.sl. = chandelier = queer), she-man, shirt-lifter (Aus.), shunter, sissy, skid-pipe plumber, skippy (US Black), so, soft boy, sperm burper, sweet (US Black), sweetcorn shiner, swish, tailgunner, tan tracker, that way, three-letter man, tonk, tooti-frooti (US Black), turd-burglar, – packer, Turk, uphill gardener, visitor to Vegemite valley (Aus.), waffle, white liver, wind jammer, wolf, woofter, woolly woofter, yoo-hoo boy; spec. fats and fems (overweight or effeminate gays, barred from many clubs)

2. *female homosexuals (derog.):*
Amy-John, charlie, dike, dyke, finger artist (UK Black), jasper (US Black), lady lover, les, lesbo, leso (Aus.), lezzie, lezzo, malflor (Sp.), nelly, pinky, Sappho, thespian; spec. bluff (bisexual lesbian); spec. beard (a man acting, for appearances, as a lesbian's husband)

3. *'masculine' lesbian:* bull, bull dagger, bull-dyke, bumper, collar and tie, daddy, dagger, diesel, diesel-dyke, drag-dyke horsewoman, jockey, mantee, pap, top sergeant, truck driver

4. *'feminine' lesbian:* fem, femme, fluff, mama, pinky, puss, ruffle, twist; spec. sil (silly about = a partner in a love affair)

5. *male homosexual types:* auntie, chicken hawk, – queen, dirty dowager, dowager, grand duchess, john, mother, mother ga-ga, Mother Superior, your mother (older men); belle, bronco, butterbox, chicken, cornflakes, daughter, debutante, ga-ga, lamb, pogue, poggler, tender box, tail, twinkie (novice or youngster); husband, pitcher ('masculine' homosexual); bitch, wife ('feminine' homosexual); peek freak, peer queer, watch queen (voyeur); church mouse (one who solicits in churches); angel, cousin, gazooney, gonsil, possesh (older man's young lover); show stopper (particularly attractive boy); body lover (homosexual frotteur); rim queen (one who practises anilingus); top man, bottom man (dominant and passive partners in a sado-masochistic couple); privy queen, tearoom queen (one who solicits in lavatories); body queen (one who prefers body-builders); ill piece (unattractive man); brilliant (ostentatious queen); drag-queen (one who dresses as a woman); kiki (an active or passive homosexual); oncer (promiscuous male, never repeating a partner); uniforms (members of the armed or uniformed services); sea food (sailors); rough trade (genuine or fantasising 'proletarian' sexual partners); size queen (one who prefers large penises); golden shower queen (one who enjoys urolagnia); toe queen (foot fetishist); felch queen (scopophiliac); angel with a dirty face, closet case, – queen (one who dare not reveal his homosexuality); breeders (married homosexuals who father children); kid simple, pee-pee lover (one who prefers very young boys); jam fag (one who is devoted only to sex); sister-act (homosexual couple, or a homosexual man copulating with a heterosexual woman); RFD (Rural Free Delivery) queen (homosexual living in the country); payoff queen (one who prefers to pay for sex); jam, straight (a non-homosexual male); pretender to the throne (one who poses as homosexual for his own purposes)

405. Gloomy or Irritable Persons

n. 1. *gloomy:* crab, crag, fuddy-duddy, gloom, meanie, misery, misery-guts, party pooper, sad sack, sourpuss, wet blanket

2. *irritable:* carpet-biter, grassfighter (Aus.), grouch, hothead, sorehead

406. Humorist; Amusing Person
n. 1. bundle of laughs, card, caution, cutup, kidder, laugh riot, Mr Laffs, stitch; spec. Carl Comedian (one whose jokes are not appreciated)

407. Stable, Conservative Person
n. 1. dodo, do-right man, eightball, grey, Mom-Dad-Buddy-and-Sis, mossyback, shell-back, square, square John, stick-in-the mud, straight; spec. heterosexual (gay use); spec. dusty bread (US Black: conventional girl)
2. *unemotional:* iceberg

408. Unstable, Irresolute Person
n. 1. bug, jellyfish, man-a-hanging (US Black), pussyfooter, shilly-shallyier, yoyo

409. Eccentric, Unconventional Person
n. 1. bat, card, cough-drop, crazo, dag (Aus.), dorf, flip-out, fruitcake, galoot, GB, geek, goof, goofball, half-saved, headcase, honker, nut, nutcase, odd stick, oddball, outfit, psycho, rum 'un, – customer, rummy, squirrel, wacko, weirdo, zod
2. spec. hippie, hipidity, mind-tripper
3. spec. little green man (extraterrestrial)

410. Enterprising, Energetic Person
n. 1. ball of fire, comer, eager beaver, fool (for), go-getter, heller, hotshot, Johnny at the rathole, Johnny on the spot, live one, – wire, mover, pisser, player, wheeler-dealer, zip; spec. -oholic (general suffix); buck private (US milit. use: a private who is 'bucking' for promotion)
2. *older:* battleaxe, warhorse
3. *hard worker:* grind, stayer, sticker

411. Lively or Passionate Young Woman
n. 1. goer, hot dish, – honey, – number, – one, – stuff, hotsy, piece, – of fluff, pushover, sassy box (US Black)

412. Lazy or Unenterprising Person
n. 1 corner cowboy, dag (Aus.), deadbeat, dead duck, – 'un, drag-ass, feather-merchant, fuck-off, goldbrick, jerk-off, lard-ass, layabout, lazybones, passenger, piker, poopbutt (US Black), skiver, sleeper, slowcoach, sooner (Aus.), weary Willie
2. *dreamer:* wanna be (US Black)

413. Successful Person
n. 1. big-timer, comer, hitter, hot-dog(ger), hotshot, it, jumping cat (US Black), knockout, Mr Shit, natural, top dog; spec. butter-and-egg man (small-town success)

414. Failure
n. 1. also-ran, back number, blind Freddy (Aus.), bum, deadbeat, dero (Aus.), dud, dudley, duffer, flake, fuck-up, gimp, goner, jerk, nebbish (Yid.), no-hoper, pooch, ring-ding, schlemiel (Yid.), schlepper (Yid), shmeggegge (Yid.), trash, washout, yesterday's papers, z-bird (see also Genral Terms of Abuse: 395, Contemptible Person: 396, Weakling: 403)

415. Wealthy Person
n. 1. fat cat, green thumb (US Black), lobster (US Black), Mr Big, pound-note geezer, silvertail (Aus.), silk stocking (US Black), tall poppy (Aus.), zillionaire; spec. nouveau, nouvy (newly rich)
2. spec. cock (one on whom one can sponge)

416. Poor Person
n. 1. broker, dosser (see also Parasite, etc.: 417)

417. Parasite; Dependant; Beggar; Borrower
n. 1. *parasite:* bludger (Aus.), crasher, freeloader, friend in need (US Black), goldbrick, leech; spec. doley (Aus. one who draws the dole)
2. *beggar:* dero (Aus.), glimmer, mooch, mook, panhandler, schnorrer (Yid.)
3. *tramp:* bag lady, bindle stiff, bum, dino, dosser, hurricane lamp (rhy.sl.), pikey, scat; spec. street people
4. *lodger:* artful dodger (rhy.sl.)

418. Praiser; Flatterer

n. 1. apple-polisher, ass-kisser, – -licker, bootlicker, brown-noser, bull artist, bum-sucker, mealy-mouth, politician, shmooser (Yid.), suck-up, tom, Uncle Tom (US Black), yes-man; spec. flack (promo man); log-roller (one who praises their friends)

419. Critic; Opposer

n. 1. Dutch uncle, knocker, Monday Morning quarterback, yenta; spec. crix (show business: critics)
2. *reformer:* bluenose, comstock, killjoy, longnose, smuthound, snoop(er), wowser (see also Meddler: 398)
3. *arguer:* rucker
4. *nag:* ball-buster, – -tearer

420. Talker

n. 1. bag of wind, blowhard, gasbag, gasser, loudmouth, spruiker (Aus.), storefront preacher, tub thumper, tummler (Yid.), windbag; spec. barrack-room lawyer (self-taught expert); (see also Vain Person: 401)
2. *gossip:* blabbermouth, gatemouth, mixer, motormouth, sack mouth (US Black), shit-stirrer, tattle-tale, whistle-blower; spec. dish queen (gay use)
3. *user of obscenity:* garbage mouth, sewer mouth
4. *barker, pitchman:* gee man (Aus.), spruiker (Aus.)
5. *teller of tales, exaggerator:* bull artist, bullshit artist, bullshitter, slickster (US Black), smoothie, wind-up merchant
6. *one who reminds:* elbow shaker (US Black)

421. Listener

n. 1. spec. dummy (deaf mute)

422. Observer; Spectator

n. 1. spec. pinktea (gay use)

423. Eater; Drinker

n. 1. barfly, chow-hound, dustbin, guts, gutso, sponge
2. *drunkard:* beerskin, brewhound, grog artist, one-pot screamer (Aus.), waste case, – product

3. *solo drinker:* Jimmy Woodser (Aus.)

424. Traveller

n. 1. *'outlaw' motorcyclists:* biker, easy rider, one percenter, ton-up boy

---

PERSONS: PHYSIQUE

425. Attractive

n. 1. *attractive woman, girl:* angel, babe, banana (US Black), beat, bit of all right, – crackling, – stuff, brickhouse (US Black), butter baby (US Black), candy, charmer, cheesecake, chick, classy chassis, cookie, creamie, crumpet, cupcake, cutes, cutesie-pie, dish, doll, doll city, dollface, dolly, donah, dreamboat, eyeful, fleshpot (US Black), frail, ginch, glamour puss, good-looking, grouse gear (Aus.), hamma, hammer (US Black), honey, hot number, jam, (little) cracker, little pretty, looker, lovely, Mercedes (US Black), mink (US Black), nifty, – piece, page three girl, pancake, patootie, peach, pie, poodle (US Black), Porsche, (US Black), poundcake, real babe, scorcher, sexpot, sleek lady (US Black), stallion (US Black), star, sweet potato pie (US Black), sweetie, talent, ten, thoroughbred black (US Black), tomato, toots, tootsie, – roll (US Black), yummy; spec. Barbie Doll (pretty and ultra-conventional); melted butter (US Black: light-skinned girl); all tits and teeth (blatantly sexual)
2. *attractive male:* beefcake, buf, glamour-puss, hunk, little pretty, sexpot, smoothie

426. Unattractive

n. 1. face like a douchebag, – like a toilet seat, fright, grub, horror, picklepuss, pretty mess, sight, sourpuss
2. *unattractive woman:* BB head (US Black), bad news, bag, bat, bear (US Black), buzzard, chicken (US Black), chromo, cow, crow, cull bird, dog, dogface, doggie, double-bagger, douchebag, drack (Aus.), grubber, hairbag, hedgehog, heifer, hog, mule, nailhead (US Black), pitch, ragmop (US

Black), Ruth Buzzy (US Black), scab, scuzz, skank, sleaze, snot, sweat hog, tackhead (US Black), thunder chicken (US Black), welfare mother (US Black); spec. PTA (US Black: pussy, tits and armpits – all smelly)
3. *unattractive male:* dick

427. According to Size
n. 1. *heavyweight:* bohunk, bozo, bruiser, brute, hunk(o), lug, lump, moose, ox, palooka, wham (US Black)
2. *fat person:* barrel, blimp, chubette, dumpling, fat-arse, fatso, fatty, guts, gutso, hully (US Black), lard-arse, pig, pudge, tick, tub of lard; spec. Miss Piggy (gay use: a fat homosexual)
3. *fat woman:* Bahama mama (US Black), butterball, Judy with the big booty (US Black), pig(ger), pigmouth, shuttlebutt, teddy bear (US Black)
4. *small person:* crumb, feather merchant, half-pint, – portion, microbe, midget, peewee, pint-size, pipsqueak, sawn-off, shrimp, squirt; spec. lofty (as nickname)
5. *tall person:* beanpole, daddylonglegs, high-pockets, lofty; spec. shorty, tiny (as nickname)
6. *thin person:* bag of bones, broomstick, long (thin) streak of piss, string bean
7. spec. gallon head, pumpkin head (person with a large head)

428. According to Hair, Facial Look, etc.
n. 1. *redhead:* bluey, coppernob
2. *bald person:* skinhead, suedehead
3. *bearded person:* beaver, fuzzface, muff
4. *according to eyes:* boss-eye
5. *similar people:* dead fetch, – ringer, – spit, spitting image
6. *left-handed person:* lefty, southpaw
7. spec. Afro (US Black: one wearing such a hairstyle); crinkle-top (US Black: woman with an Afro); duck's butt (US Black: woman with messy hair)
8. spec. long-hair (a hippie)
9. *with glasses:* four-eyes

429. Sick and Injured Persons
n. 1. *exhausted person:* burn-out, crasher, crispy

2. *cripple:* basket case, gimp, raspberry (rhy.sl. = raspberry ripple)
3. *invalid:* cot-case (Aus.), gomer, gork, vegetable
4. *alcoholics:* alky, dipso, wino
5. *corpse:* goner, stiff

PERSONS: MENTAL STATE

430. Intelligent; Experienced
n. 1. bear-leader, brain, egghead, gallon head (US Black), high-brow, know-it-all, longhair, marv, maven (Yid.), pointy-head, razor, smart cookie, smartypants, wise guy, wisenheimer; spec. old dog (US Black: expert in a given field); culture-vulture, pseud (fake intellectual)
2. *able person:* ace, clever dog, crack hand, dab, good head, hot stuff, natural, nobody's fool, no slouch, (boss) player (US Black), sensation, the cheese, the tops, up-and-comer, whiz; wizard
3. *experienced person:* old hand, old timer, vet
4 *predictor:* crystal-gazer, dopester, doper, steerer, tipster
5. *scholar:* spec. sponge (one who learns easily)

431. Stupid Person
n. 1. addlepate, airball, airhead, ass, asshole, BF (bloody fool), baarie (S.Afr.), ball, beau, berk, Berkeley hunt, Berkshire hunt, birdbrain, blockhead, bonehead, boob, boofa, boofhead, bozo, brenda, bubblehead, bugs, burg (S.Afr.), busher, butt, buttplug, butthead, buttlick, cement-head, cheese, cheese dong, chief, choad, chode, chowder-head, chucklehead, clod, clodpoll, clown, cluck, clunk, coot, crackpot, crapbrain, crudhead, deadhead, dick, dickhead, dick spanner, dicklick, dickwad, dickweed, dildo, dill (Aus.), dingaling, dingbat, diphead, dipshit, dode, dodo, donkey dick, doobie, doorknob, dope, dork, dorkbrain, dorkoff, dorkmunder, dorkus, dorkus pretentious, drongo (Aus.), Dublin University graduate, dum-dum, dumb-ass, dumb-bell,

dumbellina, dumb fuck, dumbhead, dumbo, dumbsquat, dummy, dumbski, dweeb, egg-for-fuck, eggo, fathead, flipwreck (Aus.), FNG (fucking new guy), four-oh-four, 404 (computer use; Internet error 404: 'file not found'), Fred (i.e. the cartoon figure Fred Flintstone), fruitcake, fruitloop, fuckchop, fucknob, fuckhead, fuckwit, galah (Aus.), geek, gellyhead, gerbil, get, gig (Aus.), gimp, gink, git, gob-lock, Gomer Pyle, gonus, goob, goober, goof, gook, goombah, goonhead, goop, greener, greenhorn, gumbah, guy (Aus.), hammerhead (US Black), hamshanker (rhy.sl. = wanker), head-banger, head-the-ball (Irish), herbert, hodad, ho-daddy, hodag, honch-head, horse's arse, – hangdown, – patootie, hosehead, hoser (Can.), ig man (US Black), ignant (US Black), imby (i.e. *imbe*cile), Irving, jellyhead, jerkhead, jerkweed, jock, joey, jooks (UK Black), klutz, knobber, knocka, knocker, kook, lame, lamebrain, lardhead, lift doesn't reach the top floor, log, loogan, loon(y), lug, lunchbox, lunchmeat, lunk, lunkhead, McFly (US; hero of *Back to the Future* movies), meatbrain, meathead, mental giant, – job, mo-mo, momo, mopstick, mouth-breather, muffin, mug, mummyhead, mule, musclehead, mutt, nana, nazz, nimwad, ning-nong (Aus.), nit, nitwit, nong (Aus.), no-no, noodle, nugget, numbnuts, numbskull, nutcake, nutter, one-eyed Yankee, panhandle, pinhead, poon (Aus.), poop, poophead, prat, prawnhead (Aus.), propellerhead, pud, puddinghead, pum-pum-pum (WI), quashie (WI), remo (i.e. *rem*edial), ring-ding, rookie, room to rent, rube, schlemiel (Yid.), schlub (Yid.), schmeggege (Yid.), schmuck (Yid.), schnook (Yid.), screwball, scrub, section eight, semolia (US Black), shitkicker, shitstain, sickie, silly, silly-billy, simp, slappie, spackahead, spaz, spaz-wit, sped (US; i.e. *sp*ecial *ed*ucation), speng (WI), squarebrain (US Black), squid, stumer, stupe, stupe-head, stupid fuck, sub-human, tateyfarmer, there's a kangaroo loose in the top paddock (Aus.), thickdick,

thickie, thicko, three-dollar bill, tool, toolhead, toy, twit, veg, wack, wad, wassock, wazzock, wet foot, wethead (US Black), whack, whacko, whizpop, wienie, wise, woodhead, zipalid; spec. schoolbook chump (US Black: one who is intellectual but not intelligent); spec. square-eyes (one who watches too much TV)

phr. 2. one who looks like he wouldn't piss if his pants were on fire; (to a dullard) one of these days you'll wake up dead

---

PERSONS: MORAL STATUS

432. Good; Respectable

n. 1. baa-lamb, good time, real McCoy, regular guy, right guy, square John, – shooter, straight arrow, stand-up guy, white man
2. *'good girl'*: quandong (Aus.)

433. Disreputable

n. 1 alley cat, – rat, bad egg, – hat, – penny, baddie, bar steward, bugger, cloth-ears, face-ache, freak, fucker, hard, – case, heel, hood, lare (Aus.), lowlife, naus, oik, raas, raasclat, shitbird, shithead, shitheel, shit-for-brains, shtarka (Yid.), SOB, son of a bitch, sweep, wedgeass, wrong 'un, yob(bo)
2. *foulmouthed*: salty dog, trashmouth
3. *thug*: bruiser, bucko, goon, gorilla, hard case, hard egg, hatchet man, heavy, hood, husky, lowlife, muscle, plug-ugly, punch-out artist, SAN (stop-at-nothing) man, torpedo, tough guy, – nut, ugly customer; spec. goon squad (group of hired thugs)
4. *bodyguard*: heavy, minder, muscle
5. *rebel*: cowboy (US Black)
6. *fugitive*: lamster, over the hill, runout man, skip(per); spec. draftnik (draft evader)
7. *freak*: geek
8. *assassin*: hitman

434. Dishonest

n. 1. chiseller, cowboy, gyp, hydraulic (Aus.), rip-off artist, rooker, shark, shicer, shyster, spiv, tealeaf (rhy.sl. = thief)

435. Deceitful; Untrustworthy

n. 1. actor, bad actor, Carl Rosa (rhy.sl. = poser), cross man, dreykop (Yid.), false face (US Black), fly-by-night, four-flusher, grifter, high and goodbye (US Black), merry-go-round (US Black), PhD (piles it higher and deeper), real greek, sharpie, sly slick and wicked (US Black), slyboots, snake, Spanish athlete (he 'throws the bull'), Turk McGurk, two-timer, welcher, wide boy, wrong guy, wrong 'un

2. *liar:* holy friar (rhy.sl.), one-eyed scribe (US Black), Tom Pepper

3. *informer:* abaddon, backmark, bag, baskerville (Aus.; play on *Hound of the Baskervilles*), belcher, bigmouth, blab, blabbermouth, boot-snitch, budgie (i.e. he 'sings'), buster, buzzman, cabbage-tree hat (Aus. rhy.sl. = rat), canary, carpark (rhy.sl. = nark), castle hack (Irish), cat, cheese-eater, chocolate frog (Aus. rhy.sl. = dog), conk (play on conk = nose), copper, copper's nark, dead-copper, dedos (US; Sp. *dedos* = fingers), dobber, dobber-in, dog, dog's nose, faded boogie, finger, finger man, fink, fizgig (lit. a gadabout woman), fizz, fizzer, flip, gee, gig, gnarler, gnawler, gonsel, gonsil, gonzel, grass (rhy.sl. grasshopper = shopper), grass in the park, grasser, grasshopper, grote, guinea pig, gunsel, Hyde Park (rhy.sl. = nark), impimpi (S.Afr.), Johnny Walker (rhy.sl. = talker), knark, knocker, lagger, leak, lemon (he can be 'squeezed'), lobby-gow, loose link, Miss Peach, Moreton/Moreton bay (Aus. rhy.sl. Moreton Bay fig = fizgig), mouse, mouthpiece, mule-mouth, narc, nark, narker, nightingale, noah's/Noah's ark (rhy.sl. = nark), nose, noser, peach, pen and inker (rhy.sl. = stinker), phizgig, phizzer, pig, pigeon, pimp, policeman, psalm-singer, pull dude, pussyclot, r.f. (rat fink), rat, rat fink, ratter, rounder, rusty, screamer, setter, sham, shammus, shamos, shamus, shelf (Aus./NZ), shelfer (Aus./NZ), shit-heel, shommus, shopper, singer, snitch, snitching-rascal, snout (play on snout = nose), split, spotter, squawker, squeak, squeaker, squeal, squealer, stag, stool, stooley, stoolie, stool-pigeon, stooly, supergrass, tip-off, tom slick, top-off (Aus./NZ), top-off man (Aus./NZ), – merchant (Aus./NZ), topper, tout, tuckerbox (Aus.), weasel, welcher, welsher, whiddler, whistle-blower, whistler, wrong guy, zuch (see also Crime: 473)

phr. 4. his guts are moving the wrong way, does a lot of shitting but his pants aren't down, doesn't know whether to suck or blow, – to shit or go blind, you need an ear scoop to filter his horseshit; don't pick up soap in his shower, he'd steal a rotten doughnut out of a bucket of snot, he'd fuck a snake if somebody would hold its head; you can't trust him further than you can throw a bull by the prick, – than you can see up an alligator's ass (in a dust-storm) (at midnight)

436. Sexual Choice

n. 1. *fellator:* barbecue (US Black), face-artist, fluter, French active, – passive, Frenchman, icing expert, mouth worker; spec. glutton for punishment (one who continues to fellate after orgasm)

2. *one who performs cunnilingus:* cannibal, cuntlapper, fish queen, gash-eater, high diver, meat-eater, muff diver

3. spec. sandwich man (one male plus two females)

4. spec. butt-plunger (man who enjoys inserting a dildo into his own anus)

5. *child molester:* monster, nonce, perv, secko (Aus.)

6. *exhibitionist:* flasher

7. *trans-sexual, transvestite:* TS, TV

8. *bisexual:* double-life man, switch hitter

9. *masturbator:* jack-off, jerk-off, rod walloper, wanker

10. spec. cradle-snatcher (one who prefers much younger partners)

11. *celibate:* priest

12. *voyeur:* looker, peeper

13. spec. mystery mad (one who prefers stray young girls)

437. Promiscuous

n. 1. swinger

2. *promiscuous male:* alligator (US

Black), cock-hound, cocksman, come-freak, cum-freak, rooster (US Black), saloon-bar cowboy, stud, swordsman

3. *promiscuous female:* baggage, bike, bimbo, broad, bum, carpenter's dream, charity girl, chippie, cooze, dead cert, dirty leg, easy lay, – ride, floosie, floozie, free for all, gash, girl-and-fuck-it, goer, knock, lay, leg, Little Miss Roundheels, lust dog, motorcycle (US Black), mount, nymph(o), paraffin lamp (rhy.sl. = tramp), piece, piece of ass, – tail, pig, punch, pushover, quickie, quiff, right sort, screamer and a creamer, scrubber, shack job, shack-up, shagbag, slag, sleepy-time girl, steamer, stinker, tart, town bicycle, – pump, – punch, tramp, whore; spec. groupie, band rat; snow bunny (girls who specialise in rock groups, skiers); buttered bun (girl having sex with several men in succession); splash (the victim of gang-rape)

4. *promiscuous male homosexual:* fantail, glutton

5. *promiscuous lesbian:* clithopper

phr. 6. no better than he/she should be, one who's had more arse than a toilet seat, – more pricks than a second-hand dart-board

PERSONS: SOCIAL POSITIONS

438. Friends

n. 1. abc, ace, – boom boom, – boon coon, – coon poon, asshole buddy, blood (US Black), bro (US Black), brother, buddy, butty, china (rhy.sl. = china plate = mate), chum(my), cobber (Aus.), cutty, Dutch (rhy.sl. = Dutch plate = mate), family, good ole boy, home squeeze (US Black), homeboy, homegirl (US Black), landsman, main man, mate, mellow (US Black), Mister Ed, mucker, off the block, pal, pard, PLU (people like us), road dog, running partner (US Black), splib, splib-de-wib (US Black), (main) squeeze, oppo, yardie (WI); spec. smiling faces (US Black: false friends); sight for sore eyes (a friend in need)

2. *allies:* spec. cognoscenti, sisters (gay use); friendlies (military); crew (a gang); blue-eyed soul brother, paleface nigger (US Black: white who is accepted by blacks); coon-lover, nigger-lover (derog.: a white who rejects racism)

3. *fan:* rooter

439. Hanger-on

n. 1. ligger

2. *fan:* celebrity fucker, grouper, groupie, star fucker

3. *spec. gay use:* fruit fly, fag hag, half-iron, scag hag

4. *spec. walker* (rich woman's male social companion)

5. *toady:* apple polisher, arse-kisser, – -licker, brown-noser, – -tongue, creep, suck-arse, yes-man

440. Stranger; Enemy

n. 1. *novice:* Johnny-come-lately, new fish, tenderfoot

2. *alien:* beastie, ding (Aus.), Queen's Park Ranger (rhy.sl. = stranger)

441. Lovers

n. 1. crush, dreamboat, flame, heart-throb, honeybunch, pash, sweetie, sweetie-pie

2. *male lover, boyfriend:* daddy one (US Black), Lord Right, Mr Right, old man, sweet daddy

3. *female lover, girlfriend, mistress:* chick, dolly, frail, honey, jam tart (rhy.sl. = sweetheart), Lady Right, Miss Right, main bitch (US Black), mat (US Black), monotony, mum, old lady, ordinary (US Black), Renee, Richard (the Third) (rhy.sl. = bird), steady, sweet patootie, sweetpea, toots, tootsie; spec. Mayfair Merc(enary) (using sex to succeed socially)

4. *adulterous lover:* back-door man, bit on the side, fancy man

5. *couple:* item, shack job

6. *'great lover':* fast worker, heaver (US Black), makeout artist, stallion, stickman, stud, wolf; spec. 4-F club ('find 'em, feel 'em, fuck 'em and forget 'em)

7. *former lover:* ex

8. *new lover:* fresh hide (US Black)

9. *inter-racial lovers:* coal burner,
gin-jockey (Aus.); spec. dinge queen
(gay use); gin shepherd (man who
attempts to keep races apart)
10. *physical preference:* arse man,
chubby-chaser, leg man, tit man
11. *casual partner:* it, one-night stand,
pick-up, trick
12. *flirt, teaser:* cunt-teaser (male),
cock-teaser, prick-teaser (female)

442. Sentimentalist

n. 1. sopcan; spec. moon-ass, puppy
(infatuated person)

443. Flirt; Philanderer

n. 1. *flirtatious woman:* cock-teaser,
dick-teaser, gold-digger, man-eater,
prick-teaser, vamp
2. *male philanderer:* chippy chaser, Jody
(US Black), hard-leg (US Black),
lady-killer, letch, masher, plumber,
sharp-shooter, skirt-chaser, slugger,
sport, steed, swordsman, tomcat, wolf
3. spec. MTF (must touch flesh), NSIT
(not suitable in taxis) (UK 'society' use)

444. Relatives

n. 1. *family:*
Mom-Dad-Buddy-and-Sis
2. *father:* my old guvnor, old boy,
– fellow, – man, pop(s), sorry and sad
(rhy.sl. = dad)
3. *mother:* ma, mam, mum(s), mumsie,
old lady
4. *husband:* hubbie; spec. weekend man
(US Black: one who sees his family only
at weekends)
5. *wife:* ball and chain, better half,
carving knife (rhy.sl.), Dutch, Duchess
of Fife (rhy.sl.), her indoors, old Dutch
(rhy.sl.), – lady, trouble and strife
(rhy.sl.)
6. *sister:* skin and blister (rhy.sl.)
7. *illegitimate child:* bachelor's baby
8. *grandparents:* gramps, nan(a)
9. *widow:* sod widow (as opposed to
'grass widow', whose husband is only
absent)

445. Single Person

n. 1. loner, lone wolf, stag
2. *unattached girl:* bit of spare

3. spec. fishing fleet (girls who look
abroad for husbands)

446. Sociable

n. 1. cookie-pusher, drugstore cowboy,
lounge lizard, raver, stage-door johnny,
wildcat (US Black)
2. *uninvited guest:* crasher

447. Hedonist; Pleasure-seeker

n. 1. cutup, funster, good-time Charlie,
hell-raiser, Mr Laffs; spec. nightstick
(US Black: one who enjoys night-life)
2. *tourist:* boing-boing, rubberneck

448. High Society; Elite

n. 1. blue-blood, carriage trade,
high-hat, nob, swell, toff
2. spec. glitterati (fashionable academe);
preppie (student at a US prep – UK
public – school); Wellies (upperclass
members of Exeter University, UK);
hooray, Hooray Henry (boorish
upperclass UK youth)
phr. 3. *an excess of leaders:* all chiefs and
no indians

449. Masses; Rabble; Proles

n. 1. Joe Public, John Q. Public, the
Great Unwashed

450. Fashionable; Chic

n. 1. clotheshorse, fancy pants, Mr
Firstnighter, shoe, slicker, supersoul
(US Black), swing daddy (US Black);
spec. zubber (one dressed in top hat,
tails, etc.)
2. spec. made (US Black: one who has
their hair straightened)
3. spec. glitterati (fashionable academe),
preppie (member of US prep – UK
public – schools), Sloane Ranger (British
upperclass female), yuppie (young
upwardly mobile professional)

451. Unfashionable

n. 1. boojie, boogie, cull, fish 'n' chip
mob, gape (US Black), geek, goose,
greaser, grockle, ham and egger, jello
squad, MCM (middle class monster),
Nashville (US Black), nerd, nerk, puck,
rag head (US Black), Santa Claus
(US Black), slummy, wally, zonko;

spec. nubian (US campus: black students)

2. *badly dressed:* caution sign (US Black)

452. Unsociable

n. 1. homeboy, homegirl, stay-at-home
2. *social failure:* clunk, creep, drag, drip, dumbell, dumbo, dummy, feeb, iceberg, lemon, pain in the arse, – in the behind, – in the neck, pill, schmo, schnook, stick-in-the-mud, stiff, washout, wet blanket; spec. tired woman (US Black: unsophisticated)

WORKERS

453. Worker

n. 1. jockey, wage-slave, working stiff
2. *assistant:* dogsbody, gofer, gopher, off-sider (Aus.), tickler; spec. candy-striper (US hospitals: voluntary workers); spec. head cook and bottle washer (general factotum)
3. *hard worker (at school, college):* cereb, conch, egg, gome, grub, hack, pencil geek, schoolbook chump (US Black), spider, squid, swot, throat, tool, wonk
4. *hard worker:* eager beaver, grafter, workoholic
5. *strike-breaker:* blackleg, fink, goon, – squad, scab
6. *privileged worker:* IDB (abbrev. in Daddy's business)

454. Unskilled Worker

n. 1. *beginner, novice:* butterboy, greener, greenhorn, new fish, rookie, wet foot; spec. boot, yardbird (US military: recruit); prospect (recruit to an 'outlaw' bike club); fresher (freshman at university, college)
2. spec. pearl diver (washer-up)
3. *labourer:* ape, humper, roughneck, roustabout; spec. shovel stiff (one who digs); McAlpine fusilier (worker for a construction firm); lump (freelance unskilled workers, esp. in construction industry)

455. Domestic; Servant

n. 1. biddy, daily, flunky, keep-up (US Black), shikse (Yid.)

456. Specialist

n. 1. *military:* boonie rat, dogface, doggie, doughboy, eleven-bravo, GI, grunt, swaddy, tommy (soldier); gyrene, leatherneck (US Marine); swab jockey (sailor); point (head of patrol), drag (last man); slackman (2nd man in patrol), Band-aid (corpsman); black gang (naval engine room crew); padre (chaplain); flyboy (pilot); deck ape (deck hand); grape (deck hand on carriers); early out (serviceman due for retirement); gunny (US: gunnery sergeant); bird dog (air spotter); lifer (career soldier); looie (lieutenant)
2. *medical:* croaker, medico, quack (doctor); butcher, sawbones (a poor surgeon), gynae (gynaecologist); headshrinker, looney doctor, nut doctor, shrink, trick cyclist (psycho-analyst); cock doctor (venerealogist)
3. *media:* sob sister, agony aunt (advice columnists); hack, journo, pencil pusher, scribe (writer); stringer (local correspondent); newsie (paper-seller)
4. *law:* ambulance chaser, brief, legal eagle, loudmouth, mouthpiece (lawyer); silk (Queen's Counsel); Barnaby Rudge, smear and smudge (rhy.sl. = judge); garden gate (rhy.sl. = magistrate); dick, gumshoe, shamus (private detective); repo man, skip tracer (debt collector)
5. *entertainment:* bouncer, chucker-out, wollyhumper (steward); hoofer (dancer); red (Butlins redcoat); carney (carnival worker); DJ, jock (disc jockey); muso (musician); combo (group of musicians); roadie (rock music road manager); lenser, megger (film director); gabriel (trumpeter); canary (singer)
6. *bureaucracy:* flak catcher (complaints officer); paper pusher, pencil pusher, red-taper (lowest form of civil servant); spec. sniffer (DHSS investigator)
7. *social:* walker (rich woman's companion)
8. *craftsman:* chippie (carpenter); sparks (electrician); mush faker (umbrella repairer); brickie (bricklayer); retchub (backsl. = butcher)
9. *political:* politico, flesh-presser, palm-presser; spec. lefty, parlour pink, pinko, Trot (left-wingers); lame duck

(US politican who has lost office but still serves out time); libber (feminist activist)

10. *education:* chalkie (Aus.), schoolie (teacher); lollipop man/lady (road safety supervisor)

11. *travel:* hostie, stew (air hostess); clippie (bus conductress)

12. *scientists:* back-room boys, boffins

13. *taxis:* hack(er), hackie, mushie, musher (drivers); brown coat, white coat (inspectors at London Cab Office)

14. *cleaner:* garbo (Aus.), honey-dipper, sanno (Aus.); Mary Ellen (dockyard, boat cleaners)

15. *docker:* wharfie (Aus.), yardbird

16. *business, commerce:* drummer (salesman); uncle (pawnbroker); hired gun (expert); Collins Street farmer, Pitt Street farmer (Aus.: absentee rural landlords)

17. *chemist:* druggie

18. *sportsman:* jock; slugger (boxer), tanker (boxer who deliberately loses); jock (jockey)

19. *petrol station:* pump jockey

20. *farming:* cowpoke (cowboy)

21. *oil rigs:* roughneck, roustabout (labourer)

22. *services:* milko (Aus. = milkman); saw (US Black: rooming house owner)

23. *spy:* spook

24. *general specialist:* artist, merchant, pro

25. *cook:* babbling brook (rhy.sl.)

457. Superintendent; Manager

n. 1. boss, bossman, Edmundo (rhy.sl. = Edmundo Ros = boss), gaffer, guv, guvnor, master-dog (US Black), pitch and toss (rhy.sl. = boss), skip(per), top dog

2. *military:* brass hats, white hats (officers); full bird (full colonel); topkick (first sergeant); Shake and Bake (graduate of US NCO school); mustang (officer promoted from the ranks); first skirt (senior officer in WAC); -pipper (lieutenant)

Specialist Jargons

CRIME: PERSONS

458. Persons

n. 1. *criminal:* babbler (Aus.), babbling brook (rhy.sl. = crook), bandit, body, buck, face, hardhead (Aus.), merchant, perp; spec. good people (former criminals); mooner (US: 'moonstruck' – a pathological lawbreaker); operator, the Man (major criminal); rounder (Can.: sophisticated criminal); Ten (FBI's Ten Most Wanted Criminals list) (see also Persons, Disreputable: 433, Dishonest: 434, Deceitful: 435)

2. *gang:* crew, firm, mob, push (Aus.), team; spec. the Mob, the wise guys (US Mafiosi); made man (US: member of Mafia); coolie (street gang use: an unaffiliated youth); deb (street gang member's girlfriend)

3. *small-time criminal:* cruncher (Aus.), heel, international milk thief, meter thief, parking meter bandit, pie-eater (Aus.), tearaway; spec. soldier, button man (US: lower echelon Mafioso)

4. *young or novice criminal:* JD (juvenile delinquent), schoolboy, virgin; spec. MINS (US jail use: Minors In Need of Supervision); CHINS (Children In Need of Supervision); gunsel, gonsil (criminal's young – poss. homosexual – accomplice)

5. *violent criminal:* dropper, hatchet man, hit man, stick-up artist, trigger man

6. *sex criminal:* spec. player (pimp); junior jumper (US: underage rapist); diddler, monster, short eyes, shut eyes (child molester)

7. *thief:* blagger, jump-up merchant, – man, second-storey man; spec. in-and-out man (spontaneous thief)

8. *swindler, con-man:* alias man (WI), ginnal (WI), illywhacker (Aus.), ringer, samfie (WI); spec. bait (attractive girl used to lure victims); hedge (the crowd that gathers around a street con-man); ringer (one who steals, improves, then sells cars)

9. *arsonist:* firebug; spec. blanket man (arsonist's assistant)

10. *receiver:* buyer, fence; spec. placer (middleman between thief and receiver)

11. *planner:* set-up man

12. *go-between:* bag man, bird dog

13. *look-out:* earwig

14. *pickpocket:* dip, hoister, knockabout man (Aus.), legshake artist (Aus.), whiz, wire

15. *shoplifter:* booster, hoister (US Black), blocker, stickman

16. *gambler:* KG (known gambler); spec. digits dealer (numbers racketeer); operator (controller of gambling game); subway dealer (US: card sharp)

17. spec. seducer (US Black: one who provides means of making illicit cash)

18. *court personnel:* spec. beak (judge, magistrate); interrupter (interpreter); penitentiary agent (inadequate defence lawyer)

19. *legitimate person:* pop corn

adj. 20. spec. -handed (number: three-handed, four-handed, team-handed, etc.)

CRIME: PHYSICAL

459. Health
n. 1. spec. crush-out (the obliteration of a corpse by crushing it in a junkyard metal crusher)
adj. 2. *dead:* DOA (dead on arrival), slabbed and slid, tits up

CRIME: PLACES

460. Locality
n. 1. *police station:* bill shop, cop shop, factory, pig heaven, – sty
2. *police divisions:* ground, manor, patch, toby
3. *storage enclosure:* flop, slaughter; spec. Aladdin's cave (UK: a thief's home or the hideaway for his loot)

461. Establishments; Resorts
n. 1. spec. clip joint, gyp joint (swindling night-clubs)

CRIME: PROPERTY; BOOTY

462. Money
n. 1 (see Commerce: 509); spec. California roll (US), flash (UK) (large roll of low-denomination notes, wrapped in a high-value note to give illusion of wealth
2. spec. case dough (limited funds); drops (money hidden away); earner (high-paying criminal enterprises; bribe); fall money (funds set aside for legal fees); indoor money (daily expenses)
v. 3. *to profit from crimes:* earn, score

463. Valuables
n. 1. red (gold), tom (rhy.sl. = tomfoolery = jewellery); spec. groin, groyne (UK: any ring)
2. *fake jewellery:* fool's gold, patacca; spec. mug's ticker (dud watch)
3. *safe:* can, crib, damper, peter

464. Booty; Illicit Goods
n. 1. goods, good stuff, hot stuff, swag; spec. drop (delivery of booty, money,

etc.); five-finger discount (proceeds of shoplifting); LF gear (UK: proceeds of 'long firm' fraud); overs (booty yet to be disposed of); carve-up, cut, taste (a share)
v. 2. spec. mash it on (one) (US Black: pass on contraband)
3. *to share out:* cut up touches

CRIME: IMPLEMENTS

465. Implements; Devices
n. 1. spec. autograph (blank paper used to obtain victim's signature); billy, Mr Wood, rosewood, shit-stick (billy-club, truncheon); stonicky, swailer (cosh); car key (screwdriver used to break into cars); can opener (safe-breaking tool); combo (combination lock); bracelets, cuffs, darbies (handcuffs); come-along (manacle); flash case (US Black: case holding drugs, contraband); happy bag (case carrying a shotgun); HBI (house-breaking implements); jemmy, jimmy, tool (crowbar); jigglers (skeleton keys); keister, peter (bag of tools); jumper (jump-lead); loid, lloyd (celluloid lock-pick); monkey (padlock)

466. Weapons; Explosives
n. 1. *gun:* equalizer, Roscoe; spec. crowd pleaser (US policeman's weapon); sawed off, sawn-off (sawn-off shotgun); Chicago piano, – typewriter (machine-gun)
2. *knife:* shank; spec. shin (US jail use)
3. *explosives:* dinah (nitroglycerine); jelly (gelignite)
v. 4. *to be armed:* carry, hold
adv. 5. *armed:* CCW (US: carrying a concealed weapon), carrying, holding, rodded
6. *unarmed:* clean

CRIME: FOOD; LIQUOR, ETC.

467. Food
n. 1. spec. CNR strawberries (Canadian prison-issue prunes)

468. Tobacco
n. 1. burn, snout; spec. tailormade (factory-produced cigarette)

CRIME: COMMUNICATION

469. Communication; Correspondence
n. 1. spec. batphone (UK: police radio); dep (UK: deposition); squawk (UK: petition to authorities); stiff (UK: illicit jail communication)

470. Speech
n. 1. spec. toast (US jail: long epic poem)
v. 2. spec. cut up touches (reminisce over crimes, etc.)
adv. 3. *agreed verbally:* on a promise
phr. 4. spec. on the earie! (be quiet! someone is listening); Edna! (UK: rhy.sl. = Edna May = on your way!)

471. Signals; Symbols
n. 1. spec. show out (UK: signal between policeman and an informer who meet in public)

472. Information
n. 1. bubble (rhy.sl. = bubble and squeak = speak), dope, scream, squeal, the score, tickle, tip; spec. hooking (attempting to smear the police through false information); crude (US: informer's rather than public's tip-off)
2. *informer:* backmark (US Black), canary, car park (rhy.sl. = nark), cheese-eater, dog (Aus.), dog's nose, finger, fizgig (Aus.), guinea pig, grass (rhy.sl. = grasshopper = shopper), mule mouth, nark, Noah's ark (rhy.sl. = nark), nose, pig brother (US Black), rat, singer, slim, snitch, snout, stool-pigeon, stoolie, Tom Slick (US Black), tout (IRA use); spec. narc (narcotics informer); supergrass (major informer)
v. 3. *to inform:* blow one's nose, cop out (on), copper, cough, give the man the play (US Black), grass, holler cropper, put the bubble in, QE (turn Queen's Evidence), scream, spill, – the beans; blow through (phone in information);

put it around (circulate rumours); turn one around (to persuade a criminal to turn informer)
adj. 4. *untrustworthy:* copper-hearted

473. Betrayal; Accusation
n. 1. spec. fix, frame-up (concoction of evidence)
2. *informer:* budgie, snitcher, squealer; spec. faded boogie, pig brother (US Black: black informer to white authorities)
v. 3. *to betray:* blab, blow the gaff, – the whistle on, drop a dime on, – a quarter on, – a dollar (US Black: cash sums vary as to degree of betrayal, all refer to using the telephone), finger, grass, give a body, go bent, lolly, pin on, put a body up, – a name up, – away, – in the acid, – one in (Aus.), – the nigger on, – the whisper on, rat on, rat one out, shop, snitch, squeal, tip in, tom out (US Black), top off (Aus.); spec. narc one over (betray to the drug squad)
4. *to concoct evidence:* frame, frame up, fit up, fix (up)
adv. 5. *betrayed:* bubbled, grassed up, etc. (see also Information: 472), lollied (rhy.sl. = lollypopped = shopped)

CRIME: OBSERVATION

474. Guarding
n. 1. *guard, lookout:* dogger out (US), six-man (Can.)
adv. 2. *on guard:* on the earie

CRIME: TRAVEL

475. Transportation Methods
n. 1. *driver:* wheelman; spec. skid artist, stoppo driver (UK: getaway driver)
2. *police car:* black and white, blue and white, blue dangers, hurry-up, salt and pepper; spec. nondescript, Q boat (UK: unmarked police cars); noddy (UK: police motorcycle)
3. *'Black Maria':* cattle car, go-long, hurry-up wagon, meat wagon, paddy wagon

CRIME: TRAMPING

476. Vagrancy
n. 1. *vagrant:* wag; spec. vag (vagrancy charge)

477. Begging
adv. 1. on the bow, on the earhole

CRIME: CRIME AND PUNISHMENT

478. Crime
n. 1. caper, job; spec. across the pavement (UK: any street crime); back-alley deal (US Black); rackets (underworld); the Life (US Black: the underworld); MO (modus operandi: a given criminal's 'trademarks'); ways (US: ethos and style of the Mafia); aka (false name)

v. 2. *to commit crime:* do a job, get one's feet muddy, make one, perform, pull a caper, – a job; spec. put one together (plan a crime); chip (US: carry out petty crimes); have an in (have useful contacts); make one's rep (to establish one's criminal status); row in (to enrol in a criminal plan)

3. *to give up crime:* go straight

adj. 4. *criminal:* naughty

adv. 5. *involved in crime:* at it

479. Theft
n. 1. heist, hist, screwer; spec. B&E (breaking and entering); high-wall job, second-storey job (theft involving climbing); sneak job (house-breaking); sticksing (WI: pickpocketing); boosting, hoisting (US: shoplifting); snow-dropping (stealing from washing lines); creaming, the weed (stealing from one's employer's tills); Black Power dance (looting); cartnapping (stealing supermarket trolleys); matchbox (anywhere easily robbed)

2. *thief:* gazlon (Yid.), gonef, gonnif, macer, tealeaf (rhy.sl.); spec. nighthawk (specialist in night work)

3. *specialists:* bumper, cannon, fork, hooker, nudger, stall, pick (pickpockets); moll buzzer (pickpocket who prefers female victims); jack roller, lush worker, roller (one who robs drunks); breaker, crib-man, screwsman, second-storey man (house-breaker); pete-man, peterman (safe-breaker); booster, lugger, skin worker (shoplifter); creep(er) (sneak thief); git-'em-up guy (hold-up man); reader, slow walker (US: one who follows postmen to rob them); dunnigan worker (one who robs in public lavatories); shitter (one who excretes where he has stolen)

v. 4. *to rob:* blag, clout, fleece, half-inch (rhy.sl. = pinch), kipe, knock off, – over, liberate, pinch, skank (WI), skulk, swipe; spec. dance (from upper floors); do a crib, jack in the box (to house-break); boost, hoist (to shoplift); drag, gleep a cage (US), make a car (US) (to steal from cars); work the hole, – the well (to pickpocket on public transport); drop sticks (WI), fan (to pickpocket); kiss the dog (to pickpocket face-to-face); case (the joint) (to appraise a location prior to a robbery)

adj. 5. *larcenous:* sticky-fingered

adv. 6. spec. at the wash (stealing from public lavatories); creeping and tilling (US Black: robbing from shop tills); on the bottle, on the whiz, at the push-up (working as a pickpocket); swagging (US prison: stealing prison property)

phr. 7. spec. it fell off the back of a lorry, they give them away with a pound of tea

480. Swindling
n. 1. bunco, con, flim-flam, FP (false pretences), high game, grift; spec. big con (large-scale confidence tricks); short con, – stuff (small-scale confidence tricks); slow con (slowly matured trick); fonfen (Yid. the 'line' used by a con-man); hit-and-get (moving quickly from town to town); pitch (site of a three-card monte game); bucket gaff, – job (fraudulent company); market (bait that lures the victim); donah ('the lady' in a three-card monte game)

2. *confidence tricks:* double-dooring (hotel fraud); drop game (using planted wallets); drumming (posing as a

'salesman'); the Hype, the Bill, twenties (confusing shopkeepers over change); LF, long firm (credit fraud); murphy (game) (beating and robbing of a prostitute's client); smack (coin-tossing fraud); tat (tricks using dice); tweedling (selling allegedly 'stolen' goods)

3. *confidence trickster:* artist, bat-fowler, beat, beau-trap, bilk, bite, biter, black nob, blackleg, bluff artist, boodler, bounce, bounetter, brass man, bubbler, bunco, bunco artist, – man, – -steerer, bunko, burglar, burner, bushranger (Aus.), cadator (Lat. *cado*, I fall), chiseler, chiseller, chizzer, chouse, chouser, chowse, clipster, cobweb-cheat, come-on, come-on guy, con artist, – -man, – -merchant, – -woman, coneroo, conneroo, cony-catcher (lit. rabbit catcher), – -dog, courtesy-man, crimp, cross-man, crossbiting cully, crossman, cunning man, deep-sea fisherman, diddler, dingo (Aus.), drop-cove, dud-dropper, eel, eelerspee (back.sl.), fake, faker, falconer, fast-talker, fastidious cove, fiddle, fiddler, file, flash, flat-catcher, fleecer, flim-flammer, flopper, fool trap, fool-monger, fortune-biter, forty (Aus.), foy, gagger, gambler, gamer, gazumper, ginal, ginnal, gold-dropper, – -finder, goldbrick, goose shearer, grafter, Greek, grifter, guerrilla, guinea-dropper, gyp artist, – moll, handshaker, hawk, high-flier, – -flyer, highbinder, hook, hooker, Jack of the clockhouse, jeff artist, jeff hat, Jeremy Diddler, jinal, jinnal, lamper, long-shoe (US Black), lurkman, mace, mace-cove, – -gloak, maceman, macer, megsman, mooshe-man, mosker, mushe-man, nipper, oil merchant, operator, payoff man, piker, pointer, pot-hunter, promoter, public patterer, purse-bouncer, – -emptier, queer plunger, rabbit sucker, ramp, ramper, retriever, rook, rorter (Aus.), rum bite, – gagger, samfie (WI), samfie man (WI), scammer, scamp, shark, sharp, sharper, sharpie, sharpster, sharpy, sheep-shearer, sheg-up, shifter, shuffler, slick, slick-'em-plenty, – -boy, slicker, sooner, speeler, speiler, speler, spieler,

strong man, t.b. (lit. tuberculosis; play on t.b. = '*con*sumption'), take-down, tiddlywinker, tongue pad, traffic, tweedler, twicer, two-bit hustler, verser, wheadle, wheedle; spec. amster (Aus. rhy.sl. = Amsterdam = ram); bunco-steerer, buttoner, inside man, ram (Aus.) (con-man's confederate); broadsman (card-sharp); thrower, slide (members of a three-card monte team)

4. *victim:* flop, live one, mark, mug, percher, pigeon, punter

5. *to swindle:* con, take (for a ride)

6. spec. chop the clock (turn back a mileometer); do the party (lure victims in a three-card monte game); fly a kite (pass dud cheques); reload (permit the sucker to win); cook the mark (calm down the fleeced victim)

adv. 7. spec. at the switch (swindling shops); on the knocker (posing as a salesman); on the plastic (using stolen credit cards); at the mark-up (taking an excessive share of loot or profits)

481. Illicit Business

n. 1. dodge, lay, put up job, racket, scam; spec. shakedown (blackmail, extortion); corner, lawing (confidence tricks based on selling supposedly 'stolen' goods); brooming (UK cabbies: refusing all but profitable fares); mule (amateur smuggler)

2. *false appearance:* front

3. *illicit businesses:* spec. granny (business used as a front); laundromat (a business used to 'launder' money)

v. 4. spec. launder, wash (to 'decriminalise' illicitly acquired funds); scalp (to work as a ticket tout)

adj. 5. *illicit:* moody

phr. 6. *justifying possession of stolen goods:* it fell off the back of a lorry; they give them away with a pound of tea

482. Corruption

n. 1. *corruption:* graft

2. *bribe:* bung, drink, grease

3. spec. grass-eater (US: policeman who is satisfied with the bribes he is offered), meat-eater (one who demands higher payments)

v. 4. *to take bribes:* cop, cop a drop, drink

adj. 5. *corrupt:* a bit swift, bent, dodgy, wide

adv. 6. *accepting bribes:* mumping, on a pension, – contract, – the take, – the wrist; spec. on the tin (US: free meals, gifts offered policemen)

phr. 7. spec. can I speak to you? (UK: asking a policeman: can you be bribed?)

483. Counterfeiting and Forgery

n. 1. *counterfeit money:* funny money, slush (UK)

2. *counterfeiter:* cobbler, penman, scratcher; spec. lay-down merchant, slinger (one who passes forged banknotes); kiter, paper hanger (one who passes dud cheques)

484. Kidnapping

n. 1. snatch

v. 2. snatch, sneeze

485. Violence; Coercion

n. 1 (see Rough Treatment: 337, Assault: 338); GBH (grievous bodily harm), push-in job (mugging on the victim's doorstep), RWV (robbery with violence); spec. cement kimono, – overcoat (the hiding of a corpse by burying it in cement); father and mother stuff (street gang use: attacking 'civilians')

2. spec. juice man (collector for a loan-shark); minder (bodyguard); sledge (one who carries a sledgehammer)

v. 3. *to hurt:* do a mischief (to), give it to, muscle, strongarm

4. *to rob with violence:* knock over, mug, stick up

adv. 5. *violent:* on the muscle

6. *marked for death:* on the spot

486. Evidence; Suspicion

n. 1. dope, goods, stuff (on); spec. dirty dishes (planted evidence); dabs (fingerprints); frame (general situation regarding suspicions); wild prints (prints as yet unidentified)

2. *surveillance:* ob(b)o, plant, stake-out; spec. blinker (police helicopter)

3. *identification:* ID, make; spec. mug shot (identifying photo of criminal)

4. *a suspect:* chummy

v. 5. *to suspect:* measure one's dick (for), row in

6. *to identify:* ID, make (for); mug (to take identifying photos)

7. *to plant or fake evidence:* fit up, flake, frame, plant, stitch up

8. *to hide evidence:* wax up

9. *to exonerate:* drop one out, row out

10. *to divert suspicion:* take the dairy off

adv. 11. *under surveillance:* pegged

12. *'framed up':* jobbed

13. *under suspicion:* hot, in the frame

487. Evasion

n. 1. fade, lam, powder, runout powder

2. *hiding place:* slaughter, stash

3. *escapee:* runner, take-off artist, trotter

4. spec. outfit (prison escape kit); outers (any means of escape)

v. 5. *to escape:* cop a heel, – a moke, cop and heel, do a runner, go over the hill, have it away (on one's toes), make one, make one out, take off; spec. jump bail (break one's bail conditions and flee)

6. spec. spring (to help one escape)

phr. 7. spec. one away! (UK: prison officer's cry of alarm)

488. Search; Pursuit

n. 1. *raid:* swoop

2. *search warrant:* brief, ticket, W

v. 3. *to stop and search:* fan, frisk, jack up, pat (one) down, pull, rumble, turn over; spec. spin, – a drum (to search premises)

4. spec. go out poncing (UK: to search for working pimps); house (UK: to trace a suspect to a given place)

phr. 5. the heat's on!

489. Apprehension; Arrest

n. 1. bail up (Aus.), bounce (US), bust, capture, clear-up, collar, hook, jam, pinch, pull, tug; spec. accommodation collar, flake (US: arrest simply to fill a quota); lay down (UK: remand in custody); humbug, hummer, swift 'un (false arrest)

v. 2. *to arrest:* bail up (Aus.), book, borrow, bounce, bust, capture, claim, collar, drop the hook on, feel a collar, grab, have (it) off, hook, jam, life, nab, nick, pinch, pull, put the sleeve on, run in, scoop, spear, swag, swamp, toss in the bucket, toss in the can, tug; spec. railroad (to arrest unfairly); scratch for work (UK: to need an arrest)

3. *to be arrested:* get a capture, – a tug, – one's collar felt, fall, take a fall

adv. 4. *arrested:* bagged, captured, collared, hooked, etc. (see n. 1.), done up (like a kipper), nicked, popped, tucked up; spec. on the pavement (arrested in the street)

5. *caught red-handed:* bang to rights

6. *due to be arrested:* due

phr. 7. spec. it looks like rain (an arrest is imminent)

490. Examination of Prisoners

n. 1. line-up; spec. beef (court case)

2. *hard interrogation:* heat, third degree; spec. Mutt and Jeff ('good' and 'bad' role-playing by interrogators)

3. *statement:* verbal; spec. dock asthma ('surprised' reactions of the accused on hearing their confessions in court)

4. *charge:* rap; spec. bad rap (serious or unfair charge)

v. 5. *to interrogate:* strap (interrogate harshly); spec. verbal (for police to fake a confession)

6. *to confess:* come clean, – one's cocoa, – one's fat, – one's lot, – one's guts, cough, dob in (Aus.), sing, – like a canary, sneeze (it out), spill one's guts, stand up; spec. hold the bag, take the rap, wear it (confess to another's crime)

7. *to plead innocent:* plead

8. *to withstand interrogation:* beat the rap, stand up

adv. 9. spec. very swift (of corrupt police methods)

phr. 10. *charge him!:* stick him on!

491. Sentence

n. 1. bit, bird (rhy.sl. = bird lime = time), lagging, porridge, time

2. spec. chuck (US: 'not guilty' verdict); toothbrush day (the day of sentencing: one should take a toothbrush to court)

3. spec. baby life (US: 6 yrs, 4 mths); big bit, – time, lagging, long bit, nice bit (long sentences, 3 years +); carpet (UK: 3 mths); double carpet (6 mths); fin up (US: 5 yrs to life); haircut (UK short sentence); half a stretch (UK: 6 mths);

handful (UK: 5 yrs); leggner (UK: 12 mths); maximum, minimum (US: longest/shortest times that must be served in an indeterminate sentence); nickel (US: 5 years); dime (US: 10 years), pontoon (UK: 21 mths); pound (US: 5 yrs); rofe (backsl. = 4 yrs); short time (short sentence, end of sentence); SS (UK: suspended sentence); stretch (UK: 12 mths); two (UK: 2 yrs); beggar's lagging, tramp's lagging (UK: 90 days); weekend (UK: very short sentence); woodener (UK: 30 days); zip-five (US: maximum 5 yrs)

v. 4. *to imprison:* send away, – down, – up, weigh off; spec. dish out gravy (sentence harshly); cop a plea, cop out (plea bargain)

5. *to be imprisoned:* go away, – down, pull time

6. *to be found 'not guilty':* beat the rap

adv. 7. *on trial:* standing on the top step, up the steps, – stairs

492. Capital Punishment

n. 1. *electric chair:* chair, hot chair, – seat, – squat

v. 2. *to electrocute:* bake, fry

3. *hang:* stretch (one's neck)

493. Commutation and Release

n. 1. *bail:* Royal Mail (rhy.sl.)

2. *parole:* jam roll (rhy.sl.); spec. back door parole (UK: dying in jail)

3. *rejection of parole:* blank, flop, knockback

4. *parolee:* early riser; spec. PV (parole violator)

5. spec. bleat (petition for repeal); lifeboat (pardon)

6. *release:* blue papers (UK), walking papers (US) (official statement of release date); get-up (release date); gate fever (pre-release nerves)

v. 7. spec. carry a case (to be freed on bail); on the count (US Black: walking the streets); recoup (US Black: to start post-prison life afresh); feed the bears (pay a parking fine)

494. Prison Life

n. 1. *prison:* big house, boob, brig, bucket (Can.), calaboose, chokey, clink, college, coop, cross-bar hotel, glasshouse, hoosegow, Joe Gurr (rhy.sl. = stir), joint, jug, lagging station, pen, pokey, quod, slammer, sneezer, stir, tank, Texas steel; spec. drunk tank (lockup for drunks); the Island (Parkhurst, IOW); juvie (US: juvenile prison); the Moor (Dartmoor), outhouse (US: hostel); outside (the free world); Q (San Quentin); the Scrubs (Wormwood Scrubs); upstate (prisons in New York State); the Ville (Pentonville)

2. *places in prison:* range (US/Can. open areas outside cells); block, chokey, cooler, damper, Florida (US), hole, Siberia (US) (solitary confinement); crazy alley, paddy, pads (padded cells); limbo room (Can.: corporal punishment room)

3. *cell:* cheder (Yid.), flowery (rhy.sl. = flowery dell), slot (Aus.), peter, slams; spec. Rory (rhy.sl. = Rory O'Moore = cell door)

4. *prisoners:* con, gaolbird, (old) lag, yardbird (US Black); spec. (new) fish (new inmate); flipflop (US: recidivist); short (nearing release); aces high, real man, right guy (US: popular prisoner); centreman, jointman (Can.: sycophant to guards); stoolie (informer); red band (UK: trusty); atlas, OBC (one brutal convict) (strong convicts); baron, carvie (UK: tobacco trader); sweet kid (young homosexual); prison wolf (older homosexual); bug pass (Can.: insane prisoner); politician (one who secures privileges); gaolhouse lawyer (one who studies law); wallflower (UK: one who plans an escape); lifer (serving life); three-time loser (US: serving mandatory life after a third conviction); recluse (a long-term prisoner with no outside contacts); lugger (Can.: smuggler of contraband); knight of the golden grummet (US: prison homosexual); star (UK: first offender); daddy (UK Borstal use: powerful prisoner)

5. *prison officers:* flue (rhy.sl. = screw), hack, herder, screw, twirl; spec. bully beef, screwdriver, white shirt (senior officer); bitch's bastard, caser (severe officer); bent screw, safe screw (corrupt officer); light of love (rhy.sl. = guv = governor); dep (deputy governor); particulars (US: external authorities);

tube (UK: officer who eavesdrops on prisoners); zombie (UK: sour, surly officer); Gabriel (chapel organist); convictitis (paranoid fear of prisoners)

6. *imprisonment:* porridge, time; spec. hard bit, – time (difficult sentence); first bird (first sentence); good time (remission); dead time (US: imprisonment that does not diminish the sentence); cons, jacket, mileage, PC (previous convictions); previous, rap sheet, sheet, yellow sheet (criminal record)

7. spec. bingo (Can.: riot); blanket party (US: initiation rite); break (an escape); cell task (UK: pin-up); cobitis (UK: dislike of jail food); duffer (UK: pudding, US: bread); fall money (US: legal fees); friend form (US: visiting order); grab (UK: pay); hominy gazette (Aus.: rumours); joey (UK: contraband); jo-jos (Can.: overcoat); jug-up (Can.: mealtime); bug juice, liquid cosh (Can./UK: major tranquilisers used for restraint); outfit (escape kit); pussy in a can (US: sardines); rim slide (US: fart); reader (UK: any reading matter); rower (UK: argument); scratcher (UK: match); whodunnit (UK: meat pie); wicked lady (cat o'nine-tails); kit (contraband communication; any prison paperwork); bug (Can.: homemade water-heater); KB (UK: knockback – rejection of parole); full sheet (UK: prisoner's complaint against an officer)

v. 8. *spec. (prisoners):* blow one's copper (US: lose remission); choose up (US: select a homosexual partner); do a bit (serve time); get the Book, get the glory (become religious); give (one) the office (to initiate a newcomer); flash the range (US/Can.: scan the prison landing with a mirror); go up (the river) (to be imprisoned); have some rabbit (US: yearn to escape); lay in (US: reject exercise periods); play too close (US Black: invade privacy); ride the deck, swap cans (US: have anal intercourse); cop a heel (US: attack from behind)

9. *spec. (prison officers):* bang up, dub up, chubb, miln up (UK: lock the cell door); ducket (Can.: place fellow-officer

on report); get the book (US: to be reprimanded); put the block on (UK: tighten up prison regulations); ghost (move prisoners at night); case (UK: place a prisoner on report)
adj. 10. spec. chosen (US: selected as a homosexual partner); nicked (UK: put on report); scammered (homosexual)
adv. 11. *imprisoned:* away, inside, in the nick, in chokey, – stir, etc. (see n. 1.), jugged, on jankers, on the corn (Aus.), under glass, up the river; spec. carpy (UK: locked up for the night); two-ed up, three-ed up (UK: two or three men sharing a cell); stir bugs, – crazy (insane); baroning (trading in consumables)
12. *in solitary confinement:* behind one's door, buried (US), iced, OP (Can.: off privilege); spec. in the peek (under observation); on Rule 43 (UK: in voluntary solitary confinement)
13. *escaped:* away, on the lam, over the hill
phr. 14. *aimed at a complainer:* if you can't do the time, don't do the crime

495. Policeman

n. 1. Alice Blue Gown (gay use), Babylon (WI), bear, beast-boy, Big John (US Black), Bill, blue-heeler, blue-light special, blue meanies, bluebottles, blues, bobby, bogey, bogie, Brenda (gay use), Brenda Bracelets (gay use), bull, button, casian (WI), chapper (Yid.), copman, cop(per), cozzer, deputy do-right (US Black), dibble, divine right (US Black), esclop (backsl. = cop), flatfoot, flattie, fuzz, gendarmes, gestaps (US Black), greenfly (S.Afr.), gum heel, harness bull, hawkshaw (WI), heat, Hilda Handcuffs (gay use), hood (Aus.), hoon-chaser (Aus.), irvine (US Black), John Law, John Hop (Aus. rhy.sl. = cop), Johnny-be-good (US Black), kojak, law, little boy blue (US Black), Lucy Law (gay use), mallet (US Black), nab (US Black), nail 'em and jail 'em (US Black), oinker (i.e. 'pig'), Old Bill, O'Malley, ossifer, our friend with the talking brooch (gay use), paddy, Penelope, Peter Jay (US Black), pig, rad, reppock (backsl. =

copper), robocop, rozzer, Sam and Dave (US Black), scuffer, Sherlock Holmes (US Black), Teresa Truncheon (gay use), the Man, three-bullet Joey (US Black), Tilly (gay use), uncle nabs (US Black), union wage (US Black), walloper (Aus.), weakheart (WI), whips (US Black), woodentop; spec. rusty gun (veteran); active, hungry (enthusiast); saint (uncorruptible); horseman (RCMP 'mountie'); five-day wonder (UK: graduate of police college); aid (Temporary Detective Constable); dickless Tracy (woman officer); choirboys, wollies (novices); skip (sergeant); guv, guvnor (UK: any senior rank, usually as form of address); boffin (forensic expert); bobbsey twins (gay use: squad car officers); mother superior (gay use: sergeant)
2. *detectives:* ace, brains, busy, clothes, D (Aus.), eye, filth, G-man, gumshoe, jack, mod squad, Scotland Yard (US Black), shoo-fly; spec. T-man (US Treasury agent); peeper (private detective)
3. *traffic police:* bald-tyre bandits, bear in the air (US: using a helicopter), brown bomber (Aus.), Freeway Freddie (US Black), green hornet (Can.), grey ghost (Aus.), kojak with a Kodak, pirates, Smokey
4. *group of police:* button mob, heavy mob, team; spec. heavy mob, Sweeney (rhy.sl. = Sweeney Todd = squad), the squad (flying squad); pussy posse, queer detail, Vera Vice (vice squad); narco (narcotics squad); bunco squad (fraud squad); Met (UK: Metropolitan Police); Home and Colonial (UK: regional crime squad); rubber heels, umbrella brigade (UK: Special Branch); rubber heels, shoo-fly (internal disciplinary officers); COs (UK: Commissioner's Office – taxi-cab authorities)
5. *police work:* the job; spec. batting average (US: arrest record); rubbish (UK: tedious duties); shout (an emergency call); SOP (standard operating procedure); advice (UK: a reprimand)
6. *police badge:* buzzer, potsy, tin
7. *Scotland Yard:* hollow tooth, Kremlin, the Yard

8. *police station:* Bridewell, factory, nick, old bill (see also Crime: 460)
9. spec. dido (UK: internal complaint); Kilburn (rhy.sl. = Kilburn Priory = police diary)
v. 10. spec. walk the bricks (patrol); go out with (share professional attitudes); cover the sheet (fill an arrest quota); give a coating (to reprimand); cast (UK: to be discharged); put in one's papers (UK: to resign); crash (UK: drop enquiries); plot up (UK: study a given villain); blow out (UK: for a case to collapse); shape up (for a case to develop well)
adv. 11. spec. copping on the wrist, on the take (accepting bribes); over the side (UK: shirking duty for private interests); cooping (US: sleeping on duty); on dab (UK: on a disciplinary charge)
phr. 12. derog. ACAB (all coppers are bastards)
13. spec. APB (all points bulletin: general alert); ten-four (message received and understood)
14. spec. have you got a coat? (UK: have you found a feasible suspect?)

CRIME: MISCELLANEOUS

496. Miscellaneous Terms, etc.

n. 1. spec. black (blackmail); bleeding dirt, the mouse (blackmailing homosexuals); Jewish lightning (deliberate arson for insurance fraud); bustle-punching (acting as a frotteur); moprey (exposing one's genitals to a blind woman); copper jitters (irrational fear of police); Follies (UK: Quarter Sessions)
v. 2. spec. do it for oneself (UK cabbie use: take a fare without using the meter); torch (commit arson)

PROSTITUTION

497. Prostitution

n. 1. pussy game, the Game
2. *prostitute:* ass peddler, b.o.a.t. (an enthusiastic amateur or part-timer; i.e. *b*ordering *o*n *a t*art), bangtail (US Black), bend, bimbo, bird (US Black), brass, business girl, call-girl, charlie (Aus.), chromo (Aus.), cruiser, dirt, Edie, flash-tail, flatbacker, grunter (Aus.), high roller, ho (US Black), hook(er), hoove (a part-timer), hoowah, KP (Aus.: common prostitute), kewpie (Aus. rhy.sl. Kewpie doll = 'moll'), kurve (Yid.), lady, lot lizard, meat, moonlighter, nafka (Yid.), nag, noffka (Yid.), open game (US Black), pavement princess, pro, professional woman, prossie, prosso (Aus.), puta (Sp.), run, scrub, short-time girl, stepper (US Black), stick (US Black), tackle, tom, wagon, working girl; spec. square broad (non-prostitute); industrial debutante (specialist in conventions)
3. *part-time prostitute:* B-girl, charity moll (Aus.), chippy, half-brass, weekend ho (US Black), – warrior, summertime ho (US Black)
4. *senior prostitute:* old timer, vet
5. *worn-out prostitute:* fleabag, over the hill ho (US Black)
6. *incompetent prostitute:* flaky ho (US Black), hold-out, mudkicker, nag, slouch; spec. outlaw (one who works without a pimp)
7. *experienced prostitute:* bottom woman, main bitch, rose among the thorns, star of the line, thoroughbred
8. *under-age prostitute:* baby-pro
9. *male prostitute:* ass peddler, – pro, bird taker, broad, boy, buff boy, bunny, business boy, call boy, career boy, cocksman, cocktail, coin collector, come-on boy, commercial queer, crack salesman, dick peddler, fag boy, flesh peddler, floater, foot soldier, gigolo, goofer, he-whore, Hollywood hustler, party boy, prick peddler, puto (Sp. = whore), rent, rent-boy, sport, sporting goods, two-way man, trabajadao (Sp. = worked over), trade, working girl
10. *thieving prostitute:* ginger, rip-off artist
11. *prostitutes working for a pimp:* flock, nest, stable; spec. choosing money (cash given by a prostitute to her new pimp); pimp crazy (a prostitute who prefers sadistic pimps)

12. spec. **hand gig** (gay use: prostitute who masturbates (with) client); **vegetarian** (prostitute who will not fellate); **three-way girl** (offers all bodily orifices for sex); **trapeze artist** (specialist in cunnilingus)
13. *working targets:* **catch**, **trap**; spec. **git-down time** (start of working day)
14. spec. **trick baby** (prostitute's client-fathered child)
v. 15. *to work as a prostitute:* **hawk one's fork** (Aus.), **– one's mutton**, **– one's pearly**, **hook**, **peddle pussy**, **sit on one's stuff** (US Black), **step** (US Black), **turn tricks**; spec. **break one's luck** (meet the day's first client)
16. *work as a male prostitute:* **hawk one's brown**, **peddle one's arse**
adv. 17. *working as a prostitute:* **on the bash**, **– the bat**, **– the battle** (Aus.), **– the bottle**, **– the Game**, **steppin'**, **trollin'**; spec. **on the case** (earning steadily from one client)
phr. 18. *used by prostitute to client:* **wanna do a thing?**, **– go out?**

498. Pimps and Pimping

n. 1. **mackery**, **the Life**; spec. **the Book** (verbally transmitted 'book of pimping rules')
2. *pimp:* **Alphonse** (rhy.sl. = ponce), **Charlie Ronce** (rhy.sl.), **chulo** (Sp.), **fence** (Aus.), **fucker**, **hoon** (Aus.), **hose**, **Joe Bonce**, **Joe Ronce** (rhy.sl.), **louis**, **macaroni** (US Black), **mack daddy** (US Black), **– man** (US Black), **player**, **ponce**, **sweetman**; spec. **bit of mess** (UK: a male lover, neither client nor pimp)
3. *small-time pimp:* **chili chump**, **– pimp**, **coffeeand pimp**, **popcorn pimp**, **simple pimp**
4. spec. **boss player** (superior pimp); **faggotter** (pimp for male prostitutes); **gorilla pimp** (violent pimp); **promoted pimp** (experienced, senior pimp); **sugar pimp** (kind pimp); **macaroni with cheese** (pimp who has other interests); **Madam** (male/female brothel proprietor)
5. spec. **bonds** (clothes given to his prostitutes); **copping clothes** ('best suit' used when enticing a new prostitute); **kimible** (noticeable 'pimp walk'); **pimp's arrest** (revocation of statutory bail bond for a given prostitute when she wants to leave); **pimp dust** (cocaine); **pimp fronts** (pimp-style clothes); **pimp ride** (expensive car); **pimp shades**, **– tints** (dark glasses)
v. 6. *to entice prostitutes:* **cast the net**, **cop**, **– for**, **hit on**, **take an application**
7. *to run prostitutes:* **drive one's hos**, **put one on the block**, **– one on the corner**, **turn (one) out**; spec. **cop and blow** (exploit a prostitute); **lock** (ensure a prostitute's fidelity); **ponce off** (live off immoral earnings); **work from a book** (run call – not street – girls)
8. *to discuss pimping:* **run down game**, **talk game**
9. spec. **file** (to give instruction to a prostitute); **rig a jib** (prepare a sexual con-trick); **put snow in one's game** (ensnare a white person for financial gain); **creep** (to defraud a client); **work a ginger** (Aus.: to rob a client); **drop a lug** (US Black: to confront or argue with)
adj. 10. *pertaining to pimping:* **mack**

499. Clients and Services

n. 1. **fare**, **gonk**, **john**, **trick**, **TOS** (trick off the street); spec. **freak trick**, **special** (devotee of any sexual speciality, see n. 2); **phoney** (mean client); **champagne trick** (generous client); **live one** (good client)
2. spec. **beat** (masochist); **beer bottle beat** (one who likes to be hit with a bottle); **cream-puff freak** (cake-thrower); **dress-up** (uses the girl's clothes/make-up); **facial** (the girl sits on his face); **gorilla** (sadist); **jim**, **tin soldier**, **twank** (voyeurs, 'assistants', etc.); **leapfrog** (one who watches two girls play leapfrog); **needle freak** (sadist, with needles); **no freak** (likes to simulate rape); **phone freak** (calls the girl to talk sex); **sniffer** (sniffs underwear); **talker** (only talks to the girl); **underwear** (underwear fetishist); **word freak** (listens to obscenities); **toys** (appliances used for bondage, S&M, etc.)
3. *sex show:* **circus**, **dig** (US Black), **gazoopie**, **gazupie**; spec. **T&A**, **tits and ass** (burlesque, strip-show)

4. *services:* around the world (licking, sucking of entire body); B&D (bondage and discipline); English culture, – guidance (flagellation and bondage); fifty-fifty (gay use: alternating fellatio and sodomy); fladge (flagellation); French culture (fellatio); golden showers (urolagnia); Greek culture (anal intercourse); party (any form of sex act); R/S (rough stuff, including sado-masochism, urolagnia, rubberwear, etc.); Roman culture (orgies); short time (basic intercourse); Swedish culture (rubber); telephone J/O (masturbation while listening to the telephone); tongue bath (see 'around the world'); water sports (urolagnia); middle finger (prostitute's trick that speeds up orgasms); freebie, free shot (sex for free)
5. spec. ten-two (US payment for sex: $10 for girl, $2 for room)
v. 6. *to lick and suck the client's body:* go around the world, – all over town (with), round-house
7. spec. kerb-crawl (to solicit street girls from a car)
8. spec. georgy (to hire a whore and then refuse to pay)
9. spec. freak off (offer sex for free)
10. spec. sell a boy (gay use: to hire a prostitute as a 'gift' for a third party)

500. Locations
n. 1. *brothel:* barrelhouse, benny house, call house, case, cathouse, chicken ranch, hook shop, house, knocking shop, leaning house (US Black); spec. punch house (US Black: place where pimps and whores meet); rap parlour (euphemism for 'massage parlour'); peg house, show house (homosexual brothel)
2. *pimp uses:* office (wherever a pimp conducts business); fast track (centre of whoring in a city, US East Coast cities in general); slow track (US West Coast cities)
3. *the street:* ho stroll (US Black), pitch, stroll, track
adv. 4. *on the street:* on the bricks

COMMERCIAL SEX

501. Pornography
n. 1. smut
2. *books:* eight-pager, fuck book, one-hand job, stroke book, Tijuana bible; spec. fag hots (gay-orientated material)
3. *films:* blue film, horn movie, skin-flick, stag movie
4. *spec. close-ups:* beaver shot (female genitals); flap shot, liver shot, meat shot, pink, wide-open beaver (inner labia, open vagina, etc.)
adj. 5. *pornographic:* adult, blue

DRUGS

502. Selling
n. 1. *seller:* candyman, connection, dealer, man, pusher, watermelon man (US Black); spec. seedy (US Black: seller of pills)
2. spec. buy (purchase of drugs); meet (appointment to buy drugs); green house (location, popular for buying drugs); jam house (location where cocaine is available); hop joint, shooting gallery (location where narcotics can be bought and used)
3. spec. Dr Feelgood, hungry croaker, writing doctor (doctors who write illicit prescriptions for drugs)
4. *measures of drugs:* amp (ampoule); bag (measure of narcotics); bindle, deck, paper (small fold of paper holding narcotics); birdseye (small amount of narcotics); blow, toot (one line of cocaine); brick (approx. 1 kilo of marijuana); can (1 oz of marijuana); cap (capsule); deck, dime bag ($10 worth of a drug); fifty-cent bag ($50 worth of marijuana); football (approx. 0.5 grain of a narcotic); half-lo (15 bags of heroin); jar (500/1000 pills); key (one kilo); LB (one pound weight); lid (22 gms approx. of marijuana); line (one snort of a narcotic); match, matchbox (half-oz of marijuana); mic (one microgram, used to measure LSD); oz (1 ounce weight); paper, piece (approx.

1 oz of heroin); pinch (small amount of marijuana); spoon (2 gms heroin); taste (small amount of any drug); teaspoon (1 gm heroin); ten-cent bag ($10 worth of marijuana); weight (1 oz of heroin, 1 lb of marijuana); baggie (small plastic bag to hold marijuana)

5. *adulterated drugs:* blank ('narcotics'); catnip ('marijuana'); six and four (heavily diluted heroin)

6. spec. one-shot credit (a buyer is allowed only one default in payment)

7. spec. dog tag (a legitimate prescription for narcotics)

v. 8. *to sell drugs:* deal, hustle, serve; spec. lay on (to offer free or sample drugs)

9. *to buy drugs:* connect, cop (for), score; spec. front (advance cash for a purchase)

10. spec. write script (for a doctor to write a prescription for narcotics)

11. *to measure out drugs for sale:* bag, bag up, cap (into capsules)

12. *to sell adulterated, fake or short weight drugs:* burn, rip off

13. *to adulterate drugs:* cut, hit, step on

adv. 14. *in possession of drugs:* anywhere, carrying, holding

phr. 15. *do you want drugs?:* do you need a boy?

16. *have you any drugs?:* are you anywhere?, – carrying?, – holding?

503. Use and Addiction

n. 1. *pill-taker:* a-head, downer, freak, pillhead, pill-popper, speed freak

2. *narcotic user:* spec. AD, hophead, globetrotter, hype, junkie, junk hawk, mainliner, schmecker, smack freak, – head, stuffer, unkjay, user (heroin); cokey, coke freak, – head, snow bird (cocaine); needle freak, pin-jabber (one who prefers to inject); snooter (one who prefers to sniff drugs); hog (one who uses an excess of narcotics); swellhead (US Black: one who has collapsed from drug use)

3. *soft drug user:* spec. doper, druggie, freak, head, pothead, weedhead (cannabis); acidhead, acid rapper, tripper (LSD); space cadet, zonker (an excessive user); bud sesh (smoking drugs together); teahouse (place for communal smoking); bowl, chalice, chillum, cutchie (WI) (device for smoking)

4. spec. stash (drug hiding place; thus the given drug itself)

5. *addiction to narcotics:* habit, jones, monkey (on one's back); burning down habit, oil-burner habit (very heavy addiction); coffeeand habit (mild addiction); white line fever (cocaine addiction); honeymoon (early use of heroin)

6. *withdrawal from drugs:* belly habit, bogue, cold turkey, kicking (the habit), sweats, sick; spec. detox (detoxification: post-withdrawal period); chucks, chuck horrors (excessive eating that follows withdrawal)

v. 7. *to be addicted:* be strung out, have a habit, – a jones, – a monkey on one's back, hurting (for)

8. *to stop using narcotics:* go cold turkey, kick, kick the habit

9. spec. make for a stash (to steal drugs from a fellow user)

10. spec. bogart (take an excess of marijuana)

adv. 11. *using drugs:* on the needle; spec. pinned (tiny pupils, a sign of heroin use)

adj. 12. *no longer addicted:* clean, straight

504. Pills

n. 1. *general pills, capsules, etc.:* ace, beans, blunt, candy, cap, dolls, hors d'oeuvres (US Black), jacks and jills (rhy.sl. = pills), ju-ju, M&Ms, prescriptions, rainbows, roundhead, vitamins, yum-yums

2. *stimulants:* a (amphetamine); b (benzedrine); bam (bambita = amphetamine); bennies, benny, benz (benzedrine); black beauties, – bomber, – widow, blues, bomb(er), Christmas tree (deximal); crank, crystal (powdered Methdrine); dex(y) (dexedrine); leaper, meth (methdrine); olly (rhy.sl. = Oliver Reed = speed); pep-em-ups (US Black), ph, pink lady, purple heart, rouser (US Black), speed, uppers, ups, white cross, whites, whiz, widow

3. *depressants, tranquillisers:* spec. barbs, blue angel (amytal barbiturate); borders, Christmas tree (Tuinal); downer, F-40s

(Seconal); F-60s (Histadyl); F-66s (Tuinal); goofball, gumdrop (US Black), jacket (nembutal); jiblet (US Black), Lilly (Seconal); nebbie, nembie (Nembutal); reds, sleeper, slow-'em-ups (US Black), sopor, tranks, Vallie (Valium); yellowjackets, yellows
4. *methaqualone:* ludes (Quaalude); mandies (Mandrax)
5. spec. silk and satin, up-and-downer (pill combining amphetamine and barbiturate); Mickey Finn (knock-out drug, poss. chloral hydrate); Monday pills (US milit.: malaria pills)
v. 6. *to take pills:* drop

DRUGS: TYPE

505. Hard

n. 1. *narcotics:* hard stuff, stuff; good stuff (better than average drugs)
2. *heroin:* a.i.p. (its origins in *A*fghanistan, *I*ran and *P*akistan), antifreeze, aries, Aunt Hazel, bad bundle, bad seed, beast, big bag, – H, – Harry, birdie powder, Black Power, black tar, blanco (Sp. 'white'; the colour of the powder), blue sky, bomb, bombs away, bonita (Sp., lit. 'good little girl'), boy, bozo, brain damage, brick gum, brown crystal, – sugar, bugger, bundle, butu, caballo (pun on Sp. *caballo*, a horseman/ horse), caps, carne (Sp. *carne*, meat), chi (i.e. *Chi*nese), chicle, chieva, Chinese H, Chinese no. 3, chip, climax, courage pills, crap, crop, crown crap, d.o.a. ('dead on arrival'), dead on arrival, dirt, dog food (US Black), dooley, dragon, duji, dust, elephant, estuffa (Sp. 'stuff'), ferry dust, fix, foo-foo dust, – stuff, foolish powder, Frenchman, the (ref. to the Marseilles heroin labs), galloping horse, gamot, gato, gold dust, good and plenty, gravy, H, hache (Sp. *hache*, the letter H), hairy, hammer (Aus.), hammer and tack (Aus.), henry, hero, – of the underworld, heroina (Sp.), herone, hocus, hombre (Sp. *hombre*, a man), hop, horse, isda, junk, kabayo (phon. sp. of *caballo*), Karachi (fr. its manufacture in Pakistan), little bomb, Mexican mud, mortal combat, nice and easy, oil, p-dope (i.e. *p*ure dope), – -funk,

peg, perfect high, predator, Rambo (ref. to the movie strong-man), red eagle, – rock, rocks, sack, Salisbury Crag (rhy.sl. = scag); scag, schmeck, shit, skag, skezag (pig Latin), slime, spider blue, stuff, sweet dreams, TNT, terminator, tiger, Uncle Mac, white dynamite, witch-hazel; spec. quill (heroin hidden in a matchbook cover)
3. *cocaine:* all-American drug, angie, applejack, Aunt Nora, barbs, barley, bazulco (Sp. *basuco*, cocaine base), beek, bernie's flakes, – gold dust, big bloke, – flake, – rush, billie hoke (rhy.sl. = 'coke'), birdie powder, blort (i.e. 'blow and snort'), blow, Bolivian marching powder, bouncing powder, bowser, bugle, burnese, bush, c., candy, carrie, carrie nation, cecil, cha, charlie, cholly, coconuts, coke, corinne, dama blanca, dolomite, double bubble, dream, duct, flake, flavor, Florida snow (ref. to imports of cocaine through Miami, Fla), fly, foo-foo dust, – stuff, foolish powder, freezer, Gianluca (rhy.sl. Gianluca Vialli = 'charlie'), gift-of-the-sun, giggle dust, gin, girl, girlfriend, go, gold star, golden girl, gonzo, green gold, hocus, hunter, ice, jam (US Black), king's habit, lady, lady caine, leaf, lina, loppy dust, marching dust, mujer, nose, nose candy, oats, one-on-one, paradise, paradise white, pearl, perico, Peruvian, Peruvian flake, – lady, – marching powder, pimp dust (US Black), posh (the drug's association with wealth/ success), rock, royalty, scorpion/ ski, snow, snow white, snowcones, soda, sophisticated lady (US Black), star-spangled powder (fr. its 'All-American' image), toot, turkey, tutti-frutti (play on 'ice-cream'), vitamin C, white brick, – shit, wildcat
4. *crack cocaine (all are orig. US):* b.j.s. (play on *blow j*ob), baby T, bad, ball, base, baseball, bazooka, beautiful boulders (play on 'rocks'), bebe, beemers (fr. the triple-beam scales used in dealing), Bill Blass, bings, black rock, blow-out, blue, bob, bobo, bomb, bone, bonecrusher, bones, botray, boubou, boulder, boulya, bubble-gum, bullia capital, bullion, bullyon, butter, cakes,

cap, caps, Casper the Ghost (the curling
crack smoke), caviar, cheap basing,
cheese, chemical, clicker, climax, cloud,
cloud nine, coffee coke, cookie, cookies,
crackola, crank, creamy, crib, crunch
and munch, d.o.a. ('dead on arrival'),
demolish, devil smoke, devil's dandruff,
devil, the, dirty basing, double yoke,
Eastside player, egg, eightballs,
eye-opener, famous dimes, fat bags,
fifty-one, fish scales, flake, freebase,
French fries, fries, fry, glo, gold, golf
ball, gravel, grit, groceries, hail (orig.
use = ice cubes), hamburger helper (i.e.
MSG, which resembles cocaine),
handball, hard line, hard rock, hotcakes,
hubba, hubba, I am back (rhy.sl.), hydro
(fr. the manufacturing process), I am
back (rhy.sl.), ice cube, ice-cream, issues,
jelly beans, johnson, juice, kangaroo,
kokomo (play on 'coke'), kryptonite, lido,
lightning, love, nuggets, one-fifty-one,
pee-wee, piedras, pony, press, raw, ready
rock, readywash, red caps, regular p (i.e.
pure), roca, rock, rocks, rocks of hell,
rocky, Rocky III (play on the movie title
+ 'rocks'), rooster, rox, roxanne, roz,
schoolcraft, Scotty (ref. to *Star Trek*'s
engineer Scotty, who 'beams you up'),
scramble, scruples, Serpico (ref. to the
movie *Serpico* 1973), Serpico 21,
seven-up, sleet, smoke, snood, snoodge,
snort, snow soke, snowflake, speed boat,
square time bob, stone, sugar block,
supercharge, supercloud, superwhite,
swell-up, teeth, tension, tissue, top gun,
tornado, troop, ultimate (ref. to its
effects), wash, washed rock (fr. the
manufacturing process), wave, we are
the world, white ghost, white sugar,
white tornado, whiteball, wrecking crew,
yahoo, yale, yeaho, yeyo (synon. Sp.),
yimyom
5. *opium:* black, brown stuff, button,
canned stuff, card, green ashes, high hat,
hop, mud, O, red smoker, san lo, tar,
yen pok
6. *morphine:* cube, Dr White, dolly,
God's Own Medicine, GOM, M, Miss
Emma, mojo, sweet Jesus, white nurse,
– stuff
7. spec. PG (paragoric); paracki
(paraldehyde)

8. *drug cocktails:* 'Frisco speedball
(heroin, cocaine & LSD), speedball
(heroin and cocaine)
9. *drug injection:* bang (in the arm), fix, hit,
Jimmy Hix (rhy.sl. = fix), jolt, shot; spec.
wake-up (first injection of the day); main,
mainline (the vein into which one
injects); joy bang, – pop (occasional use);
ab (an abscess caused by injecting);
marks, tracks (scars of regular injections);
hot shot (injection of poison deliberately
used to murder a drug addict)
10. *hard drug paraphernalia:* gun, hypo,
spike (hypodermic syringe); fit, gizmo,
outfit, works (needle plus other
equipment for making an injection);
collar (wrapper that ensures needle and
dropper fit tightly); cooker (a container
in which a mixture of heroin and water
can be heated); cotton (cloth through
which heroin is sucked into the syringe);
tie-up (a means of tying off the vein
prior to injection); rope (a vein)
v. 11. *to inject drugs:* bang up, crank
(up), do a thing, – in, – up, fix, geeze,
jack up, hit the mainline, mainline, pop,
shoot up, take off, use; spec. chippy (to
use narcotics occasionally); tie off (to
isolate the vein); skinpop (inject under
the skin rather than into a vein); fire up,
shoot gravy, jack off (pump the mixture
of blood and heroin into the arm); spill
(to miss the vein); get one's wings (to
start injecting drugs); brew, cook (heat a
mixture of heroin and water prior to
injecting oneself)
12. *to sniff or inhale drugs:* blow, get one's
nose cold, horn, jam (US Black), sniff,
snort, toot; spec. base, freebase (to
inhale cocaine mixed with ether); chase
the dragon, kick the gong around (inhale
heated heroin); toot (a device for
inhaling cocaine)
13. *to addict to drugs:* hook
adj. 14. *narcotic:* heavy
adv. 15. spec. caught in a snowstorm
(under the influence of cocaine); on the
sleeve (injecting narcotics)

506. Soft
n. 1. *hashish:* af, aff, Afghan/Afghani,
ash, bang, bar, biccies, bikkies, black,
black hash, – pak, – rock, – Russian,

blades (lumps of hashish heated on a knife blade), brown, brownie, charas, chitral, chocolate, chocolate stuff, churus, citrol, commersh, dope, double zero, finger, gold seal, goma de moto, half-moon (the hashish is moulded in a half-moon shape), hash-cake, – -monster, Jack Flash (rhy.sl. = hash), jibb, Johnny Cash (rhy.sl. = hash), key, kief, kif, leb, Lebanese, Lebanese Gold, – Red, Nep, Nepalese, oil, Pakistani black, potten bush, quarter moon, soles (fr. the smuggling of hashish in the soles of purpose-built shoes), spots (NZ), sweet Lucy (hashish dissolved in wine), temple balls

2. *marijuana:* ace, ashes (i.e. the residue), Aunt Mary, baby, baby bhang, bad seed, bale, bamber, bar, bash, belyando spruce (Aus.), benny mason, bitchweed, black bart, – gungeon, – moat, – Russian, blend, block, blonde, blowing smoke, blue sky blond, bobo, bobo bush, bohd, bomber, boo, boogie, brand X (US Black), brick, broccoli, bu, buda, buddha, bullion, bullyon, bush, butter, butter flower, cabbage (NZ), cavi, cavvy, cess, charge, cheever, Chicago black, – chronic, co, cochornis, coli, coliflor tostao (synon. Sp. sl.), collie, Colom (Colombian), Colorado cocktail, commercial, commersh, cosa (Sp., lit. 'thing'), cryp, crystal bud, Culican, dagga, dak, dank, dank nuggets, – nugs, dawamesk (Arabic), dew, dimba (West African), dirt grass, ditch, ditchweed, djamba (West African), don jem (West African), doobage, dope, doradilla (Sp., lit. 'a small fern'), double bubblegum, duby, endo (Indonesian), esra (Turkish *esra*, cannabis), esrar, fine stuff, fir, four-twenty (US), gage, ganga, gangja, gangster (US Black), gash, gauge gear, geeba, geek, gimmie, gizzy, gold, gold star, grass, greapha, greefo, green, green tea, greenbud, greenery, greenhouse special, greens, greeny, grief, griefo, griff, groceries, gunja, gunny, hay, hemp, herb, hocus, hocus-pocus, homestone, houbini, houdini (like Harry *Houdini*, the smoker 'escapes'), huckleberry, hydro, Indo, Indonesia, Indonesian bud, jarpot, Jim Jones (cult leader Rev. Jim Jones, 1933–78), johnson, joy, juanita, k.g.b. (*killer green bud*), kali mist, kaya, kill, kumba, l (i.e. 'loc'), l.l. (from rapper *L.L.* Cool J.), la, lah, lakbay diva (pig Latin for 'black weed'), liesca (Sp.), lima, loaf, loc (abbrev. 'locoweed'), locoweed, love boat, lubage, machinery, magic smoke, maharishee, mariweegee, Mary Warner, Mary, Maryanne, Maryjane, Mr Mason, moocah, mootah, mooter, mother nature's own tobacco, mother nature, mu, mud-bud, muggle, muggles, Northern Lights, nugs, nuke, olly (rhy.sl. = Oliver Reed = weed), pakalolo (from Hawaii), pocket rocket, pot, pretendica (poor quality; i.e. it 'pretends' to be good), pretendo, Queen Ann's lace (usu. in UK cow parsley, in US wild carrot), reefer, rooibaard (S.Afr. 'red beard'), root, rose mane, sen, sense, sensi, sensimillia (Sp., lit. 'seedless'), shake, silver pearl, smoke, spear, speed boat, spots, square mackerel (fr. seaborne smuggling of containers of drugs), stickies (NZ; the flowering tops), super bio (play on washing-powder name), superskunk, taima, takkouri, tea, tical (abbrev. SE practical), trees, trom (abbrev. SE traumatize), turbo, turnip greens (US Black), twist, Viking, vitamin T (i.e. *t*etrahydrocannabinol), 'wana, weed, whacky baccy, whacky weed, wheat, white widow, – -haired lady, x, yeh, Yellow Submarine (ref. to the Beatles' song), Zambi (i.e. Zambesi), zombie (Aus.), zoom; spec. sinsemilla, Mexican green, Durban poison, Congo bush, Acapulco gold, Acapulco red (geographical 'trade' names); homegrown (home cultivated); bad shit (better-than-average drugs)

3. *marijuana or hashish cigarette:* bag of bones, bomber, bones, doobie, dubee, duby, j, joint, ju-ju, no-brand cigarette, no-name cigarette, off-brand cigarette, skoofer, skoofus, skroofus, spliff, stencil, stick, stogie, toke, toothpick (US Black), tuskie (US Black); spec. burnie, roach (remains of a cigarette); crutch, roach clip (gadget to hold the hot 'roach'); papers, skins (cigarette papers); makings

(content of a 'joint'); hit, toke (puff of a cigarette)
4. *hallucinogens:* acid, LSD; spec. clear light, mellow yellow, Owsley, strawberry fields, sunshine, window pane ('trade names); angel dust, hog, steam (phencyclidine); businessman's trip (DMT); mesc (mescalin)
5. *MDMA:* acid, Adam, apples, big brown ones, biscuit, burgers, clarity, decadence, disco biscuit, doctor, dollar, domex, double-M (i.e. *MDMA*), dove, E (i.e. 'ecstasy'), ecky, ecstasy, eggs, elkies, energiser, essence, fantasia, grey biscuit, hamburger, hammer and sickles, hug drug (its users 'love' each other), Kinder Eggs, Kleenex (it blows one's mind rather than nose), love dove, love drug, M25 (ref. to the site of many 'orbital raves'), New Yorkers, orbit (i.e. orbital), pink flamingoes, – studs, rhubarb and custards, rolling, running, snowballs, speed for lovers, swans, vitamin A (i.e. *a*cid), – E (i.e. *e*cstasy), – X (i.e. *e*cstasy), white callies, – dove, whizz-bomb, x (i.e. *e*cstasy), XTC (i.e. ecstasy), yellow callies
6. *amyl nitrate:* aroma, poppers
v. 7. *to smoke drugs:* blast, do a number, take a hit, toke (down); spec. bogart, double-clutch (take more than one's share), shotgun (blow smoke into another's mouth); cuff (to hide a burning cigarette)

507. Experience and Effects
n. 1. *hard drug use:* rush (immediate effects of a narcotic injection); spec. OD (overdose)
2. *soft drug use:* charge, high, stone, turn-on; spec. hashover (cannabis hangover); trip (LSD experience)
3. *bad experience:* bring-down, bummer, bum trip, freak-out, horrors
v. 4. *to take a drug:* do, do up, get behind
5. *to 'get high':* blow one's mind, do one's head, fly, get Chinese, – high, – low, make one right (US Black), ride the wagon (US Black), – tough (US Black), toot one's horn; spec. freak out (have an unpleasant drug experience; come down (to feel the effects of the

drug end); go on the nod, nod, nod out (to fall asleep when using heroin)
6. *to look after a drug user:* babysit
adj. 7. *'drugged':* spacey, trippy, weird
adv. 8. *experiencing drugs:* annihilated, bent out of shape, blocked, bombed, charged up, destroyed, fried, fucked up, goofed, have the slows (US Black), high, hopped up, loaded, messed up, on it, ossified, out of it, – of one's brain, – of one's gourd, – of one's mind, – of one's nut, – of one's skull, pilled up, psychedelic to the bone (US Black), ripped, skulled, spaced (out), toasted, twisted, wasted; on the nod, smacked out (intoxicated with heroin)
phr. 9. DFFL (dope forever, forever loaded); someone blew out his/her pilot light

---

COMMERCE

508. Commerce
n. 1. *large sum of money:* big bucks, bundle, fat knot (US Black), megabucks, packet, pile, sting, wedge
2. *small sum of money:* chickenfeed, grubstake, pin money, razoo (Aus.), walk-about money
3. *cheque:* goose's neck (rhy.sl.), total wreck (rhy.sl.); spec. bum map, frog, kite, leaper, rubber cheque, stumer (bad cheque)
4. *rent:* burton (rhy.sl. = Burton-on-Trent), Duke of Kent (rhy.sl.)
5. *corruption:* lurkola (Aus.), payola (payoffs for media exposure); gayola (payoffs that permit the running of gay clubs)
6. spec. California bankroll, Chicago bank roll, flash roll, Kansas City roll, nigger's bankroll (a roll of small bills wrapped in one large one); divvy (dividend); loose ends, mad money, money to burn (spare money); OPM (other people's money – invested in business); quick (instantly available money); rainy-day money (savings); slush fund (contingency fund); whip-round (instant collection of money); whack (a share)

7. *businessmen:* spec. breadhead (obsessed with money); damager (manager); jobber (freelance cabbie); Mr Ten Per Cent (an agent or middleman)

8. *locations:* Arthur (rhy.sl. = J. Arthur Rank), iron tank (rhy.sl.), jug, kaynab (backsl. = bank); Ma and Pa store, Mom and Pop store (corner shops); rip (off) joint (an exorbitantly expensive store); schlock shop (flashy dress shop)

9. *industrial relations:* compo (Aus.: industrial compensation); con and coal (rhy.sl. = dole); dole-bludger (Aus.: dole scrounger); greens (rhy.sl. = greengages = wages), rock of ages (rhy.sl.); time and a half (overtime); sweetheart contract, yellow-dog contract (contracts that favour the company)

10. *cost, bill:* Beecham's pill (rhy.sl.), damage, nut, tab; spec. swindle sheet (expense account)

11. spec. action (business deal); bottom line, real deal (end result, basis); cherry-picking (reviewing rival business ideas); dog (unsaleable item); Jewish piano, – typewriter (cash register); quick and dirty, quick fix (instant remedy); bob a nob (a shilling each)

v. 12. *to spend money:* push the boat out, splurge; spec. blew in, do one's dough (waste money); bounce (pass a dud cheque or have the bank refuse payment on the cheque); catch a cold, hold the baby (lose money on investments)

13. *to invest:* bankroll; spec. pick up the tab (pay a bill)

14. *to earn money:* knock out (plus sum), make change (US Black), pull down (plus sum)

15. *to become rich:* carve a slice, coin (it), make a bomb, – a killing, rake it in, scoop the pool, strike it rich

16. *to sell:* flog, hype, push; spec. whack for (to charge); go like hot cakes (for a commodity to sell fast)

17. *to cost:* set (one) back

18. spec. headhunt (to recruit executives)

adj. 19. *expensive:* pricey, through the nose

20. *free:* buckshee, on the house

adv. 21. spec. hanging-up (cab use: refusing to take unprofitable fares); on the clock (freelance taxi-driving); in the barrel (about to be dismissed); staked long and deep (US Black: investing heavily)

phr. 22. *deriding a small sum of money:* don't spend it all at once

509. Names for Money

n. 1. *money:* ace, ackers, beans, bees and honey (rhy.sl.), big coin, billies, billys, boodle, brass, bread, buff c.r.e.a.m. (*cash rules everything around me*), cabbage, cake, cargo, cheese, clams, cod, cod's roe (rhy.sl. = dough), coin, crumbs, dibs, dinero, do-re-mi, dough, drop-dead money, duckets, duckettes, duckies (US Black), fetti (abbrev. SE con*fetti*), floss, fuck-you money, gangsta roll, gelt, gold, gravy, green, greenbacks, greenies, grip, grits, guineas, gusto, hard money, hoot (Aus.), Jimmy O'Goblins, juice, kale, kylege (WI), lean green, lettuce, link, lolly, long, long green, loot, mail, maphepha (S.Afr.), mass, mazuma, mephepha (S.Afr.), mitt, moolah, mulla, n's (US Black; i.e. 'notes'), nut roll, oscar (rhy.sl. = Oscar Asche = cash), paper, papes, potatoes, readies, ready, rhino, Robert Dinero, roll, samosa, sausage and mash (rhy.sl. = cash), scramble, scratch, scrill, scrilla, shekels, simoleons, slotties, smash, snaps (one 'snaps' a dollar bill), spondulicks, stackola, sugar, swag, tusheroon (US Black), wallpaper, wampum, whistle and toot (rhy.sl. = loot), wong, wonga, yennom (backsl.); spec. crackle, folding stuff, soft money (paper money); long-tailed 'un (large sterling note); paper (money orders, etc.)

2. *pound sterling:* bar, doonups (backsl.), funt (Yid.), oncer, nicker, note, quid, smacker, smackeroo, sov

3. *dollar bill:* clam, skin, slab (see also: green, greenbacks, long green, etc. in n. 1)

4. *small cash sums:* spec. Abergavenny (rhy.sl. = penny), yenep (backsl. = penny); Susy (rhy.sl. = Susy Anna = tanner), tanner (sixpence); tosheroon (half a crown); caser, dollar, Oxford scholar (rhy.sl.) (five shillings); calf

(rhy.sl.), cows (rhy.sl. = cow's calf = half), half a bar, – a sheet (ten shillings, 50p); pony in white (£1.25 in silver); deuce ($2.00); nickel (5 cents); dime (10); quarter (25)

5. *five pounds, five dollars:* fin, finnif, pound note ($5.00); half a cock (rhy.sl. = half a cock and hen = half of ten), Jacks (rhy.sl. = Jack's alive = five)

6. *ten pounds, ten dollars:* sawbuck, sawski ($10.00); cock and hen, cockle and hen (rhy.sl. = ten)

7. *twenty dollars, twenty pounds:* double sawbuck, double sawski ($20); score (£20)

8. *twenty-five pounds:* macaroni (rhy.sl. = pony), pony

9. *fifty dollars:* half a yard

10. *one hundred pounds, one hundred dollars:* big one, C, c-note, century, hun, one bill, yard ($100); big one, century (£100)

11. *one hundred and fifty dollars:* buck and a half

12. *two hundred pounds:* twoer

13. *five hundred pounds:* monkey

14. *one thousand pounds, one thousand dollars:* g, grand, K

510. Loans; Debts, etc.

n. 1. *usurer:* loan shark, shark, shy, shylock; spec. Uncle (pawnbroker)

2. *credit:* drip, never-never, slate, sub, tick; spec. lay-by (Aus.: deposit paid in a shop); sharking (practising usury)

3. *interest:* juice, vig, vigorish

4. *location:* hockshop

v. 5. *to loan:* spot, sub (for); spec. nail (charge with a debt); hold paper on (stand as creditor)

6. *to pawn:* hock

7. *to purchase on credit:* drip it up, put on the slate, – on tick, etc. (see adj. 11)

8. *to pay one's debts:* ante up, brass up, pony up; spec. welch (to refuse to pay debts)

adj. 9. spec. financial (Aus.: in credit, solvent); in hock, to the bad, up the spout (in debt)

10. *owing:* into (one for)

11. *on credit:* on the cuff, – the slate, – tick; spec. on the drip, the never-never (on hire purchase); on appro (on approval)

GAMBLING

511. Gambling and Wagering

n 1. action; spec. Lombard Street to a China orange (the longest possible odds); cert, dead cert, million (certain winner); on the Murray cod (Aus. rhy.sl.), on the nod, payday stakes (betting on credit)

2. *gambler:* high roller, punter; spec. mug punter (foolish gambler)

3. *money:* bundle (large sum); short-end money (betting on a loss); smart money (bets made by experts)

4. *locale:* spieler (gambling club); plot (site of a three-card monte game); blower (tannoy system in a betting shop)

v. 5. *to bet:* play, punt, put one's shirt on, spiel (Yid.), splosh it on; spec. go for the doctor (Aus.), shoot for the sky, – for the moon (bet all one's money)

6. spec. make book (work as a bookmaker)

adj. 7. big (multiples of ten thousand; thus 'big nickel' = $5,000)

adv. 8. *at stake:* on the line; spec. on the short end (the unfavourable end of the odds)

phr. 9. spec. put up or shut up (bet, don't talk)

512. Winning and Losing

n. 1. *a win:* motsa (Aus.), skinner (Aus.); spec. dirty money (dishonourable gains)

2. *loss:* tap city

3. *loser:* provider, pooch

v. 4. *to lose:* dog it

5. *to beat:* clean out, take to the cleaners

6. *to pay debts:* come across; spec. welch (to refuse to pay debts)

adj. 7. *impoverished:* skinned, tapioca, tapped out

adv. 8. *winning:* hot, in the money, on a roll, – a rush

9. *losing:* in the hole

513. Persons

n. 1. *gambler:* punter; spec. hustler (professional gambler)

2. spec. hot dog (successful); hardnose (cautious); knocker (one who defaults on debts); kibitzer, railbird, sightseer (watchers, not players); shill, steerer (house player); sucker-bait (female used to lure gamblers); take-out guy (member of card-sharping team)

514. Horse-racing

n. 1. airs and graces (rhy.sl. = races)

2. *horses:* gee-gees; spec. pelter (fast horse); dead cert (a winning horse); dead 'un (Aus.), quitter, stiff 'un, undertaker job (a losing horse); closer (horse on whom odds shorten); underlay (horse on whom odds increase)

3. *locations:* canal boat (rhy.sl. = the Tote); flapping track (small, unlicensed track); smoked haddock (rhy.sl. = the paddock)

4. *people:* chalk eater (one who bets on favourites only); horseplayer (better); hot walker (groom who walks horses after the race)

5. *the race:* boil over (Aus.: an upset); dead cert, romp (absolute certainty); the off (start)

6. *betting:* dope sheet, morning line, scratch sheet (racing form); Heinz (a combination bet); on the nose (a bet to win rather than place or show)

v. 7. spec. dope, dope out, – the ponies (to work out bets); go for the doctor (Aus.: for a horse to draw ahead); go through the card (bet on every horse); nobble (interfere with a horse); play the gee-gees (bet on races); pull (deliberately pull up a horse)

515. Cards

n. 1. bladder of lard (rhy.sl.), broads, flats, Wilkie Bard (rhy.sl.); spec. readers (marked cards); case card (last card of the four suits in each denomination to turn up); bullet (ace), deuce (two), trey (three), trips (three of a kind), whore (the queen)

2. *card games:* skin game (US Black); spec. find the lady, monte, three-card monte ('the three-card trick')

3. spec. mechanic (cardsharp); tells (tics and mannerisms that betray poker bluffing)

v. 4. *to play cards:* spread the broads; spec. kibitz (watch a game)

5. *spec. poker uses:* bring it in (for the lowest card to start betting); coffeehouse (to bluff); fold (cease betting on a hand); sandbag (bluff by checking the bet); tight-weak (weakness in play)

adj. 6. *marked deck:* spooked

excl. 7. *deal the cards!:* hit me!

516. Dice; Bingo, etc.

n. 1. *dice:* African dominoes, bones, tatts; spec. flats, tops (doctored dice)

2. *dice player:* gunner, shooter

3. *playing dice:* fading game (players bet against each other and not against a bank); hard way (throwing pairs to make even points in craps); jacking off (shaking dice up and down)

4. spec. numbers, policy ('numbers' gambling); April fools (rhy.sl. = football pools)

5. *names of points in craps:* snake-eyes (pair of one 1s; 2); ace-deuce, trey (3); little Josie, little Joe (from Kokomo) (4); fever in the South, five in the South, (Little) Phoebe (5); Jimmy Hix, sixty days (6); craps (2, 7 or 12 as a loss); natural (7 as a win or 11); Ada from Decatur, eighter from Decatur (8); Nina from Carolina, Nina with her hair down (9); big Dick (from Boston) (10); box cars (12)

6. *names of numbers in bingo (many are rhy.sl.):* buttered scone, Kelly's eye (1); dirty old Jew, me and you (2); you and me (3); knock at the door (4); God's in heaven (7); garden gate, Harry Tate (8); doctor's orders (9); cock and hen, Downing Street (10); legs eleven (11); monkey's cousin (12); unlucky for some (13); rugby team (15); never been kissed (17); blind twenty (20; thus 'Blind thirty', 'Blind forty', etc.); all the twos (22; thus 'all the threes', 'all the fours', etc.); two ducks, dink-do (22); Pompey whore (24); bed and breakfast, half a crown (26); speed limit (30); all the steps (39); half-way house (50); all the

beans (57); stop work (65); clickety click (66); was she worth it? (76); two little crutches (77); two fat ladies (88); top of the house (99 or 100)

phr. 7. *toss the dice!:* roll them bones!

Guide to Using the Index

1. This Index has been prepared on a computer database and as such conforms in its alphabetical order to the rules that are part of the standard ASCII (American Standard Code for Information Interchange) data transmission system. In practical terms, as experienced by the user of such an alphabetical system, ASCII listings work as follows.

Assuming that a list contains a number of examples of the same word, differentiated by capitals, punctuation marks and so on, the ASCII system will sort them thus: Fully capitalised words, initially capitalised words, lower case words, words incorporating a bracket, words incorporating a punctuation mark (!?*), words incorporating a hyphen. Thus:

AND 76.3	and 20.15	and! 94.5
And 234.1	and (and) 23.1	and-some 272.3

This order, when capitals, punctuation marks, etc. have to be considered, supercedes any non-computer-based alphabetical rules. Other than these differences, the basic alphabetical listing of individual words remains as would be expected in any dictionary.

2. For the purposes of this Thesaurus, the words listed in this Index have been designated typographically as follows.

LOVE 123–127: a comprehensive section of the book, comprising a number of subsections and identifying a wide-ranging topic which has been broken down into a number of more specific sections.

Love 123: a single sub-section of the book dealing with a single specific topic.

Love 125.1: a keyword as listed within a specific sub-section; usually one of the parts of speech defined within that sub-section.

love 125.17: the slang words included at large within the Thesaurus.

Index

act of surpassing 20.1
act on the square 305.3
act suspiciously 161.3
act the nigger 298.2
act unpleasantly 278.3
act up 276.6
act your age 146.7, 230.3
action 49.1, 276.2,
  508.11, 511.1
action piece 71.1
active 495.1
ACTIVITY 236–243
Acton Hilton 195.6
actor 435.1
acts like shit wouldn't melt
  in her mouth 401.3
AD 503.2
ad lib 12.2
Ada from Decatur 516.5
Adam 506.5
Adam and Eve 86.27,
  160.2
Adam and Eve on a raft
  86.27
Adam and Eve on a raft
  and wreck 'em 86.27
Adam's ale 67.1
Addicks 179.1
addict 145.3
addict to drugs 505.13
addiction to narcotics 503.5
addle-pated 169.5
addled 101.3, 169.5
addlepate 431.1
adjust one's set 118.14
adjust the bowl of fruit
  118.14
admirable person 394
admitting ignorance 145.5
adrift 169.5
adult 306.5, 357.10,
  501.5
adulterate drugs 502.11
adulterated drugs 502.5
adulterous lover 441.4
advantage 259
advertise 299.2
advice 495.5
advisor 400.5
af 506.1
aff 506.1
affected 142.4
AFFIRMATION 199–200
afflicted 101.3
affliction 101.1
Afghan 506.1

Afghani 506.1
afloat 101.3
afraid 296.7
African dominoes 516.1
African golf ball 86.14
afro 120.1, 428.7
afro set 47.3
Afs 384.1
after 2.6
after 349.4
afterlife 326
afternoon 3.8
afternoon delight 359.3
agates 116.36
age 111
age before beauty 345.2
aggravation 284.1
aggressive 344.7
aggro 338.1
agony 179.8
agony aunt 456.3
agree 340.2
agreed verbally 470.3
agreement 340
agreement 340.4
ahead of the game 20.5,
  216.6, 257.5
aid 495.1
ailments 125
ain't holding no air 311.6
ain't it the truth! 199.3
ain't long enough 376.2
ain't love grand 273.7
ain't that a fact 164.12
ain't that a fact! 199.3
ain't that so 164.12
ain't that so! 199.3
ain't that something 273.7
ain't that the truth 164.12
ain't we got fun 273.7
ain't worth wiping your
  ass on 235.10
air 146.3, 353.1
air hose 82.15
air out 59.2
airball 431.1
aircraft 75.7
airhead 431.1
airmail 235.2
airs and graces 83.14,
  116.5, 514.1
airy-fairy 19.6
aka 478.1
Al Capone ride 75.2
Aladdin's cave 460.3
Alan Whickers 82.10

alcohol seller 92.1
alcohol: general types
  94, 95
**alcohol: manufacture,
  sale** 103
alcohol: types 95
alcoholic 429.4
alderman's nail 115.6
aled up 101.3
alert 148.7
Alf 383.2
alias 306.3
alias man 458.8
alibi out of 317.4
Alice Blue Gown 495.1
alien 440.2
alive and kicking 123.3,
  148.7
alkied 101.3
alky 94.1, 429.4
all and then some 378.2
all anyhow 40.1, 151.7
all at sea 101.3, 168.5,
  169.5
all at sixes and sevens
  168.5
all balled up 169.2, 250.2
all behind like a fat
  woman 169.4
all bets are off 10.3, 10.8,
  112.10
all chiefs and no indians
  448.3
all done by mirrors 310.2
all dressed up and
  nowhere to go 282.5
all dressed up like a pox-
  doctor's clerk 142.2
all fine and dandy 27.3
all fingers and thumbs
  254.6
all for 267.4
all gummed up 250.2
all hands 378.2
all hopped up 172.3
all in 243.4
all in one 360.6
all kidding aside 161.6
all kidding aside! 199.3
all mops and brooms
  101.3
all mouth and trousers
  299.3, 401.1
all my eye and Betty
  Martin 146.2
all of a doodah 262.7

all of a heap 173.6
all of a tiswas 262.7
all of a tizzy 262.7
all on one's lonesome
  213.6
all out (of) 25.5
all out 49.11
all over 41.8
all over bar the shouting
  10.8
all over oneself 273.5,
  297.3
all over the board 147.5,
  231.6
all over the map 41.8
all over the place 5.5
all over the shop 5.5, 41.8,
  51.5
all piss and wind 299.3
all points bulletin 283.1
all reet 275.4
all reet! 199.3
all right! 199.3
all right for some 333.2
all screwed up 250.2
all shot 7.15, 25.5, 124.5,
  127.2, 243.4
all sorts 18.2
all that jazz 24.2
all the beans 516.6
all the steps 516.6
all the twos 516.6
all the way 49.11
all the way! 285.5
all the way live 275.6
all the world and his
  brother 378.2
all the world and his wife
  378.2
all there 123.3, 143.5
all there (with the goods)
  148.7
all thumbs 254.6
all tits and teeth 425.1
all to cock 5.5
all to fuck 127.2
all to hell 7.15
all to pieces 7.15
all to shit 169.4
all to smash 7.15
all to the good 123.3
all torn up 10.8
all up (with) 10.8
all up 112.10
all washed out 112.10
all washed up 112.10

all ways to hell 232.5
all ways to shit 232.5
all wet 7.14, 101.3
all wind and piss 401.1
all wool and a yard wide
  27.3, 139.5, 164.8,
  305.8
all yours! 288.5
all-American drug 505.3
all-fire(d) 189.4
all-fired 18.10
all-originals 384.2
alley cat 433.1
alley rat 433.1
alley whipped 376.4
alley-oop! 55.3
Allied Irish 360.9
allies 438.2
alligator 437.2
allow 204.4
allurement 220
almighty 18.8
almond 116.34
almonds 83.5
alone 213.6
along 38.1
Alphonse 498.2
already 2.4
also-ran 414.1
altar 79.1
alter 11.2
alter one's opinion 209.4
alternative 212.2
am I lying? 312.4
amateur hour 254.5
amaze 173.3
amber fluid 95.1
amber liquid 95.1
amber nectar 95.1
ambidextrous 357.9
ambition 269
ambitious 236.8
ambulance 75.11
ambulance chaser 456.4
ambush (v.) 338.7
American 383.1
amigo 328.10
ammo 72.1
ammunition 72
amount 16
amp 502.4
amscray 54.3, 211.3
amster 480.3
amuse 277.2
amusing person 406
Amy-John 404.2

amyl nitrate 506.6
an Indian 86.26
an excess of leaders 448.3
anchors 76.2
and don't you forget it!
  199.3
and how 18.9, 273.7,
  340.5
and how! 159.4
and no mistake 164.12
and that's a fact! 199.3
and then some 18.2,18.9
and you! 292.7
Andy Cain 66.4
Andy Capp 119.7
angel 180.1, 400.2, 404.5,
  425.1
angel dust 506.5
angel kisses 116.27
angel with a dirty face
  404.5
angel-face 180.1
anger 280
angie 505.3
angle 163.4, 232.1, 232.3
angry 280.6
anilingus 360.4
animal 395.1
animal house 48.4
animals 115
ankle along 59.2
ankle-biter 381.2
Anna Maria 79.5
Annie Oakley 190.2
annihilated 507.8
anno domini 111.1
annoy 280.4, 284.2
annoyance 284
annoyed 284.5
annoying person 397
anoint 318.5
anointing 318.3
another story 26.1
answer the last muster
  112.5
answer the last roll-call
  112.5
answer the last round-up
  112.5
ante up 510.8
anticipation 172
antifreeze 505.2
antique 382.1
ants in (one's) pants
  263.1
antsy 263.4

bamboozle 168.3, 219.5, 310.4
bamboozler 168.2
banana 425.1
banana bender 385.1
banana oil 146.2, 183.2, 287.1
bananaland 45.1
bananas 147.5, 404.1
band 380.1
band in the box 125.10
band of hope 69.8
band rat 437.3
Band-aid 456.1
bandit 458.1
bang (in the arm) 505.9
bang 2.11, 18.10, 32.3, 94.8, 164.11, 236.2, 262.2, 273.1, 337.2, 359.1, 359.6, 506.1
bang around 236.4
bang away (at) 205.2
bang away 241.7
bang like the shithouse door in a gale 359.7
bang off 2.11, 337.7
bang on 27.3, 164.9, 164.10, 184.2, 275.4
bang out 151.3, 239.3
bang the bishop 360.19
bang the drum for 286.2
bang to rights 159.3, 162.7, 164.10, 489.5
bang up (against) 38.6
bang up 22.7, 27.3, 164.9, 494.9, 505.11
banger 75.3
bangers 116.36
bangtail 497.2
banjaxed 7.13
banjo 69.11, 337.4
banjy boy 404.1
bank on 159.2, 160.4
banker 60.2
bankroll 508.13
bannocks 116.36
banter 293
bar 506.1, 506.2, 509.2
bar steward 433.1
barbecue 436.1
barber 196.3
Barbie Doll 425.1
barbs 504.3, 505.3
barcoo salute 118.15
bare-ass 85.6, 117.6
bareback 359.16

barf 118.13
barf! 189.5
barf city 278.1
barf me out! 189.5
barfly 92.3, 423.1
bargain basement 19.7
bargain bucket 116.40
barge 116.40
barge in 53.1, 249.2
barge into 162.4
bark up the wrong tree 316.3
barkeep 92.2
barker 420.4
barker 71.1
barking up the wrong tree 165.4
barley 505.3
barman 92.2
barminess 147.1
barmy 138.4, 147.5
Barnaby Rudge 456.4
barnet (fair) 116.2
barney 116.34, 338.1, 344.1
baron 494.4
baroning 494.11
barrack 188.2
barrack-room lawyer 420.1
barrel (it) 49.4
barrel 337.4, 427.2
barrel of money 375.1
barrelass 204.2
barrelhouse 500.1
barrels 18.2
barrels of fun 276.1
barrels of laffs 276.1
base 292.3, 505.4, 505.12
base! 135.1, 284.
baseball 505.4
bash 7.9, 33.3, 318.5, 337.4, 363.1, 506.2
bashed 101.3
basic 28.2
baskerville 435.3
basket 116.33, 395.1
basket case 429.2
basket picnic 350.1
basketeer 352.5
bastard 252.4, 377.1, 396.1
baste 318.5
baste the tuna 118.14
basted 101.3
basting 318.3

bat (it) around 186.6
bat (it) out 241.6
bat 98.1, 276.3, 409.1, 426.2
bat and wicket 190.2
bat around 58.2, 276.5
bat out of hell 49.3
bat the breeze 183.7, 196.3
bat-fowler 480.3
bate 280.1
bath bun 65.2
bathouse 147.5
bato 383.15
batphone 469.1
bats 138.4, 147.5
bats about 270.5
bats (in the belfry) 124.7
bats in one's belfry 138.2
bats in the belfry 147.1, 147.5
batshit 147.5
batter 98.1
batti 116.30
batting average 495.5
battle 241.6
battle of the purple-helmeted warrior 118.14
battle-cruiser 78.6, 104.1
battleaxe 382.3, 410.2
batty 124.7, 138.4, 147.5
batty about 270.5
battyman 404.1
bawl out 291.2
bawl the (living) hell out of 291.2
bawling out 291.1
Bay City 43.1
bazoo 116.7
bazooka 116.30, 116.34, 505.4
bazoom 116.31
bazoomas 116.31
bazulco 505.3
be a coward 296.3
be a devil! 295.6
be a dickhead 145.2
be a dorkbrain 145.2
be a dumbo 145.2
be a man 295.2
be able 253.3
be about one's speed 137.3
be addicted 503.7
be addled 101.2

black nob 480.3
black on black 76.7
black pak 506.1
Black Power 505.2
Black Power dance 479.1
black rock 505.4, 506.1
black Russian 506.1,
  506.2
black sensibility 260.2
black tar 505.2
black taxi 75.2
black 360 degrees 384.2
black widow 504.2
black wings 360.4
blackjack 217.2
blackleg 241.9, 453.5,
  480.3
blacks (by blacks) 384.2
blacks (by whites) 384.1
blacktop 47.1
bladder 194.3
bladder of lard 515.1
blade 69.9
blades 506.1
blag 310.4, 479.4
blagger 458.7
blah (on) 146.6
blah 19.2, 124.4, 146.3,
  185.1, 185.2, 299.2
blah! 292.8
blam 2.11, 135.1, 164.11
blame 18.10
blame 316
blame unfairly 316.3
blamed 28.2, 189.4
blamelessness 305.2
blanco 384.12, 505.2
Blanco 179.8
blank 150.2, 200.1, 200.2,
  224.3, 493.3, 502.5
blanket man 458.9
blanket party 494.7
blankety 18.8, 18.10,
  28.2, 189.4
blap 164.11
blarney 183.2, 183.19,
  184.1, 287.1, 287.2
blart 116.40, 183.9
blast 113.4, 276.3, 337.7,
  363.1, 506.7
blasted 101.3, 189.4
blat 183.9
blate 116.40
blather 146.3, 184.1
blatherskite 146.2, 299.1,
  401.1

blaze on 338.4
blazes 326.2
blazing (down) 66.1
blazing 18.8
bleary 101.3
bleat 188.1, 188.2, 289.2,
  493.5
bleed (white) 368.3
bleed 384.2
bleed the liver 119.8
bleeder 377.1
bleeding 18.10, 189.4
bleeding dirt 496.1
blend 506.2
bless me! 189.5
bless my heart! 189.5
bless my soul! 189.5
bless you! 285.5
bless your little cotton
  socks 328.10
blessed 18.8, 189.4
blessed event 110.1
blew in 508.12
blighter 377.1
blighty 45.1
bliksem! 395.1
blikskottel 395.1
bliksom! 395.1
blimey! 189.5
blimp 427.2
blind 18.10, 98.1, 101.3,
  116.37, 311.2, 317.2
blind Freddy 414.1
blind pig 104.2
blind staggers 101.1
blind twenty 516.6
blinder 344.1
blinding 27.3
blindside 173.3
blinker 195.9, 486.2
blinking 18.8, 18.10, 22.6,
  189.4
blip 164.11
blister 397.1
blithering 189.4
blitzed 101.3
blob 16.2, 95.11
block 116.4, 494.2, 506.2
blockbuster 18.1, 386.4
blocked 507.8
blocker 458.15
blockhead 431.1
blockheaded 145.3
bloke 377.1, 379.1
blonde 506.2
Blondie 179.11

blood 116.28
blood 384.2, 438.1
blood claat 396.1
blood oath! 199.3
blood wagon 75.11
bloody 18.8, 18.10, 96.1,
  189.4
bloody-minded 206.2
blooey 258.4
blooey! 146.11
blooie 7.4
bloomer 165.1
blooming 18.8, 22.6,
  189.4
blooper 183.1
blop 41.5, 135.1, 164.11
blort 505.3
blossom 180.1
blot 116.29
blot one's copybook 165.3
blotch 69.18
bloviate 183.9
blow (it) 233.4
blow (it)! 54.6, 189.5
blow (n.) 337.2
blow (off) 184.2
blow (oneself out) 89.7
blow (out) 25.4
blow (up) 7.4
blow 7.8, 54.1, 54.3,
  183.7, 211.3, 235.4,
  360.12, 502.4, 505.3,
  505.12
blow a fuse 147.4, 280.3
blow a gasket 280.3
blow a raspberry 292.3
blow ass 49.4
blow away 113.4, 173.3,
  337.7
blow Black 299.2
blow by 361.4
blow down one's ear 183.8
blow fire 239.4
blow great guns 66.8,
  289.2
blow hard 183.9, 299.2
blow heavy 299.2
blow in 52.1, 52.2, 53.1
blow in one's ear 202.4
blow it 127.1, 216.5,
  280.3
blow it out (your arse)!
  292.7
blow me down (with a
  feather)! 173.7
blow my nose! 173.7

bodily fluids 116.28
bodily functions 118
BODY 116–121
body 458.1
body and soul lashing
  69.23
body lover 404.5
body odour 125.18
body queen 404.5
body-snatching 194.6
bodyguard 433.4
boff 274.2, 277.1, 337.4,
  338.5
boffin 495.1
boffins 456.12
boffo 27.3
boffola 277.1
bog 48.6, 79.1, 107.2,
  119.7
bog in 238.4
bog person 395.1
bogart 503.10, 506.7
Bogey 179.8
bogey 495.1
bogeyman 325.4
bogie 495.1
bogman 395.1
bogtrotter 383.12
bogue 12.4, 503.6
bohd 506.2
boho 147.5
bohunk 390.3, 427.1
boil 88.4
boil over 280.3, 514.5
boiled 101.3
boiler 77.1, 382.3
boilerplate 4.8
boiling 18.8
boing-boing 447.2
bo-jack 116.34
boko 116.4, 116.9
bold 347.4
bold as brass 347.4
boldacious 231.5
Bolivian marching
  powder 505.3
bollick 291.2
bollix up 254.2
bollixed 7.13
bollock 364.2
bollock naked 117.6
bollockbrain 395.1
bollocking 291.1
bollocko 117.6
bollocks 116.36, 146.2
bollocks up 254.2

bollocksed (up) 7.13
bollox 146.2
bologna 146.2
boloney 19.2, 146.2
bolshy 342.4
BOLTOP 191.5
bomb 28.1, 258.2, 504.2,
  505.2, 505.4
bomb off 258.2
bomb out 258.2
bombed 101.3, 507.8
Bomber 179.8
bomber 504.2, 506.2,
  506.3
bombs away 505.2
bombshell 173.1
bonaroo 27.3
bonce 116.4
bonds 498.5
bone 116.35, 505.4
bone idle 245.1
bone to pick 334.2
bone up (on) 190.9
bone smuggler 404.1
bone yard 48.6, 112.3
bone-shaker 75.3
bone-stroker 404.1
bonecrusher 505.4
boned 337.10
bonehead 431.1
boneheaded 145.3
boner 118.4
bones 505.4, 506.3, 516.1
bong 73.1, 135.1
bonified 253.7
bonita 505.2
bonkers 145.3
bonzer 27.3
boo 165.1, 506.2
boo-boo 165.1
boob 165.1, 165.3, 390.3,
  391.1, 431.1, 494.1
boob-tube 82.21, 195.1
booboisie 390.1
booby hatch 147.2
boodle 116.40, 509.1
boodler 480.3
booed and hissed 101.3
boofa 431.1
boofer box 69.25
boofhead 431.1
booful 180.1
boog 384.1
boogaloo 276.5, 364.3
boogie 116.40, 276.5,
  364.3, 384.1, 506.2

boogie-woogie 54.3
boogieman 325.4
boogying 364.1
boohonged 101.3
boohoo 281.3
boojie 451.1
book (the joint) 132.6
book 190.7
book 54.3, 194.3,
  489.2
book it 190.9
book up 190.9
boola-boola 188.1
boolhipper 82.12
boom 73.1
boom-boom 119.3
boomer 18.1
boondocks 46.1
boondoggle 235.3
boonie 390.2
boonie hat 82.17
boonie rat 456.1
boonies 46.1
booshwah 146.2
boost 285.2, 286.1,
  286.2, 341.1, 341.2,
  341.3, 479.4
booster 458.15, 479.3
boosting 479.1
boot (around) 337.4
boot (out) 24.5, 63.2
boot 32.3, 63.1, 94.8,
  118.13, 224.2, 242.4,
  384.2, 454.1
boot-hill two-step 119.5
boot-out 63.1
boot-snitch 435.3
booted 63.4
bootlick 287.3
bootlicker 418.1
booty 116.40, 380.1
booty-buffer 404.1
booze 94.1, 97.3
booze artist 92.3
booze hound 92.3
booze it up 97.3
booze joint 104.1
booze-up 98.1
boozed 101.3
boozed up 101.3
boozer 78.6, 92.3, 104.1
boozing 97.1
bop 41.5, 56.1, 59.2,
  73.1, 135.1, 338.3,
  338.5
bopper 381.5

break loose 276.5
break my heart 271.7
break one's arse 241.6
break one's balls 291.4
break one's chops 183.7, 184.2
break one's luck 497.15
break one's neck 238.5, 241.6
break squelch 183.14
break the bank 215.5, 257.2
break up 274.4, 274.5, 331.2
break up with 331.2
break wind 118.8
break-up 331.1
breaker 479.3
breakfast 89.3
breakfast cereals 86.17
breaking 364.3
breaking wind 118.2
breaks 214.1, 215.1
breathe down one's neck 344.2
breathing down one's neck 38.6
breed 383.11
breeders 377.1, 404.5
BREEDING 141–142
breeze 251.1
breeze along 53.1
breeze in 52.2, 53.1, 249.3
breezer 118.2
breezy 274.9
brekker 89.3
Brenda 495.1
Brenda Bracelets 495.1
brew 87.2, 95.1, 505.11
brew dog 95.1
brew up 88.1
brewer's droop 118.4
brewha 95.1
brewhaha 95.1
brewhound 432.3
brewski 95.1
bribe (n.) 372.2, 482.2
bribe (v.) 372.3
bribery 372
brick 68.5, 394.1, 502.4, 506.2
brick gum 505.2
brickhouse 425.1
brickie 456.8
bricks 47.2

Bricktop 179.11
bridewell 495.8
brief 456.4, 488.2
brig 494.1
Brigham 179.8
bright 384.4
bright and early 2.13
brill 27.3
brilliant 404.5
bring down 220.3, 279.5, 282.2, 300.4
bring down the house 257.2
bring home the bacon 239.5, 257.2, 371.5
bring it in 515.5
bring one up 291.2
bring oneself off 118.14, 360.19
bring the house down 274.5
bring-down 282.1, 300.2, 507.3
briny 67.2
Bristol City 116.31
bristols 116.31
bro 438.1
broad 380.1, 437.3, 497.9
broad in the beam 37.3, 117.1
broadcast 183.9, 299.2
broadcasting 183.1
broads 515.1
broadsman 480.3
broccoli 116.39, 506.2
brodie 7.4, 56.1, 258.1
broke (to the wide) 376.5
broken 7.13
broker 416.1
brolly 69.21
bronco 404.5
Bronx cheer 293.1
broom 49.4, 54.3
brooming 481.1
broomstick 427.6
brothel 500.1
brothel creepers 82.15
brothel stompers 82.15
brother 273.7, 438.1
brothers 384.2
Brough 179.1
brougham 75.2
brought down 279.7
brown 360.15, 506.1
brown artist 404.1

brown bomber 495.3
brown coat 456.13
brown crystal 505.2
brown dirt cowboy 404.1
brown envelope 224.2
brown family 404.1
brown hatter 404.1
brown off 284.2
brown pipe engineer 404.1
brown stuff 505.5
brown sugar 505.2
brown wings 360.4
brown-eye 116.29, 360.5
brown-nose 287.3
brown-noser 418.1, 439.5
brown-slice 338.5
brown-tongue 439.5
brownbag 97.3
browned off 284.5
brownie 95.5, 116.29, 506.1
brownie point 303.1
browning 360.5
Browning family 404.1
Browning sisters 404.1
bruce 404.1
bruiser 427.1, 433.3
brummagem 311.5
brummy 28.2, 385.1
bruno 44.2
brush 116.39, 348.1, 353.1
brush (off) 63.1
brush off 113.4, 150.1
brush one's teeth 360.13
brush-off 25.2, 348.1
Brussel sprouts 378.3
brute 252.4, 427.1
BS 146.2, 183.2, 183.19, 299.1, 299.2, 310.7, 312.1, 312.2
BSHs 116.31
BTM 116.30
bu 506.2
bub 178.3, 381.3
bubble 83.2, 193.4, 383.9, 472.1
bubble and squeak 119.2
bubblebutt 116.30
bubble-gum 505.4
bubble-gummer 381.5
bubbled 193.8, 473.5
bubblehead 431.1
bubbler 480.3
bubbly 95.4

bubby 178.3

Buck 179.8, 179.10

buck (against) 289.2

buck (for) 205.2, 238.5

buck 72.1, 210.2, 458.1

buck and a half 509.11

buck for 238.5

buck private 410.1

buck up 128.4, 148.2, 274.6, 274.7, 295.3, 295.6

buck's night 3.3

bucket 116.29, 116.30, 116.40, 292.4, 494.1

bucket down 66.7

bucket gaff 480.1

bucket job 480.1

bucketing down 66.3

buckled 101.3

bucko 231.5, 433.3

buckshee 508.20

buckwheat 384.4

bud 381.5

bud sesh 503.3

buda 506.2

buddha 506.2

buddy 116.34, 178.3, 438.1

buddy up 328.2

buddy-buddy 328.7

buddyseat 76.4

budgie 435.3, 473.2

buf 425.2

buff (n.) 509.1

buff boy 497.9

buff one's helmet 118.14

buff the banana 118.14

buff the bishop 118.14

buff the happy lamp 118.14

buffalo 218.3, 336.2

buffalo piss 95.1

buffer 382.2

bufu 404.1

bug 69.26, 116.40, 284.2, 408.1, 494.7

bug-eyed 101.3

bug juice 494.7

bug out 54.3

bug pass 494.4

bugger (it) up 165.3

bugger 252.4, 379.1, 396.1, 404.1, 433.1, 505.2

bugger! 189.5

bugger about 146.4

bugger all 23.3

bugger me! 173.7, 189.5

bugger off 54.3, 54.6

bugger off! 278.7

bugger up 7.8, 33.3, 254.2

bugger you! 189.7

bugger's grips 120.2

buggeration! 284.8

buggered 173.6, 252.12, 258.4

buggered up 7.13, 126.2

buggering 189.4

buggerlugs 328.10

buggin's turn 8.2

buggins 180.1

buggle 180.1

buggy 75.1

bughouse 146.2, 147.2, 147.5

bughutch 78.8

bugle 116.9, 505.3

bugs 431.1

bugs about 270.6

buick 118.13

build a log cabin 119.7

build-up 285.2, 287.1

building 78.1

BUILDINGS 78–81

built 35.4, 117.11, 117.12

built like a brick outhouse 32.6, 37.3, 117.12

built like a brick shithouse 32.6, 37.3, 117.12

built that way 137.3

bulbs 116.36

bull (along) 310.7

Bull 179.10

bull 146.2, 146.3, 146.6, 183.2, 183.19, 287.1, 287.2, 293.5, 299.1, 299.2, 310.1, 312.1, 312.2, 404.3, 495.1

bull! 146.11

bull and cow 344.1

bull artist 418.1, 420.5

bull dagger 404.3

bull muffin 146.1

bull sesh 186.1

bull session 186.1, 196.2

bull-dyke 404.3

bull-fiddle 69.24

bullcrap 146.2

bulldog 194.3

bulldoze 336.2

buller 404.1

bullet 62.2, 515.1

bullet-proof 32.6

bullia capital 505.4

bullion 505.4, 506.2

bullnecked 206.2

bullpen 48.1

bullrag 336.2

bullsh 146.2

bullshine 146.2

bullshit 146.2, 146.6, 183.2, 183.19, 219.5, 287.2, 299.1, 299.2, 310.1, 310.7, 312.1, 312.2

bullshit! 146.11

bullshit artist 401.1, 420.5

bullshitter 420.5

bullwash 146.1

bully (for you)! 285.5, 292.7, 345.2

bully 27.3, 123.3, 273.6

bully beef 494.5

bullyon 505.4, 506.2

bullyrag 294.3, 294.6

bum 28.1, 28.2, 60.7, 116.30, 311.5, 396.1, 414.1, 417.3, 437.3

bum around 58.2, 244.1

bum chum 404.1

bum deal 258.1

bum fodder 79.3

bum map 508.3

bum off 368.2

bum plumber 404.1

bum soup 119.5

bum steer 165.1, 192.4, 192.7

bum trip 258.1, 507.3

bum's rush 63.1

bum-boy 404.1

bum-fluff 116.10

bum-freezer 82.12

bum-rap 196.3

bum-sucker 418.1

bumchat 352.7

bumf 79.3, 191.4

bumhole 116.29

bummed 101.3

bummed out 279.7

bummer 258.1, 507.3

bump (off) 113.4

bump 63.1, 63.2, 242.5, 359.2

bump into 162.4, 362.3

bump oneself off 112.7

bumper 18.7, 106.3, 404.3, 479.3

bumper kit 116.30
bumpers 116.31
bumpity-bump 57.1
bumps 252.3
bunch of fives 116.16
bunch punch 360.6
bunco 310.2, 480.1, 480.3
bunco artist 480.3
bunco man 480.3
bunco squad 495.4
bunco-steerer 480.3
bundle 375.2, 505.2,
  508.1, 511.3
bundle of laughs 406.1
bunfight 363.1
bung 62.3, 116.29, 372.2,
  372.3, 482.2
bung-ho! 99.1
bungalow 255.6
bunged up 124.4
bunghole 116.29, 116.30,
  116.40, 360.15
bungo 384.12
bungy 69.18
bunk 54.2, 146.2, 183.2,
  211.1, 211.3, 310.1
bunk down 247.3
bunk off 54.3
bunk-up 359.1
bunker 404.1
bunko 480.3
bunkum 146.2, 183.2,
  310.1, 311.1
bunny 180.1, 183.1,
  183.7, 497.9
buns 116.30
bunty 382.3
buoyant 101.3
burbed out 227.3
burble 135.2, 183.7,
  184.1, 184.2
bureaucracy 191.4
bureaucrats 456.6
burg 42.1, 431.1
burgers 506.5
burglar 404.1, 480.3
burgle 360.15
burgoo 86.17
buried 494.12
BURMA 191.5
burn 106.2, 113.3, 144.4,
  280.4, 282.2, 284.1,
  284.2, 301.1, 310.6,
  353.3, 468.1, 502.6
burn down 243.1
burn one's shoulder 101.2

burn out 243.1, 243.3
burn rubber 60.4
burn up 284.2
burn with a low blue flame
  101.2
burn-out 429.1
burn-up 60.2
burned (at) 280.6
burned down 243.4
burned out 124.6, 243.4
burner 480.3
burnese 505.3
burnie 506.3
burning down habit 503.5
burnt 79.4, 282.4
burnt offering 86.2
burp the worm 118.14,
  360.19
burrito 116.34
burro 115.8
burst 274.4, 337.4
burst one's bubble 300.4
bursting (for) 268.4
burton 508.4
bury (it) 171.1
bury 112.8
bury a quaker 119.7
bury the hatchet 330.2
bush 21.3, 116.39, 505.3,
  506.2
bush league 28.2
bush patrol 351.1, 359.1
bush telegraph 196.2
bushed 243.4
bushel and peck 116.21
busher 431.1
Bushey Park 276.3
bushranger 480.3
bushwa 19.2, 28.1, 146.2
business 119.1
business 22.3
business boy 497.9
business end 234.1
business girl 497.2
businessman 456.16
businessman's trip 506.4
businessmen 508.7
Busky 179.8
bust (one) up 337.4
bust (out) 54.2
bust (up) 7.13, 10.5,
  331.2, 356.2
bust 7.4, 7.6, 73.1, 162.5,
  165.1, 218.3, 242.5,
  258.1, 276.3, 363.1,
  489.1, 489.4

bust a blood vessel 280.3
bust a grape 238.5, 241.6
bust a gut 205.2, 238.5,
  280.3
bust caps 73.3
bust in 53.1, 53.2
bust loose 309.3
bust loose on 318.4
bust one's arse 205.2,
  238.5, 241.6
bust one's hump 238.5,
  241.6
bust one's nuts 238.5,
  241.6
bust some booty 359.6
bust-out 18.10, 89.5
bust-up 7.4, 10.2, 331.1,
  356.1
busted 376.5
buster 178.3, 382.1, 435.3
busting 263.4, 264.3
bustle-punching 496.1
busy 241.10
busy 495.2
busy as a one-armed
  paper-hanger (with the
  itch) 241.10
but good 27.1
Butch 179.10
butch 404.1
butcher 456.2
butcher knife 116.34
butcher's 124.4, 132.1
butcher's window 116.40
butt 106.2, 106.3, 116.30,
  431.1
butt in 183.15
butt out 249.4
butt out! 201.6, 292.7
butt plug 431.1
butt-fuck 360.15
butt-plunger 436.4
butter 116.30, 116.40,
  380.1, 505.4, 506.2
butter baby 425.1
butter flower 506.2
butter one's corn 360.19
butter up 287.2
butter-and-egg man
  413.1
butterball 427.3
butterbox 383.5, 404.5
butterboy 454.1
buttercup 180.1, 404.1
buttered 84.3
buttered bun 437.3

can't find one's arse with both hands 101.3
can't get it together 33.1
can't hack it 33.1, 254.3
can't hit the ground with one's hat 101.3
can't knock the skin off a rice-pudding 33.1
can't see through a ladder 101.3
can't sus 167.2
can't take it 33.1
can't win them all 258.5
Canadian 383.3
canal boat 514.3
Canaries 179.1
canary 435.3, 456.5, 472.2
cancel one's ticket 113.4
cancer 125.8
candy 425.1, 504.1, 505.3
candy stick 116.34
candy-ass 33.8, 403.1
candy-butt 381.6
candy-striper 453.2
candyman 502.1
cane 83.3
cane 83.3
canned 101.3
canned stuff 505.5
cannibal 436.2
cannon 71.1, 116.34, 479.3
cannot understand 167.2
canoodle 351.3
Canuck 383.3
canyon 116.40
cap 502.4, 502.11, 504.1, 505.4
cap on 294.5
Cape of Good Hope 69.8
caper 478.1
capital punishment 492
caplump 164.11
caplunk 2.11, 164.11
capper 10.3, 20.2, 183.4
caprice 208
caps 505.2, 505.4
capsules 504.1
Captain Cook 132.1, 190.7
capture 489.1, 489.2
captured 489.4
car 75.1
car key 465.1
car park 472.2
caravan 60.4

carb 76.1
card 144.7, 406.1, 409.1, 505.5
card games 515.2
card up one's sleeve 259.1, 374.1
care 149
career boy 497.9
careless 151.5
careless person 393
careless work 151.2
carelessly 151.7
carelessness 151
caress (v.) 351.3
caressing 351
cargo 509.1
Carl Comedian 406.1
Carl Rosa 435.1
carne 505.2
carney 456.5
carnies 114.2
carpark 435.3
carpenter's dream 437.3
carpet 116.39, 291.2, 491.3
carpet-biter 405.2
carpy 494.11
carriage trade 448.1
carrie 505.3
carrie nation 505.3
carriers 69.20
carrot cruncher 390.2
Carrots 179.11
carry 466.4
carry 61.1
carry a case 493.7
carry a torch 353.6
carry on (about) 270.3
carry on 231.4, 276.6, 353.4
carry the can (for) 316.4
carry-on 231.1, 280.2, 280.3
carry-out 78.7
carrying 466.5, 502.14
carrying a load 101.3
cart 61.1
cartnapping 479.1
carve a slice 508.15
carve-up 308.1, 464.1
carvie 494.4
carving knife 444.5
cas 27.3
case (it) around 58.2
case (the joint) 479.4
case 28.1, 494.9, 500.1

case card 515.1
case dough 462.2
case off 54.6
case out 339.2
case over 132.11
case the joint 156.3
caser 494.5, 509.4
cases 164.3
cash and carried 355.7
cash in (on) 234.2
cash in one's chips 112.5
cashed up 375.4
casian 495.1
casmack 164.11
Caspar Milquetoast 403.1
casper 384.4
Casper the Ghost 505.4
cast 495.10
cast nasturtiums 293.4
cast one's optics (at) 132.6
cast one's peepers (at) 132.6
cast the net 498.6
castle hack 435.3
casual partner 441.11
cat 118.13, 377.1, 435.3
cat and mouse 48.2
cat around 58.2, 352.5
cat's pee 94.6
cat's piss 94.6
cat's pyjamas 27.1
cat's whiskers 27.1
catch (merry) hell 318.6
catch (on) 166.2
catch 162.5
catch 134.2, 148.3, 497.13
catch a bite 89.8
catch a buzz 118.14, 360.19
catch a cold 125.16
catch a cold 252.5, 508.12
catch a listen 134.3
catch asleep at the wheel 173.2
catch bending 162.5, 173.2, 259.3
catch cold 162.5
catch flat-footed 173.2
catch forty winks 247.5
catch hell 291.3
catch it (hot) 291.3
catch it 318.6
catch off-base 173.2
catch on the hop 162.5

cheer up – the worst is yet to come! 295.6
cheerfulness 274
cheerie-bye 346.4
cheerio 346.4
cheerio! 99.1
cheers! 99.1
cheese 18.1, 116.28, 118.8, 118.12, 146.1, 164.4, 431.1, 505.4, 509.1
cheese 86.15
cheese dong 431.1
cheese it 211.3
cheese it! 10.9, 201.5
cheese off 284.2
cheese-eater 435.3, 472.2
cheesecake 194.5, 251.5, 425.1
cheesed off 279.7, 284.5
cheesy 7.14, 311.5
cheesy-feet 395.1
cheever 506.2
chemical 505.4
chemist 456.17
chepooka 146.1
cheque 508.3
cherry 1.6, 116.40, 381.7
cherry hogs 78.8
cherry splitter 116.34
cherry-picking 508.11
cherrypop 359.11
chevy chase 116.5
chew (the fat) 183.7
chew face 351.3
chew on that! 153.11
chew one's balls off 291.2
chew out 291.2, 294.6
chew the cud 153.4
chew the fat 152.3, 186.6
chew the rag 184.2, 186.6
chi 505.2
chi-ike 310.4
chic people 450
Chicago bankroll 508.6
Chicago black 506.2
Chicago green 506.2
Chicago lightning 73.2
Chicago piano 71.2, 466.1
Chicago typewriter 71.2, 466.1
chichi 116.31, 358.7
chick 180.1, 380.1, 425.1, 441.3
chickabiddy 381.2

chickadee 180.1
chicken 115.2
chicken 180.1, 296.6, 403.1, 404.5, 426.2
chicken hawk 404.5
chicken out 33.2, 209.3, 296.3
chicken queen 404.5
chicken ranch 500.1
chicken run 60.2
chicken scratchings 190.4
chicken-hearted 296.6
chicken-plucker 395.1
chickenfeed 19.6, 508.2
chickenshit 33.8, 296.6, 403.1
chickenshits, the 119.5
chicky 180.1
chicle 505.2
chico 383.15
chief 431.1
chieva 505.2
child 381.3
child molester 436.5
chili chump 498.3
chili pimp 498.3
chill 112.1, 113.4
chill out 265.3
chiller 198.4
chilli 86.30
chillum 503.3
chilly 95.1
chilly dog 95.1
chimes 116.36
chimney 82.17
chin 116.23
chin-chin 346.4
chin-chin! 99.1
china 438.1
Chinaman's chance 158.2
chinee 190.2
Chinese 383.4
Chinese chance 158.2
Chinese ducket 190.2
Chinese fire drill 5.1
Chinese H 505.2
Chinese no. 3 505.2
chingazo 359.6
chingus 116.34
chink 383.4
chink chow 86.26
chinky 374.4, 383.4
CHINS 458.4
chinwag 152.3, 186.1
chip 478.2, 505.2

chip in 183.15, 341.2, 367.2, 370.2, 370.3
chipper 123.3, 148.7, 236.7, 274.9
chippie 353.3, 437.3, 456.8
Chippy 179.8
chippy 48.6, 344.7, 497.3, 505.11
chippy chaser 395.1, 443.2
chippy on 353.3
chips 116.30
chirp up 274.6
chirpy 236.7
chisel 310.6
chisel out 365.4
chiseler 434.1, 480.3
chiseller 480.3
chitral 506.1
chiv 69.9, 70.5
chive 337.6
chizz 310.6
chizzer 480.3
choad 116.34, 431.1
chocky jockey 404.1
chocolate 384.1, 506.1
chocolate chutney 119.5
Chocolate City 44.1
chocolate frog 435.3
chocolate runway pilot 404.1
chocolate speedway rider 404.1
chocolate stuff 506.1
chode 431.1
choff 86.1
CHOICE 212–213
choice 27.3
choirboys 495.1
choke (it) down 222.2
choke a darkie 119.7
choke off 201.2
choke the chicken 360.19
choke the chook 118.14, 360.19
choked 101.3, 279.7
choked down 84.3
choker 282.1
chokes and croaks 179.4
chokey 494.1, 494.2
chokka 22.2
cholly 505.3
cholo 383.15
chomp at the bit 248.4
choof 54.3

clever 12.3
clever dog 430.2
click (with) 273.3, 328.3
click 233.3, 257.2, 340.1
clicker 505.4
clickety click 516.6
cliffhanger 198.4
climax 505.2, 505.4
climb all over 291.2, 351.3
climb the rigging 280.3
climb the walls 263.2, 280.3
climb trees to get away from it 359.10
climb-down 140.2, 300.2, 302.1
climbing the walls 263.5
clinch 115.4
clincher 10.3, 163.1
clink 494.1
clinkers 119.3
clinking 18.8
clip 337.4
clip joint 78.7, 461.1
clipped 116.38
clippie 456.11
clipster 480.3
clit 116.42
clithopper 437.5
clitoris 116.42
clitty 116.42
clobber 82.1, 337.4
clobber one with 217.2
clobbered 101.3
clock 116.5, 132.6, 337.4
clock 69.17, 81.7
clock a daffy 312.2
clock in 52.2
clock off 241.8
clod 390.2, 431.1
clodpoll 431.1
close 38.6
close but no cigar 27.5
close call 211.2
close shave 38.3, 211.2
close up 202.2
closer 514.2
closet 202.5
closet case 404.5
closet queen 404.5
cloth-ears 433.1
clothes 495.2
clothes 82
clotheshorse 450.1
clotty 395.1
cloud 46.3, 505.4

cloud nine 505.4
clout 116.40, 216.1, 219.1, 479.4
clouting 318.3
clown 395.1, 431.1
clown around 276.6
club 70.2, 78.7
clubs 378.3
cluck 431.1
clucky 109.4
clue (one) in 197.1
clueless 145.3
clumsy 254.6
clunk 337.4, 390.3, 431.1, 452.2
clunker 75.3
clutch 364.2
CNR strawberries 467.1
co 506.2
COs 495.4
coal burner 441.9
coat 82.12
coat and badge 368.2
Coats and 'Ats 179.2
cobber 438.1
cobbler 483.2
cobblers 7.2, 146.2
cobitis 494.7
cobs 116.36
cobweb-cheat 480.3
cocaine 505.3
cochealed 366.4
cochornis 506.2
cock (it) up 165.3, 254.2
Cock 179.8
cock 116.34, 116.40, 146.2, 178.3, 379.1, 380.1, 415.2
cock a deaf 'un 210.2
cock a snoot (at) 347.3
cock a weather eye 149.4
cock and hen 16.3, 509.6, 516.6
cock block 353.2
cock doctor 456.2
cock linnet 3.11
cock movie 195.3
cock off 258.2
cock pluck 351.3
cock sparrow 69.20
cock up 165.3
cock-and-bull story 198.2
cock-eyed 101.3
cock-hound 437.2
cock-locker 116.40
cock-tease 352.8

cock-teaser 352.2, 441.12, 443.1
cock-up 7.2
cockamamie 169.4
cockeyed 5.5, 7.13, 33.5, 40.1
cockface 395.1
cockhead 395.1
cockle and hen 16.3, 509.6
cockmunch 395.1
cocksman 437.2, 497.9
cocksuck 395.1
cocksucker 395.1, 396.1, 404.1
cocksucking 189.4
cocktail 497.9
cocktails 119.5
cocky 178.3, 297.3
coco 116.4
cocoa 87.3
cocoa-shunter 404.1
coconuts 505.3
cod 310.3, 310.5, 310.7, 509.1
cod trench 116.40
cod's roe 509.1
codger 382.2
codology 293.2
cods 116.36, 146.2
cods up 254.2
codswallop 146.2
coffee 87.1
coffee and cocoa! 146.11
coffee coke 505.4
coffee grinder 75.7
coffeeand 28.2
coffeeand habit 503.5
coffeeand pimp 498.3
coffeehouse 515.5
coffin 112.4
coffin nail 106.2
cognoscenti 438.2
coin (it) 508.15
coin 509.1
coin collector 497.9
coitus interruptus 359.5
cojones 116.36, 295.1
coke 505.3
coke freak 503.2
coke head 503.2
coke stare 132.1
cokey 503.2
col 28.1
cold 31.2, 125.3
cold 27.3, 28.1, 28.2,

crackers 138.4, 147.5
crackle 509.1
cracko 147.5
crackola 505.4
crackpot 431.1
crackup 258.1
cracky! 189.5
cradle-snatcher 436.10
craftsmen 456.8
crag 405.1
cram 89.7
cramber 119.7
cramp 125.4
cramp one's style 250.1
crank (up) 236.5, 505.11
crank 76.1, 504.2, 505.4
crank it out 190.8
crank one's shank 360.19
cranny 116.40
crap (all) over 5.4
crap (on) 146.6
crap 19.2, 28.1, 86.2,
    119.3, 119.6, 119.7,
    146.2, 235.2, 310.1,
    312.1, 312.2, 505.2
crap! 146.11
crap around 252.10
crap on 5.4, 299.2
crap out 7.6, 112.5, 215.6,
    243.1, 258.2
crapbrain 395.1, 431.1
craphouse 46.2
crapout 258.1
crapped out 243.4, 247.7
crapper 48.6, 79.1
crappo 28.2
crappy 7.14, 28.2, 235.9
craps 516.5
crapshoot 214.3
crash (out) 247.4, 258.2
crash 119.3, 119.7, 247.3,
    258.1, 495.10
crash 75.15
crash in 53.2
crash out 211.3
crash time 3.9
crash-pad 78.2
crasher 397.1, 417.1,
    429.1, 446.2
crawfish 209.3, 302.3,
    399.1
crawl out from under
    252.9
crawling (with) 5.6
crawling with 22.4
craze 270.2

craze-o 228.3
crazo 409.1
crazy 147.5
crazy 27.3, 268.4
crazy alley 494.2
crazy for 148.8, 268.4,
    270.5, 349.4
crazy house 147.2
crazy to 268.4
crazy-arse 147.5
cream 20.2, 116.28,
    257.2, 338.5, 359.8
cream one's jeans
    262.3
cream-puff freak 499.2
creamie 425.1
creaming 479.1
creampuff 403.1
creamstick 116.34
creamy 505.4
crease (one) up 277.2
crease 338.5
crease up 274.4
creased 243.4
create 231.4, 280.3
create 240.1
creation 240
cred 160.1
credence 160
credit (n.) 510.2
creep 287.3, 363.2, 396.1,
    439.5, 452.2, 479.3,
    498.9
creeper 479.3
creeping Jesus 403.1,
    403.2
creeping and tilling 479.6
creeps 129.1, 263.1, 296.2
creepsville 46.2
creepy 278.5
creepy crawly 115.4
crevice 116.40
crew 378.1, 438.2, 458.2
crewed up 339.6
crib 48.4, 78.2, 310.2,
    463.3, 505.4
crib-man 479.3
crikey 325.2
crikey! 189.5
CRIME 458–496
crime: accusation 473
crime: arrest 489
crime: begging 477
crime: betrayal 473
crime: booty 464
crime: coercion 485

crime: communication
    469
crime: correspondence
    469
crime: corruption 482
crime: devices 465
crime: establishments
    461
crime: evidence 486
crime: examination of
    prisoners 490
crime: explosives 466
crime: food 467
crime: general 478
crime: health 459
crime: illicit goods 464
crime: illicit business
    481
crime: implements 465
crime: information 472
crime: locality 460
crime: money 462
crime: observation 474
crime: persons 458
crime: pursuit 488
crime: search 488
crime: signals 471
crime: speech 470
crime: suspicion 486
crime: tobacco 468
crime: transportation
    methods 475
crime: vagrancy 476
crime: valuables 463
crime: violence 485
crime: weapons 466
Crimea 95.1
criminal 458.1, 478.4
criminal go-between 458.12
criminal planner 458.11
criminal sentence 491
criminal specialists 479.3
criminy 325.2
criminy! 189.5
crimp 218.1, 218.2, 480.3
crimson 44.2
crinched 40.1
crinkle-top 428.7
cripes 325.2
cripes! 189.5
cripple 429.2
crisp 1.6
crispy 429.1
criss-cross 310.4
critic 419
criticise 290.2

cut down to size 291.2
cut gas! 201.5
cut in 367.3
cut it 239.5, 253.3, 257.3
cut it out 146.7
cut it out! 10.9, 146.11
cut it up 363.3
cut loose (with) 62.3, 183.10
cut loose 9.3, 25.4, 54.3, 113.4, 209.2, 213.3, 276.5
cut loose with 239.2
cut no ice 19.4, 271.4
cut off at the pass 249.2
cut one's cable 112.5
cut one's own throat 213.2
cut out 211.3, 350.6
cut that out! 146.11
cut the cake 359.11
cut the chat! 201.5
cut the comedy 146.7, 230.3
cut the crap 146.7, 230.3
cut the crap! 146.11, 201.5
cut the funny business 230.3
cut the mustard 239.5, 253.3, 257.2, 257.3, 275.2
cut the noise! 201.5
cut the rug 364.3
cut up 25.3, 98.2, 276.6, 290.2, 367.2
cut up old scores 170.2
cut up rough 231.4, 337.3
cut up rusty 231.4, 337.3
cut up the cake 339.5
cut up touches (with) 198.8
cut up touches 25.3, 464.3, 470.2
cut-throat 384.5
cutchie 503.3
cute 35.7, 273.6
cutems 180.1
cutes 425.1
cutesie 35.2, 35.7, 180.1
cutesie-pie 35.2, 180.1, 425.1
cutie 425.1
cuts and scratches 69.16
cutter 69.9
cutting the rug 364.1
cutty 438.1

cutup 276.3, 406.1, 447.1
cuz 178.3
CYA 230.2, 255.3
cystitis 125.9

D 495.2
d 27.3
D&D 97.4, 125.14
d.j. 82.3
d.o.a. 505.2, 505.4
DA 120.1
dab 135.1, 238.2, 430.2
dachsie 115.1
dad 178.3, 325.1
dad and dave 120.11
dad-blasted 189.4
dad-gasted 189.4
daddy 273.7, 404.3, 494.4
daddy one 441.2
daddy-o 178.3
Daddylonglegs 179.12
daddylonglegs 427.5
dadgummed 189.4
daffy 138.4, 145.3, 147.5, 165.5
daffy about 270.5
daffydown dilly 145.3
daft 145.3
dag 409.1, 412.1
dagga 506.2
dagger 116.34, 404.3
dago 43.1, 383.13, 383.15
dago red 95.3
dags 119.3
daily 455.1
Daily Excess 179.5
Daily Getsmuchworse 179.5
Daily Mail 116.30, 196.1, 198.1
daily food 89.1
daily grind 226.1
daily-daily 128.3
dairies 116.31
daisy 27.1, 35.2, 273.6
daisy roots 82.15
daisy-chain 360.6
dak 506.2
daks 82.11
dama blanca 505.3
damage 508.10
damaged 101.3
damager 508.7
dame 380.1
Dame Fortune 215.1
damn! 189.5

damn my stars! 189.5
damn right! 199.3
damn your hide 189.7
damn-sakes! 189.5
damnation 189.4
damned clever these Chinese 240.3
damned if I know 145.5
damnit! 189.5
damnit to hell (and back)! 189.5
damp 101.3, 116.40
damper 218.1, 278.1, 463.3, 494.2
Dan 179.8
dance (n.) 364.2
dance (v.) 364.3
dance 479.4
dance on one's lips 337.4
dance on the mattress 359.6
dance with johnnie one-eye 118.14
dancing 364
dandy 27.3
dandy! 285.5
dang(ed) 189.4
danger 256
dangerous 256.5
dangler 116.34
dank 506.2
dank nuggets 506.2
dank nugs 506.2
dap 84.3, 164.11, 346.1
daps 82.16
darbies 465.1
Darby Kelly 116.13
dark complexioned black (by blacks) 384.3
dark meat 384.1
darkie 384.1
darkness at noon 179.4
Darky 179.8, 179.11
darling 273.6
darn! 189.5
darn right! 199.3
darnedest 238.2
darry 132.1
dash 372.1
dash! 189.5
dash in the bloomers 359.1
dash it (all)! 189.5
dashed 28.2, 189.4
date 116.29, 116.30, 354.2, 362.1

do a bunk 54.3, 54.4
do a crib 479.4
do a dry waltz with oneself 360.19
do a fade (on) 209.5
do a fade 211.3
do a fair lick 49.4
do a favour 341.7
do a job 119.7, 478.2
do a job for oneself 119.7
do a job on 7.10, 310.6, 337.4
do a jobbie 119.7
do a kindness 359.6
do a mischief (to) 485.3
do a number (on) 219.4
do a number 54.3, 263.3, 506.7
do a powder 54.3
do a rear 119.7
do a runner 54.3, 211.3, 487.5
do a rural 119.7
do a shift 119.7
do a shit 119.7
do a solid 341.7
do a thing 505.11
do a ton 60.4
do a twos 107.4
do a vanishing act 132.9
do an agricultural 119.7
do any which way 151.3
do as one damn well pleases 213.2
do as you like 75.10
do big jobs 119.7
do brown 7.10, 310.4, 310.6
do down 310.4
do easily 251.4
do everywhichway 151.3
do for 318.4
do handiwork 118.14
do in 7.10, 113.4, 243.3, 505.11
do in the eye 310.4
do it for oneself 496.2
do it like Mommy 239.2
do it one's own way 118.14
do it up (right) 239.4
do like a dinner 259.3
do one dirt 308.2
do one's best 238.6
do one's bit 339.4
do one's block 280.3

do one's business 119.6, 119.7
do one's darnedest 238.6
do one's dirty 119.7
do one's dough 508.12
do one's duty 119.7
do one's head 507.5
do one's level best 238.6
do one's nails 118.14
do one's nut 280.3
do one's own thing 213.2, 230.2
do one's share 339.4
do one's stuff 239.4
do one's thing 212.3
do oneself in 112.7
do oneself off 360.19
do over 7.10, 33.3, 243.3, 252.10, 310.6, 337.4, 338.5
do rag 83.11
do roughly 239.3
do say! 173.9
do skippers 247.4
do something for one's chapped lips 118.14
do something stupid 146.5
do successfully 257.3
do tell! 173.9
do the bachelor's shuffle 118.14
do the backstroke roulette 118.14
do the business on 33.3, 113.4
do the crazy act 146.5
do the dirty (on) 308.2, 314.2
do the disappearing act 211.3
do the do 359.6
do the Dutch 112.7
do the full sesh 204.2
do the Han Solo 118.14
do the handsome thing 305.4
do the honours 363.4
do the job (on) 113.4
do the lolly 280.3
do the nasty 359.6
do the natural thing 359.6
do the party 480.6
do the pussy 359.6
do the vanishing act 211.3
do the whole bit 239.4

do the works 239.4
do to a turn 259.3, 338.5
do up (brown) 7.8, 33.3, 338.5
do up (like a kipper) 7.10, 162.5
do up 4.4, 6.3, 33.3, 338.4, 505.11, 507.4
do up right 162.5
do well 239.4, 253.4
do with 268.2
do you get me? 166.6
do you get my meaning? 166.6
do you need a boy? 502.15
do you read me? 166.6
do you understand? 166.6
do you want drugs? 502.15
do your own thing 118.14
do-dad 69.2
do-hickey 69.2
do-jigger 116.34
do-re-mi 509.1
do-right man 407.1
DOA 459.2
dob in 193.4, 252.8, 370.2, 490.6
dobber 435.3
dobber-in 435.3
dobbin 115.10
dock 41.4, 218.2
dock asthma 490.3
docker 456.15
doctor (up) 203.7, 234.3
doctor 506.5
doctor's orders 516.6
doctored (up) 203.9, 311.5
doctors 456.2
doddle 251.1
dode 431.1
dodge 210.1, 307.1, 310.2, 481.1
dodge the column 210.5
Dodger 179.8
dodgy 28.2, 482.5
dodo 407.1, 431.1
does a bear shit in the woods? 199.3
does a lot of shitting but his pants aren't down 435.4
does the bear shit in the woods! 299.4
does the Pope shit in the woods? 199.3, 299.4

egghead 430.1
eggo 431.1
eggs 506.5
eggs in the basket 116.36
ego trip 231.1
egocentric 399.2
EGYPT 191.5
eight-pager 194.4, 501.2
eightball 95.1, 384.1, 407.1
eightballs 505.4
eighteen-carat 164.8
eighter from Decatur 516.5
eighty-six 63.2
einstein 116.39
ejection 63
el disappearo 211.1
elbow 63.1, 63.2, 210.1, 224.1, 242.2
elbow grease 32.2
elbow shaker 420.6
electric 27.3
electric chair 492.1
electrocute 492.2
elephant 115.9
elephant 505.2
elephant and castle 116.30
elephant's trunk 101.3
elevated 101.3
eleven-bravo 456.1
eli 44.2
eliminate 25.4
elkies 506.5
elly-bay 116.13
elsewhere 153.9
elwoff 86.7
emag 307.1
embalmed 101.3
embarrass 301.1
embarrassment 301
embellish 298.3
eminence in degree 18.4
eminent 139.6
emok 116.28
emok nye! 53.3
emotion 260
emotional freedom 265.2
employment 241
employment bonuses 242.1
empty bottle 105.4
empty one's trash 359.6
empty the cannon 118.14
enclosure 48
encore! 27.4
encourage 295.3

encourage oneself 295.4
end 10
end 10.5
end 48.6, 116.30, 116.34
end an affair 353.5
end of the ball game 112.1
end of the line 10.1, 163.2
end work 241.8
end-around 10.3
endanger 256.4
ended 10.8
endo 506.2
endure 266.2
endure tedious work 241.7
enemy 440
energetic person 410
energiser 506.5
energy 236.2
enforcer 70.1
engage in safe sex 118.14
engaged 354.4
engagement 354
engaging sixth gear 360.9
engine 76.1
engine 77
English culture 360.7, 499.4
English guidance 499.4
Englishman 383.6
engrossed 148.8
enjoy 276.4
enjoyment 276
enliven 236.5
enmity 332
enob 116.34
enough! 136.4
enough and then some 22.2
enough said! 201.5
enquiries as to health 122.3
enter 53.1
enter forcibly 53.2
enterprising person 410
entertain 239.8, 363.4
enthroned 358.10
enthuse 286.2
enthusiasm 236.3, 270
enthusiastic 236.8, 270.4
enthusiastic about 270.5
entice 220.2
enticement 220
entice prostitutes 498.6
enticing 220.4
entrance 53
entrap 315.2
entrapment 315

enuff 22.1
equality 26.1
equalizer 71.1, 466.1
equipment 116.33
equipment 69.1
er 9.2, 177.3
er? 167.4
erase 113.4
erect penis 116.35
erection 118.4
-erino 10.4
-eroo 10.4
Errol Flynn 116.23
error 165
esaff 116.5
escape (v.) 211.3, 487.5
escape 211, 487
escape from trouble 252.9
escape punishment 318.9
escaped 494.13
escapee 487.3
esclop 495.1
-ese 176.1
eskimo 384.8
esky 69.20
esra 506.2
esrar 506.2
essence 506.5
essentials 164.3
ESTATE 375–376
estimate (n.) 163.3
estimate (v.) 163.4
estimated 163.6
estrangement 331
estuffa 505.2
etc. 135.1
ethno 385.1
-ette 10.4, 19.4
euchred 243.4
evade 210.2
EVASION 207–211
evasion 210, 487
Even Stephen 179.9
even steven 26.2, 367.1, 367.6
ever so 18.10
even the score 335.2
every Tom Dick and Harry 378.2
every man jack 378.2
every mother's son 378.2
everyone 378.2
everything 22.3
everything but the kitchen sink 22.3
everything's cool 275.7

everything's hotsy-totsy
  275.7
everything's jake 275.7
everything's OK 275.7
everywhere 41.8
everywhichway 5.5, 40.1,
  51.5, 151.7, 232.5
evidence 162.1
evil 306
ex 27.3, 441.7
exaggerated 312.3
exaggerator 420.5
exalted 101.3
examination 156
exceedingly 18.10
excellent 18.11
excellent 27.3
excessive 22.5
exchange stories 198.8
EXCITABILITY 262–264
excite sexually 357.4
excited 262.7
excitement 262
exciting 262.6
exciting story 198.4
excluded from a share 367.7
excuse (n.) 317.2
excuse my French 189.3
excuses to leave 317.6
execution 113.3
exercise the ferret 359.6
exercising 121.2
exert strength 32.4
exhaust 243.3
exhausted 124.6, 243.4
exhausted person 429.1
exhib 132.10
exhibitionist 436.6
exonerate 486.9
expat 383.6
expect 172.2
expectant 172.3
EXPECTATION 172–173
expectation 262.8
expensive 508.19
experience 11.1
experienced 253.7
experienced person 430
experienced person 430.3
experienced prostitute 497.7
experiencing drugs 507.8
experiment 156.4
explain 197.1
explanation 186.4
explanation 197
explosion 73

explosion of rage 280.2
EXPLOSIVES 70–74
expose 193.5
expose the genitals 357.6
express yourself 118.14
exterior 76.8
extort 368.3
extract the michael 293.5
extravagance 373
eye 156.1, 495.2
eye doctor 404.1
eye-opener 97.2, 505.4
eyeball 132.6
eyeful 35.2, 425.1
eyes (characteristics) 117.4
eyes 116.12
eyes 116.31
eyes like pissholes in the
  snow 117.4
Eyetie 383.13
eyewash 146.2, 183.2,
  287.1, 310.1

f.b.i.! 395.1
F-40s 504.3
F-60s 504.3
F-66s 504.3
faastie 347.4
fab 27.3
face 116.5
face 295.1, 347.1, 377.1,
  458.1
face fungus 116.10
face like a douchebag
  426.1
face like a toilet seat 426.1
face the music 318.7
face the nation 360.13
face-ache 433.1
face-fucking 360.2
faced 101.3
facer 168.2, 252.1
facial 499.2
facial characteristics 117.8
FACILITY 251–254
factory 460.1, 495.8
facts 164.1
fad 270.2
fade 7.5, 211.3, 259.3,
  384.6, 487.1
fade away 54.3
faded 101.3
faded boogie 384.6, 435.3,
  473.2
fadeout 112.1, 258.1
fading 20.1

fading game 516.3
fag (out) 243.3
fag 106.2, 241.1, 272.2
fag boy 497.9
fag tag 82.18
fag your face! 292.7
fag-end 106.3
fagged (out) 243.4
faggot 395.1
faggotter 498.4
faggy 33.6
fag hots 501.2
fail 258.2
fail to agree 343.1
failed 258.4
failing 258.3
failure 258
faint 125.17
fair crack of the whip!
  305.9
fair dinkum 159.4,
  305.9
fair dos! 285.5
fair enough! 285.5
fair go 214.2
fair go 305.1
fair one 338.1
fair pop 214.2
fair shake 305.1
fair shake of the dice!
  305.9
fair to middling 123.4
fair-haired boy 387.1
fairy snuff! 285.5
fairy story 198.2
fake (up) 203.7, 233.1
fake 311
fake 480.3
fake evidence 486.7
fake illness 124.3
fake it 311.4
fake jewellery 463.2
fake on (one) 150.1
fake up 232.4
faked 311.6
faker 480.3
falconer 480.3
fall (all) over oneself 49.5
fall (for) 160.2, 258.1,
  489.3
fall 56.1, 56.2
fall about 274.4
fall apart 127.1, 283.2
fall by 361.4
fall down on 282.2, 307.2
fall down on the job 258.2

gannet 399.3
gaol break 1.4
gaolbait 381.5
gaolbird 494.4
gaolhouse lawyer 494.4
gap 116.40
gape 116.40, 451.1
garbage 19.2, 86.2, 146.2
garbage mouth 420.3
garbage wagon 75.6
garbo 456.14
garden 116.39, 116.40
garden 48.5
garden gate 456.4, 516.6
Garden of Eden 116.40
gargle 87.6, 94.1, 97.2, 97.3
Garudnia 179.5
Gary Glitter 116.29
gas 67.5, 146.3, 183.1, 183.7, 184.1, 184.2, 185.1, 276.4, 299.1, 299.2
gas and run 310.6
gas-guzzler 75.2
gasbag 420.1
gash 116.40, 235.7, 380.1, 437.3, 506.2
gash-eater 436.2
gasper 106.2
gassed 101.3
gasser 420.1
gassy 184.4
gat 71.1
gate 63.1
gate fever 493.6
gatecrash 53.2
gatemouth 420.2
gato 505.2
gauche 254.6
gauge 506.2
gawd 325.2
gawdelpus 381.3, 397.1
gawk 132.8
gawp 132.6, 132.8
gay 404.1
gay and frisky 95.5
gay gothic 198.5
gayola 404.1, 508.5
gazlon 479.2
gazoo 116.29
gazooney 404.5
gazoopie 499.3
gazump 310.6
gazumper 480.3
gazungas 116.31

gazupie 499.3
GB 409.1
GBH 485.1
gd 189.4
gear 27.3, 69.1, 116.33, 506.2
gear up 237.2
geared 360.23
gee 116.40, 325.2, 359.6, 435.3
gee man 420.4
gee up 334.4
gee whillikers! 189.5
gee whillikins! 189.5
gee whiz! 189.5
gee-gee 115.10
gee-gees 514.2
geeba 506.2
geechie 167.3
geed (up) 101.3
geek 132.6, 390.3, 409.1, 431.1, 433.7, 451.1, 506.2
geepie 381.4
geetoh 75.4
geez 325.2
geeze 505.11
geezer 379.1
gellyhead 431.1
gelt 509.1
gen 194.1
gendarmes 495.1
gender-bender 404.1
general forms of address 178.3
General Smuts 116.36
general specialist 456.24
general terms of abuse 395
generous 370.7
genials 116.32
genital area 116.32
genteel 141.1
gentility 141
genuine 164.8
GEOGRAPHICAL CONDITIONS 64–66
George 69.23
georgia 359.12
georgy 359.12, 499.8
gerbil 431.1
geri 382.1
Germaine Greer 95.1
German 383.8
German bands 116.15
gerry riddle 119.2

gertcha! 146.11
gessump 310.6
gestaps 495.1
gesture of derision 293.3
gesuip 101.3
get (his, yours, etc.) 112.5
get (it) off one's chest 193.3, 319.2
get (it) off one's mind 319.2
get (it) on 204.2
get (it) out of one's system 193.3, 319.2
get (one) going 168.3
get 301.1, 431.1
get! 292.7
get a bang out of 276.4
get a bee in one's bonnet 262.3
get a black eye 140.3
get a boner 118.11
get a capture 489.3
get a cut 367.4
get a guernsey 257.2
get a hair up one's arse 280.3
get a haircut 310.8
get a hard (on) 118.11
get a jag on 101.2
get a kick out of 276.4
get a laugh 274.5
get a line on 132.7, 144.4, 162.2, 162.3, 163.4, 166.2, 192.8
get a load of 132.6, 134.2
get a load off one's behind 119.7
get a load off one's mind 119.7
get a load on 97.3
get a move on 49.5
get a noseful 131.3
get a piece 367.4
get a result 257.2
get a rise out of 280.4
get a shot of leg 359.6
get a slant on 162.2
get a slice 367.4
get a snootful 97.3
get a swelled head 297.2
get a tug 489.3
get above oneself 297.2
get across 257.2, 284.2, 359.12
get along (with you)! 146.11, 161.6

give it to 318.4, 337.7, 485.3

give jiggs 149.5, 255.4

give lumps 338.5

give one Larry Dooley 318.4

give one a (good) talking to 291.2

give one a (nasty) jolt 173.2

give one a (nasty) turn 173.2

give one a headache 278.4

give one a miss 362.4

give one a pain (in the neck, arse) 284.2

give one a razoo 278.4

give one a pain in the arse 278.4

give one a song and dance 186.7

give one a tumble 359.6

give one in the neck 278.4

give one rocks 357.4

give one some curry 291.2

give one some funny business 313.2

give one some stick 291.2

give one the belt 348.2

give one the brush (off) 348.2

give one the brush 331.2

give one the brush-off 331.2

give one the business 291.2, 293.5

give one the cold shoulder 348.2

give one the creeps 283.4

give one the freeze (out) 348.2

give one the frost 348.2

give one the go-around 348.2

give one the leather 337.4

give one the leg 293.5

give one the pink slip 370.2

give one the runaround 348.2

give one the shaft 313.2

give one the works 291.2

give one's best shot 204.2

give one's bum an airing 119.6

give one's come-uppance 371.4

give one's deserts 371.4

give orders 216.4

give over! 292.7

give some body 359.6

give some skin 346.2

give some spli 346.2

give the (old) heave-ho 25.4, 63.2

give the E 224.3

give the OK 222.2

give the air 25.4, 63.2, 353.5

give the all-clear 285.3

give the belt 63.2

give the big razoo 292.3

give the bird 293.4

give the boot 224.5

give the brown envelope 63.2, 224.5

give the brush 353.5

give the brush-off 25.4, 209.5

give the bullet 242.6

give the bump 25.4

give the business 113.4, 318.4, 350.3

give the chop 113.4, 338.5

give the come-on (to) 220.2

give the dog a bone 359.6

give the dogs a rest 56.3

give the dope on 192.5

give the double-shuffle 259.4

give the drummer some 346.2

give the duke 290.2

give the elbow 25.4, 63.2, 224.3

give the eye (to) 132.6

give the eye 156.3

give the finger 148.5, 292.3, 293.6

give the glad eye 350.4

give the go-ahead 222.2, 285.3

give the go-around 209.5

give the go-by 210.2, 210.4

give the goods on 192.5

give the green light (to) 222.2

give the hard word 224.3, 294.6

give the heave 25.4

give the high sign 182.3

give the hook 25.4

give the knife 25.4

give the leather 337.9

give the man the play 472.3

give the miss 210.4

give the needle 284.2

give the nod 288.3

give the once-over 156.3, 132.6

give the pip 284.2

give the rap 113.4

give the red light (to) 224.3

give the rough edge of one's tongue 294.6

give the runaround 210.2, 210.4

give the sack 63.2, 224.5

give the slip 25.4

give the thumbs-up (to) 222.2

give the thumbs-down (to) 200.2, 224.3, 288.3

give the time of day 267.2

give the works (to) 338.3

give the works 113.4, 318.4

give the works to 338.5

give up 209.2

give up as a bad job 302.2

give up crime 478.3

give up one's face 360.11

give up rhythm 352.5

give up the ship 112.5

give up the store 209.2

give your face a rest! 201.5

give yourself a low five 118.14

giveaway 193.1

giving 370

giving up 209

giz 116.40

gizmo 69.2, 505.10

gizzard 116.13

gizzum 116.28

gizzy 506.2

glad 101.3

glad eye 132.1, 352.3

glad hand 328.1, 328.5

glad rags 82.4

glads 114.2

glamity 116.40

glamour 229.1

I mean! 199.3
I mean it 204.7
I pass 145.5
I refuse! 223.1
I should be so lucky 158.7, 285.5
I should care 271.7
I should cocoa 146.11
I should live so long 158.7
I should say so! 199.3
I should worry 271.7
I suppose 116.9
I understand 166.5
I've won! 20.7
I want work 242.9
I want! 365.5
I wouldn't fuck her with a borrowed prick 359.20
I wouldn't fuck her with your prick 359.20
I wouldn't know 271.7
I wouldn't touch it with a (ten-foot) barge-pole 288.6, 359.20
I wouldn't touch it with yours 288.6, 359.20
I wouldn't trust him/her as far as I could throw him/her 307.5
I'll be a Dutchman! 189.6
I'll be a (lowdown) son of a bitch! 189.6
I'll be a Chinaman! 189.6
I'll be a dirty word! 189.6
I'll be a monkey's uncle! 173.7, 189.6
I'll be blowed 189.6
I'll be consarned! 189.6
I'll be damned (if I will)! 223.1
I'll be damned if! 200.3
I'll be danged (if I will)! 223.1
I'll be darned! 189.6
I'll be dashed (if I will)! 223.1
I'll be fucked 173.7
I'll be fucked if! 200.3
I'll be hanged (if I will)! 223.1
I'll be hanged 189.6
I'll be jiggered! 189.6
I'll be shot (if I will)! 223.1
I'll be shot 189.6

I'll be . . . ! 189.6
I'll eat my hat! 161.6, 199.3
I'll eat my head! 199.3
I'll freeze 345.5
I'll go for that 340.5
I'll say 340.5
I'll say! 199.3
I'll say she does 164.12
I'll say you do 164.12
I'll see you in hell first! 223.1
I'm bored 272.7
I'm on 340.5
I'm with you 340.5
ibble out 89.7
IBM 116.34
IC 379.1
ice 83.10, 113.4, 505.3
ice 67.4
ice cream 86.29
ice cream machine 116.34
ice cube 505.4
ice-cream 505.4
iceberg 407.2, 452.2
iced 494.12
iced to the eyebrows 101.3
icing expert 436.1
icky 36.2, 130.2, 235.9, 261.5, 278.5
icky-poo 278.5
icy pop 95.1
ID 116.34, 144.2, 486.3, 486.6
IDB 453.6
idea 153.2
identification 486.3
identify 144.2, 486.6
idiosity 138.1
idiosyncracy 138
idiot board 195.1
idiot box 195.1
idiot girl 195.1
idle (v.) 244.1
idleness 244
idrin 378.1
if it moves salute it, if it doesn't, paint it 216.8
if that doesn't beat the band! 173.7
if you can't beat 'em join 'em 302.5
if you can't do the time don't do the crime 494.14
-iferous 10.4

iffy 28.2, 151.6, 256.5, 307.3
ig man 431.1
ignant 431.1
ignite the lightsaber 118.14
ignore 150.1
ikey mo 384.8
ill 124.4
ill piece 404.5
ill-bred person 392
ill-tempered 280.5
illegal liquor 94.7
illegitimate child 444.7
illegitimis non carborundum 241.12
illicit 481.5
illicit business 481.3
illicit drinking establishment 104.2
illness 124
illnesses 125
illywhacker 458.8
ILUVM 191.5
imaginary cities 43.2
imagination 175
imagine 175.2
imagine it! 173.8
imby 431.1
imitation 15.3
immature youngster 381.6
immediately 2.10
immoral 306.3
immorality 306
impairment 7
impatience 264
impatient 264.3
impimpi 435.3
implements 69
important facts 18.3
important person 387
impossibility 158.2
impossible 158.5
impoverished by gambling 512.7
imprison 491.4
imprisoned 494.11
imprisonment 494.6
IMPROBITY 306–309
improve 6.1
improve one's health 128.4
IMPROVEMENT 6–7
Imps 179.1
impudence 347
impudent 347.4
in Dutch (with) 332.4

indulge oneself 309.3
industrial debutante 497.2
industrial relations 508.9
inequality 26.1
'inevitable' nicknames
  (UK) 179.8
INEXCITABILITY
  265–266
inexpectation 173
inexperienced 254.5
infanticipating 109.4
infatuation 349.1
inferior 21.3
inferior liquor 94.6
inferiority 21
infested 5.6
influence 219
influence emotionally 219.7
info 192.1, 194.1
inform 192.5, 472.3
inform on 193.4
INFORMATION 192–198
informer 435.3, 472.2,
  473.2
INHABITANTS 383–386
inhale (a snort) 97.3
inhale 87.6
inhale drugs 505.12
inject drugs 505.11
injured 126.2
injured persons 429
ink 340.3
inked 101.3
inkslinging 190.1
inky-dinky 384.3
inner man 90.1
-ino 10.4
INQUIRY 154–157
inquisitive 155.2
inquisitive person 398
inquisitiveness 155
ins and outs 215.1
insane 147.5
insects 115.4
inside 202.5, 494.11
inside dope 192.2
inside information 192.2,
  192.10
inside man 480.3
inside stuff 192.2
inside tip 192.2
inside track 164.2, 259.1
insignificance 19
insignificant 140.6
insignificant 19.6
insignificant person 388

-inski 10.4
instrument (guitar) 135.6
insufficiency 23
insufficient funds 376.2
INTEGRITY 303–305
intellectual 143.2
intellectually demanding
  153.7
intelligence 143
intelligent 143.5, 144.9
intelligent person 430
intelligibility 166
intense 263.6
inter-racial lovers 441.9
interest (n.) 510.3
interest (v.) 267.3
INTEREST 267–270
interested 267.4
interfere 249.2
interfere in a relationship
  353.2
interfere with courtship
  350.7
interference 249
interior 76.7
interior decorating 359.1
international milk thief
  458.3
interrogate 154.3, 490.5
interrogation 154
interrupt 183.15
interrupter 458.18
intestinal fortitude 295.1
intimate 328.8
intimidate 336.2
intimidation 336
into (one for) 510.10
into 148.8, 166.4, 204.6,
  267.4, 328.9
introductory word 177.3
intrude in a conversation
  249.3
invalid 429.3
invertebrated 101.3
invest 508.13
investigate 156.3
investigation 156
invitation 191.2, 361.2
invitations to drink 99.2
involve 339.3
involved in crime 478.5
irey 27.3
iris out 54.3, 54.4
Irish 383.12
Irish confetti 68.5
Irish fortune 116.40

Irish hurricane 66.6
Irish jig 120.5
Irish root 116.34
Irish screwdriver 69.6
Iron 179.8
iron 71.1, 75.1, 404.1
iron cross 252.3
iron mikes 70.3
iron tank 508.8
irregular motion 57
irresolute 207.3
irresolute person 408
IRRESOLUTION 207–211
irrigate the tonsils 97.3
irritable person 405
irritated 284.5
Irvine 495.1
Irving 431.1
is a bear a Catholic?
  199.3
is that good or is that
  good! 285.5
is that . . . or is that . . . !
  199.3
is the Pope a Catholic!
  199.3, 299.4
is the bear a Catholic?
  299.4
isda 505.2
island-hop 58.2
Isle of Wight! 199.3
isn't ready for people
  145.2
issue 22.3
issues 505.4
it 139.1, 413.1, 441.11
it fell off the back of a
  lorry 479.7, 481.6
it looks like rain 489.7
it shouldn't happen to a
  dog 278.7
it takes two to tango
  359.19
it will all come out in the
  wash 295.6
-itis 10.4, 270.2
it's (all) Greek to me
  145.5
it's a great life if you don't
  weaken! 295.6
it's been a slice 276.9
it's been fun 276.9
it's got me 167.5
it's my story and I'm
  sticking with it 206.4
it's not my funeral 271.7

leo-time 3.4
les 404.2
lesbo 404.2
Leslie 116.40
leso 404.2
less of it 347.5
less of it! 10.9, 146.11
less than no time 1.3
let (it) go 150.1
let (it) ride 150.1, 248.3
let (it) slide 150.1
let (one) have it 291.2
let (one) in 192.5
let (one) in on the ground
  floor 192.5
let down 282.2, 282.4
let down easy 193.7,
  282.2, 329.3
let down one's hair 283.3
let go (of) 62.3
let have it 337.7
let her go 60.4
let her out 60.4
let her rip 49.7, 276.5
let it all hang out 262.3
let it sweat 150.1
let loose (with) 183.10
let loose 309.3
let loose on 294.6
let me hold some change
  368.5
let off hot air 146.6
let off some hot air 299.2
let off the hook 213.3
let one have it 113.4,
  318.4
let one have it in the neck
  318.4
let one have what-for
  318.4
let one's game slip 244.1
let one's hair down 276.5
let oneself go 183.12,
  309.3
let oneself in for it 318.8
let rip 241.5
let slide in one ear and out
  the other 171.1
let someone get on with
  341.6
let the cat out of the bag
  184.3
let the daylights into 337.6
let the dog see the rabbit
  341.6
let up on 329.3

let's be having you! 247.8
let's boogie 54.3
let's co-operate 339.7
let-down 258.1, 282.1,
  353.1
let-go 276.3
let-off 317.1
let-on 193.1
let-out 317.1
letch 443.2
letter 177
letter 191.1
lettuce 509.1
letup 25.1
level (with) 319.2
levy 360.19
lezzie 404.2
lezzo 404.2
LF 480.2
LF gear 464.1
liar 435.2
libber 456.9
liberate 479.4
lick (it) 239.7
lick 20.3, 49.1, 238.2,
  337.2, 338.5
lick and a promise 151.2
*lick and suck the client's
  body* 499.6
lick into shape 237.3
lick my froth! 292.7
lick the dick 118.14
lick the hell out of 318.5
lick the pants off 318.5
lick the tar out of 318.5
lick to a frazzle 318.5
licked 21.2
lickety-split 49.9
licking 20.1, 318.3
licorice stick 116.34
lid 218.1, 502.4
lido 505.4
lie (v.) 312.2
lie 312
lie dead 203.6
lie doggo 149.5, 203.6
lie down 246.3
lie low 203.6, 300.3
lie of the land 4.1
liesca 506.2
LIFE 108–111
life of Reilly 361.1
life preserver 70.2
lifeboat 493.5
lifer 456.1, 494.4
lift 94.8, 489.2

lift doesn't reach the top
  floor 431.1
lift one's game 239.5
ligger 439.1
light 133
light 197.1
light a cigarette 107.3
*light complexioned black (by
  blacks)* 384.4
light into 241.5, 291.2,
  318.4
light of love 494.5
light off 118.12
light out 54.3
lighten the load 118.14
lighten up 265.4, 265.7
lightning 505.4
lights 69.22
lightweight 140.6, 388.1,
  403.1
like 177.3
like a bat out of hell 49.9
like a dose of salts 49.9
like a good 'un 270.5
like a house on fire 18.4,
  251.6
like a rat up a drain 49.9
like a shot 2.10, 221.2
like a shot out of hell 2.10
like crazy 151.8, 270.5
like fuck! 146.11, 165.5,
  200.3
like fuck I will! 223.1
like fun! 165.5, 200.3
like fun I will! 223.1
like hell! 165.5, 200.3
like hell on wheels 151.8
like it or lump it 217.3,
  266.2
like it? 153.12
like nobody's business
  18.4
like shit I will! 223.1
like winking 49.9
likely story 312.1
likeness 15.1
likkered 101.3
Lilley and Skinner 89.4
lilly 504.3
lily 27.1, 384.12, 404.1
lima 506.2
limbo room 494.2
limey 383.6
limo 75.2
limp-dick 403.1
lina 505.3

low down 28.2
low in the saddle 101.3
low rent 7.14, 28.2, 140.6
low-down 140.5, 306.3,
  308.3
low-life 140.5, 278.5
low-rent 278.5, 306.3,
  308.3
lowdown (on) 162.1
lowdown 192.1, 192.2,
  194.2
lower (it) 89.6
lower one's flag 300.5
lower than a snake's belly
  279.7
lower than the spots on a
  snake's ass 396.1
lower than whale shit
  396.1
lower the boom on 291.2
lowest of the low 140.5
lowlife 392.1, 433.1,
  433.3
lox jock 384.8
LSD 506.4
LTR 355.2
lubage 506.2
lube 67.6
lubricated 101.3
luck 215
luck into 215.5
luck out 215.5
lucky 215.8
Lucozade 384.1
Lucy Law 495.1
Lucy Locket 82.19
ludes 504.4
lug 116.11, 390.3, 395.1,
  427.1, 431.1
luggage 366.2
lugger 479.3, 494.4
lughole 116.11
lulu 27.1
lumber 250.1, 312.2
lumme! 173.7
lummocks 395.1
lump 119.7, 337.4, 390.3,
  427.1, 454.3
lump of shit 395.1
lumpy chicken 134.6
lunch 116.34, 360.1,
  360.2
lunchbox 431.1
lunchmeat 146.1, 431.1
lunchtime intercourse
  359.3

lunchy 145.3, 229.5,
  274.9
lungs 116.31
lunk 431.1
lunkhead 390.3, 431.1
lunkheaded 145.3
lurk 307.1
lurkman 480.3
lurkola 508.5
lurky 307.4
lush 92.3, 97.3
lush it around 97.3
lush it up 97.3
lush worker 479.3
lushing (it up) 97.1
lushy 101.3
lust dog 437.3
lying low 203.8
lyricising 352.4

M&Ms 504.1
M&S 179.2
M 505.6
M25 506.5
M-way 47.1
m.f. 395.1
MA 71.3
ma 444.3
Ma and Pa store 508.8
mac 178.3
mac out 89.7
macaroni 498.2
macaroni with cheese
  498.4
mace 310.3, 310.6, 480.3
mace-cove 480.3
mace-gloak 480.3
maceman 480.3
macer 479.2, 480.3
machine 75.6
machine-gun 71.2
machinery 506.2
macing 310.10
mack 186.2, 350.3,
  498.10
mack daddy 498.2
mack man 498.2
mack on 352.7
mackery 498.1
macking 350.1
mad 27.3, 280.6
mad about 349.4
mad as a cut snake 280.1
mad as a wet hen 280.6
mad money 508.6
madam 498.4

made 450.2
made man 458.2
made of money 375.4
madness 147
mag 71.1
magazines 194.3
Maggie's drawers 182.2
maggot 116.34, 395.1
maggotty 101.3
maggoty 101.3
magic 27.3
magic 327
magic smoke 506.2
magoozlum 146.2
maharishee 506.2
mahogany flat 48.2
mail 509.1
main 505.9
main bitch 441.3, 497.7
main chance 214.1
main drag 47.3
main man 387.1, 438.1
main squeeze 438.1
main stem 47.3
main street 47.3
mainline 505.9, 505.11
mainliner 503.2
majigger 69.2
major 27.3
make (for) 486.6
make (it) 257.2
make (it for) 144.4
make 162.3, 166.2,
  359.12, 486.3
make a (great) to-do 280.3
make a Federal case (out
  of) 262.3, 289.2
make a beeline (for) 51.2
make a bloomer 146.5,
  165.3
make a bomb 508.15
make a boo-boo 165.3
make a break 211.3
make a car 479.4
make a clean breast (of it)
  193.3
make a cobblers of 254.2
make a cods of 254.2
make a dead set for 267.2,
  350.4
make a deal 339.5
make a dog's dinner (out
  of) 5.2
make a dumb play 146.5
make a fool of 146.8
make a fuss 263.3

Mexican foxtrot 119.5
Mexican green 506.2
Mexican mud 505.2
Mexican stand-off 344.1
Mexican toothache 119.5
Mexican two-step 119.5
mic 502.4
mick 383.12
mickey 105.2
Mickey Finn 504.5
Mickey Mouse 28.2, 132.2
micky/mike bliss 119.2
micro-beer 95.1
microbe 403.1, 427.4
middle finger 499.4
middle leg 116.34
midget 427.4
midi 82.9
midnight 384.3
midnight lace 116.34
miff 284.2
miffed 280.6, 284.5
mike-mike 38.7
mileage 253.1, 494.6
military forces 456.1
military leaders, officers 457.2
military nicknames 179.3
milk 95.1, 310.6
milk 87.4
milk and water 19.6, 261.1
milk bar cowboy 395.1
milk the chicken 360.19
milkers 116.31
milkman 116.34
milko 456.22
milksop 403.1
mill 16.4
million 511.1
million dollar wound 122.2
miln up 494.9
milquetoast 403.1
mince 86.9
mind 255.2
mind one's Ps and Qs 227.2
mind-blowing 27.3
mind-tripper 409.2
minder 433.4, 485.2
mindfucked 101.3
mine host 92.1
minge bag 380.1
mingy 374.4

mini 82.9
minimum 491.3
mink 425.1
minnow 105.3
MINS 458.4
minute 3.11
mirror 81.6
misbehave 231.4
misbehaving 231.6
misbehaviour 231
miscellaneous criminal terms 496
miscue 165.1
misery 279.2
misery 405.1
misery-guts 279.1, 405.1
misfire 165.1, 282.1
mishegaas 146.2
miss 178.3, 258.1
miss a lover 353.6
Miss Amy 384.13
Miss Ann 383.13
Miss Emma 505.6
Miss Lillian 384.13
Miss Peach 435.3
Miss Piggy 427.2
Miss Right 441.3
miss the boat 258.2, 282.3
miss the bus 258.2
Miss Thing 346.3
mistake 165
mistaken 165.4
mister 178.3
Mister Ed 192.3, 438.1
Mister Laffs 447.1
mistress 441.3
mitt 509.1
mitt man 323.3
mittens 83.1
mix (it) 252.6
mix it 338.3
mixed drinks 96
mixer 420.2
mixologist 92.2
mizzled 101.3
MO 478.1
mo 1.3
mo-mo 431.1
mob 378.1, 458.2
mob up with 328.6
mob-handed 339.6
moch 384.8
mockie 384.8
mod 229.4
mod squad 495.2
mod to the bone 84.4

mods 378.3
mogador 338.5
moisture missile 116.34
mojo 219.1, 505.6
moke 115.8
mole 116.34
molest sexually 360.18
molest the mole 118.14
moll 380.1
moll buzzer 479.3
Molly Malone 195.5
mollycoddle 403.1
mollydooker 393.1
mollyfock 395.1
mollyfock! 189.5
mollyfocking 189.4
mollyfogging 18.8
Mom and Pop store 508.8
Mom-Dad-Buddy-and-Sis 407.1, 444.1
momma 178.3
momma's game 294.1
momma-hopper 395.1
momo 431.1
momser 377.1, 395.1
Monday Morning quarterback 419.1
Monday Night at the Movies 179.4
Monday pills 504.5
mondo 22.5, 27.3
money 509.1
money for jam 251.1
money for old rope 251.1
money to burn 508.6
money: names 509
mong 395.1
mongrel 395.1
monicker 178.1
monkey (on one's back) 503.5
monkey 16.4, 69.7, 116.34, 116.40, 465.1, 509.13
monkey business 146.1
monkey spank 395.1
monkey suit 82.3
monkey with 249.2
monkey's cousin 516.6
monkey's tails 69.15
monkeys to junkies 179.4
monotony 441.3
mons 7.2
monster 18.1, 436.5, 458.6

Mr/Mrs/Miss/Ms/Master
  Knowitall 179.17
Mr/Mrs/Miss/Ms/Master
  Smartarse 179.17
Mr/Mrs/Miss/Ms/Master
  Smartypants 179.17
Mrs Palm and her five
  daughters 360.9
MTF 443.3
mu 506.2
much goo about nothing
  360.9
muck 294.2
muck about 244.1
muck in 339.2
muck in with 367.2
mucker 396.1, 438.1
muckhole 46.2
muckrake 193.5
mucky-muck 387.1
mud 68.2, 294.2, 505.5
mud snake 116.34
mud-bud 506.2
mudcrusher 397.1
muddle 169.1, 169.3
muddled 169.5
Muddy 179.8
mudkicker 497.6
mudslinging 294.2
muff 258.1, 428.3
muff diver 436.2
muffin 431.1
muffishness 254.1
mug 276.6, 277.6, 351.3,
  391.1, 395.1, 431.1,
  480.4, 485.4, 486.6
mug book 195.6
mug punter 511.2
mug shot 486.3
mug up 54.3, 170.5
mug's game 146.1
mug's ticker 463.2
muggle 506.2
muggles 506.2
mujer 505.3
mule 77.1, 399.4, 426.2,
  431.1, 481.1
mule mouth 472.2
mule-mouth 435.3
mulish 206.2
mulla 509.1
mullah 338.5
mulled (up) 101.3
mulligan stew 86.8
mulligrubs 279.2
mum 201.4, 441.3, 444.3

mumbo-jumbo 146.2
mummy 338.5
mummyhead 431.1
mump 368.2
mumper 58.1
mumping 482.6
mums 444.3
mumsie 444.3
munchies 90.2
munga 86.1
munger 86.1
munt 384.1
murder 113
murder 7.10
murphies 86.11
murphy (game) 480.2
muscle 32.2, 337.1, 433.3,
  433.4, 485.3
muscle in 53.2, 249.2,
  338.4
muscle into 367.4
musclehead 431.1
mush 178.3
mush faker 456.8
mushe-man 480.3
musher 456.13
mushie 456.13
mushy 261.5
musical instruments 69.24
muski 95.3
muso 456.5
must have swallowed the
  dictionary 143.7
must-I-holler 116.40
mustang 380.1, 457.2
muteness 201
mutt 115.1, 431.1
Mutt and Jeff 134.5, 490.2
mutton bayonet 116.34
mutton musket 116.34
muttonheaded 145.3
muzziness 169.1
muzzle 215.2
muzzler 404.1
muzzy 101.3, 169.5, 243.4
my (giddy) aunt! 161.6
my (holy) aunt! 189.5
my cripes! 189.5
my eye! 146.11, 161.6
my eyes! 189.5
my foot! 146.11, 161.6
my gosh! 189.5
my hat! 189.5
my man 178.3
my old guvnor 444.2
my sainted aunt 189.5

my shout 370.5
my stars (and garters)
  189.5
my word! 173.7
MYOB 249.4, 292.7
Myrtle the Turtle 179.9
mystery 380.1
mystery mad 436.13

n's 509.1
nab 162.3, 365.2, 489.2,
  495.1
nabes 46.1
nadgers 116.36
naff 28.2
naff off! 54.6
nafka 497.2
nag 291.4
nag 497.2, 497.6
nagging 291.5
nagging person 419.4
nail 41.5, 162.3, 166.2,
  310.6, 337.7, 359.12,
  510.5
nail 'em and jail 'em 495.1
nail it 164.5
nail to the wall 318.4,
  318.5
nailed 101.3, 162.7
nailhead 426.2
nails 69.15
naked 259.5
naked 85.6
naked! 199.3
nam 379.1
namby-pamby 403.1
name 178
name of the game 164.3
NAMES 178–180
names of affection 180.1
names of endearment 180.1
names of numbers in bingo
  516.6
names of points in craps
  516.5
nammo 380.1
nan 444.8
nana 431.1, 444.8
nance 33.6, 404.1
nancy-boy 404.1
nanny goat 82.12
nanny-goating 350.1
nap 247.2
Nap Town 43.1
nappy 120.13
narc 435.3, 472.2

nigger-bashing 338.1
nigger-driving 241.6
nigger-flicker 69.9
nigger-lover 438.2
nigger-pot 94.7
nigger-rich 376.5
niggerish 245.1
niggerlip 107.2
niggly 280.5
night 3.9
night clothes 82.1
night exercises 360.9
night-cap 97.2
night-club 363.2
nighthawk 479.2
nightingale 435.3
nightstick 447.1
nignog 384.1
-nik 10.4
nimrod 116.34
nimwad 431.1
Nina from Carolina
  516.5
Nina with her hair down
  516.5
nine 95.1
nine day blues 125.10
nine-to-five 226.1, 241.1
nineteenth hole 78.6
ning-nong 431.1
ninnies 116.31
nip 162.3, 337.8, 365.2,
  383.14
nipper 381.3, 480.3
nisht 16.2
nit 431.1
nit-nit 201.5
nitro 67.5
nitty gritty 18.3, 144.1,
  162.1, 164.1, 164.3
nitwit 431.1
nitwitted 145.3
nix 200.1, 200.2, 224.1,
  225.1, 288.1, 288.3
nix! 200.3, 225.3
nix on that (stuff) 225.3
no! 200.3, 225.3
no account 235.8
no better than he/she
  should be 437.6
no big deal 28.1, 388.1
no biggie 271.7
no bon 28.2
no can do 254.3
no can see 167.2
no chance 214.4

no chance! 214.11
no chicken 111.4
no deal 343.2
no deal! 223.1
no dice 158.7, 258.1,
  282.1, 343.2
no dice! 200.3, 223.1
no fear 158.7
no flies on (him, her, etc.)
  143.6, 253.7
no freak 499.2
no go 28.2, 258.1, 343.2
no go! 223.1
no great catch 19.4, 140.6
no great shakes 19.1, 19.4,
  140.6, 388.1
no holds barred 213.5
no ifs and buts 159.3
no ifs or buts 164.8
no joy 282.1
no kick 275.4
no kid(ding)! 199.3
no kidding 161.6, 204.7
no laughs (laffs) 252.11
no longer addicted 503.12
no muss no fuss 265.7
no oil painting 36.1
no picnic 252.11
no prize 36.1
no punches pulled 213.5
no rest for the wicked
  241.11
no risk 199.3
no sale 258.1, 343.2
no sale! 200.3
no savvy 167.2
no shit 159.4, 161.6,
  164.12, 204.7
no shit! 173.9, 199.3
no siree (bob) 200.3
no skin off my arse 271.7
no skin off my nose 271.7
no slouch 35.7, 430.2
no soap 158.7, 258.1,
  282.1, 343.2
no soap! 200.3, 223.1
no squawk 275.4
no strings (attached)
  213.5
no stuff 305.1
no sweat 251.6, 275.4,
  345.4
no sweat! 285.5
no thank you 345.5
no two ways (about it)
  159.3

no two ways about it
  212.2
no way 158.7, 343.2
no way! 146.11, 200.3,
  225.3, 288.5
no-brand cigarette 506.3
no-hope 278.5
no-hoper 140.5, 414.1
no-name cigarette 506.3
no-no 158.2, 200.1,
  200.2, 306.1, 431.1
noah's 435.3
Noah's ark 435.3, 472.2
nob 116.34, 448.1
nobbing 359.1
nobble 7.4, 514.7
Nobby 179.8
nobby 141.1
nobody to write home
  over 388.1
nobody's fool 430.2
nobscratch 395.1
Nocky 179.8
nod 182.1, 507.5
nod and a wink 285.1
nod out 507.5
noddy 475.2
noffka 497.2
noise (light, splashing)
  135.2
noise (loud) 135.3
noise (of a blow) 135.1
noise (of a crash) 135.1
noise 183.1
noisy 131.5
nola 404.1
Nola the Bowler 179.9
nommus! 256.6
non 393.2
non compos 147.5
non-Jews (by Jews) 384.10
non-alcoholic drinks 87
nonce 436.5
nonchalant 271.6
nondescript 475.2
nong 431.1
nonsense 146
nonsense 146.2
noodle 431.1
noogies 116.36
nookie 359.1
nooner 359.3
nope! 200.3
norks 116.31
north end of a southbound
  horse 395.1

out of one's chump 124.7
out of one's gourd 124.7, 507.8
out of one's head 101.3, 124.7, 147.5
out of one's mind 101.3, 147.5, 507.8
out of one's misery 112.10
out of one's nut 507.8
out of one's onion 147.5
out of one's skull 507.8
out of one's tree 147.5
out of order 5.5, 142.2, 231.6, 278.5
out of order 7.13
out of pocket 231.6
out of sight 22.5, 27.3
out of sorts 124.4, 280.5
out of state 27.3
out of the blue 173.5
out of the box 27.3
out of the game 367.7
out of the money 21.3
out of the picture 21.3, 112.10, 367.7
out of the running 367.7
out of this world 27.3
out of trouble 251.7
out of whack 5.5, 7.13, 126.2, 147.5
out on a limb 252.12
out on one's arse 63.4
out on one's ear 63.4
out on one's feet 243.4
out to lunch 101.3, 145.3, 147.5, 153.9
out with (it) 183.14, 319.2
out with 183.10, 278.6, 332.4
out-and-out 395.1
outasite 22.5, 27.3
outers 278.1, 278.5, 487.4
outfit 14.1, 378.1, 409.1, 487.4, 494.7, 505.10
outfront 305.6
outhouse 494.1
outlaw 497.6
outside 494.1
outside lavatory 79.2
over a barrel 218.5
over easy 86.27
over one's head 167.3
over the fence 18.9
over the hill 1.7, 111.4, 433.6, 494.13
over the hill ho 497.5

over the moon 273.5, 274.9
over the side 495.11
over the top 22.5, 101.3, 142.2, 151.8, 228.3, 231.6
overboard 270.4
overs 464.1
owing 510.10
Owls 179.1
Owsley 506.4
ox 390.3, 427.1
Oxford scholar 509.4
oyster 380.1
oz 502.4

p 116.40
P check 144.2
p.h.a. 116.34
p-dope 505.2
p-funk 505.2
P-Town 43.1
pa 187.1
pace 262.4
pachuco 383.15
pack (it) in 209.2, 239.6
pack 58.2, 61.1, 366.8, 378.1
pack a gat 74.2
pack a rod 74.2
pack 'em 296.4
pack iron 74.2
pack one's palm 360.19
pack peanut butter 360.15
package 116.40
packet 508.1
packing a gat 74.3
packing 'em 296.7
packing iron 74.3
pact 340.3
pad (a bill) 311.3
pad 48.2, 78.2
padding crib 48.4
paddle one's own canoe 213.2
paddy 383.12, 494.2, 495.1
paddy wagon 475.3
padre 456.1
pads 494.2
page three girl 425.1
pain 278.1, 284.1
pain (in the arse) 28.1, 272.2, 252.4
pain in the arse 252.2, 278.1, 284.1, 396.1, 397.1, 452.2

pain in the behind 452.2
pain in the neck 28.1, 278.1, 284.1, 397.1, 452.2
paint one's ceiling 360.19
paint the town red 98.2, 276.5
pair of spectacles 16.2
paisan 383.13
pakalolo 506.2
Paki 383.17
Paki-bashing 338.1
Pakistani 383.17
Pakistani black 506.1
Pakki 383.17
pal 178.3, 438.1
pal up (with) 328.2
pal up to 287.3
paleface 384.12
paleface nigger 438.2
pally 328.7, 361.5
palm 372.3
palm presser 456.9
palooka 390.3, 427.1
palsy 361.5
palsy-walsy 328.7, 361.5
pam 73.1, 135.1
Pam and her five sisters 360.9
pan 132.6, 132.11, 292.3, 293.4, 318.5
pan out 11.3
pancake 425.1
panhandle 431.1
panhandler 41.72
panic stations 262.1
panning 292.1, 293.1
pansy 33.6, 404.1
panther piss 94.7
pants 85.5, 146.1
pantywaist 33.6, 403.1
papa 404.3
paper 190.6
paper 502.4, 509.1
paper hanger 483.2
paper pusher 456.6
papers 106.5, 506.3
papes 509.1
par for the course 172.4
paracki 505.7
Paraders 179.1
paradise 505.3
paradise white 505.3
paraffin lamp 437.3
parallel parking 359.1
paralytic 101.3, 274.9

pep up 236.5, 274.6, 274.7
pep-'em-ups 504.2
pepper and salt 384.12
pepper 'em up 101.2, 237.2
pepper one up 337.4
pepper-kissing 18.8
peppy 236.7
perch 41.6, 105.1
percher 480.4
percy 116.34
perfect high 505.2
perfectionist 284.7
perfecto! 27.4
perforate 337.7
perform (something) carelessly 151.3
perform 478.2
perform a self-test 118.14
performance 239
perico 505.3
period of time 1.1
perish the thought! 288.5
perishing 18.8
perk up 6.2, 128.4, 274.7
perky 274.9
permanence 13
permit sodomy 360.16
perp 458.1
perplexity 168
perseverance 205
persevere 205.2
persevering 205.3
person with a large head 427.7
person with a squint 428.4
person with glasses 428.9
personal assistant 456.6
personality 137.2
PERSONS 377–452
persons according to hair, facial features, etc. 428
persons according to size 427
persons by physical preference 441.10
persons by sexual preference 436
PERSONS: BY AGE 381–382
PERSONS: GENERAL 377–380
PERSONS: MENTAL ATTRIBUTES 430–431

PERSONS: MORAL STATUS 432–437
PERSONS: PHYSIQUE 425–429
PERSONS: SOCIAL POSITIONS 438–452
PERSONS: TYPES 387–424
persuade 219.4
persuader 70.1
persuasive 'line' or 'pitch' 186.2
pertaining to pimping 498.10
Peruvian 505.3
Peruvian flake 505.3
Peruvian lady 505.3
Peruvian marching powder 505.3
perv 436.5
perv about 352.5
pervin' 101.3
pet 180.1
pet lamb 180.1
pet names 180
pet one's pussycat 118.14
pet the poodle 360.20
pete-man 479.3
peter 116.34, 463.3, 465.1, 494.3
Peter Jay 495.1
peter out 7.5, 243.1
Peter the Poof 179.9
peterman 479.3
petrified 101.3
petrol 67.5
petrol station worker 456.19
petrols 82.11
PG 505.7
PH 504.2
PhD 435.1
pheasant plucker 395.1
phew 131.1, 131.3
Phil the Dill 179.9
philander 352.5
philanderer 443
philandering 352
philandering 352.1
Philippino 383.18
phizgig 435.3
phizog 34.1
phizzer 435.3
phlegm-cutter 97.2
phone freak 499.2
phoney 499.1

phonus balonus 146.2, 311.1
phony 311.1, 311.5
phooey! 146.2, 292.8
photo finish 95.1
photographer 195.9
phut 135.1
physical breakdown 127
physical condition 122
physical exercise 121
physical injury 126
physical strength 32.2
physically affectionate 351.4
physics for poets 179.4
pi 303.3, 321.3
piano 86.5
piccolo and flute 82.2
pick 479.3
pick a bone with 344.3
pick 'em up 49.6
pick the daisies 119.6
pick the plums 371.5
pick up 350.3
pick up 352.7
pick up brownie points 139.4
pick up fag ends 183.15
pick up the soap for 360.16
pick up the tab 304.1, 370.5, 508.13
pick up the vibrations 360.22
pick-me-up 97.2
pick-up 441.11
pickaninny 384.1
pickings 365.1
pickle kisser 404.1
pickled 101.3
picklepuss 426.1
pickles 86.21
pickpocket 458.14
picnic 11.1, 251.1
piddle 119.2, 119.4, 119.8
piddle about 244.1
piddle around 244.1
piddle away 235.4
piddling 19.6
pie 251.5, 425.1
pie and mash 119.2
pie in the sky 175.1, 371.1
pie-eater 458.3
pie-eyed 101.3
piece (of the action) 23.1
piece 14.1, 38.1, 38.3, 70.1, 71.1, 116.34,

pisser 277.1, 410.1
pisshole 48.8, 79.1
pisshouse 79.1
pissing 189.4
pissing down 66.3
pissing oneself 296.7
pisspoor 28.2
pisspot 92.3
pissy-ass 19.6
pistol 116.34
pit 5.1, 116.40
pit city 278.1, 279.8, 281.1
pit-a-pat 57.1
pita 497.1
pitch 312.1, 426.2, 480.1, 500.3
pitch a bitch 298.2
pitch and toss 387.1, 457.1
pitch camp 41.6
pitch in 89.7, 241.5
pitch in! 89.9
pitcher 404.5
pitchman 420.4
pits 278.1, 279.2
Pitt Street farmer 456.16
pitty 36.2
pixie 404.1
pixillated 101.3
pizza 86.20
pizzazz 229.1, 236.2, 269.1
pjs 82.14
PLACE 41–48
place 41.4
place of entertainment 78.8
place of intercourse 359.4
placer 458.10
places in prison 494.2
placket 116.40
plaguey 189.4
plain 95.1
plain sailing 251.5
plan 232
plan (v.) 232.3
PLAN 232–233
plank 41.5, 359.6
plant 41.4, 112.8, 203.5, 315.2, 486.6, 486.7
plant evidence 486.7
plant oneself 246.3
plants 114
plaster 113.4, 287.2, 337.4
plastered 101.3

plastic 15.6
plastic job 128.2
plate 360.12
plates 135.5
Plato to NATO 179.4
platters 135.5
plausible 160.5
play (along) 310.7
play (it) for all its worth 234.2
play (one) dirty 308.2, 313.2
play 165.1, 236.1, 511.5
play a flute solo on one's meat whistle 360.19
play a hunch 214.5
play around (with) 156.4
play around 352.5
play ball (with) 339.2
play cards 515.4
play checkers 352.5
play chick 255.4
play chicken 255.4, 353.2
play dead 203.6
play dumb 311.4
play fathers and mothers 359.6
play footsie 351.3
play for a sucker 310.4
play funny buggers 276.6
play gooseberry 350.7
play hard to get 352.6
play hardball 204.2
play hide-and-seek (with) 210.2
play hookey 210.3
play hoop-snake with 360.12
play it cool 252.9, 271.3
play it square 305.3
play it straight (down the line) 305.4
play Judas 314.2
play mummies and daddies 359.6
play night baseball 359.6
play one too close 249.2
play one's cards right 257.2
play one's hand 214.9
play one's tune 275.2
play out of the pocket 310.8
play past 239.5
play pocket billiards 118.14, 360.19

play possum 203.6
play practical jokes 277.5
play records 135.8
play ring a rosie 244.1
play second fiddle 302.3
play silly buggers 276.6
play stuff 312.2
play the Tom 302.3
play the chill (for) 209.5
play the con 310.4
play the dozens 294.4
play the duck 210.2
play the dummy 202.2
play the field 352.5
play the fool 146.4, 276.6
play the game 305.4
play the gee-gees 514.7
play the giddy goat 309.2
play the heel 278.3
play the male organ 360.19
play the nut role 310.4
play the piano 135.7
play the white man 305.4
play too close 494.8
play truant 210.3
play up to 287.3
play with a clean deck 305.3
play with oneself 118.14, 360.19
play-away 3.4
played out 243.4
player 410.1, 430.2, 458.6, 498.2
playful 276.7
playing chopsticks 360.9
playing dice 516.3
playing possum 203.8
playing with the big boys (now) 254.3
plead 490.7
plead innocent 490.7
plead the Fifth 210.2
pleasant 273.6
pleasant situation 273.2
please (v.) 273.3
please one's pisser 360.19
pleased 273.5
pleased as heck 273.5
pleased as hell 273.5
pleased as punch 273.5
pleased as the devil 273.5
PLEASURE 273–277
pleasure and pain 66.4
pleasure-seeker 447

pop (off) 73.3

pop 2.11, 87.5, 95.4, 135.1, 274.8, 382.2, 444.2, 505.11

pop a cherry 359.11

pop corn 458.19

pop in 53.1, 361.4

pop off (at the mouth) 299.2

pop off (at) 184.2

pop off 54.3, 280.3

pop one's cork 280.3, 359.8

pop one's nuts 118.12

pop the question 354.3

pop-eyed 101.3

popcorn 19.6

popcorn pimp 498.3

poppa lopper 395.1

popped 498.4

popped off 112.10

poppers 506.6

poppycock 146.2

pops 382.2, 444.2

popsicle 116.34

popular black nickname 179.19

popular with 328.9

pork 359.6

pork out 89.7

pork sword 116.34

porky 312.1

porno film 195.3

pornographic 357.10, 501.5

pornographic books 501.2

pornographic films 501.3

pornography 501

porridge 491.1, 494.6

porridge gun 116.34

porsche 425.1

port 95.9

portable pocket rocket 116.34

posh 141.1, 505.3

posish 41.1

positively 159.4

posse 378.1

possesh 404.5

POSSESSION 365–376

POSSIBILITY 158–159

possible 158.6

possum-guts 395.1

post a letter 119.7

postponement 248

pot (of) 18.2

pot 77.1, 506.2

pot and pan 382.2

pot of dough 375.1

pot-bellied 37.3

pot-hunter 480.3

potato 380.1

potato jack 94.7

potatoes 86.11

potatoes 509.1

potatoes in the mould 66.2

potboiler 198.4

pothead 503.3

pothooks and hangers 190.4

potshot 174.1

potsy 181.1, 495.6

potted 101.3

potten bush 506.1

potty 138.4, 147.5

poultry 86.7

poultry scratchings 190.4

pound (one's) brains 153.4

pound 491.3

pound note 509.5

pound off 118.14

pound one's ear 247.4

pound one's flounder 360.19

pound one's pork 360.19

pound one's pud 360.19

pound sterling 509.2

pound the brains 170.3

pound-note geezer 415.1

poundcake 425.1

pour (it) on 318.4

pour it on (heavy/thick) 287.2

pour it on 49.4, 241.6

pour on the oil 183.19

poverty 376

pow 73.1

pow-pow 186.1, 186.3, 186.6

powder 54.2, 211.1, 487.1

powder one's nose 119.6

powder puff 404.1

powee 2.11, 94.8

powerful 18.10

powie 32.3, 135.1

pox 125.10

poz 159.4

pozzy 159.4

practise anilingus 360.14

practise cunnilingus 360.13

praise 286

praise of a passing woman 286.3

praiser 418

prang 75.14, 75.15

prat 431.1

praties 86.11

pratt for 360.16

prawnhead 431.1

pray to the porcelain gods 118.13

preacher 323.3

prearrange 233.1

prearrangement 233

precious 180.1

precious heart 180.1

precisely 164.9

predict 174.2

predator 505.2

predictor 430.4

preface 9.2

preggers 109.4

pregnancy 109

pregnant 109.4

prep 237.2

preparation 237

prepare 237.2

prepared 237.5

preparing food 88

preppie 448.2, 450.3

prescriptions 504.1

presentiment 172.1

press 505.4

press flesh 328.5

press ham 85.4

press one's hair 120.9

pressed 84.3

pressie 370.1

pressure 219.4

pretence 311.2

pretend 311.4

pretender to the throne 404.5

pretendica 506.2

pretendo 506.2

pretty 180.1

pretty mess 252.2, 426.1

pretty muddle 252.2

pretty pickle 252.2

pretty up 4.4

previous 2.13, 494.6

prezzie 370.1

pricey 508.19

prick 116.34, 395.1, 396.1

prick peddler 497.9

prick-tease 352.8

pull something funny 308.2

pull strings 219.2

pull the juice 133.1

pull the other one (it's got bells on it)! 146.11, 278.7

pull the plug (on) 10.6

pull the pope 360.19

pull the rug from under 193.7

pull the wool over one's eyes 219.5, 310.5

pull through 6.2

pull time 491.5

pull to a set 98.2

pull to pieces 290.2

pull together 274.7

pull up stakes 54.3

pull wires 219.2

pull your head in! 292.7

pum-pum 116.40

pum-pum-pum 431.1

pummelled 101.3

pump 71.1, 154.3

pump jockey 456.19

pumping iron 121.2

pumpkin head 427.7

pumps 116.31

punch 94.8, 236.2, 359.6, 437.3

punch house 500.1

punch in the mouth 360.3

punch out 241.8

punch the clock 1.8, 241.4

punch up 236.5

punch-out artist 433.3

punch-up 338.1

punchy 145.3

punctual 2.14

puncture one's balloon 193.7, 282.2, 300.4

punish 318.4

punishment 318

punishment 360.2

punk 7.14, 124.4, 360.15

punk out 296.3

punks 378.3

punt (around) 214.5

punt 244.1, 511.5

punt it (up) 214.5

punt off 210.2

punter 377.1, 480.4, 511.2, 513.1

pup 381.4

puppethead 391.1

puppy 105.1, 116.34, 381.4, 381.7, 442.1

puppy dog 381.6

purchase on credit 510.7

purler 56.1

purple heart 504.2

purple ridgeback 116.34

purple-headed avenger 116.34

purse-bouncer 480.3

purse-emptier 480.3

pursue 344.2

push 209.1, 236.3, 286.1, 286.2, 353.1, 378.1, 458.2, 508.16

push along 54.3

push off 54.3

push off! 54.6

push one's face through the back of one's neck 338.5

push the boat out 508.12

push the thumb 60.7

push up the daisies 112.5

push-in job 485.1

pushed (for) 376.5

pushed out of shape 280.6

pusher 502.1

pushing iron 121.2

pushing up daisies 112.10

pushover 251.1, 391.1, 411.1, 437.3

pushy 236.8, 347.4

puss 404.4

puss gentleman 403.1

pussums 180.1

pussy 82.12, 380.1, 403.1

pussy fodder 116.34

pussy game 497.1

pussy hair 116.39

pussy in a can 494.7

pussy posse 495.4

pussy-whipped 355.8

pussycat 400.1

pussyclot 435.3

pussyfoot 8.3, 207.2

pussyfooter 408.1

put (it) across 239.5, 257.3

put (it) away 10.7, 239.6

put (it) in cold storage 239.6

put (it) on ice 239.6

put (it) over 239.5, 257.3

put (one's business) on front street 196.3

put (one) away 337.5, 338.5

put (one) down 300.4

put (up) against the wall 251.10

put 41.4

put a body up 473.3

put a crimp into 218.2

put a few back 97.3

put a few down 97.3

put a flea in one's ear 291.2

put a hurting on 337.4

put a name up 193.4, 473.3

put a notice on 113.6

put a sock in it 136.3, 201.1

put a sock in it! 201.5

put a spell on 327.2

put a word in one's ear 192.5

put all at sea 169.3

put at a disadvantage 259.3

put at sixes and sevens 169.3

put away (the groceries) 89.6

put away 20.3, 87.6, 113.4, 274.5, 473.3

put down 290.2, 294.6

put down a routine 310.4

put down the soft pedal 136.2

put down with force 41.5

put in a (good) word for 285.4

put in a flat spin 169.3

put in cold storage 374.3

put in lights 18.6

put in one's papers 495.10

put in one's two cents 183.17

put in one's two cents' worth 249.3

put in one's two pennorth 249.3

put in shtuck 252.10

put in stitches 274.5

put in the acid 473.3

put in the bag 233.1

put in the club 109.3

rebellious 342.4
rebellious black (by blacks) 384.5
recce 132.5
receiver 458.10
reckless 151.6
reckless person 402
recklessly 151.8
recklessness 151
reckon 16.6, 172.2, 204.4
recluse 494.4
recognize 144.4
RECOLLECTION 170–171
recommend 285.4
recommendation 285.2
reconcile 330.1
reconciliation 330
record players 69.25
records 135.5
recoup 493.7
recover 6.2, 128.4
recovery 128
rectal ranger 404.1
rectum ranger 404.1
Red 179.11
red 86.30, 383.19, 390.2, 456.5, 463.1
Red Sea pedestrian 384.8
red arse 279.2
red ass 280.1
red band 494.4
Red Biddy 95.3
red caps 505.4
red eagle 505.2
red light 224.1
red pants 280.1
red rock 505.2
red smoker 505.5
red stuff 68.3, 83.10
red tape 191.4
red wings 360.3
red-hot 402.1
red-hots 86.6
red-light 352.10
red-taper 456.6
redball 47.1
redeye 95.6
redhead 428.1
redloch 116.19
redneck 390.2
Reds 179.1
reds 504.3
reeb 95.1
reefer 506.2
reek with 366.3

reeking 101.3
reel in the biscuit 359.12
reelin' and rockin' 173.6
reet 166.5
reffo 383.25
reform (v.) 320.2
reform 320
reformer 419.2
refresh the memory 170.3
refusal 224
region 46
register 257.2
regular 22.6, 305.8
regular Joe 379.1
regular guy 394.1, 432.1
regular p 505.4
rehash 186.9
rehearsals 195.6
reimburse 113.3
reject (v.) 224.3
rejection 224
rejection of caresses 351.5
rejection of parole 493.3
rejig 234.3
relative time 2
relatives 444
release 493.6
release from jail 493
reliable 192.11
reliable information 192.3
RELIGION 321–327
religion 384
religious 321.2
religious activities 322
religious buildings & organisations 324
religious person 323
relinquish 209.2
relinquishment 209
reload 480.6
remain 244.2
remain calm 265.3
remark (v.) 183.10
remark 183.4
remember 170.4
REMF 395.1
remind 170.6
reminisce 170.2
remo 431.1
renee 441.3
rent 497.9
rent 508.4
rent-boy 497.9
rep 139.1
repair 6.3
repap 190.6

REPARATION 319–320
repel sexually 356.3
replace 12.2
replying to enquiries as to health 123.4
repo man 456.4
reppock 495.1
representative 400.3
reptiles 82.15
reputable 139.5
REPUTATION 139–140
repute 139
request for something 368.1
rescue station 104.1
RESEMBLANCE 14–15
resemble 15.4
reside 41.6
residence 48.4
resident 386.3
resignation 258.5
RESOLUTION 204–206
respectable girl 432.2
respectable person 432
response 186.5
responsibility 304.1
rest (v.) 246.2
rest 246
resting 244.4
restrain 218.2
restrain oneself 218.4
restrained 218.5
restraint 218
result 163.2
result 257.1
retaliation 335
retchub 456.8
retired 242.8
retract one's words 209.3
retriever 480.3
rette 106.2
rev 6.3, 60.4, 234.3
revamp 6.3, 234.3
reveal 132.10, 193.3
reveal a plan 233.2
reveal one's homosexuality 358.3
reveal one's intentions 193.6
reveal one's worries 283.3
revenge 335
revolution 228.1
reward 371
RF 310.4
RFD queen 404.5
rhino 509.1
rhubarb 146.2

sneeze 97.3, 365.2, 484.2

sneeze in the cabbage 360.13

sneeze in the canyon 360.13

sneezer 494.1

snicket 116.40

snide 311.1, 311.5

sniff 23.2, 193.2, 505.12

sniff drugs 505.12

sniff out 157.1, 162.3

sniffer 456.6, 499.2

sniffy 131.5, 271.5

snifter 97.2

Snip 179.8

snip 251.1

snipe 106.3, 113.4

snipe on 294.6

snippiness 297.1

snippy 289.3

snips 69.10

snitch 193.4, 435.3, 472.2, 473.3

snitcher 473.2

snitching-rascal 435.3

snob 401.4

snobbish abbreviations 392.2

snobby 297.3

snockered 101.3

snog 351.3

snood 505.4

snoodge 505.4

snooks 180.1

snookums 180.1

snoop 132.7, 249.2, 419.2

snooper 419.2

snoopy 155.2

snooter 503.2

snootered 101.3

snootful 22.2, 101.1

snooty 297.3

snooze job 272.1

snorker 86.6

snort 97.2, 505.4, 505.12

snorter 198.4

snot 28.1, 426.2

snot-locker 116.40

snotnose 381.3

snotrag 83.2

snotty 297.3, 347.4

snotty nose 125.3

snout 106.1, 435.3, 468.1, 472.2

snow (job) 183.2

snow (under) 183.19

snow 310.4, 312.1, 383.25, 384.13, 403.1, 505.3

snow bird 503.2

snow bunny 437.3

snow job 186.2, 310.1, 312.1

snow soke 505.4

snow white 505.3

snow-dropping 479.1

snowballs 506.5

snowcones 505.3

snowed over 349.4

snowed under 241.10

snowfall 310.1

snowflake 505.4

snub (v.) 348.2

snub 348

snuff (out) 113.4

snuff it 112.5

snuff movie 195.3

snuggies 82.10

so 404.1

so busy I've had to put a man on to help 359.10

so dumb he couldn't find his ass with two hands at high noon 145.3

so dumb he couldn't piss out of a boat 145.3

so long 346.4

so low he can look up a snake's asshole and think it's the North Star 396.1

so what? 271.7

so's your old man! 292.7

so-and-so 69.2, 395.1

soak 92.3, 368.2

soaked 101.3

soap 183.2

soap dodger 384.1

soap opera 195.1

SOB 252.4, 395.1, 433.1

sob sister 456.3

sob story 198.3

sob stuff 183.2, 261.1, 281.1

sober 93.3

sociability 361

sociable 361.5

sociable person 446

social elite 448

social engagement 362

social entertainment 363

social error 231.3

social failure 452.2

SOCIAL LIFE 361–364

social remarks 345.2

socially inept 390.4

sock 32.3, 41.5, 94.8, 135.1, 164.11, 257.1, 292.2, 318.5, 337.4

sock it to me! 173.7

sock the clock 241.4

sockerino 257.1

sockeroo 32.3, 257.1

socking 18.10

socko 2.11, 27.3, 135.1, 236.2, 257.1

sockola 257.1

socks 83.5

sod 252.4, 395.1, 396.1

sod about 146.4, 244.1

sod all 23.3

sod off 54.3, 211.3

sod off! 54.6, 278.7

sod that (for a lark) 167.5

sod widow 444.9

sod you! 189.7

soda 87.5

soda 505.3

sodded 101.3

sodding 18.10, 189.4

sodomise 360.15

sodomy 360.5

soft (in the head) 145.3

soft 275.5, 329.4

soft boy 404.1

soft drug use 507.2

soft drug user 503.3

soft drugs 506

soft money 509.1

soft number 251.1

soft on 349.4

soft pedal 218.4

soft soap 183.19, 287.1, 287.2

soft touch 391.1, 400.1

soft-cop 391.1

softie 400.1

softy 403.1

soggies 86.17

SOHF 395.1

soil 5.4

soixante-neuf 360.1

sold 160.6

sold on 160.6, 268.4

soldier 210.5, 458.3

speler 480.3

spend a penny 119.8

spend money 508.12

spend time 1.5

speng 431.1

sperm burper 404.1

spew (it out) 183.10

spew 118.13

spew one's guts 118.13

spew one's ring 118.13

spic 383.15

spick 179.4, 383.15

spicy 306.5

Spider 179.8, 179.12

spider 453.3

spider blue 505.2

spiel 183.2, 183.7, 186.2, 198.1, 511.5

spieler 480.3, 511.4

spiff (oneself) up 84.2

spiff 35.1

spiff up 35.6

spiffed (up) 84.3

spifflicate 113.4, 169.3, 318.4

spifflicated 101.3

spiffy 27.3

Spike 179.10

spike 48.6, 505.10

Spikey 179.8

spill (it) 319.2

spill (one's guts) 193.3

spill 56.1, 472.3, 505.11

spill a line 183.7

spill it out 319.2

spill one's breakfast 118.13

spill one's guts 319.2, 490.6

spill the beans 193.3, 283.3, 319.2, 472.3

spill the beans on 314.2

spill the works 193.3

spillin' 338.1

spin 49.2, 60.1, 75.13, 488.3

spin a drum 488.3

spin a line 198.7

spin a yarn 198.6

spin discs 135.8

spine-tingler 198.4

spirit 236.2

spit (it out) 193.3

spit 66.7

spit out of the window 360.12

spit-bit 183.2

spitting image 428.5

spiv 434.1

spivmobile 75.2

splang 152.1

splash 298.1, 437.3

splash it about 373.2

splash it on 185.2

splash the boots 119.8

splendiferous 27.3

splib 438.1

splib-de-wib 438.1

splice the mainbrace 97.3

spliced 355.7

spliff 506.3

splish and splash 186.6

split (with) 331.2

split 23.1, 54.3, 356.2, 367.1, 367.2, 435.3

split kipper 116.40

split the cup 359.11

split with 367.3

splitsville 311.1, 356.1

splosh 87.2

splosh it on 373.2, 511.5

splurge 298.1, 373.2, 508.12

splurging 373.1

spoil 7.8, 7.12

spoil for 268.2

spoiling 194.6

spoiling for 268.4

Spokey 179.8

spondulicks 509.1

sponge 423.1, 430.5

spontaneous 240.2

spontaneous intercourse 359.2

spontaneous thought 153.8

spook 296.5, 325.4, 384.1, 456.23

spooked 296.7, 515.6

spoon 89.6, 502.4

sport 379.1, 443.2, 497.9

sporting goods 497.9

sporting life 361.1

sportsman 456.18

sportswear 82.20

sporty 309.4

spot 41.4, 78.1, 241.2, 510.5

spot on 27.3

spot one out 166.2

spots 506.1, 506.2

spotter 435.3

spout (off) 184.2

spray the tonsils 360.12

spread 89.5

spread a tehnicolour rainbow 118.13

spread it about 298.2

spread it on (thick) 287.2

spread oneself 370.6

spread the broads 515.4

spread the bull 299.2

spreads 86.10

spree 98

spring (it) 233.2

spring (v.t.) 487.6

spring 317.3

spritz 183.13

sprog 381.3

sprout 381.3

spruik 184.2

spruiker 420.1, 420.4

Spud 179.1

spud 395.1

spud-bashing 88.3

spuds 86.11

spunk 236.3, 295.1

spunk-gullet 395.1

spunk-head 395.1

spunk-pot 116.40

spunko 143.6

spunky 236.8, 295.5

Spurs 179.1

spy 456.23

spy on 132.7

SQPQ 392.2

square (it) 335.2

square 253.6, 254.4, 390.1, 391.1, 407.1

square John 407.1, 432.1

square away 163.5

square broad 497.2

square mackerel 506.2

square one 9.1

square one off 372.3

square rigger 95.1

square shake 305.1

square shooter 432.1

square time bob 505.4

square to the wood 254.4

square up 330.1

square-eyes 431.1

squarebrain 431.1

squaredom 390.1

squarehead 383.8

squash 300.4

squashed 101.3

squat 16.2, 119.7

squawk 188.1, 188.2,

suck it and see! 292.7
suck off 360.12
suck on 107.2
suck the bottle 97.3
suck up to 287.3
suck wind 258.2
suck-arse 287.3, 439.5
suck-ass 28.2
suck-up 418.1
sucka 395.1
sucker 310.2, 391.1, 395.1
sucker bait 220.1, 513.2
sucks to you! 292.7
suddenly 2.11
suds 95.1
Sue City 342.2
suede 384.2
suedehead 428.2
suffering cats! 189.5
sufficiency 22
suffixes used in slang words 10.3
sugar 180.1, 509.1
sugar! 189.5
sugar 86.16
sugar block 505.4
sugar daddy 382.2
sugar pimp 498.4
sugar-bun 180.1
sugar-pie 180.1
sugar-plum 180.1
suit 82.2
suitable 253.8
suited (down) 84.3
sullen 279.6
sullenness 279
sumbitch 395.1
summertime ho 497.3
summon 188.3
sun 65.2
sunbathe 65.3
sunbeam 91.1
Sunday punch 238.2
sunk 235.8, 252.12
sunny side up 86.27
sunshine 328.10, 506.4
super bio 506.2
supercharge 505.4
supercloud 505.4
superfluity 22.2
superfly 27.3
supergrass 435.3, 472.2
superhonkie 384.12
superintendent 457
superior liquor 94.5
superior person 394

superior to 20.5
superiority 20
supernatural beings 325
superskunk 506.2
supersoul 450.1
superwhite 505.4
supplied 366.4
support (v.) 286.2, 341.3
SUPPOSITION 174–175
suppress 202.3
sure as God made little
   green apples 159.3
sure as eggs is eggs 159.3
sure bet 192.3
sure enough 164.8
sure thing 159.1, 192.3
sure-as-shit 305.8
sure-fire 305.8
surf 60.8
surpass 20.3
surprise (v.) 173.2
surprise 173
surveillance 486.2
sus 161.4, 256.5
sus out 144.3, 166.2,
   192.8
susfu 5.5
suspect (n.) 486.4
suspect (v.) 486.5
suspicion 161
suspicious 161.4
sussed (out) 144.9
sussed out 162.7
sussy 161.4
Susy 509.4
swab 390.3
swab jockey 456.1
swack 32.3, 41.5, 116.34,
   135.1, 318.5
swacked 101.3
swacko 101.3, 135.1
swaddy 456.1
swag 94.1, 464.1, 489.2,
   509.1
swagging 479.6
swags 86.6
swailer 465.1
SWAK 191.5
SWALCAKWS 191.5
SWALK 191.5
swallow (hook, line and
   sinker) 310.8
swallow (it) 222.2
swallow 160.2
swallow the dictionary
   185.2

swamp 489.2
swan around 58.2
SWANK 191.5
swank 185.2, 298.1,
   298.4, 299.2, 311.4
swanky 141.1, 298.5
swans 506.5
swap cans 494.8
swap spit 351.3
swartzer 384.1
swear 189.3
swear and cuss 75.12
swear blind 164.7
swear till one's blue in the
   face 199.2
swear to God 164.7
sweat (it) out 205.2
sweat 154.3, 252.1, 262.1,
   264.1, 280.2, 283.2
sweat hog 426.2
sweat it out 241.6, 248.4
sweats 503.6
swede 390.2
Swedish culture 360.7,
   499.4
Sweeney 495.4
sweep 433.1
sweep the board 20.3,
   365.3
sweet (as a nut) 251.5
sweet (bleeding) Jesus
   189.5
sweet 27.3, 180.1, 404.1
sweet chance 158.2
sweet daddy 441.2
sweet dreams 505.2
sweet FA 16.2, 23.3
sweet Jesus 505.6
sweet fuck all 23.3
sweet kid 494.4
sweet Lucy 506.1
sweet on 349.4
sweet patootie 441.3
sweet potato pie 116.32,
   425.1
sweet savagery 198.5
sweet talk 219.4
sweet-talk 352.7
sweetcakes 116.30
sweetcheeks 116.30
sweetcorn shiner 404.1
sweetheart contract 508.9
sweetie 35.2, 180.1,
   425.1, 441.1
sweetie-pie 180.1, 441.1
sweetman 498.2

tetchy 284.6
teuf-teuf 346.4
Tex Ritter 95.1
Texan rude 38.6
Texan rude nam 386.2
Texas steel 494.1
textiles 377.1
texture 30
TF much 273.6
TGIF 3.2
thank you 345.3
thank-you letter 191.3
thank-you note 191.3
thanks 191.3
thanks a bunch 292.7,
 345.3
thanks a million 292.7,
 345.3
that 17.2
that and this 119.2
that finishes me 272.7
that way 404.1
that's (for) me 340.5
that's a big ten-four 275.7
that's a good one 277.8
that's a laugh 277.8
that's absurd 146.11
that's affirmative 275.7
that's cool 345.4, 345.5
that's funny 277.8
that's impossible! 158.7
that's it! 285.5
that's just too bad! 278.7
that's news! 173.7
that's satisfactory 275.7
that's so ill! 288.5
that's telling them 164.12
that's telling them! 285.5
that's the ball game 302.5
that's the shot! 199.3
that's the stuff (to give the
 troops)! 285.5
that's the stuff 164.12
that's the ticket 27.3
that's the ticket! 199.3
that's the way the cookie
 crumbles 302.5
that's the way! 285.5
that's torn it 7.16
that's your bad luck 271.7
that's your funeral 271.7
that's your lot 10.10
that's your problem 271.7
that's your tough tits
 271.7
THC 506.1

the (grim) reaper 112.1
the (real) McCoy 305.8
the (real) McKay 305.8
the (real) goods 94.5
the air 63.1
the all-clear 285.1
the altogether 85.2
the Andrew 179.3
the answer is a lemon!
 292.7
the axe 63.1
the berries 27.1
the big chill 113.1
the big E 25.2
the Bill 480.2
the Book 498.1
the bump (off) 113.1
the burn 121.3
the Bush 44.1
the business 113.1
the cheese 387.1, 430.2
the chill 113.1
the Coathanger 44.1
the con 183.2
the creature 94.1, 95.5
the deal's off 10.10
the deuce 17.2
the Devil 323.3
the devil 17.2
the devil to pay 252.2
the dirt farm 196.2
the dirty 308.1
the doings 32.2
the double 49.1
the Drain 44.1
the dust 25.2
the Earie 134.1
the Erie 134.1
the elbow 25.2
the fade 54.1
the fast lane 309.1
the fast track 309.1
the finger 293.3
the first hundred years are
 the hardest 295.6
the fuck I will! 223.1
the fuck with you 189.7
the Game 497.1
the Gate 44.1
the go-ahead 285.1
the goods 27.1, 164.2,
 192.3
the gorilla 387.1
the Grand Tour 58.2
the Great Unwashed
 449.1

the Grove 44.1
the gun 71.3
the handsome thing 305.1
the hard word 294.3
the heat's on! 488.5
the hell 17.2
the hell I will! 223.1
the hell to pay 252.2
the hell with it 278.8
the hell with it! 189.5,
 292.8
the hell with you 189.7
the hell with you! 292.8
the hell you say 161.6
the hell you say! 173.9,
 223.1
the Hype 480.2
the Island 44.3, 494.1
the job 495.5
the Junction 44.1
the kiss-off 113.1
the Life 309.1, 478.1,
 498.1
the life of Riley 276.2,
 309.1
the likes (of) 137.1
the liquor's talking 183.4
the Man 458.1, 495.1
the man 387.1
the Mob 458.2
the Moor 494.1
the mouse 496.1
the no 288.1
the nod 285.1
the off 514.5
the OK 285.1
the old this and that 137.2
the pip 279.2, 284.1
the pits 125.18, 229.5
the rabbit died 109.4
the real McCoy 94.5
the real stuff 94.5
the Revo 228.1
the rubout 25.2
the runaround 25.2
the score 472.1
the Scrubs 44.3, 494.1
the shaft 308.1, 313.1
the show on the road
 9.3
the sky's the limit 213.5
the slip 25.2
the Smoke 43.1
the Squad 495.4
the street 500.3
the tape 156.1

tub thumper 420.1
Tubby 179.8, 179.13
tube 95.1, 105.3, 195.1, 258.2, 494.5
tube it 195.12
tubed 101.3
tubesteak 116.34
tubesteak of love 116.34
Tubs 179.13
tubular 27.3
tuck 86.1
tuck in one's tail 300.5
tuck up 310.6
tuck-in 89.5
tucked up 489.4
tucker 86.1
tucker out 243.1, 243.3
tuckerbox 435.3
tuckered 243.4
tude 260.1
Tug 179.8
tug 489.1, 489.2
tumble (for) 160.3
tumble (to) 144.4, 162.3, 166.2
tumble 156.2, 161.2, 359.6
tumble for 267.2, 310.8, 340.2
tummler 420.1
tummy banana 116.34
tummyache 125.1
tump over 337.4
tuna 380.1
tune in 166.2
tune off 265.5
turbo 506.2
turd 119.3, 396.1
turd in the punchbowl 395.1
turd-burglar 404.1
turd-packer 404.1
turf 46.1
turf out 63.2
turk 404.1
Turk McGurk 435.1
turkey 258.1, 395.1, 505.3
turkey neck 116.34
turkey on a string 391.1
turking 359.1
Turkish pollen 506.1
turn (one) around 219.4
turn one's crank 273.3
turn (one) out 498.7
turn 173.1, 363.1

turn 8.2
turn a trick 239.5
turn against 314.3
turn in 247.3, 314.2
turn inside out 154.3, 318.4
turn into fish food 112.6
turn it on 49.4
turn it up 241.5
turn it up! 146.11
turn off 136.2, 356.3
turn off lights 133.1
turn off one's lights 112.7
turn on 273.3, 357.4
turn on the heat 73.3, 238.5
turn on the waterworks 261.4, 281.3
turn one around 472.3
turn one's crank 273.3
turn one's face to the wall 112.5
turn one's nose up at 224.3
turn one's stomach 278.4
turn one's tum 278.4
turn out 360.17
turn over 488.3
turn the corner 358.5
turn the set 231.4
turn the tables 358.3
turn tricks 497.15
turn up one's nose at 288.3
turn up one's toes 112.5
turn up trumps 215.5, 257.2
turn upside down 157.1
turn-on 262.2, 273.1, 507.2
turn-up 173.1
turned on 143.6
turnip greens 506.2
turnout 34.1
turnup (for the book) 215.2
turps 97.2
turtle 83.1
turtle-dove 180.1
tusheroon 509.1
tuskie 506.3
tutti-frutti 505.3
tux 82.3
TV 436.7
twack 95.1
twaddle 146.2
twang 359.6

twang one's wire 118.14, 360.19
twange 116.40
twak 499.2
twat 395.1
twat-rug 116.39
twat-scourer 395.1
tweak one's twinkie 360.19
tweaked 101.3
tweedler 75.4, 480.3
tweedling 480.2
tweeked 101.3
twenties 480.2
twenty dollars 509.7
twenty pounds 509.7
twenty-five pounds 509.8
twenty-nine and a wake-up 1.5
twerp 388.1
twicer 480.3
twig 132.6, 162.3, 166.2
twink 404.5
twinkies 404.5
twirl 255.1, 494.5
twist 160.1, 380.1, 404.4, 506.2
twist one's arm 217.2, 219.4
twisted 101.3, 147.5, 169.5, 284.5, 507.8
twister 69.13
twit 431.1
two 491.3
two and eight 262.1
two bricks short of the load 147.5
two cents worth 153.3
two down 86.27
two ducks 516.6
two fat ladies 516.6
two fingers of scorn 293.3
two hundred pounds 509.12
two jumps ahead 20.5
two little crutches 516.6
two looking at you 86.27
two on a slice of squeal 86.27
two other guys 26.1
two pence short of a bob 147.5
two shakes of a lamb's tail 1.3
two with their eyes closed 86.27
two-bit 19.7, 28.2

wipe out 7.10, 113.1, 258.2, 338.5
wipe-out 258.1, 369.1
wiped out 258.4, 376.5
wire 116.34, 458.14
wire up 197.1
wired 147.5, 283.6
wires 219.1
wise (to) 144.9
wise (up) 192.5
wise 143.6
wise 431.1
wise guy 401.1, 430.1
wise up 144.5, 170.3, 192.6, 202.4, 230.2, 237.3
wise-arse 401.1
wise-ass 347.4
wisenheimer 401.1, 430.1
wish on 304.3
wish upon 304.3
wit 277
witch-hazel 505.2
with a head like a sieve 171.2
with a hole in the head 171.2
with it 143.6
with knobs on! 292.7
with one foot in the grave 124.5
with one's tail between one's legs 279.7
withdrawal from drugs 503.6
withhold information 201.3
without rules 213.5
withstand interrogation 490.8
wizard 27.3, 430.2
wobbler 125.12
wobbly pop 95.1
wodge 29.1
wog 384.1
wog box 69.25
Woler 75.4
wolf 404.1, 441.6, 443.2
wolf it 299.2
wolf-pussy 131.2
wollied 101.3
wollies 495.1
wollyhumper 456.5
women 380
womon 380.1
wonelly 18.10
wong 116.34, 509.1

wonga 509.1
wonk 453.3
wonk one's conker 360.19
wonkiness 169.1
wonky 33.5, 124.4
wood 116.34
wooden 337.4
wooden ears 395.1
wooden kimono 112.4
wooden overcoat 112.4
wooden road to Bedfordshire 79.6
wooden spoon 21.1, 181.3, 371.3
woodener 491.3
woodentop 495.1
woodhead 431.1
woodie 75.4
woof 118.13, 184.2
woofer 116.34
woofter 404.1
wool 380.1
Woolies 179.2
woolly woofter 404.1
Wooloomooloo Yank 385.1
woollyback 390.2
Woop Woop 43.2
Wootsie 180.1
wooziness 169.1
woozy 101.3, 169.5
wop 383.13
woppitzer 400.5
word 177
word! 199.3
word freak 499.2
word up! 199.3
work (on) 220.2
work (v.) 241.4
work 241
work 259.4, 310.4
work a crowd 368.2
work a ginger 498.9
work as a male prostitute 497.16
work as a prostitute 497.15
work for 365.4
work from a book 498.7
work hard 241.6
work hard or don't waste time 241.11
work keenly 241.6
work like a black 241.6
work like anything 241.6
work like billy-o 241.6
work on 219.4

work one's arse off 241.6
work one's butt off 241.6
work one's tail off 241.6
work one's ticket 124.3, 244.1
work out 239.7
work over 154.3, 219.4, 337.4
work over good 338.5
work shift 241.3
work the hole 479.4
work the room 184.2
work the well 479.4
work time 1.4
work to excess 243.2
work up (a head of) steam 280.3
work up a circulation 262.3
work up a lather 262.3
worked up (about) 270.5
WORKERS 453–457
workers in entertainment, show business 456.5
workers in travel 456.11
working as a prostitute 497.17
working girl 497.2, 497.9
working out 121.2
working stiff 390.1, 453.1
workaholic 453.4
workout 156.2
workover 154.2
works 69.1, 505.10
world 64
worm 116.34
wormbait 112.2
worn-out prostitute 497.5
worried 283.6
worry (v.) 283.4
worry 283
worry about 283.5
worrying 283.7
worse things happen at sea 295.6, 329.5
worth a punt 158.3
wotcher 346.3
would I shit you (you're my favourite turd) 199.3, 204.7, 312.4
wouldn't tell you the time of day 140.5
wound (v.) 337.8
wounded 126.3
wow 35.7, 173.3, 273.4

READ MORE IN PENGUIN

In every corner of the world, on every subject under the sun, Penguin represents quality and variety – the very best in publishing today.

For complete information about books available from Penguin – including Puffins, Penguin Classics and Arkana – and how to order them, write to us at the appropriate address below. Please note that for copyright reasons the selection of books varies from country to country.

In the United Kingdom: Please write to *Dept. EP, Penguin Books Ltd, Bath Road, Harmondsworth, West Drayton, Middlesex UB7 0DA*

In the United States: Please write to *Consumer Services, Penguin Putnam Inc., 405 Murray Hill Parkway, East Rutherford, New Jersey 07073-2136.* VISA and MasterCard holders call 1-800-631-8571 to order Penguin titles

In Canada: Please write to *Penguin Books Canada Ltd, 10 Alcorn Avenue, Suite 300, Toronto, Ontario M4V 3B2*

In Australia: Please write to *Penguin Books Australia Ltd, 487 Maroondah Highway, Ringwood, Victoria 3134*

In New Zealand: Please write to *Penguin Books (NZ) Ltd, Private Bag 102902, North Shore Mail Centre, Auckland 10*

In India: Please write to *Penguin Books India Pvt Ltd, 11 Community Centre, Panchsheel Park, New Delhi 110017*

In the Netherlands: Please write to *Penguin Books Netherlands bv, Postbus 3507, NL-1001 AH Amsterdam*

In Germany: Please write to *Penguin Books Deutschland GmbH, Metzlerstrasse 26, 60594 Frankfurt am Main*

In Spain: Please write to *Penguin Books S. A., Bravo Murillo 19, 1°B, 28015 Madrid*

In Italy: Please write to *Penguin Italia s.r.l., Via Vittorio Emanuele 45Ia, 20094 Corsico, Milano*

In France: Please write to *Penguin France, 12, Rue Prosper Ferradou, 31700 Blagnac*

In Japan: Please write to *Penguin Books Japan Ltd, Iidabashi KM-Bldg, 2-23-9 Koraku, Bunkyo-Ku, Tokyo 112-0004*

In South Africa: Please write to *Penguin Books South Africa (Pty) Ltd, P.O. Box 751093, Gardenview, 2047 Johannesburg*

READ MORE IN PENGUIN

LITERARY CRITICISM

The Practice of Writing David Lodge

This lively collection examines the work of authors ranging from the two Amises to Nabokov and Pinter; the links between private lives and published works; and the different techniques required in novels, stage plays and screenplays. 'These essays, so easy in manner, so well-built and informative, offer a fine blend of creative writing and criticism' *Sunday Times*

A Lover's Discourse Roland Barthes

'May be the most detailed, painstaking anatomy of desire we are ever likely to see or need again . . . The book is an ecstatic celebration of love and language . . . readers interested in either or both . . . will enjoy savouring its rich and dark delights' *Washington Post*

The New Pelican Guide to English Literature Edited by Boris Ford

The indispensable critical guide to English and American literature in nine volumes, erudite yet accessible. From the ages of Chaucer and Shakespeare, via Georgian satirists and Victorian social critics, to the leading writers of the twentieth century, all literary life is here.

The Structure of Complex Words William Empson

'Twentieth-century England's greatest critic after T. S. Eliot, but whereas Eliot was the high priest, Empson was the *enfant terrible* . . . *The Structure of Complex Words* is one of the linguistic masterpieces of the epoch, finding in the feel and tone of our speech whole sedimented social histories' *Guardian*

Vamps and Tramps Camille Paglia

'Paglia is a genuinely unconventional thinker . . . Taken as a whole, the book gives an exceptionally interesting perspective on the last thirty years of intellectual life in America, and is, in its wacky way, a celebration of passion and the pursuit of truth' *Sunday Telegraph*

READ MORE IN PENGUIN

LANGUAGE/LINGUISTICS

Language Play David Crystal

We all use language to communicate information, but it is language play which is truly central to our lives. Full of puns, groan-worthy gags and witty repartee, this book restores the fun to the study of language. It also demonstrates why all these things are essential elements of what makes us human.

Swearing Geoffrey Hughes

'A deliciously filthy trawl among taboo words across the ages and the globe' *Observer*. 'Erudite and entertaining' Penelope Lively, *Daily Telegraph*

The Language Instinct Stephen Pinker

'Dazzling . . . Pinker's big idea is that language is an instinct, as innate to us as flying is to geese . . . Words can hardly do justice to the superlative range and liveliness of Pinker's investigations' *Independent*. 'He does for language what David Attenborough does for animals, explaining difficult scientific concepts so easily that they are indeed absorbed as a transparent stream of words' John Gribbin

Mother Tongue Bill Bryson

'A delightful, amusing and provoking survey, a joyful celebration of our wonderful language, which is packed with curiosities and enlightenment on every page' *Sunday Express*. 'A gold mine of language-anecdote. A surprise on every page . . . enthralling' *Observer*

Longman Guide to English Usage
Sidney Greenbaum and Janet Whitcut

Containing 5000 entries compiled by leading authorities on modern English, this invaluable reference work clarifies every kind of usage problem, giving expert advice on points of grammar, meaning, style, spelling, pronunciation and punctuation.

READ MORE IN PENGUIN

REFERENCE

The Penguin Dictionary of the Third Reich
James Taylor and Warren Shaw

This dictionary provides a full background to the rise of Nazism and the role of Germany in the Second World War. Among the areas covered are the major figures from Nazi politics, arts and industry, the German Resistance, the politics of race and the Nuremberg trials.

The Penguin Biographical Dictionary of Women

This stimulating, informative and entirely new Penguin dictionary of women from all over the world, through the ages, contains over 1,600 clear and concise biographies on major figures from politicians, saints and scientists to poets, film stars and writers.

Roget's Thesaurus of English Words and Phrases
Edited by Betty Kirkpatrick

This new edition of Roget's classic work, now brought up to date for the nineties, will increase anyone's command of the English language. Fully cross-referenced, it includes synonyms of every kind (formal or colloquial, idiomatic and figurative) for almost 900 headings. It is a must for writers and utterly fascinating for any English speaker.

The Penguin Dictionary of International Relations
Graham Evans and Jeffrey Newnham

International relations have undergone a revolution since the end of the Cold War. This new world disorder is fully reflected in this new Penguin dictionary, which is extensively cross-referenced with a select bibliography to aid further study.

The Penguin Guide to Synonyms and Related Words
S. I. Hayakawa

'More helpful than a thesaurus, more humane than a dictionary, the *Guide to Synonyms and Related Words* maps linguistic boundaries with precision, sensitivity to nuance and, on occasion, dry wit' *The Times Literary Supplement*

READ MORE IN PENGUIN

REFERENCE

The Penguin Dictionary of Troublesome Words Bill Bryson

Why should you avoid discussing the *weather conditions*? Can a married woman be celibate? Why is it eccentric to talk about the aroma of a cowshed? A straightforward guide to the pitfalls and hotly disputed issues in standard written English.

Swearing Geoffrey Hughes

'A deliciously filthy trawl among taboo words across the ages and the globe' Valentine Cunningham, *Observer*, Books of the Year. 'Erudite and entertaining' Penelope Lively, *Daily Telegraph*, Books of the Year.

Medicines: A Guide for Everybody Peter Parish

Now in its seventh edition and completely revised and updated, this bestselling guide is written in ordinary language for the ordinary reader yet will prove indispensable to anyone involved in health care: nurses, pharmacists, opticians, social workers and doctors.

Media Law Geoffrey Robertson QC and Andrew Nichol

Crisp and authoritative surveys explain the up-to-date position on defamation, obscenity, official secrecy, copyright and confidentiality, contempt of court, the protection of privacy and much more.

The Penguin Careers Guide
Anna Alston and Anne Daniel; Consultant Editor: Ruth Miller

As the concept of a 'job for life' wanes, this guide encourages you to think broadly about occupational areas as well as describing day-to-day work and detailing the latest developments and qualifications such as NVQs. Special features include possibilities for working part-time and job-sharing, returning to work after a break and an assessment of the current position of women.

READ MORE IN PENGUIN

DICTIONARIES

Abbreviations
Ancient History
Archaeology
Architecture
Art and Artists
Astronomy
Biographical Dictionary of
  Women
Biology
Botany
Building
Business
Challenging Words
Chemistry
Civil Engineering
Classical Mythology
Computers
Contemporary American History
Curious and Interesting Geometry
Curious and Interesting Numbers
Curious and Interesting Words
Design and Designers
Economics
Eighteenth-Century History
Electronics
English and European History
English Idioms
Foreign Terms and Phrases
French
Geography
Geology
German
Historical Slang
Human Geography
Information Technology

International Finance
International Relations
Literary Terms and Literary
  Theory
Mathematics
Modern History 1789–1945
Modern Quotations
Music
Musical Performers
Nineteenth-Century World
  History
Philosophy
Physical Geography
Physics
Politics
Proverbs
Psychology
Quotations
Quotations from Shakespeare
Religions
Rhyming Dictionary
Russian
Saints
Science
Sociology
Spanish
Surnames
Symbols
Synonyms and Antonyms
Telecommunications
Theatre
The Third Reich
Third World Terms
Troublesome Words
Twentieth-Century History
Twentieth-Century Quotations